The Other Islanders

The Other Islanders

People Who Pulled Nantucket's Oars

Frances Ruley Karttunen

Thanks to the generous cooperation of Spinner Publications and the Nantucket Historical Association, a fully footnoted version of *The Other Islanders,* together with appendixes of primary documents for each Part and a comprehensive bibliography, is accessible from the Nantucket Historical Association's Eprint Archive at www.nha.org.

Noncirculating printed copies of the annotated version are located in the Nantucket Historical Association Research Library reading room, the Great Hall of the Nantucket Atheneum, and the Nantucket Public Schools' Suzanne T. Gardner Library.

Cover design: Jay Avila

Text © 2005 Frances R. Karttunen
All rights reserved.
© Spinner Publications, Inc.
New Bedford, Massachusetts 02740
Printed in the United States of America

Library of Congress Cataloging-in-Publication Data

Karttunen, Frances Ruley, 1942-
    The other islanders : people who pulled Nantucket's oars / by Frances Ruley Karttunen.
        p. cm.
    Includes bibliographical references and index.
    ISBN 0-932027-93-8 (pbk.)
    1. Minorities—Massachusetts—Nantucket Island--History. 2. Occupations—
Massachusetts—Nantucket Island--History. 3. Nantucket Island (Mass.)—History. I. Title.
    F72.N2K37 2005
    974.4'97004--dc22   2005013018

To all the people who came to Nantucket and became part of Nantucket.

And for all the island's children, who are Nantucket's future.

Contents

Acknowledgments

I am indebted to a great many people: first to my great-great-grandmother and my grandmother, uneasy partners in transmitting our Nantucket heritage.

Because Ellen Ramsdell and Esther Gibbs bequeathed to me the house I live in, I have written this history upstairs in what was the old Sylvaro homestead. The planning and research for *The Other Islanders* began, however, many years ago during the time when I worked off-island and could come home only now and then.

In early days, John Mendonça and I had long, memorable conversations in Pocomo. A while later Eunice Sjölund took up the story of Nantucket's fishing families with me in her sunny parlor on Pine Street. Lifelong friend Eileen McGrath has been a generous helper in my efforts to reconstruct recent Nantucket history from school records, newspaper articles, and photos, as have Ruth Grieder; Arline Bartlett; Richard and Catherine Mack; Francis Pease; and Constance Indio, who gave me access to the whole history of the *Town Crier* and its publisher, Joseph Indio.

Among Nantucket's Cape Verdeans I owe a special debt to Viola (Cabral) Howard and Pauline (Cabral) Singleton, Norma (Cabral Teixeira) Nunes, Theran Singleton, Falynn Correia, and Augusto Ramos for sharing with me their life experiences in this community where we all reside without, sometimes, knowing much about one another. Carl Cruz of New Bedford has supplied books, references, genealogical information, and good cheer.

Lonn Taylor and Dedie Uunila Taylor provided a much appreciated pied-à-terre when research took me to Washington, D.C.

I have been blessed with what can only be described as *aloha* from John Charlot, Noelani Arista, Ikaika Hussey, and Laura Lehuanani Yim. Our sharing of the Hawai'i–Nantucket connection has been moving beyond words. Frederick G. S. Clow was the sensitive photographer on the solemn occasion of the singing of Hawaiian chants for the dead on Nantucket.

I appreciate Patricia Loring's donation of Jared Coffin's account book to the Nantucket Historical Association's manuscript collection, and thank Bette Spriggs for acquainting me with the autobiography of Mrs. Nancy Prince in the rare-book collection of the Nantucket Atheneum. Without those records I would have remained ignorant of Nantucket's connections with Jamaica in the eighteenth and nineteenth centuries.

It was through Wilhelm Higginbotham's commitment to Nantucket history that the African Meeting House, at the corner of York Street and Pleasant Street, began the journey back toward its original form and function. He and Angeleen Campra have responded to my queries with a flow of family history that has deepened and enriched my understanding.

All my fellow Friends of the African Meeting House on Nantucket have encouraged me, particularly Helen Seager, Elizabeth Oldham, Jean Duarte, and Joan Wilson-Godeau. I have also enjoyed material support in the form of a grant from the Nantucket Arts Council and a year-long James Bradford Ames Fellowship. I am deeply indebted to Adele Ames for her personal interest in this work and to my companion Ames Fellows Isabel Kaldenbach and Aminah Pilgrim for sharing the results of their research.

Likewise, I have benefited from the collegiality of scholars Elizabeth Little, Franklin Dorman, Barbara Linebaugh White, James Traue, and Susheel Bibbs, all of whom shared their work with me without reservation and even undertook new research to advance mine. Lincoln Thurber kindly helped with maps.

For help with Parts III and IV of *The Other Islanders*, I am already deeply indebted to the kindness and interest of Ethel Anastos, Olga (Anderson) Hansen, Genevieve Booth, Mildred Collatz, Eugene Collatz Jr., Justine (Collatz) Connors, Ada (Der) Andrews and Leland Der, Lisa Dias, Robert Erler, Leonora Gaspie, Joan (Genesky) Rubin, Ellen (Gibbs) Holdgate, John and Elizabeth Gilbert, William Haddon, Jean Hughes, Roland Huyser, Morton and Robert Kaufman, Lillian Khouri, Ethel (Larsen) Hamilton, Melvin Lash, Morgan Levine, Betsy Lowenstein, Betty MacDonald, Grace (Nicholson) Marshall, Albert Ottison, Barbara (Petumenos) Thomas, R. Andrew Pierce, Clarissa Porter, Karsten Reinemo Jr., Francina (Reyes) Gibbs, Koren Reyes, Sol and Lucy Salomon, Morton and Reva Schlesinger, Raymond Senecal, Carl and James Sjölund, Georgia Ann Snell, Frank Spriggs, Robert and Molly Sziklas, Frieda Thurston, Beverly Topham, Jeanette Topham, Joan Wilson-Godeau and Vivian (Wilson) Richardson.

Work in primary sources would have been impossible without the cooperation of the staffs of the Nantucket Town and County offices. Town Clerk Catherine Flanagan Stover, Clerk of Courts Patricia Church, Clerk of Deeds Catherine Ancero, and Register of Probate Sylvia Howard, together with all the staff members in those offices, have made room for me, put up with me, and expressed positive interest in what I have been up to.

The staffs of the Nantucket Atheneum and the Nantucket Historical Association's Research Library have helped me along month in, month out with unfailing interest and care. No matter how esoteric my interlibrary loan requests have been, the Atheneum staff has cheerfully looked to my needs. When I have had microfilm to scan, a reader has always been available. At a crucial moment, Ben Simons of the NHA identified an obscure piece of writing by Herman Melville, thereby saving me from embarrassment. Marie Henke has done wonders with illustrations from the NHA image collection.

The NHA collections databases have led me to unanticipated treasures of information. My thanks must extend beyond the NHA staff to the volunteers who have read through the manuscripts and summarized their content for the databases and to everyone who has deposited family papers, scrapbooks, ships' logs, business records, research papers, theses, and dissertations in the NHA Research Library. First among researchers deserving of praise are Nantucket historians Edouard A. Stackpole and Grace Brown Gardner. Stackpole's immense Collection 335 and Gardner's scrapbooks constituting Collection 57 have been mainstays of my research.

Financial support for the production of this volume was provided by contributions from Augusto Ramos, Colleen McGrath, Clarissa Porter, Georgia Ann Snell, Richard and Elizabeth Bretschneider, the members of the steering committee of the Friends of the African Meeting House on Nantucket, and a Nantucket foundation that wishes to remain anonymous. A donation by Robert Reed honors Willie House, the Chicken Box, and the Sons and Daughters of Arquipelago de Cabo Verde. Publication was also supported in part by a grant from the Nantucket Cultural Council, a local agency which is supported by the Massachusetts Cultural Council, a state agency.

Through generous cooperation between Spinner Publications and the Nantucket Historical Association, a fully annotated scholar's version of *The Other Islanders* with appendices of primary documents is accessible at www.nha.org.

Finally, I return to my family with thanks to the two historians on Nantucket with whom I have daily contact: my husband Alfred W. Crosby and my cousin Maurice Gibbs. Without their wisdom and support, this project would have gone nowhere.

Strangers, Coofs, and Washashores

When Sarah (Pinkham) Bunker died at home on a Saturday in 1902, the *Inquirer and Mirror* reported that "the funeral took place Wednesday, relatives from abroad coming on to attend."

Sarah P. Bunker's relatives from "abroad" hadn't made a warp-speed transatlantic voyage to Nantucket for her funeral; they came by steamboat across Nantucket Sound. At the beginning of the twentieth century Nantucketers still divided the whole globe into on-island and off-island. Off-island was "abroad," and off-islanders were spoken of as "strangers" or less politely as "coofs."

There was no doubt in the minds of the readers of the *Inquirer & Mirror* that Sarah P. was a "descended Nantucketer." Just short of ninety-four at the time of her death, she was recognized as the island's oldest resident. Moreover, she shared a pedigree with people who for centuries had formed the influential majority on the island. Through her father, Hezekiah Pinkham, she was descended from one of Nantucket's founding-settler couples, Tristram and Dionis Coffin, in no less than seven different lines. Jethro Coffin and Mary Coffin, for whom Nantucket's "Oldest House" had been built in the 1680s, were Hezekiah's great-great grandparents. Progeny of Tristram and Dionis had intermarried with Starbucks, Gardners, Bunkers, and Pinkhams through six generations to bring forth Sarah P.'s father.

Her mother, Eunice Pinkham, was descended from the same people, as was her husband, Elisha Bunker. Sarah P. was the product of one of those proverbial old local families whose genealogical trees do not branch.

Nantucket's "Oldest House" was built by the Coffin and Gardner families for the wedding of Jethro Coffin and Mary Gardner in 1686.

Not only was Sarah P. old in years and of old settler stock, she also shared what was recognized as true Nantucket life experience. Through the China trade her father grew sufficiently wealthy to move his family from the house on North Liberty Street where Sarah P. had been born to a grander house on the Cliff with a view of the harbor. But in marriage her good fortune foundered, as it had for many other women. Her husband, Elisha Bunker, seeking to gain yet more riches from a long whaling voyage, was lost at sea in 1841, leaving behind his widow and a two-year-old whom he had never seen. In the self-reliant tradition of Nantucket women, Sarah P. maintained the Pinkham homestead property and supported herself, her widowed father, her daughter, and eventually a grandson by taking in roomers and going out to nurse Nantucket's sick and dying. As she passed through the town's dark streets at night carrying a lantern to find her way, her tall figure was known jocularly as "the walking Sankaty Light."

The *Inquirer & Mirror* reported most of this in her obituary, and the rest has been passed down as part of family history, the stories told and retold to her great-grandchildren as part of their Nantucket heritage.

What the newspaper didn't report, and what would not have been thought to be Nantucket heritage, is that Sarah P. had a familiar stranger truly "from abroad" living right under her roof. Sarah P.'s grandson, Maurice Gibbs, had married Hilda Österberg of Finland, and Hilda had assumed the running of the household.

A fall at age 80 had left Sarah P. unable to get about easily, and she rarely left the upstairs north bedroom where she received visitors and followed the construction of a grand summer mansion across the street as it rose to close off her sea view.

Every afternoon Hilda climbed the stairs with a tray to serve tea to Sarah P. on Hezekiah's Limoges china. Hilda lived in fear of breaking a teacup and incurring the wrath of Sarah P. and all the ghosts of Nantucketers past who seemed to palpably inhabit the north rooms. Intimidated by her husband's family, she felt that in this house she would forever be regarded as a foreign maid, a stranger, a coof, a person outside Nantucket history.

In the 1930s, three decades after Sarah P.'s death, Guy Loman Jr., an interviewer for the New England Dialect Atlas project, came to collect samples of Nantucket speech. Fieldworkers had been directed to interview elderly descendants of old local families and middle-aged people with a high school education but no extensive travel or college education away from home. They were reminded that it was "of supreme importance" that the people interviewed should be from "various generations and diverse social and racial" groups, but the editors of the final report had to admit that several fieldworkers, especially Loman, "showed a preference for the interesting old-fashioned local type."

Although Loman was supposed to interview a representative sample of islanders, he chose just two men and one woman, all around eighty years old and all connected with the village of Siasconset. He could not interview any Nantucket Indians, since the last two speakers of the local variety of Eastern Algonquian had died within two months of each other in the winter of 1854–55. Nor were there on-island in the 1930s any descendants of African Nantucketers whose families had come to the island in the 1700s. There were, for sure, Nantucket-born children and grandchildren of families who had moved to Nantucket from the Azores and Cape Verde Islands and from Ireland, but Loman ignored them.

Each interview could take as long as three days to complete, and Loman, who was operating on a Depression-era budget, had to move on to other communities on Martha's Vineyard and Cape Cod. Another reason for the narrowness of the survey was Loman's acknowledged love of talking to old-timers. He would have been delighted to have taken tea with Sarah P. Bunker upstairs in her home on the Cliff, but he had come thirty years too late.

The operating definition of "Old New England" had taken shape in the latter part of the nineteenth century in reaction to economic and demographic changes in the region. Industrialization had created a labor market far outstripping the supply of rural New England millgirls who had originally left their families' farms to work and save money for their futures. The mills had drawn to New England a labor force from beyond the borders of the United States. Among the first had been the Irish fleeing the potato famine of the 1840s. Beginning in the 1880s intense immigration brought workers from Canada, Northern and Southern Europe, and the Middle East. By 1912, when strikes shut down the textile mills of Lawrence and Lowell, Massachusetts, the workers demanding better wages and working conditions were French Canadians, Italians, Greeks, Portuguese, Lithuanians, Poles, Belgians, Armenians, Turks, and Syrians, as well as Irish and English. In the Fitchburg mills the workers were mainly Finns. Just a few descendants of New England farmers were still working there.

With the turn of the century Finns and Cape Verdeans were working cranberry bogs on Cape Cod and Nantucket. Fishing boats heading out

to the Georges Banks were crewed and captained by Azoreans, Cape Verdeans, and Scandinavians, whose relatives on-shore worked for weekly wages as laborers and domestics and aspired to operate their own small businesses.

In 1910 fifteen per cent of the population of the United States was foreign-born, and about a third of those immigrants did not yet speak English. Anti-immigrant feeling ran high and was freely expressed in newspapers, public lectures, and legislation, ultimately leading to the restrictive immigration quotas established in the wake of World War I.

In the early 1930s a search was under way for how people had talked in old New England. Even in Nantucket, which had a long multiethnic and cosmopolitan history, there was nostalgia for old-time ways of speaking. This nostalgia had found its expression in *The Nantucket Scrap Basket*, a 1916 book containing anecdotes, turns of phrase, and an alphabetic glossary of quaint Nantucketisms. The compilers, William Macy and Roland Hussey,

Steamboat Wharf as it appeared when Hilda Österberg of Finland arrived on-island in the early 1890s.

dedicated the book to "all the sons and daughters of Nantucket." Those sons and daughters probably did not include, in Macy's and Hussey's view, the Nantucket-born who lived in Nantucket's New Guinea neighborhood, those who spoke Portuguese at home, or those who attended Mass in Nantucket's new Church of St. Mary, Our Lady of the Isle. It has taken the Nantucket community a long time to grow beyond this.

Another thirty years into the century, when Sarah P. Bunker's Finnish granddaughter-in-law Hilda herself passed the age of 90, more changes had taken place. Early in the century, her husband's old Nantucket line—through generations of infant mortality, "galloping consumption," and accidents at sea—had dwindled to just one person short of extinction. In the second half of the twentieth century, apparently benefiting from hybrid vigor, it was swelling like yeast dough in a warm kitchen. Today the roster of Sarah P.'s descendants, on-island and off-island, is still expanding exuberantly. Through

repeated marriages with off-islanders, few of them have old Nantucket surnames.

The house on Cliff Road, ghosts and all, has been sold out of the family. Meanwhile the Nevins mansion across the street has become venerable in its own right, surviving a century of change as a guest house, then back into private hands as Innishail (Gaelic for 'Haven of Rest'), and lately renovated by yet another newcomer to the island.

But most of all, at the dawn of a new millennium, who is a Nantucketer and what constitutes Nantucket heritage have been transformed. This has been accomplished not only by the integration of many arrivals who have been called at various moments in Nantucket history "strangers," "coofs," and "washashores" (the current pejorative), but also by the belated recognition of people who have lived on Nantucket throughout its centuries without being given place in its public history.

These are the Other Islanders, and here is some of their history.

Nantucket Historical Association

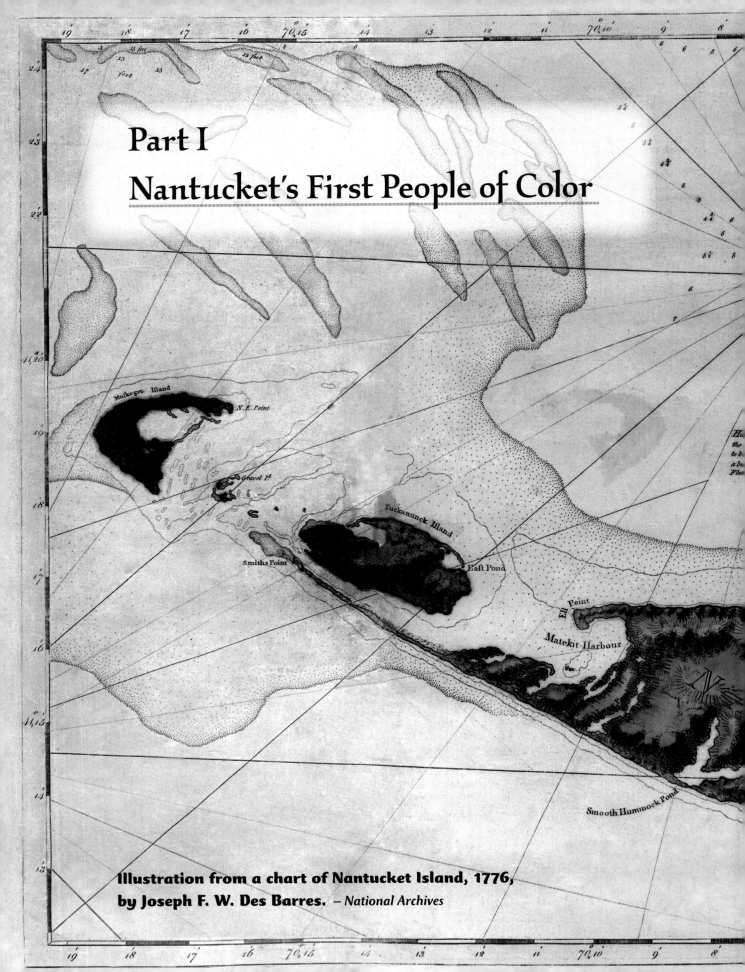

Part I
Nantucket's First People of Color

Illustration from a chart of Nantucket Island, 1776, by Joseph F. W. Des Barres. — *National Archives*

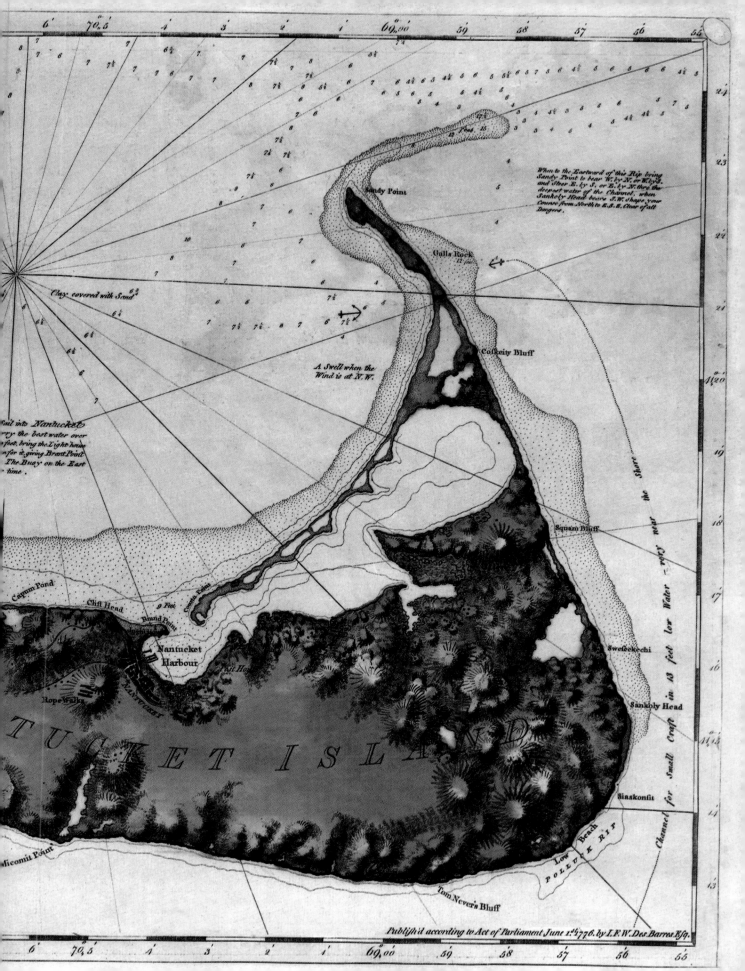

Sandy Point

Gulls Rock
12 fm

When to the Eastward of this Rip bring
Sandy Point to bear W. by N. or W. by S.
and Steer E. by S. or E. by N. thro the
deepest water of the Channel, when
Sankoty Head bears S.W. shape your
Course from North to E.S.E. clear of all
Dangers.

Coskeity Bluff

Clay covered with Sand

A Swell when the
Wind is at N.W.

Sail into Nantucket
rry the best water over
feet, bring the Light house
n for it, giving Brant Point
The Buoy on the East
time.

Squam Bluff

Capum Pond
Clift Head
Brand Point   9 Feet
Nantucket
Harbour   Coatu Point

Rope Walks

Swessekechi

Sankoly Head

Micomit Point

TUCKET ISLAND

Siaskonsit

Low Beach

POLLUCK RIP

Channel for Small Craft in 13 feet low Water — very near the Shore

Tom Never's Bluff

Publish'd according to Act of Parliament June 1ˢᵗ 1776. by I.F.W. Des Barres Esq.

CHAPTER ONE

Wampanoags: The Ancient Proprietors

— Library of Congress.
Algonquians in a dugout canoe,
from a 1650 map of New England.

Witnesses

Bones buried in the earth, discolored by minerals in the soil and disarticulated over time by frost heaves and moving water, become unintelligible to all but the most practiced eye. Our skulls are another matter. When a human skull is found, the question is not "What?" but "How long ago?" These days when a skull comes to light, the site is treated as a crime scene until the medical examiner and an archaeologist determine its age. Nantucket has been peopled for so long—for many thousand years—that the origin of such a find may be far in the past. If it predates the 1600s, then it is of the Nantucket people who have been called the island's "ancient proprietors."

As summer turned to autumn in 1894, Sarah P. Bunker watched from her upstairs bedroom window as workmen dug an immense hole across the street. They were preparing to lay a foundation for the Nevins mansion on the very brink of the Cliff. In the course of their work, they unearthed two human skulls that David Nevins conveyed to the Nantucket Historical Association. Albert Folger, Sarah P.'s neighbor up the street, had come upon others a dozen years earlier.

In December of 1987, a backhoe operator excavating for the foundation of public housing at the head of Miacomet valley dug into another

Human remains were unearthed during the construction of the Nevins mansion in 1894. Tradition locates a Wampanoag cemetery at this place.

Nantucket Historical Association

unmarked cemetery. Subsequently a worker with a shovel unearthed a skull. Unlike the old interments found a century earlier, the deceased in this cemetery had received burial in wooden coffins. Remains of the 222 victims of a massive epidemic in the winter of 1763–64 had been rediscovered. The wonder was that they had lain forgotten so long in the pine woods on the very edge of Surfside Road.

Inadvertent disinterments bear witness to Nantucket's first people in all stages of their history: from long before the coming of Europeans to these shores, during the transition from traditional life to a European-defined form of community, and at the near-termination of their existence on the island. Traces of their life on Nantucket dating back several thousand years show that the first stage had continued for a very long time before English settlers arrived. The last part—the population plunge toward extinction—took barely a century.

Their language, changed in pronunciation but still recognizable as theirs, is in our mouths a dozen times a day in familiar island names, many ending in *t*: 'Sconset, Madaket, Quidnet, Wannacomet, Miacomet. More of them used to have the *t*: Coatue

was once *Coatuet* and Capaum was *Capamet*. Eighty-six place names can be found in Nantucket deeds and wills, and a third of these remain in everyday use, a very high density when compared with even the most "Indian" of off-island locales.

Their artifacts turn up constantly. Construction sites unearth the dumps where they disposed of bones and shells from their meals, and to this day heavy rains continue to wash arrowheads from sand banks. We are reminded by the occasional emergence of their skeletal remains from eroding bluffs and from dirt roads worn deep into the moors that Nantucket's history did not begin in 1659.

Wampanoags and their Language

Living descendants of the people who once inhabited Cape Cod and its neighbor islands still form communities at Aquinnah (Gay Head) on Martha's Vineyard and Mashpee on the Cape. Today they identify themselves as Wampanoags. An alternative name for the indigenous people of Cape Cod and areas immediately to the southwest is "Pokanokets," while people of the outer Cape, thought to have special connections with those on Nantucket, have been identified as "Nausets."

1874 Ewer map of Nantucket, Tuckernuck, and Muskeget. The density of Eastern Algonquian place names is remarkable even for New England.

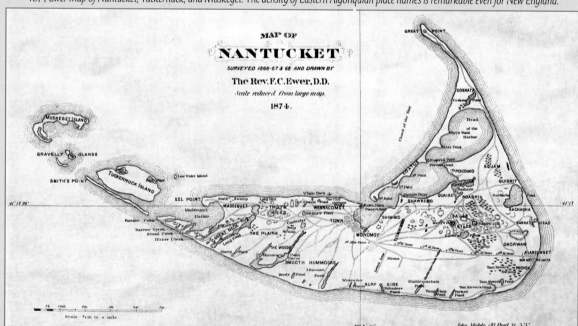

Nantucket Historical Association

It is difficult to sort out the political affiliations of the people living on the Cape and islands just before English and Dutch exploration of the area began. The native peoples left almost no records of themselves from that time, and the English and Dutch writers, having their own difficulties distinguishing among the various peoples they encountered, contradict each other and themselves. For the most part they called everyone they met "Indians," which would have dismayed the Pokanokets, who believed themselves to be as different from the Massachusetts as they were from the English and the Dutch.

Roger Williams, writing of the nearby Narragansetts with whom he had lived through the winter of 1636, remarked, "I cannot observe that they ever had (before the coming of the English, French or Dutch amongst them) any Names to difference themselves from strangers, for they knew none; but two sorts of names they had, and have amongst themselves." The first sort were words which simply meant "people," and the other sort were specific names for their neighbors such as *Massachusett* and *Pequot*. Williams continued, "They have often asked me why wee call them Indians."

The English, who would have been mortally offended to hear their own language and Dutch described as just a couple of local dialects of Low German, nonetheless perceived a New World full of Indians who spoke one Indian language. To negotiate with them and to preach to them it was necessary to learn to understand and to speak "Indian." To this end Williams published *A Key Into the Language of America* in 1643, and John Eliot published *The Indian Grammar Begun; or, An Essay to Bring the Indian Language into Rules* in 1666. Little did they know that the continent upon which they had intruded but a footstep was filled with languages as different from one another as are Russian, Chinese, Arabic, and Swahili. Unlike the French fur traders and Catholic missionaries at work in the St. Lawrence River valley, they had not yet come face to face with the Iroquois.

The first Europeans on the scene can be forgiven their cultural and linguistic short-sightedness, and we can be excused from belaboring the question of whether Nausets were Pokanokets and if in retrospect they should be called Wampanoags. Setting aside political alliances, which could shift in a matter of years, coastal New England emerges as a culturally and linguistically homogeneous place. The languages spoken in the area were all Eastern Algonquian languages, and the major division was between two languages: Massachusett and Narragansett. People on the Cape and islands spoke Massachusett, and people in what are today Rhode Island and Connecticut spoke Narragansett. Beyond the speakers of Narragansett were people who spoke yet another Eastern Algonquian language, Pequot-Mohegan. The differences among them were probably comparable to the differences among Italian, Spanish, and Portuguese.

Guy Loman Jr. and his fellow dialectologists mapped local differences in English speech around Southern New England early in the 1900s. Just so, in its time, Massachusett varied in pronunciation

Title page to A Key into the Language of America by Roger Williams.

A KEY into the
LANGUAGE
OF
AMERICA:
OR,
An help to the *Language* of the *Natives* in that part of A M E R I C A, called
NEW-ENGLAND.

Together. with briefe *Observations* of the Customes. Manners and Worships, &c of the aforesaid *Natives*, in Peace and Warre, in Life and Death.

On all which are added Spirituall *Observations*, Generall and Particular by the *Authour*, of chiefe and speciall use (upon all occasions,)to all the *English* Inhabiting those parts; yet pleasant and profitable to the view of all men:

BY ROGER WILLIAMS of Providence in New-England.

LONDON,
Printed by *Gregory Dexter*, 1643.

and vocabulary from place to place. Martha's Vineyard speech was said to be difficult for off-islanders to understand, and Nantucket, being farther from the mainland, probably even more so. But the language was Massachusett, nonetheless, as can be seen from wills, grave markers, transfers of land, and bills of sale written in it during the 1600s and 1700s.

There are current efforts to resurrect the language, but Massachusett has not been spoken in over a century. We learn about it through related languages that are still spoken and through written records. We owe a debt of gratitude to two Nantucket Quakers, Richard Macy and Richard Mitchell, who presented a collection of seven documents from Nantucket written in Massachusett to the Massachusetts Historical Society for preservation.[1] They did this in 1802, nearly four decades after the great epidemic, at a time when very few speakers of the language remained living on Nantucket. Had the documents stayed on Nantucket and come to rest in the original Atheneum, they would have gone up in flames in the Great Fire of 1846, and Algonquian studies would have been the poorer. Today the surviving writings in Massachusett, including the precious Nantucket documents that Macy and Mitchell preserved, are in print and available to library users in Nantucket and on the mainland.

What are Eastern Algonquian languages like? The word for skunk sounds pretty much like *skunk*, and the word for squash sounds like *squash*. To English these languages have also contributed the words *moose*, *wigwam*, *moccasin*, *papoose*, *sachem*, *sagamore*, *wampum*, and *powwow* as well as the now less common words *succotash* (corn stew) and *mugwump* (a person of dubious loyalty). Despite the ugly connotations that became attached to the word *squaw* and despite the bitter assertion by many Indian people that the English adopted an Iroquois word meaning 'female genitals' or 'prostitute' to refer to women, Roger Williams recorded

squaw in Narragansett as 'woman' and *keegsquaw* as 'young woman,' while the Massachusett documents have *squa* for 'woman' and *ussqua* meaning 'young woman.' The wife of a sachem was called *saucksqua* in Narragansett. None of these are used with any implicit insult by speakers of Narragansett or Massachusett.

Most Algonquian words are long, and English speakers have shortened them by dropping off syllables from the front. Tuckernuck was once *Petockenock,* Squam was *Wanisquam*, and Quidnet was *Aquidnet.* The practice continues today with the pronunciation of Siasconset as '*Sconset* and Sesachacha Pond as '*Sacacha.*

Personal names were shortened in the same way. The descendants of Sachem Nickanoose used Noose as a surname, while those of Sachem Wanackmamack went by the family name of Mamack. Descendants of the first native pastor on Martha's Vineyard, Hiacoomes, have continued the name in the form Coombs.

Lifeways

Daily life in Nantucket before the coming of English settlers differed from life on the mainland. European explorers along the New England coast remarked on the extensive gardens and cornfields they observed, and the Pilgrims exploring Cape Cod came upon a large buried cache of corn that they used for themselves. Little evidence for extensive cultivation of corn has been found on Nantucket, however; just a few kernels have been recovered from old trash pits. Nor are there signs that land was cleared for extensive planting prior to the mid-1600s. English settlers may have been the ones to introduce field agriculture to the island.

Wigwams were light and easy to dismantle, and Algonquians in general moved frequently. In the winter the mainland Wampanoags and their neighbors withdrew from the coasts to the forests to hunt deer, which provided them with abundant

1. Zaccheus Macy, justice of the peace, was most likely the last Englishman on Nantucket to speak the Massachusett language. His son Richard (named after his grandfather) was one of the donors of the documents to the Massachusetts Historical Society. Before his death in 1797, Zaccheus had probably passed the documents on to Richard for safekeeping. Both elders of the Nantucket meeting of the Society of Friends, Richard Macy lived until 1813 and Richard Mitchell until 1819.

meat, skins, and horn. Deer-hunting was a major occupation even as nearby as Mashpee on Cape Cod, but deer were scarce or absent from Nantucket for periods of time, and the cottontail rabbits that are so plentiful these days originated in Europe and were not introduced to Nantucket until 1891. While people may have moved their wigwams seasonally on the island, from summers along the beaches to sheltered winter sites in protected spots like Masquetuck on Polpis Harbor, their cold-weather hunting was for ducks and geese. Woven grass mats took the place of skins for clothes and wigwam coverings, and trash pits yield few enough deer bones to suggest that whatever venison people ate was obtained by trade with the mainland. Many migratory birds passed through in fall and spring, but Nantucket's year-round land-animal population consisted of hardly more than voles, bats, snakes, and the Wampanoags' dogs. There were no foxes, wolves, bears, skunks, moose, or even squirrels.

What did people eat besides water fowl? Middens where they dumped their refuse tell us that the original Nantucketers were shellfish eaters. They especially liked to eat the *poquauhock*, which we have shortened to "quahog," and they don't seem to have had much use for mussels, which surprised Europeans, who considered them good food. English settlers adopted this local prejudice; their Nantucket descendants have eaten quahogs, scallops, and oysters but not until quite recently mussels.

Other food from the sea included lobsters, bluefish, herring (which are really alewives), eels, and meat and blubber from sea mammals—including seals and the blackfish that have periodically beached in large numbers on the island. Gull and turtle eggs, seaweeds, and plants from the tidal marshes were other available sources of nutrition.

Wampanoag women were gardeners and gatherers. Although their gardens may not have been extensive, the island offered an abundant natural harvest including cranberries, beach plums, and the tasty nodules that form on the roots of nut grass. Only pollen analysis from layers of centuries-old sediment and peat can sort out which of the many useful plants that grow uncultivated on the island today were here before the English settlers brought their cuttings, seeds, and inadvertent

Nantucket Wampanoags were heavily dependent on shellfish for nutrition. They also benefited from the frequent beaching of blackfish (pilot whales).

weeds. Of all the useful edible and medicinal plants that have grown on the island for the last century or more, only some were available for use before the mid-1600s. Many that we consider characteristic of Nantucket—the rugosa rose with its vitamin-rich scarlet rose hips, for instance—are attractive, useful, well-adapted aliens.

On their diet of shellfish from the shores, migratory birds from the air, and the original fruits of Nantucket's sandy soil, the island Wampanoags[2] lived healthy lives. They were tall, well-nourished people, whose teeth were undamaged by sugar or a diet over-reliant on corn. One thing is certain: in order for two or three thousand people to maintain wholesome lives on Nantucket, the resources of the entire island—shores, woods, swamps, and grasslands—had to be available to everyone at all times, different spots offering different resources throughout the year.

The reported population just prior to the first English settlement in 1659 was about 3,000. This density (and a similar density on Martha's Vineyard) contrasts with an eerie emptiness across the Sound. The coastal mainland had been swept by epidemics introduced by European fishermen and explorers, the worst having completely depopulated the area where the *Mayflower*'s passengers finally disembarked. The off-shore location of Nantucket and Martha's Vineyard protected their inhabitants from contagion, and it is possible that refugees from the affected areas had swollen the island populations to the brink of their carrying capacities shortly before the English began to arrive. The 1600s were hardly normal times for anyone, indigenous or European. In any case, Nantucket's ancient proprietors needed every square foot, every nook and cranny of their island in order to carry on their way of life.

Wampanoag society was governed by sachems, community elders who bore the responsibility of making decisions, creating alliances, and carrying out policies for everyone under their jurisdiction. They were also personally responsible for executions. In return for their services, sachems received loyalty and gifts from their people to support them in their work. Sachems' families were more influential than most families, but a sachem, unlike a European monarch, did not automatically pass on his position to his eldest son. Moreover, consensus-building among community members played as great a role as authority from the top of a chain of command. Europeans looking for Wampanoag equivalents of their kings and princes misunderstood and misrepresented what they encountered in southeastern New England, and in time, as the English sought to replace the sachems' authority with that of their King, those misunderstandings caused trouble for everyone.

From around the area—including Nantucket—there were also reports in the 1600s of "queen-sachems." These were wives, sisters, and daughters of sachems who exercised considerable authority themselves as well as conveying power to their husbands and sons. During English settlement of the island, Nantucket's queen sachem was Askammapoo, daughter of Sachem Nickanoose. Her husband's name, Spoospotswa, was shortened by English speakers to Spotso, and their son Daniel Spotso was an active broker between the early English settlers and the Wampanoags. Among the documents given by Richard Mitchell and Richard Macy to the Massachusetts Historical Society is a power of attorney written in Massachusett by which Askammapoo delegated Daniel to appear in court on her behalf.

Among the Wampanoags power resided in the sachems and also in their spiritual leaders. The meaning of the word *powwow* has changed. It originally referred to individuals, not to gatherings of people—men and women who had experienced visions calling them to serve as healers and seers. To find the cause of illness and

---

2. The native people of Nantucket did not call themselves Wampanoags, nor are there documented instances of anyone else using this term in reference to them prior to the epidemic of 1763–64. But Wampanoag is now used by the descendants of the native peoples of Martha's Vineyard and Cape Cod, as it would be by descendants of the native peoples of Nantucket if they returned to the island today.

to predict the outcome of important events such as harvests and wars, powwows made spiritual journeys outside their bodies, wafted along by tobacco smoke and in the company of companion birds and animals. In their travels they might encounter the powerful thunderbird, the horned serpent, and the sacred turtle, symbol of motherhood and fertility. Powwows traveled to the spirit world at great risk to themselves, and in return their people rewarded them with gifts and reverence, just as they rewarded their sachems. As a result, sachems and powwows accumulated wealth and influence through public service.

Most Wampanoags were not of sachems' or powwows' families. They lived out their daily lives on the island in ways that remain familiar to us today—hunting ducks, digging quahogs, and gathering cranberries on warm autumn days; surviving winter storms, bitter cold, and lean times long enough to produce new generations of native Nantucketers. As generations succeeded generations, they left behind their homesites, their tools, and their shell dumps for us to puzzle over.

Passings

In one view of Nantucket history the ancient proprietors' presence ceased in the winter of 1763-64 when their numbers were reduced by half in a matter of a few months. In another view, the last truly native Nantucketers passed into history in the mid-1800s with the deaths of Abram Quary and Dorcas Honorable.

The disappearance of the Nantucket's indigenous population can be attributed to various pernicious practices of the English settlers who had arrived on Nantucket in 1659. Prominent among them are the appropriation of land, the introduction of alcohol, and the institution of a money economy, leading inevitably to failure of the Wampanoags' traditional way of life and thence to debt-servitude, the whipping post, and the gallows beyond the edge of town.

Or the responsibility can be laid at the door of sachems who, through incomprehension or personal greed, sold out their own people.

Or it can be attributed to impersonal and uncontrollable forces that were at that time utterly beyond human understanding or control: the failure of Wampanoag families to reproduce and the mystery of the deadly epidemic.

Or one can take the position that the disappearance of Nantucket's first people was a typical nineteenth-century social construction and that there have been no "last Indians." But history is never simple, and none of those stories quite covers all the ground.

First Acquaintances

The Wampanoags and their neighbors enter documentary history with the arrival of European explorers along the New England coast, followed by English settlers—the Pilgrims of Plymouth, the Puritans of Massachusetts Bay, and eventually an odd lot of individuals who, having for one reason or another become marginal in the mainland colonies, sought refuge and new beginnings for themselves beyond the Massachusetts Bay Colony: in Rhode Island and on the offshore islands. It is through the writings of these Europeans—opportunistic, often adversarial, and at best patronizing—that we have first records of the Algonquians.

The Pilgrims were not the first Europeans the peoples of coastal New England had ever seen. Before they arrived, some Eastern Algonquians had already visited Europe, not by their own design. Much of the early history of Algonquian–European contact involves kidnapping. In 1524 Giovanni da Verrazzano, in the service of France, explored the coast from Manhattan to Narragansett Bay and described his visit with two local leaders who were either Wampanoags or Narragansetts. The very next year Estevão Gomes, a harbinger of things to come, showed up in the same waters, captured more than fifty Algonquians from the shore, and carried them off to Spain for sale as slaves.

And so it went. Trade with Breton and Basque fishermen who frequented the waters provided useful goods. Exploring along the coast in 1602,

Bartholomew Gosnold, who has been credited as the first European to record the existence of Nantucket, was met by Wampanoags in a Basque-style sailboat.

For the Wampanoags, however, the desirability of useful trade items was tempered by the unpredictability of what next might come under sail over the eastern horizon. After Gosnold's visit, French and English explorers—including Captain John Smith, famous for his account of having been saved by Pocahontas from death in Virginia—began to frequent the coastal waters. In fact, John Smith took credit for first naming the area "New England." Contacts that began as peaceful opportunities for trade sometimes exploded into violence. Resentments grew, and there were attacks and killings on both sides as the local people tried to drive off European explorers and the explorers tried to protect their material possessions and their lives.

In 1604 Martin Pring, working for a company of English merchants, built a fort at the tip of Cape Cod, where Provincetown is now located, and took to loosing his two large dogs on Nausets who came to see what he was up to. In frustration, the Nausets set fire to the surrounding woods to burn him out.

In 1606 on Monomoy Point, at the elbow of Cape Cod, a French party put on a show of force to intimidate the people onshore. The obnoxious intruders were run off, losing a man in the fight, while the angry local residents demonstrated their contempt by flinging beach sand at them and yapping like a pack of wolves.

There were more kidnappings. Among them, the English captains George Waymouth, Edward Harlow, Nicholas Hobson, and Thomas Hunt carried off close to thirty people, including a Martha's Vineyard sachem named Epinow.

Hugo Allard's 1673 "True and Exact Map of All New Netherlands" shows Cape Cod, Nantucket, and Martha's Vineyard. In the general area of Providence and New Bedford appears the word "Wampanoos."

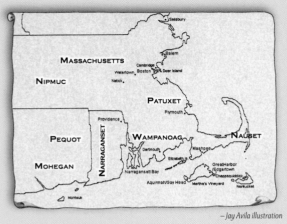

– Jay Avila illustration

Locations on the New England mainland, Cape Cod, and the islands of special significance to Nantucket history.

Accounts of what happened next don't entirely agree. Apparently Hunt, like Gomes before him, tried to sell his captives in Spain, but Spanish authorities confiscated them. Some of the Algonquians who had been snatched from their own shores lived for a while in England and eventually returned home.

According to Sir Fernando Gorges, also exploring for England, Epinow ended up as the property of yet another English captain, Henry Harley, who exhibited him as a curiosity in London. By 1614, when the Dutch and the English were both mapping New England's coastal waters, Epinow had acquired a serviceable command of English. He, Assacomet (a servant of Gorges), and Wenape (another Wampanoag, who had landed somehow on the Isle of Wight) were sent with Captain Hobson back to the Vineyard to serve as interpreters for the English. Thwarting efforts to keep him captive aboard ship, Epinow managed to break loose from his captors and swim ashore. Epinow survived to tell his story to his people and to enlighten them about the world from whence his captors came. The kidnapping of Epinow and the others (including Nausets from the outer Cape and Patuxets from the Plymouth area) was fresh in people's minds when the English settlers began arriving in the 1620s. The memory of the English raids inspired local resentment toward the newcomers, who were the washashores of their day.

In the early spring of 1621, three months after the *Mayflower* had delivered its Pilgrim passengers to the place they named New Plymouth, a man walked out of the woods and greeted them in English, introducing himself as Samoset. Through association with fishermen and traders along the Maine coast, he spoke English and probably bits of other European languages as well. He may have been to Europe and back in advance of the Pilgrims. On his next visit, Samoset brought Tisquantum (a name the English predictably shortened to "Squanto"), a local Patuxet who had been carried off to be sold in Spain. Like Epinow, however, Tisquantum had ended up in London, living with an English merchant named John Slany before making more transatlantic voyages, ultimately in the service of Fernando Gorges.

Considering what he knew first-hand about the English, it seems little short of miraculous that Tisquantum attached himself to the struggling Plymouth Plantation and made himself useful to people he had every reason to consider his enemies. The English at the time and historians since have had reason to question his motives, but Squanto was now a man alone. He had returned home to a silent, empty land.

Sometime around 1616, in horrific foreshadowing of what was to happen in Nantucket a century and a half later, an epidemic had broken out and raged for two years along the coast from Narragansett Bay to Penobscot Bay. Before the *Mayflower* arrived, the Patuxet had perished. Their fields stood uncultivated, shoulder-high in grass, ready for the English settlers to reclaim for themselves with minimum effort. Scavenger birds—crows, gulls, and the vultures that gave their name to Buzzards Bay—had cleaned away the human carrion, but bones lay unburied, witness to the horror that had come in advance of the sails of the diminutive *Mayflower* with its seemingly insignificant human cargo.

However, what the Pilgrims observed at Plymouth was deceptive. The epidemic had not swept inland or reached out to the islands. There were far more Massachusetts, Nipmucks, Abenakis,

Narragansetts, Pequots, and Wampanoags than they imagined, and in the years to come these peoples and the English would engage in mutual bloodletting.

Before the century was out, the mainland had been shaken by two devastating conflicts, the Pequot War of 1637 and King Philip's War of 1675–76. Nantucket and Martha's Vineyard had not seen their first English settlers at the time of the Pequot War, however, and the violence of Philip's War didn't touch them. Philip himself did visit Nantucket a decade before the war that bears his name, and at about the same time—to put it in the words of an English footnote to a document written in Massachusett—"Indians ware hanged on Nantucket."

Out to the Islands

English reach to the islands had begun at the opening of the 1640s, after the Pequot War. Thomas Mayhew, a Puritan businessman, faced bankruptcy in the Massachusetts Bay Colony. His son Thomas Jr. and his employee of several years, Peter Folger, had both been learning to speak Massachusett. Thomas Jr. studied the language as part of his training for the ministry. Peter Folger learned it for practical business purposes, but in the course of time, he too became an evangelist. When Thomas Mayhew Sr. decided to rebuild his lost fortune outside the colony on Martha's Vineyard, both young men, with their special language skills, were indispensable to the enterprise.

Mayhew's first act was to legally clear his new off-shore land holdings. This included obtaining from the Earl of Sterling in 1641 a deed to Nantucket, Tuckernuck, and Muskeget for himself and his son. Then, concluding that the outer islands didn't suit his plans, he soon after obtained a separate deed to Martha's Vineyard and the Elizabeth Islands.

The Earl of Sterling did not hold undisputed title to the land in question, however. Despite a broad royal grant of coastal lands to Sterling in 1635, the explorer Sir Fernando Gorges had a competing claim, and for security's sake Thomas Mayhew also sought confirmation from him of the right to settle the islands.

In 1659, Mayhew sold Nantucket to the "original proprietors" (as contrasted with the ancient proprietors). These new proprietors were Tristram Coffin, Thomas Macy, and their fellow investors—residents of Salisbury, a town on the northern edge of the Massachusetts Bay Colony. They paid to Mayhew the famous price of thirty pounds and two beaver hats "one for my self and one for my Wife."

Within a year the Nantucket sachems Wanackmamack and Nickanoose signed a deed as well. For the price of twenty-six pounds (twelve already paid and fourteen more to come), they sold to Mayhew and the Nantucket proprietors the west end of Nantucket; one half of the remainder of the meadows and marshes on the island; rights to "what grass they shall need to mow" from the remainder of the island's marshes and meadows; liberty to take timber and wood from any part of

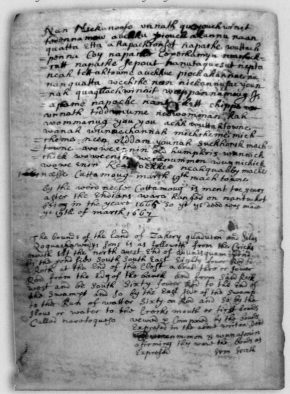

Deed of land by Sachem Nickanoose to Quaquachwinnit, written in Massachusett language with English note about Indians being hanged on Nantucket in 1665.

Kevin Crosby photograph, courtesy of Nantucket Registry of Deeds

25

The 1660 deed by which Nantucket sachems Wanackmamack and Nickanoose
conveyed part of Nantucket to Thomas Mayhew, Tristram Coffin, and the other English investors.

The tenth day of May 1660

These presents witness that we Wanachmamuck & Nikanoose, head Sachems of Nantucket Island do give grant bargain & sell unto Mr Thomas Mayhew of Martins vineyard Tristram Coffin Senr Thomas Macy Christopher Hussey Richard Swain Peter Coffin Stephen Green Leaf Thomas Barnard John Swain and William Pile all the land meadows & Marishes Timber and wood and all appurtenances thereto belonging being and lying from the west end of the Island of Nantucket unto the pond called by the Indians waquittaquaag and from the head of that pond upon a strait line unto the pond situate by Monument harbour or Creek now called wheelers Creek and so from the North East Corner of the so pond to the sea that is to say all the Right that we the aforesd Sachems have in these tract of land provided that none of the Indian Inhabitants in or about the wood land or whatsoever Indians inhabit within the last purchase of land from the head of the pond to Monument harbour shall be Removed without full satisfaction and also we the aforesd Sachems do give grant bargain and sell the one half of all the Remainder of the Meadows & Marishes upon all other parts of the Island and also that the English people that have what Grass they shall need for to mow out of the Remainder of the Meadows and Marishes on the Island so long as the English Remain upon the Island and also free liberty for Timber and wood on any part of the Island within our Jurisdiction and also we the aforesd Sachems do fully grant free liberty to the English for feeding all sorts of Cattle on any part of the Island after Indian harvest is Ended until planting time or until the first day of may from year to year for ever for and in Consideration of twelve pounds already paid and fourteen pounds to be paid within three months after the date hereof to have & to hold the aforesd purchase of land and other appurtenances as aforementioned to them the aforesd Mr Thomas Mayhew Tristram Coffin Thomas Macy and the Rest aforementioned and their heirs and assigns for Ever In witness whereof we the aforesd Sachems have hereunto set our hands and seals the day and year above written

Signed Sealed & delivered   the sign of Wanachmamah
in the presence of   the sign of Nikanoose

Peter Foulger
Felix Kuttahamaquat   Wanachmamuck & Nikanoos acknowledged the
Edward Starbuck   above written to be their act & deed in the presence
                                         of the General Court this 12th of June 1677 as attests
                                                                          Matt mayhew Cler to the General
                                                                          Court

I do witness this deed to be a true deed according to the Interpretation of felix the Interpretor also I heard Wanachmamah but two weeks ago affirm the Sale of the neck and he do say that he will so do what Ever Come of it witness my hand this 17 1 mo 64
                                                                          Peter Foulger
witness
Mary Starbuck
the mark of John E C Coffin   a true Coppy Attest Eleaz Foulger
                                                                          Regr

Nantucket Historical Association

the island; and liberty to graze livestock anywhere on the island from after the Wampanoags' harvest in the fall until planting began in May.[3] To this deed of sale Wanackmamack and Nickanoose placed their marks in the presence of Peter Folger, Edward Starbuck, and Felix Kuttashamaquah, interpreter.

A year later, Wanackmamack signed a second deed covering all that is in the previous deed and adding that "likewise I…doe sell unto the English… the property of the rest of the Island belonging unto mee." For this he received forty pounds more.

The sachems had, so to speak, given away the farm. With the signing of these deeds, which were further confirmed with additional witnesses in 1664 and 1677, Nantucket was forever alienated from its ancient proprietors. Subsequent petitions to the General Court of Massachusetts in the first half of the 1700s for the recovery of their lost land would not prevail. The court pointed out that English title to the island had been triply obtained: from the Earl of Sterling, from Sir Fernando Gorges, and from the Nantucket sachems.

How could such a thing have happened in the wink of an eye, when the number of English settlers actually resident on the island could be counted on one's fingers? The case has been made that the sachems did not grasp what such a sale meant; that perhaps they understood the money presented to them as tribute comparable to what they received from their own people; and that they believed they were temporarily renting out their sachem rights. From their viewpoint such agreements were not made in perpetuity but were subject to frequent renewal. Granted that a phrase appearing in the 1660 deed, "so long as the English remain on the Island," implies that the sachems regarded the deal as temporary, still both deeds also state that the land was conveyed to the purchasers, their heirs, and their assigns "forever."

Peter Folger, the Massachusett-speaking agent of Thomas Mayhew, and Felix Kuttashamaquah, the English-speaking Wampanoag interpreter, knew between them what the deed meant, and if they failed to make this intelligible to Wanackmamack and Nickanoose, then they were jointly responsible for a grave injustice. In obtaining the sachems' marks on the deeds before witnesses, they were taking away for all time the only means of independent living the ancient proprietors of Nantucket had or could have on the island. In the future, following the signing of the deeds, their only means of subsistence would be as dependents of the English. This was not immediately evident in 1660, when Wampanoags overwhelmingly outnumbered English on what had been their island. But they would soon see the light.

English Insecurities

The period from Thomas Mayhew's purchase of Nantucket in 1641 to his sale of the island to the English proprietors in 1659 was a time of great change and anxiety for the English as well as for the Wampanoags. In 1641 Oliver Cromwell considered leaving England for a new life in Connecticut. Had he departed, and had King Charles I averted the English revolution against its monarchy, Massachusetts and Connecticut would have been flooded with thousands more Puritans following Cromwell's lead and abandoning their homes in England for new lives across the seas. But parliamentary winds shifted, and Cromwell stayed in England to head up the civil war that broke out the following year.

Instead of experiencing an influx of new settlers, the New England colonies lost population as men returned to England to fight against their king and his party. Harvard College had been founded in 1636. Between 1640 and 1650, more than fifty percent of the young men graduating from the college departed for England to support the revolution. The conflict culminated in the execution of Charles I in 1649, and Oliver Cromwell became Lord Protector of the English republic until his death in 1658.

---

3. The practice of clearing title in all directions was not novel to Nantucket. It had been a policy of the Massachusetts Bay Colony from the beginning, and already in the 1630s the towns of Boston, Cambridge, Charlestown, Concord, and Ipswich had made payment for lands they occupied. Roger Williams was a gadfly of the Massachusetts Bay Colony, insisting that it was immoral to occupy the land of indigenous peoples without purchasing it from them.

Then the political tide turned once again. With the restoration of the monarchy in 1660, the New England Puritans who had returned to their old country to assume positions of power were once again vulnerable. Some, including the Reverend Hugh Peters, who had exerted considerable influence on the young Peter Folger, were executed for treason. Even the deceased Cromwell was not safe; his body was exhumed from the grave for posthumous beheading.

A local consequence of this turn of history is that the given name Cromwell became popular among the offspring of English settlers in Nantucket for generations, persisting well into the 1800s. The Coffin family must drive genealogists to despair with its four Cromwell Coffins, four Oliver Cromwell Coffins, and two Oliver C. Coffins, whose birthdates range from 1709 to 1823.[4]

Strangers and Their Religion

During the English political and religious upheaval that unsettled the New England colonies, the Wampanoags of Martha's Vineyard and Nantucket were also swept up in a revolution on their home islands. Thomas Mayhew Jr., who had been ordained into the clergy, went to the islands as an evangelist just at the time when John Eliot began his preaching ministry to the native peoples of Natick. During the following decade a primer for teaching how to read in Massachusett was produced on the printing press in Harvard Yard, and Eliot set about translating the Bible into Massachusett. Seven "praying towns," including the flagship community of Natick, were established along the western frontier of the Massachusetts Bay Colony. Because the Puritans believed that all Christian communities required spiritual leaders with a mastery of Latin and Greek as well as Protestant theology and English, young men from the praying towns were sent to be prepared for a college education in Cambridge in order for them to return to their peoples as ministers.

The task at hand for Thomas Mayhew Jr. was to organize the Wampanoags of Martha's Vineyard and Nantucket into Christian communities like those on the mainland. Members of these communities were to be self-governing, literate in their own language, and orthodox according to Puritan beliefs. In addition to Mashpee and nine other praying towns on Cape Cod, there came to be ten on Martha's Vineyard and five on Nantucket, the accomplishment of the Mayhews together with Peter Folger.

The first step was for the Mayhews and Folger to take up residence on Martha's Vineyard. As they built English frame houses at Great Harbor (later renamed Edgartown), no one attacked them. The island's sachems and powwows were not receptive to evangelization, however, and their people reacted dramatically to the stress of having English settlers among them. Experience Mayhew, writing later about his grandfather's and great-grandfather's first year on the Vineyard, recounted an incident in 1643 when the Wampanoags blackened their faces as though in mourning, shouted, brandished weapons, and "ran up and down as if delirious till they could run no longer." Yet they offered the Mayhews no harm.

Meeting opposition to the Christian message from the sachems and powwows, Thomas Mayhew Jr. found his first convert from outside the elite Wampanoag families. Hiacoomes was a young man with a wife and two children when he began his association with the English in the mid-1640s. Experience Mayhew described him as a gifted but marginal member of his own society. The Mayhews provided him an intellectual outlet for his unrecognized talents by giving him one of the new "Indian Primers" and some instruction in how to use it. In a small reading class in 1645, Hiacoomes advanced so much faster than the others that he took over their instruction from Thomas Mayhew Jr. Within the year the two men were preaching jointly to the sachems, and

---

4. There were also an Oliver Cromwell Hussey, an Oliver Cromwell Barnard, an Oliver Cromwell Gardner, an Oliver C. Gardner, an Oliver C. Swain, an Oliver C. Folger, a Cromwell Barnard, a Cromwell Macy, a Cromwell Pinkham, and a Cromwell Folger. Even the Boston family, descendants of Nantucket Africans and Wampanoags, produced an Oliver C. (1836–1872).

Hiacoomes was engaging the Vineyard powwows in public debates. Having begun his ministry in 1646, Hiacoomes was formally ordained as a minister in 1670 and continued his career in public speaking nearly to his death in 1690.

The informal reading group of 1645 gave place to a regular school established in 1651 with Peter Folger as schoolmaster. He taught reading and writing in both Massachusett and English along with church doctrine. Although the "Indian school" operated only sporadically, it produced a number of Wampanoag preachers for the Vineyard's praying towns, and according to Experience Mayhew, reading became widespread among the island's men, women, and children.

Being reckoned as a Christian among the Puritans was hard even for the English. Once accepted, one could easily misstep and be ejected again, as Roger Williams learned painfully during his first years in the Massachusetts Bay Colony.

For Wampanoags the cultural leap was orders of magnitude greater. They had to learn to abase themselves, shed tears over their inherent unworthiness, and look to death as deliverance from this sinful world in the hope of a better one to come. Experience Mayhew wrote a book about the lives, last words, and deaths of godly Wampanoags to show how men and women, young and old—those who had lived lives of prayerful good behavior and those who had engaged in scandalous backsliding—all were brought humbly to final resignation. A formulaic deathbed confession of unworthiness appears often in the book, as for instance in the last hours of Jonathan Amos, when reportedly, "He confessed himself to be a Sinner, and utterly unworthy of God's Mercy; and yet declared that he had Hopes of attaining eternal Mercy thro' Jesus Christ, our only Savior."

As an early test of faith and a triumph for Christianity, Mayhew described the death in 1650

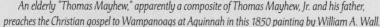

An elderly "Thomas Mayhew," apparently a composite of Thomas Mayhew, Jr. and his father, preaches the Christian gospel to Wampanoags at Aquinnah in this 1850 painting by William A. Wall.

of one of the young sons of Hiacoomes and his wife. The child was buried without the traditional rites of face-blackening, lamentation, and burial of grave goods with the body. Mayhew preached at this new kind of funeral and praised the bereaved parents for presenting such a good example of patient Christian acceptance of their child's death.

The English evangelists tacitly assumed that the people they sought to convert were not their moral and intellectual equals. Experience Mayhew wrote, "It must indeed be granted that the Indians are generally a very sinful People: Iniquity does abound among them."

Three bulwarks of defense against unchristian behavior were established in praying towns: church, home, and civil authority.

Constant admonition, a feature of Puritan religious life, was instilled as a practice among the new converts. From their ministers, members of praying towns received weekly reinforcement of the notion of their deep and inherent sinfulness. Japheth Hannit took the occasion of his own impending death to issue the following denunciation of his fellow Wampanoags: "God is constantly calling us to Repentence, and has offered repeatedly his Chastisements on us, by grievous Sicknesses, but this notwithstanding, how full of Wickedness has he seen all our Towns, for both Men and Women, young Men and Maids, do all delight in Sin, and do things therein greatly grievous."

Parents were expected to carry on spiritual instruction at home as well. Long before his final illness, Jonathan Amos "used his Endeavors to bring up his Children in the Knowledge and Fear of God; to this end he used to make useful Observations on the Scriptures when he read them to his Family, and to exhort them to the Duties mentioned in them, and did often at other times instruct and admonish them."

And finally, each praying town had native magistrates and constables to enforce good behavior and punish wrongdoing. Sometimes the whippings imposed by the magistrates struck the English as excessive. When Thomas Mayhew, Sr. suggested to Wampanoag magistrate William Lay of Chilmark that he was too severe, Lay replied that unlike guilt-wracked Englishmen, Indians had no sense of shame and so had to be mercilessly punished for crimes they committed.

On Nantucket there is a legend of "Corduda's Law." According to this, the Wampanoag justice of the peace would arbitrarily have both plaintiff and defendant whipped before they were granted a hearing. The original source for this, however, tells a different story from the one that has developed through retellings. On one occasion Nantucket's "great justice" Corduda had a conversation with a Massachusett-speaking Englishman named Nathan Coleman, who happened to be present when a Wampanoag sought an appeal of a previous ruling. It was Coleman who suggested that the man be punished for coming to court. The original report refers to Coleman as a "crank" for inserting himself into Wampanoag judicial proceedings. Yet folklore has suppressed the role and even the name of the Englishman and perpetuated the story as a joke at the expense of the Wampanoag magistrate and, presumably, his imperfect mastery of English principles of justice.

Interpreters and *Patrones*

Many are the jokes about the relentless monolingualism of English speakers. For example: a person who speaks several languages is multilingual; a person who speaks two languages is bilingual; a person who speaks one language is an American. In fact, Europeans abroad in the world have generally placed the burden of language learning on other people, generally by kidnapping them for a period of total-immersion language learning before employing them as interpreters. In any contact situation of any duration, however, someone among the newcomers does manage to learn the local language. In the 1620s Edward Ashley offered to broker a trade partnership between the English and the native people of the Penobscot area of Maine because he "had for some time lived among the Indians as a savage and went naked amongst them and used their manners, in which time he got their language." The religious dissident Roger Williams could write his *Key into the Language of America* and establish his Providence colony because he had lived with the Narragansetts while evading deportation to England. A profound sense of religious obligation impelled John Eliot to learn Massachusett, organize the native people on the western edge of the Massachusetts Bay Colony into praying towns, and keep issuing religious books in their language from the Harvard Yard printing press. Captain Daniel Gookin, Superintendent of the Indians of Massachusetts Bay for 30 years from the mid-1650s to the mid-1680s, came to his position from a military career in Ireland and Virginia, posts where he had become accustomed to dealing first with speakers of Irish Gaelic and then with speakers of Powhatan.

These atypical Englishmen, moving with familiarity, relative comfort, and a modicum of appreciation among the indigenous peoples of southern New England, became spokesmen and negotiators before English civil and military authority. This gave them power over indigenous society (although less than they might have wished for) and at the same time exposed them to hostility from other Englishmen who did not share their concerns for the material and spiritual well-being of "savages." Their lives were often threatened by their fellow Englishmen. At the same time they wrought enormous and often detrimental and irreversible changes in the lives of the people they intended to serve or to exploit.

In Latin America men who speak an indigenous language as well as their native Spanish or Portuguese and who look out for and control people they consider theirs are called *patrones*. The word has connotations somewhat different from the English *patron*, although the English definition of a patron as a source of financial support touches on one aspect of this sort of relationship. The word is derived from the Latin root meaning 'father,' and being a father implies that one has moral authority over people considered to be one's children. *Patrones* are on hand to get their people out of trouble, to intervene in community affairs, to call in favors and debts, to mediate disputes, to take over people's lives on a direct one-to-one basis. In the case of missionaries who claim to be gatekeepers of the hereafter, this control extends even beyond death.

In their various ways, Ashley, Williams, Eliot, and Gookin functioned as *patrones* in New England in the 1600s. However much they valued and admired their indigenous friends, as Europeans and as Christians they did not for a moment doubt their own intellectual and moral superiority or their right to radically remake other people's lives.

The first Massachusett-speaking Englishmen operating on Nantucket and Martha's Vineyard were, as we have seen, Thomas Mayhew Jr. and Peter Folger. Mayhew and Hiacoomes preached together on the Vineyard, while—beginning in 1651—Folger served as schoolmaster there. The Mayhews and Folger became the first English *patrones* of the islands' native peoples.

In 1657 Thomas Mayhew Jr. embarked for England. The ship on which he took passage sailed off to the east and was never seen again. Thereafter his father, Thomas Sr., his son Matthew, and eventually his grandson Experience, all continued his religious mission.

Before Thomas Jr.'s ill-fated voyage, he, Peter Folger, and Hiacoomes had made evangelical visits to Nantucket. Thomas Sr. had decided against business operations there, but other settlers were certain to come. In the meantime, the groundwork was laid for Christian praying towns on Nantucket similar to the ones forming on the Vineyard and Cape Cod.

Peter Folger was undergoing a religious conversion himself. Although he taught the Wampanoags Puritan doctrine in the school on the Vineyard, he was attracted to ideas of the sort Roger Williams espoused and was leaning toward the beliefs of the people who at that time were called *antipedobaptists*. This led Peter Folger to resign his membership in the church at Great Harbor (Edgartown) in October 1659, just when the first English settlers arrived on Nantucket.

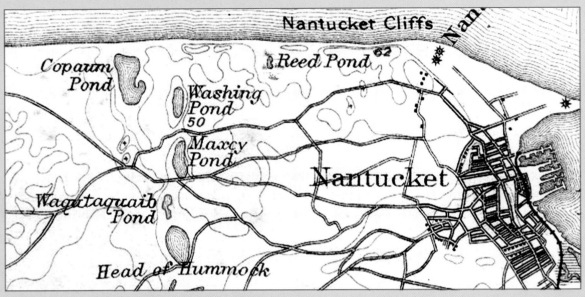

Waqutaquaib Pond was near Maxcy's Pond. – U.S. Geological Survey, 1893, National Archives

Although he assisted Nantucket's new proprietors as interpreter and surveyor of land, Folger did not immediately move to Nantucket himself, nor was he one of the shareholders in the new venture. Instead, he remained with his family on the Vineyard for three years, disenfranchised from local government by his resignation from the church. Then he packed up his household and departed for Rhode Island, a place where being a Baptist was not an impediment to full citizenship.

The next summer, however, the Nantucket proprietors offered Folger and his son Eleazar a half-share in their enterprise if they would move to the island permanently. Peter was to serve the settlers as interpreter, surveyor, and miller and Eleazar as shoemaker.

No longer constrained by his former employer Thomas Mayhew, Sr., Folger gave free rein to his religious beliefs. A couple of generations later Nathaniel Starbuck, Jr. paused to comment to Hezekiah Cartwright as they passed by a pond near the Madaket Road, that in this place "through blind zeal Peter Folger dipped my mother and thy grandmother all under."[5]

From his base in Nantucket, Folger boldly returned to the Vineyard to preach the need for rebaptism to the Wampanoags there. Eventually the Baptist faith became the preferred form of Christian worship among Wampanoags both on the Vineyard and in Mashpee.

On Nantucket through the end of the 1600s and into the first years of the 1700s, religious pluralism prevailed among the English settlers, who sometimes referred to themselves as Electarians. Organized religion on the island was the domain of the praying Wampanoags, who were said to be "very solid and sober in their meetings of worship." From time to time they would complain that the English settlers did not observe the Lord's Day in decent prayer and worship but instead engaged in everyday work, went rambling all over the island, and—if a whale came into view from the shore— troubled the Wampanoags to leave their devotions and launch their boats for the pursuit.

Indian Superintendent Gookin reported in 1674 that there were three places where the native peoples of Nantucket worshipped: Oggawame (near 'Sconset), Wammasquid (possibly Miacomet), and

5. Nathaniel Starbuck, Jr.'s mother was Mary (Coffin) Starbuck, daughter of Tristram Coffin. Later she became instrumental in establishing a Friends Meeting on Nantucket. Cartwright's grandmother was Peter Folger's daughter Dorcas. Mary Coffin is said to have been twenty years old at the time of her pond baptism. The pond is identified as Waqutaquaib Pond on what is now the Sanford Farm property, owned and maintained by the Nantucket Conservation Foundation.

Squatesit. Twenty years later, shortly after Peter Folger's death, there were five assemblies of praying Wampanoags on the island with three churches, two of them Congregational and one Baptist.

If Folger rebaptized English settlers and sought to do the same for his former students on the Vineyard, he doubtless shared his convictions with the Nantucket Wampanoags, and their Baptist Church may have been part of his island legacy. Another Folger legacy was the popularity of the baptismal name Dorcas among the Wampanoags. Of the two English women Peter Folger had zealously dunked in Waqutaquaib Pond, one was his own daughter Dorcas. Records exist of at least fifteen Wampanoag women who subsequently bore her name.[6]

There was more than evangelism, however, to Peter Folger's three decades of interaction with Nantucket's ancient proprietors. He was an agent of the settlers, the new proprietors who had made him a half-shareholder in their corporation in exchange for his services. He carried out the surveys and wrote the deeds by which Wampanoag land passed into the possession of the English settlers, and he was indispensable to both sides as a conduit of information, especially when dealing with the mainland Wampanoag leader Metacom, who had become known by his English given name Philip.

Late in life, smarting from a power struggle with the English proprietors that landed him in jail for half a year, Folger warned that the Nantucket Wampanoags were upset by his incarceration. Stating that "I have been interpreter here from the beginning of the Plantation, when no Englishman but myself could scarce speak a word of Indian," he went on to say that he had on occasion stepped in to avert violence against English settlers who had committed offenses. In concert with the Wampanoag elders, he said, he had kept peace on the island. Now, as his confinement dragged on, he couldn't answer for what might happen.

When Folger wrote those words, King Philip's War had been over for less than a year. During that time English towns had been burned, farmsteads had suffered deadly attacks, and English settlers had been gruesomely killed or carried off into captivity. Precisely the same fate befell the native inhabitants of mainland praying towns. Worse still, Christian residents of the praying towns who did not join the insurgents were interned by the English colonists on desolate Deer Island in Boston harbor, ostensibly for their own safety. During the winter of 1675–76, half of them died there of starvation and exposure, and massacre of the survivors by an English lynch mob was barely averted. As for Philip, his allies, and his family, defeat by the English in the summer of 1676 brought death for some, long terms of involuntary servitude for others, and for those considered too dangerous to remain in New England, export to the Caribbean slave markets. Like Oliver Cromwell, Philip was beheaded after death. His head was mounted on a pole for public viewing in Plymouth, where his father Massasoit had celebrated with the Pilgrims their first harvest in 1621. Mainland New England had been knocked reeling by its second Indian war of the century, and more of the same lay ahead in the century to come.

Peter Folger read a lesson into this war as it ravaged the mainland while sparing the islands. He was inspired to write a long poem entitled *A Looking Glasse for the Times* in which he lay the blame for the war on Puritan intolerance and persecution of people who held religious beliefs different from their own. In his view, Philip and his allies were instruments of God's wrath, and the sooner the Puritans stopped harassing Baptists and other dissidents, the sooner the war would end.

In traditional Wampanoag society, the burden of punishing wrongdoers rested with the sachems. In the new context of Christian praying towns, the responsibility belonged to Wampanoag magistrates, who—as we have seen—might lay on whippings so severe as to disturb English observers. English punishment and execution of Wampanoags, on the other hand, were profoundly troubling to Wampanoags. Of the ten or more

---

6. Dorcas Caine, Dorcas Corduda, Dorcas Homney, Dorcas Jacob, Dorcas Kenny, Dorcas Levi, Dorcas Mingo, Dorcas Punkin, Dorcas Quabe, Dorcas Timmit, Matakeken's daughter Dorcas, Oqua's daughter Dorcas, Matthew Jenkin's servant Dorcas, "Limping Dorcas," and Dorcas Esop (later Honorable).

hangings that have taken place in the course of Nantucket history, the tradition is that all those "dropped" were Wampanoags. A number of lists of the ten have been published with minor variations. Despite misdatings, misreadings, and lack of complete documentation for all cases, there is no doubt that English settlers and their descendants did hang Wampanoags in the 1700s. There is also that cryptic reference to Indians being hanged on Nantucket in 1665, within two years of Peter Folger's taking up residence there. At about the same time King Philip put in a brief, threatening visit to Nantucket, and Peter Folger negotiated his departure. Both the obscure hangings of 1665 and the much better-known visit of King Philip that same year seem to have ties to an off-island institution, Harvard College.

Harvard Indians

The founding of Harvard College in 1636 came just a half-dozen years after the founding of the Massachusetts Bay Colony itself. The Indian College did not come into existence, however, until the 1650s, and by 1698 its building—underutilized and in disrepair—was demolished.

A major figure associated with the Indian College was John Eliot, who had come from England in 1631 and set about learning Massachusett. In teaching literacy in both Massachusett and English, his aim was that new converts should form independent Christian communities with their own native clergy, teachers, and civic leaders.

Harvard College intended to play a role in the process. In the 1640s the college sought funds within the colony and from England for education and conversion of the native peoples of the area. At the end of the decade, with the incorporation of the Society for the Propagation of the Gospel in New England, Harvard finally received financial support and a new charter, providing for "the education of the English and Indian youth of this country." The Society proposed to begin with six scholars and agreed to build a two-story brick hall in Harvard Yard to eventually house twenty scholars and a printing press.

Although no painting or drawing survived the demolition of Harvard's Indian College, the structure probably resembled this "Conjectural Restoration of the Indian College by H. R. Shurtleff, Esq."

The Indian College was the fourth hall built in the Yard, and construction took until 1656, yet when it was completed, there were no Massachusett-speaking scholars to form a class. For the first five years of its existence it was used to house sons of the English colonists.

In the meantime, boys from Massachusett-speaking communities around eastern New England, including the Cape and islands, were sent to preparatory schools in Dorchester, Roxbury, and Cambridge to study English, Latin, and Greek, which were entrance requirements for Harvard College.

One of the first of Eliot's protégés was John Sassamon. When the first English came to Massachusetts Bay in 1630, Sassamon's parents lived among them in Dorchester and converted to Christianity. Eliot is said to have known Sassamon since childhood, so Sassamon must have been at most a teenager when the Pequot War broke out in 1637. Despite his youth, he went to that war as an interpreter for the English, serving under the command of Richard Callicott of Dorcester. Returning from that campaign, they brought a captive Montauk boy named Cockenoe. Cockenoe was immediately put to work as an interpreter and assistant Bible translator for John Eliot. It was not until the late 1640s that he at last managed to return home to Long Island.

John Eliot's work in Cambridge ran parallel to the work of Thomas Mayhew Jr. and Peter Folger on the Vineyard and Nantucket. During the 1640s they all acquired Massachusett-speaking

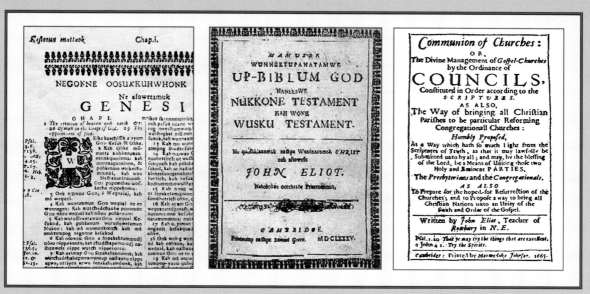

Publications by John Eliot. The Massachusett translation of the Bible was published in 1663 and reissued in 1685. Left, the first page of the Book of Genesis. Center, the title page of the New Testament. Right, Eliot's Indian Grammar (1666). — Millicent Library, Fairhaven

associates to help with teaching and preaching, and in Cambridge Eliot produced his publications, notably the Bible, in Massachusett. These were used throughout eastern New England, including the Cape and islands. By the mid 1640s, Eliot, Mayhew, and Folger were preaching in the language, and so were some converts—Sassamon as well as Cockenoe in the Massachusetts Bay Colony, and Hiacoomes on Martha's Vineyard.

Next the evangelists began recruiting boys to prepare for education at Harvard. Eliot also made an investment in some Harvard education for Sassamon, who was what today would be called a "student older than average." During Sassamon's time at Harvard, the Charter of 1650 mandating Indian education was already in effect, but the Indian College building had not been built. There was no special place for men like Sassamon, and there was not yet a special press room for the production of books in the Massachusett language. Nonetheless, the same year that Sassamon was a temporary student there, Eliot's *Indian Catechism* was printed at Harvard.

Soon after, two boys from Martha's Vineyard were sent to Daniel Weld's preparatory school in Roxbury. Caleb Cheeshahteaumuck was eleven

when he left his island home for Cambridge, and Joel Hiacoomes was just ten. The career of almost everyone who went to the Harvard Indian College during its less than half-century of existence took an unforeseen turn.

Sassamon left his position as schoolmaster in Natick and beginning around 1660 served as secretary to the mainland Wampanoag sachems, producing written documents for them in their dealings with the English. This does not seem to have been what John Eliot had in mind for him, but insofar as Sassamon could keep the English apprised of what was going on with the sachems, it was not entirely against the interests of his mentor. But Sassamon's bilingualism and ease with written documents, on which the Wampanoags had become dependent, made him an object of suspicion and resentment on both sides. When his body was found in February 1675 stuffed under the ice of a pond near Plymouth, the English demanded that the guilty parties be found and brought to justice. Three of Philip's chief counselors were accused, tried by a jury of twelve Englishmen and six Wampanoags, found guilty, and hanged. Three weeks later King Philip's War was under way.

In 1666 John Wampus entered the college, but he left the next year. Of his later career, Daniel Mandell writes that residents of Natick and two other enclaves "would contest bitterly a string of land sales made by a Nipmuck, John Wampus, who apparently betrayed his position as the Indians' interpreter to sell large chunks of the territory." This was surely not what Eliot had in mind.

In the year of the outbreak of King Philip's War, a young man named Eleazar matriculated as a freshman at the college. There he contracted smallpox and died, leaving behind as an artifact of his short life an essay composed in Latin and Greek, both of which he had studied in order to gain entrance to the college.

One other Massachusett-speaker was active at Harvard through this period without ever being a registered student. That was James Printer, Eliot's associate in the production of the Massachusett Bible and other publications printed in Harvard Yard.[7]

By 1661 Caleb Cheeshahteaumuck and Joel Hiacoomes had completed their preparatory education, matriculated at Harvard, and been admitted into the class of 1665. Their studies apparently moved along uneventfully. A Harvard monitor's bill lists them both in their sophomore year. Joel Hiacoomes signed his name on the flyleaf of a book he owned in college. Governor Winthrop reported in 1663 that he had heard them take part in an oral examination conducted in Latin, where they acquitted themselves well, and that they could also express themselves in Greek. The New England Company was sponsoring their education, and to the governor of the company Winthrop sent Latin essays by each of them. Caleb Cheeshahteaumuck's essay survives to this day in the archives of the Royal Society in London.

But graduation time in 1665 brought tragedy. Daniel Gookin wrote:

These two were hopeful young men, especially Joel, being so ripe in learning, that he should, within a few months have taken his first degree of bachelor of art in the college. He took a voyage to Martha's Vineyard to visit his father and kindred, a little before the commencement; but upon his return back in a vessel, with other passengers and mariners, suffered shipwreck upon the island of Nantucket; where the bark was found put on shore; and in all probability the people in it came on shore alive, but afterwards were murthered by some wicked Indians of the place; who, for lucre of the spoil in the vessel, which was laden with goods, thus cruelly destroyed the people in it; for which fault some of those Indians was convicted and executed afterwards. Thus perished our hopeful young prophet Joel.

Caleb Cheeshahteaumuck marched without Joel at his side in the 1665 commencement procession in Harvard Yard and was welcomed into the company of educated men. Some months later in the Watertown lodgings where he had been placed under the care of a physician, he turned his face to the wall and died.

A full decade before the outbreak of King Philip's War, Philip is said to have come to Nantucket to kill a local man whose Massachusett name was Assassamough, but who had taken the English name John Gibbs. According to Eva Folger, Gibbs was educated at Harvard by the Mayhews. There is no record of him at Harvard College, however. Possibly he had been sent to a preparatory school in Cambridge, in the same wave of recruitment that swept up young Caleb and Joel from the Vineyard. More boys were sent to the preparatory schools than the very few who actually matriculated at the college.

Philip's anger at John Gibbs is said to have been stirred by Gibbs's mention of his father Massasoit's name after his death. This is in accordance with Roger Williams's report that, "they abhorre to

---

7. In 1675 Printer was taken captive by the Nipmuck allies of King Philip. A few months later Mary Rowlandson, wife of a Puritan minister, survived an attack on her town only to be carried off by the same people. She lived and traveled with them from February to early May 1676, when she was finally ransomed and released. Once restored to her family, she wrote and published one of the best known of New England's captivity narratives. James Printer had done the writing for the Nipmucks as they negotiated her ransom. Then he managed to extricate himself from captivity. Finally back at work at the Harvard press, he set the type for Mary Rowlandson's book about the experience they had shared.

name the dead.…In that respect I say, if any of their Sáchims or neighbors die who were of their names, they lay down those Names as dead." It is also consistent with the sachem's responsibility to perform executions with his own hands.

Matters took an unexpected turn, however. Philip, who had started life as Metacom and taken the name Philip in the Plymouth court in 1660, had grown angry with English pressure on himself and his people, and he was returning to traditional Wampanoag ways. It was a time of ambivalence even as he continued to affix his initial "P" to written documents. He came to Nantucket to act as a sachem, but he was dissuaded by Peter Folger from claiming John Gibbs's life and accepted a cash ransom from the English settlers instead. Escaping this close call, John Gibbs went on to serve as Christian pastor of the church at Oggawame.[8]

There may have been more to Philip's visit that has been lost in the retelling of the story. He apparently came to the island just when Wampanoags were hanged in connection with the death of Joel Hiacoomes. Whether or not Philip's jurisdiction extended to the island in more normal times, this appropriation by the English of a sachem's responsibility for exacting justice must have rankled. A decade later a similar act in Plymouth, the execution of three of Philip's advisors accused of Sassamon's murder, precipitated his devastating war against the English.

English Introductions

Beginning in 1659, the English introduced all sorts of new things to the island. One of the first was livestock. Having obtained rights to the grass on the island through the deed signed by the Nantucket sachems Wanackmamack and Nickanoose, the settlers brought foraging animals: sheep for wool, cows for milk, draft oxen for plowing, horses for transportation, and hogs for pork and lard. A portion of the lambs and calves produced on the island would provide more meat for the English diet. The English did not intend to eat shellfish except in emergencies. There came to be a saying among them: "First a feast and then a famine. Then out on the flats a-clammin'."

The proprietors had a plan for regulating the numbers and kinds of animals let loose on the commons, the undivided land where all their livestock grazed mingled together. In 1669 a shareholder was permitted to graze either forty sheep, six cows, or one horse per share. The proportion changed over time. At another time one horse equaled two cows equaled twelve to sixteen sheep. According to Zaccheus Macy, writing Nantucket history in the next century, the owners initially slaughtered one half their lambs each spring and added the other half to their breeding stock.

Although the Wampanoags took up the spinning and weaving of wool, they had no pastoral experience and did not aspire to keeping sheep of their own. Horses were another matter. Just as the peoples of the Great Plains took to Spanish horses that spread north from Mexico, so did the native peoples of Nantucket take to English horses. They acquired horses for themselves and demanded their own grazing rights from their sachems. Having already granted winter grazing rights for the whole island to the English, the sachems spent the next thirteen years negotiating grazing rights for themselves and some of their own people. Finally, the four major sachems in power in 1682 regranted all their grass to the English and received in return eighty-seven horse commons. Recipients of the commons were free to lease or sell them, and they frequently did so to English settlers, soon losing the advantage for which the sachems had campaigned so assiduously. Daniel Spotso alone sold off thirty-five of the eighty-seven horse commons.

It was over horses that some of the seeds of discord between Wampanoags and settlers were first sown. Within ten years of their arrival, the English already felt that the island had become overrun by livestock, horses being the main problem. At a 1669 town meeting they discussed

8. The stream known as Philip's Run, which meanders from Gibbs's Pond toward the south shore, is said to be the route by which Philip had to run for his life from indignant Nantucket Wampanoags, but this is a piece of folk etymology. "Run" is an English synonym for "stream."

"clearing the Island of horses, mares and goats or to keep a smaller number than now are." It was decided that each household could keep one horse or mare (using "horse" to specifically mean 'stallion') and that the rest were to be taken off-island or destroyed. After a few months' grace period, a warden was delegated to impound unauthorized animals and get rid of them. The town meeting also directed that "no man shall sell a Living horse, mare, or colt to any Indian on the Island." Anyone who did so would be fined five pounds.

Exceptions were made. The town bent the rule to allow Nickanoose's son to buy a horse, but how could it not have offended the Wampanoags that a sachem's son needed permission from the English? Nor was the local injunction against selling horses to the Wampanoags effective. They bought mares on the Vineyard and brought them home, presumably to breed.

Wampanoags who did not have horses of their own still yearned to be up and astride. In 1715 English settler Daniel Russell took Wampanoag Tom Cain to court for riding his mare without permission. Russell wanted a large award for damages (four pounds) and had to settle for a small one (fifty shillings). The trouble wasn't over, because very soon after, Wampanoags Joe Shinny and John Moab were in court for taking and riding Russell's mare repeatedly and also burning Russell's hay, perhaps in retaliation for Russell's complaint against Tom Cain. Outraged, the English court sentenced Shinny and Moab "to be severely whipt."

Not only did the English seek to prohibit Wampanoags from having horses, but soon after arriving on the island they issued the first of repeated orders to kill all the Wampanoags' dogs on the grounds that the dogs ran down sheep and killed lambs. The court's defense of property rights was clearly reserved for the new English proprietors and did not extend to the island's ancient proprietors, whose own domestic animals were now branded a nuisance.

The nuisance of English livestock to the Wampanoags was an order of magnitude greater.

Not only did protection of the English sheep occasion the slaughter of the Wampanoags' dogs, but the foraging animals of the English—sheep, goats, cows, and horses alike—grazed their way through Wampanoag crops despite provisions written into the original deeds that protected Wampanoag fields and gardens from planting time until harvest each year. A flood of complaints appears in court records over the years. In 1672, at the suggestion of Eleazar Folger and others, the town ordered the settlers to erect a fence to keep their animals from invading the Wampanoags' cornfields and to pay the salary of a cowkeeper to watch the animals. Still, Wampanoag complaints continued.

Animals loose on the commons also menaced Wampanoag homes. Lightly built and easy to move, wigwams were vulnerable to trampling by cows. A petition notes that John Jethro's "wequam house" had been broken down by English cattle in 1741 at the same time that they devoured a half-acre of his crop of rye. It's hardly any wonder that the Wampanoags early began securing lumber and nails to build English-style frame houses, which—although lacking the easy portability of wigwams—were not easily moved off their foundations.

The Wampanoags' fields planted with corn, wheat, and rye had been broken with English plows. According to James Freeman, reporting long after the fact in 1807, they were impressed by the efficiency of English plows and asked the settlers to plow land for them as well. Account books and complaints from the preceding century bear out his assertion. English settlers who owned plows and oxen bartered their labor for goods, while Wampanoags complained that the English deprived them of draft animals with which they could have plowed their land for themselves.

Subsequent to clearing and plowing land, the local court would hear trespass complaints from time to time in which one Wampanoag would complain against another about planting fields they both claimed as their own. At the same time, the English would respond to accusations that they had usurped Wampanoag land by asserting that

Wampanoags had abundant land for their own use but failed to "improve it" so that it went to brush and brambles, yielding nothing. In order to keep Wampanoag women and children from starving, the settlers claimed, they had to take it upon themselves to plant and tend land for them.

Members of elite Wampanoag families signed deeds, but just about anyone might come before the English magistrates and justices of the peace, and the courts kept meticulous records. So did those English men and women who imported buttons, kerchiefs, greatcoats, cured tobacco, sugar, molasses, rum, wooden boards, iron nails, fishhooks, and rope—things the English considered necessities of life and the Wampanoags soon felt need of as well. The traders kept account books that balanced debits against credits. There wasn't much currency available to anyone on the island—English or Wampanoag—and much of what appears in the account books is barter: goods in the debit column over against days of labor, bushels of grain, barrels of fish, and the like in the credit column. The value of each item was reckoned in pounds, shillings, and pence, with the sums added up on both sides of the page. Everyone doing business—English or Wampanoag—was recorded by name and credit history. When an account fell deeply into the red and remained there for a long time, resort was made to court, and then a court record came into existence as well. At death, if the deceased owned anything of value—a house, livestock, tools of a trade—an inventory was made for probate. Among the items listed in probate inventories were debts the deceased owed at death and debts owed to him by others.

At least a thousand different Wampanoag individuals are documented by name in the various written records of the town. The majority of the names are themselves English introductions. English record-keeping required given names plus family surnames, and there were several different ways of making them. Some combined Christian baptismal names with fabricated surnames such as Harry Britain, Simon Dutchman, James and William Cowkeeper,

— *Nantucket Historical Association*

Entries in Mary (Coffin) Starbuck's account book from the early 1700s detail many transactions with Wampanoag men.

and Mary Seahorse. A longer Algonquian name such as Nickanoose, Wanackmamack, or Wannanahumma might be shortened for that person's descendants, yielding names such as Paul Noose, Hannah Mamack, and George Humma. Another type was what is known as a patronymic: the son of a man might have "-*son*" added to his name. Peter Musaquat's son Isaac was known as Isaac Peterson, and other families took the names Samsson, Thomasson, and Jepthason. Algonquian family names ending in -*son* (Nosson, Pampusson, Suppason, Weyapasson, Womhomasson, and Wunnohson) are probably also patronymics. Yet another strategy was to approximate the sound of an Algonquian name to an English word or phrase: Peekeyes, Toughskin, Short Chin, Turkey, Scotsbonnet, Orange, and Pumpkin. Alternatively a person might just take a wholly English name, as Assassamough did upon baptism, exchanging his Algonquian name for "John Gibbs." The records also identify George and John Bunker, Micah Coffin, and Joe Starbuck as "Indians." Occasionally a place-name was attached to a given name. There was Tuckernuck Dave, who got into trouble for an unauthorized salvage operation, and Madequecham Micah, who had an English-style house, ran an account with an English merchant, and left enough of an estate to have it go through probate.

Zaccheus Macy wrote of the Nantucket Wampanoags that, "some of them were weavers, some good carpenters," and probate records show them owning looms and carpentry tools, signs of their early integration into the labor force for the English settlers' business enterprises. This integration was problematic, however. When a creditor took a Wampanoag to court for unpaid debt and brought an account book along as evidence, it was common for the defendant to insist that the debt simply couldn't be as great as the creditor said it was. The justice of the peace invariably believed figures in the account book rather than the protestations of the debtor, who then was required to pay the outstanding debt and the court costs as well.

The First Half Century of Coexistence

When the ominous events of 1665 took place—murders, hangings, and King Philip's visit to Nantucket—the number of English settlers living on the island was minuscule. They remained outnumbered by Wampanoags for a half century or so until their high birthrate and longevity intersected with the Wampanoags' diminishing fertility and life expectancy to bring their respective numbers to parity. During the first fifty years the Religious Society of Friends did not yet have a foothold on the islands, and, with the exception of Peter Folger, the settlers did not evangelize. They appear to have been typical frontiersmen—intensely individualistic, resistant to outside interference, and tenacious of their personal rights. Although they quarreled among themselves and with the half-share men they had brought in, in large measure the share-holding proprietors left one another alone, and they left the Wampanoags alone, relying on Peter Folger and his offspring to serve as intermediaries.

During the last decades of the 1600s, while English-speakers were still a minority of the population, Massachusett continued as the principal language on the island. In their meeting houses, the Wampanoags gathered to hear their own ministers preach in their language, and at home they read and reread their Massachusett Bibles. Under the influence of Eliot's translation, their language was changing. On-island and off-island, spoken Massachusett was becoming more like the language of their Bibles, and this standardization facilitated communication among speakers from different places. The Nantucket variety of the language was less distinctive than it had been, more readily understood by off-islanders from Mashpee to Natick.

As other English settlers learned Massachusett and their children grew up naturally bilingual, Peter Folger and his family no longer had the monopoly on intergroup communication. Zaccheus Macy recorded the conversation in Massachusett that went on between Nathan Coleman and Justice of the Peace Corduda, and J. Hector St. John de Crèvecoeur in his famous description of Nantucket claimed that "The young Europeans learn it with the same facility as their own tongues and ever after speak it with ease and fluency." The settlers learned some of the traditional stories told in Massachusett and incorporated them into their own oral history, telling and retelling them until they were finally written down in English.

A remnant of Wampanoag rhetoric unmediated by retelling in English can be found in documents written down in Massachusett that are apparently verbatim records of speech. As an example, Paul Noose, son of the sachem Nickanoose, and Quequenab, a Christian minister, made two declarations that Ukkahdeahohamun and his brother owned a particular piece of land, which they located in terms of its boundaries and the name of land that lay adjacent to it. The first time they did this, in October of 1691, Wuddashioo transcribed their declaration. A dozen years later they made the same statement again, and this time Quequenab wrote it down himself and six Wampanoags witnessed it. The first-person statements, the naming of the adjoining pieces of land, the mention of forefathers, and—in the second event—the affirmation of the truth of what was said by six other Wampanoags probably reflect the way sachems had traditionally made public proclamations. English innovations

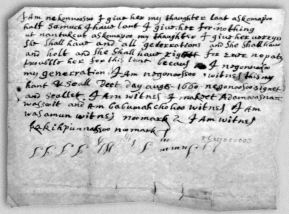

*English-language version of a deed by which Sachem Nickanoose trans-
ferred land to his daughter Askammapoo.*

include the recording of the spoken statements in
writing, the dates given according to the European
calendar, the borrowed English word *witness*, and
the appeal to the authority of the King of England,
who is, however, referred to by the Massachusett
word *ketahsoot*, 'great man'—a word John Eliot
had chosen to use in the translation of the Old
Testament First Book of Kings.

A dozen such Nantucket documents written
in Massachusett survive. They are dated between
1667 and 1729 and record statements about ownership or transfer of land and whale rights among
Wampanoags. They differ from English-language
documents signed by the sachems, such as the
1659 deed by which Nickanoose and Wauwinet
transferred land and rights to the English settlers. In the Massachusett-language transactions,
owners, donors, recipients, and witnesses are all
Wampanoags. Forefathers are mentioned but, in
accordance with Wampanoag practice, not by
name. Places are designated by Massachusett
names mostly long since forgotten on Nantucket
such as Kuppanachasuh and Potupootuppummeh.
Donors state that they are transferring land
because of their love for the recipients. English
presence goes all but unacknowledged. In his
capacity as chief magistrate, Tristram Coffin
certified one document and William Worth certified another. Eleazar Folger made a copy of one at
the request of the recipient of some land. A small

number of English loanwords appear repeatedly:
acre, witness, day, month, and the names of months.
Others only come up once: *judge, wheat, barley,
money, half.* In one document the English phrase
"at Nantucket" stands in the middle of a sentence
otherwise in Massachusett. The most significant
English influence to be found in these documents
produced by and for Wampanoags in the late 1600s
is the fact that they were written down.

The English kept order among themselves and
settled disputes (or attempted to settle them) by
a system of constables and magistrates or justices
of the peace. The constables were sent to bring
people accused of wrongdoing before the magistrate or justice, who heard the case and made a
ruling with or without a trial by jury. On Martha's
Vineyard and then on Nantucket, the English
sought to replace the sachems' traditional rule of
law with their own English-style system in which
authority descended to the local level from the
King of England. They chose native magistrates
and constables and gave them imported staffs of
office bearing the King's arms. In principle, the
Wampanoag and the English judicial systems
should have operated independently, but from as
early as the 1665 hangings, Wampanoags were
subjected to trial and punishment imposed by
English judges and juries even if no English settlers were directly involved.

In 1704, a jealous husband named Sabo hacked
his wife Margaret to death in their wigwam at
Madequecham. Abigail Gardner was first on the
scene and saw the victim's body. Then Edward
Coffin came upon Sabo burying the murder
weapon in the sand. Everyone else who had contact
with Sabo as he fled to Tuckernuck and Muskeget
was Wampanoag, which is hardly surprising
given that at the time the Wampanoags consider-
ably outnumbered the English. A grand jury was
called that included four Wampanoag men, but the
trial jury was entirely composed of Englishmen.
Besides Abigail Gardner and Edward Coffin, eight
Wampanoag witnesses (including one woman)
testified, as did a Wampanoag constable. Sabo was
found guilty and sentenced to be hanged.

As many as nine other Wampanoag men would follow Sabo to the gallows in the years to come, but their trials were not recorded on Nantucket. From 1671 on, the island's court had been authorized to sentence convicted offenders to be pilloried or whipped, but capital cases were supposed to be referred to mainland courts. The Sabo murder trial, carried out on the island with Wampanoag participation, was unique. Subsequent murder trials were recorded off-island with the sentences returned to the island and carried out at Gallows Field beyond the Newtown Gate, which separated the English town from the open commons.

Environmental Degradation

Herman Melville, writing in the mid-1800s, enumerated some of the tall tales that people told about Nantucket: that it was nothing but a sand-heap, "all beach and no background," treeless and grassless, where weeds had to be imported, mushrooms served as shade trees, and people carried around bits of wood as holy talismans. The island is not like that today nor was it before the 1650s, but old photographs from soon after the time when Melville wrote *Moby-Dick* bear out the view of Nantucket as treeless, sandy, and barren. What had happened to the Wampanoags' island home?

When they first arrived, the English settlers had not yet settled on sheep as their source of livelihood. They expected to carry on diversified farming with grain crops and dairy cattle as well as sheep. In their first decade on the island, they found that grain could be grown on the plains on the south side of the island, and they could cut hay from the stonier north side and from the salt marshes. This sort of subsistence farming yielded no surpluses, however, so in 1672 they voted to concentrate on sheep raising and the export of wool. The number of sheep on Nantucket rose to between eight and ten thousand, and at one point even little Tuckernuck Island sustained a herd of about a thousand.

Plows and sheep remade the landscape, cutting through and gobbling up the native vegetation. Saws and axes made quick work of denuding the island of trees, depriving home sites and livestock of windbreak protection. Exposed to the salt-laden wind, the sandy soil became less fertile than it once had been. Zaccheus Macy wrote of the changes he had witnessed in the course of his long lifetime that "our farming business is become poor by reason of hard winters and wood all gone and shrubs almost gone so there is no shelter to keep off the hard cold winds." He went on to say that corn yield per acre had

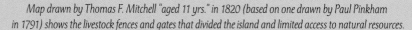

Map drawn by Thomas F. Mitchell "aged 11 yrs." in 1820 (based on one drawn by Paul Pinkham in 1791) shows the livestock fences and gates that divided the island and limited access to natural resources.

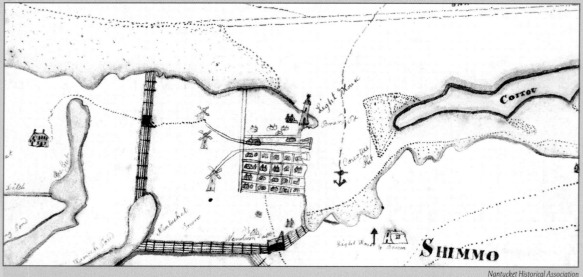

dropped by a third and that rather than reserving half the spring lambs each year for breeding stock, it had become necessary to keep 70 percent or more. Fifteen years later, that number was approaching 85 percent, indicating high annual mortality for animals out on the open moors without shelter.

Wampanoags and English settlers alike were increasingly enclosed and immobilized by the sheep industry. Instead of being penned in, the animals were fenced out of places where they were not to graze. They were fenced out of fields and gardens; fences were put up to keep them from roaming onto Wampanoag land; and the whole town was fenced around, with gates controlling access to and from the commons.

All this fencing limited access to resources the Wampanoags had traditionally used, and in any case, the sheep were busily nibbling many of those resources to oblivion. Bit by bit the Wampanoag population was concentrated into year-round villages and kept from traditional foraging. Although they themselves had largely given up on farming in 1672, the English settlers were, nonetheless, of the opinion that the Wampanoags still had plenty of land to support themselves and their families if they would just settle down to planting and harvesting crops in the English fashion.

The island's damaged ecosystem could no longer support the Wampanoag way of life nor could it enrich the burgeoning English population, much less do both. Local legend has it that before the end of the 1600s, a settler watching whales off the south shore remarked to a companion that their descendants' green pastures lay out there on the sea. In the same year that the town had voted in sheep, it had also extended an invitation to a Long Islander named James Loper to come to Nantucket to set up a whaling operation. As the mainland slid into King Philip's War, Nantucket would have been safe for Loper, but he did not come immediately upon receipt of the invitation, and then it was too late. Whaling did not get a start on the island until after New England emerged from the maelstrom of that war. When it did, it engaged every part of the island's male population: English, Wampanoag, and African.

Sheep in Quaise in the late 1800s. As long as Nantucket supported grazing sheep, the island remained nearly treeless.

Whaling

The sea had always cast up useful things on Nantucket's beaches. Until the arrival of the English settlers, the Wampanoags, under their sachems' regulation, had made use of anything and everything that came ashore, including dead whales. In a document written in Massachusett in 1696, the sachem Matekekin conveyed whale rights as well as land at a place called Pukquotanussut on Nantucket to fellow Wampanoag Koshkuhtukquainnin. But Englishmen and Wampanoags had long since begun to contend for drift whales. The sachem Musaquat and Eleazar Folger took a dispute over such a whale to court, and Eleazar was ordered to pay a cash settlement to Musaquat. Despite the confirmation of Musaquat's claim to that particular whale, however, as early as 1668 Peter Folger was engaged in negotiating on behalf of the English town for "all the whales that come on shore on the island." Nor did the English stop at the appropriation of drift whales. They also proclaimed in 1672 that they reserved for themselves all goods washed ashore from shipwrecks "to be equally divided to the English inhabitants."

The Wampanoags did not readily acquiesce to being cut off from salvage as well as from land resources. Tristram Coffin and his associates made a great profit from their first salvage operation and expected those in the future to be equally lucrative. But when a cargo of cattle hides washed on shore from a wreck, the Wampanoags carried off a share of them for themselves. The New York admiralty court held Coffin, as chief of the salvage operation, responsible for the whole cargo, which he was unable to deliver, resulting in painful financial reverses for him.

Coffin was taken aback by this fiasco, but surely no more so than was Tuckernuck Dave when he was hailed into court and sentenced to be whipped for helping himself to rum and pork from a boat cast ashore on his island. How could the English have so thoroughly usurped the Wampanoags' traditional rights? How could the Wampanoags take the English claims seriously?

— Nantucket Historical Association

1775 sketch of a shoreline whaling station in Nantucket Proprietors' Records, Book 1. Early whaling on Nantucket was carried out by lookout teams who manned such rudimentary stations and kept watch for drift whales from an observation mast.

Between 1700 and 1750 whaling practices evolved rapidly. From staking claim to dead whales that washed up on the beach or stranded ones dying in the shallows, the islanders moved on to killing live whales. To begin with, this was a shore-bound operation. Stations were set up along the ocean side of the island and manned by crews of six who took turns watching from a lookout mast. When whales were sighted, the crew would launch their boat from the beach, row out, and attempt a kill by first harpooning the whale and forcing it to drag around a heavy weight (a "drug" or "droge"), then lancing the exhausted animal until it bled to death. If successful, the crew would tow the huge carcass to land and strip it of its blubber, which was carted off to tryworks located at people's homesteads. Oil extracted from the blubber would turn up on the credit sides of account books, having been traded locally for goods and services and ultimately shipped off-island, commonly to London.

While drift-whaling involved little risk, alongshore whaling, in light twenty-foot boats against huge living animals out on the water in winter weather, was another matter. More hazardous still was the next development: offshore whaling. As whales became scarce close to shore and those surviving more wary, sloops with crews of thirteen or so started carrying pairs of whaleboats out to "the deep," searching for right whales and the even larger and more lucrative sperm whales. Voyages to the open sea south of Nantucket and the Vineyard lasted as long as six weeks. Now the islanders began to pay for their new industry in money, in social reorganization, and in lives.

A sperm whale washed up on the bach at Siasconset in 1998.

Building, outfitting, and provisioning sloops to spend weeks at sea was a costly business. Only the most prosperous of Nantucket men could afford the investment to become an owner or a partner in ownership. With the development of offshore whaling, Nantucket male society divided into those who stayed on land and sent their sloops out after whales and those who went to sea for a percentage of the take. The owner or the partners kept half the profits, and the crew shared in the other half, with the captain and the harpooneer receiving double shares. As in agricultural share-cropping, this "lay" system rewarded productivity, but it paid least to the people who did the heavy work while providing the owners with the capital to expand their investments. Of the nascent whaling industry Obed Macy wrote, "The Indians, ever manifesting a disposition for fishing of every kind, readily joined with the whites in this new pursuit, and willingly submitted to any station assigned them. By their assistance, the whites were enabled to fit out and man a far greater number of boats than they could have done of themselves."

Nantucket sachems became valued whalemen, but not a one had the capital to acquire and operate a sloop. To be a working Nantucket man—Wampanoag or English—was to spend much of one's life out on the water apart from one's family and in peril of not returning. According to Obed Macy, Wampanoag men about to go to sea plowed as much land as their wives and children could manage in their absence, and English settlers assisted in plowing Wampanoag land for the benefit of absent husbands and fathers. Despite their dependence on Wampanoag crew members in their boats, the English settlers took on the burden of providing for the welfare of whalemen's families only grudgingly. They expected English and Wampanoag women to manage for themselves in their husbands' absence, temporary or permanent. The relatively high number of female heads of households on Nantucket—widows and never-married women of all ethnicities—began in the early 1700s and persisted as long as Nantucket men went to sea.

Wampanoag men had few practical alternatives to this work and made up half or more of the thirteen-member crew aboard a whaling sloop. They were excellent boatsmen and so highly valued for their whaling skills that the English sloop owners exerted intense economic pressure to keep them out on the water. Going to sea certainly must have had its attractions. On the deep a man could be a man among men, and courage and skill were positively rewarded. In the mutual dependence of men in a small vessel there was an egalitarianism not to be found on land. Practically speaking, whaling was a way of acquiring cash to function in the money economy that had replaced subsistence and barter on the island. Nonetheless, whaling was a carrot-and-stick situation. The rewards for going were backed up by English penalties for refusing to go, straitening the already limited options of the Wampanoags.

During the period from 1700 to 1750, the number of vessels going to sea after whales doubled and redoubled. With this growth of offshore whaling came losses of life such as had not previously been experienced on the island. A private record of Nantucket deaths lists a dozen or so whaling-related losses between 1722 and 1756, ranging from a single man struck by lightning to ten boats lost with all hands "at sea," "in the shoals," and most frequently "awhaling to the southard."

Except for one notable case, the Indians, Africans, and "strangers," who drowned when Nantucket whaling boats went down remain anonymous in the record. They were counted but not named. In 1731, for instance, all thirteen members of a crew lost their lives: "Thomas Hathaway,

Benjamin Starbuck, Wm Burgess, & one Stranger with one Negro and 8 Indians lost awhaling to the Southard." In 1743 Daniel Paddack, Obed Bunker, and Joseph Trott went down with their fellow whalemen, "the Remainder of the Crew being strangers and Indians." The years 1755 and 1756 each saw the loss at sea of three whaling crews with the usual complement of strangers and Wampanoags. Isaac Coffin was moved by one of the losses in 1755 to make a note on the front page of his record that "Ebenezer Corduda was the Great Indian Justice. He was lost with Peter Bunker in the year 1755 and his Son James Corduda was lost with him at the same time." Whaling had carried off the authority of the Wampanoags' own court, not just for a season of offshore whaling, but father and son forever.

Transformations

Sometime between 1710 and 1720 the English population on Nantucket surpassed the Wampanoag population. From a tiny group of first settlers, there had proceeded a population explosion almost entirely by natural increase. From the first, the English proprietors had maintained control of who might join them from off-island. Participation in their Nantucket enterprise was by invitation only. This did not keep down the English population, however, because the settlers enjoyed large families, low mortality, and remarkable longevity. Tristram Coffin, whom Zaccheus Macy referred to as "the old grandfather of almost all of us" by virtue of his seventy-five grandchildren, himself attained the age of 76, dying on Nantucket in 1681. Peter Folger outlived him by nine years, dying in 1690 at the age of 73, and Peter's wife Mary survived into the new century, living until 1704. Of their nine children, Bethiah drowned with her husband soon after their marriage and four others moved off-island, but the remaining four contributed thirty-three more Folgers to the English population. Zaccheus Macy was the great-grandson

of another first settler couple, Thomas and Sarah (Hopcott) Macy. Four of the six children of Thomas and Sarah produced island families. Zaccheus was one of eleven children, while his uncle John and John's wife Deborah (Pinkham) Macy provided Zaccheus with eight first cousins. Zaccheus and his wife added fourteen more children to the English population. Zaccheus's eighty-four years spanned most of the 1700s, making him a fit eyewitness historian of his century.[9]

The English population on Nantucket had grown from eleven in the winter of 1659–60 to 3,000 by the mid-1700s. This was the size the Wampanoag population is said to have been a century earlier. In the meantime, the ancient proprietors had dwindled to fewer than a thousand. In their lifetimes they had gone from majority status, to parity with the English, to being outnumbered three to one. For them something had gone terribly wrong. Everyone, then and after, agreed that the lethal enemy was rum. Experience Mayhew wrote of the ravages of rum on Martha's Vineyard, and on Nantucket Zaccheus Macy wrote that by drinking so much rum the Wampanoags decayed very fast.

Early on, the proprietors had sought to prevent Wampanoag access to "spirits," but this colonial-period selective prohibition was no more effective than the modern experiment with prohibition that tried and failed to dry out the nation between 1920 and 1933. In both cases, the effect was to enrich rumrunners and bootleggers, to clog the courts, and to criminalize the behavior of people whose lives had already been rendered wretched by alcoholism.

The quantity of stolen rum mentioned in court cases is staggering. One wonders how Tooth Harry and Joe Bone managed to carry off eight gallons of rum with one stolen bucket in 1713. In another case, four Wampanoag men were convicted of making off with fourteen gallons. Then four other men were found guilty of stealing thirty gallons. In 1717 a constable with a search warrant for illegal liquor impounded eighty-one gallons of rum

9. At least five Englishmen and women of the 1700s lived into their nineties. In the course of the eight decades of her life Nantucket midwife Rachel Bunker, who died in 1795, had assisted other women in the delivery of 2,994 babies and had given birth to twelve of her own. At her death she had contributed 128 grandchildren and 98 great-grandchildren to Nantucket's population.

found in an Englishman's house. Clearly, anyone—Wampanoag or English—with a container and a strong arm had access to practically unlimited quantities. Rum was stolen from storehouses, from vessels in the harbor, and from homes. It was run from Rhode Island to Tuckernuck, where Wampanoag men gathered in the winter months to hunt ducks, drink, and avoid their creditors. The Wampanoags themselves brewed "very good strong beer" according to Zaccheus Macy.

English men and women served rum, cider, and beer illegally from their homes and were frequently turned in by their Wampanoag customers for a bounty. Generally the court fined the seller. In 1726, the alleged seller was Africa, "a free negro." Africa denied that he had sold rum to his accuser, Tupasha, but in the end he confessed and was remanded to jail until he paid his fine. In 1730, Isaac Aosawa accused Nathan Chase not only of selling rum to him and his friends but of overcharging them. Chase said he had no recollection of having done so, but the court fined him anyway.

Now and then a case was dismissed for lack of evidence or because the accused cleared himself or herself by taking an oath. On the other hand, sometimes the collection of evidence was documented with particular care. In 1749 Sarah Humphrey accused an Englishman of selling her cider and rum. He denied it, but Sarah had three Wampanoag witnesses to the sale. They came as a group to testify in court, and the Englishman had no choice but to pay his fine. In the most detailed set-up, in 1755 Abraham Weenhop took three witnesses—two men and a woman—with him when he went to buy rum from an English woman. The witnesses testified that they saw the woman put the rum into jugs for Weenhop, who then carried the jugs directly to the house of the justice of the peace, who tasted the contents. The woman could offer no defense and was found guilty.

The court records also witness the consequences of alcoholism—from the nuisance of public intoxication to matters more grave. Drunken brawling resulted in beatings and stabbings that put men out of work for months at a time. Micah Phillips had the bad luck to be stabbed on two occasions three years apart. Drunkenness led to domestic violence and invasions of other people's homes. In 1736 Ben Jusap broke into a house at night and terrorized the English family who lived there. By the sober light of day he could offer no explanation beyond that he had been drunk at the time and didn't know why he had done it.

The English settlers who were so fearful of the effects of alcohol on the Wampanoags and so anxious to keep it out of their hands nonetheless felt it to be an absolute necessity to themselves. They imported rum and made beer and cider in great quantities for themselves and to sell to each other. Before their move to Nantucket, Tristram Coffin's wife Dionis had been in trouble with the authorities of the Massachusetts Bay Colony for brewing premium beer for her paying customers in Salisbury. Captain John Gardner had been invited by the English proprietors in 1672 to come to the island to set up a codfishing enterprise, but within three years he was in trouble with the local magistrates because—at the height of King Philip's War—he felt it right and necessary to provide a drink to every man, Wampanoag as well as English, first thing in the morning before they all went out to fish.

With considerable variability from year to year, from 1700 to 1763 roughly half the cases before the English court involved Wampanoags. They were in court for drunkenness, violence, theft, sheep rustling, and debt. Sometimes they brought complaints against each other. On rare occasions they won a case against an Englishman. Beginning around 1745, nearly two decades before the epidemic, the percentage of court appearances by Wampanoags began to fall because there were proportionally fewer of them, and because a rapidly expanding English economy engaged the court in two new types of business: the granting of licenses for public houses, inns, and tea and coffee houses on the one hand, and on the other the expulsion of English men, women, and families from off-island who tried to take up residence and do business on Nantucket without an invitation from the proprietors.

Endgame

In the first half of the 1700s Nantucket's economy evolved rapidly as English enterprise expanded in several directions. The sheep industry provided employment for spinners (or "spinsters" as the women were called, regardless of their marital status) and weavers—English, African, and Wampanoag. Wool and woven cloth were stored and shipped off-island, and dealers came to Nantucket to buy directly. The whaling industry needed every able-bodied man available, and men came over from the Vineyard and the Cape to fill out the crews of "Strangers, Blacks, and Indians." Whale oil was processed on the island and coopers were kept busy making barrels for its export to London. Codfishing, originally set up to pay Nantucket's taxes to New York, continued with fish-drying racks spread out along the beaches. The English town, named Sherburne from 1673 to 1795, had relocated from little Capaum to its new waterfront on the big harbor, and was growing rapidly with new homesteads, wharves, oil sheds, and warehouses. To meet the demand, Wampanoag men had become skilled carpenters as well as whalemen. Sarah P. Bunker's home on the Cliff and the mill that still stands on the south edge of

town, both built in 1746, may have been framed by Wampanoag builders.

As the Wampanoags erected frame houses for themselves, they furnished them with the same sort of utilitarian items to be found in the English households: chairs, tables, chests, beds, and looms. But between 1700 and 1750 the inventories of English households expanded to many pages in length, including large mirrors, curtains, bed spreads, tablecloths, pewterware and chinaware, silver spoons, chocolate ladles, and collections of books (especially dictionaries).

As in the merchants' account books, everything in the probate inventories was assigned a value in English pounds, shillings, and pence. Nantucket was now a thoroughgoing money economy, and the Wampanoags were failing in it. The value of their labor was figured in pounds, shillings, and pence, and they had to buy lumber, nails, rope, meat, flour, and even tobacco with the same currency. In the new economy they seldom earned enough to cover their needs, much less their wants. The endless theft of rum manifests their cravings, but other types of theft reveal their unmet needs. More and more, as the century progressed, Wampanoag men and women were brought to

Early 19th-century representation of the town after its relocation from Capaum to Nantucket Harbor. Subsequent to the American Revolution, the town meeting petitioned the Massachusetts legislature to change the name from Sherburne back to Nantucket. Permission was granted in 1795.

Engraving by Benjamin Tanner, after a drawing by Joseph Sansom, National Archives

court for stealing food. They broke into mills and carried off grain. They broke into warehouses and homes for mutton and pork. Wampanoag men were ever more often brought in for butchering Englishmen's sheep. Many a man and many a woman was cited for receiving, cooking, and consuming illicit mutton.

Sheep rustling grew to epidemic proportions. To begin with, it amounted to a lamb here and a lamb there, a sheep or two now and then. By the late 1740s sheep were being taken and slaughtered twenty at a time on Coatue, and in the 1750s a gang of three with a juvenile sidekick was operating on Tuckernuck.

Wampanoags also took tools they needed and could not afford. In 1731 a handsaw belonging to Richard Macy disappeared. Nine years later Zaccheus Macy took Panchame (Benjamin), a Wampanoag elder, to court for being in possession of it, and a jury convicted Panchame of theft and fined him. In 1734 Betty Pon, a young girl, was accused of taking three files from a shop. Her only response was that she had taken only one file, and the other two had been taken by a Wampanoag boy named Caleb. The court ordered that Betty pay triple restitution for the files, that she should be whipped (ten stripes on her back), and thereafter that she should be bound in service for a year to the shopkeeper whose files she had taken.

And then there were the saddest of petty thefts: a coat, a quilt, a blanket—signs of misery and desperation. That sort of pilfering didn't inspire pity among the English Nantucketers, however. They were purely outraged and blamed the Wampanoags bitterly for failure to keep their heads above water in the sink-or-swim economy. Many of the English proprietors were inclined then and for long after to regard the descendants of the ancient proprietors as vermin who would make off with anything that wasn't nailed down. In reporting the discovery of a list of the Wampanoag victims of the 1763–64 epidemic in an old Bible sold to a "Cliff Cottager" in 1890, a writer for the *Inquirer and Mirror* remarked, "very likely there is more sentiment lavished upon the Indians of to-day, out upon the Western

Plains, than the great grand-parents of the present Islander bestowed upon his dirty, thriftless and thieving Indian neighbor."

William Lay, the Wampanoag magistrate at Chilmark, had told the Mayhews that since his people were not so inclined to shame as the English were, they had to feel punishment in their bodies. On this point he and Nantucket's Justice Corduda were in agreement, as they laid on whippings for offenders among their people. But how were the English to deter drunkenness and theft? Branding was tried for a while. Before the practice was given up around 1730, a half dozen or so Wampanoag men and boys convicted of burglary— Tooth Harry and Joe Bone among them—were branded in the middle of the forehead with the letter "B."

Whipping went on without respite. It was dealt out in stripes—ten, fifteen, twenty, or thirty laid on the bare backs of men and women, boys and girls. Some people were simply sentenced to be "severely whipt." Between 1707 and 1760 about seventy people were sentenced to whipping. A few were English men and women—John Harper and William Percy, for instance, for stealing a boat in 1718—but most were Wampanoags. In 1708 Alice Jude was found guilty of being an accomplice to theft and sentenced to ten stripes. She begged for mercy, however, and was given the alternative of a fine, which her fellow Wampanoag, John Bunker, paid for her. In 1726, Sarah Paine, wife of Benjamin Tashama, was also sentenced to ten stripes for participating in a large-scale meat theft, and once again, because of the intercession of a number of people, the court allowed substitution of a fine. By the 1740s the option of paying an additional fine to avoid whipping had become more the rule than the exception. For people with no money of their own, however, the only way to avoid the pain was to agree to work for free for someone else who would pay the fine.

Eliza Mitchell wrote in her memoirs of what she believed was the last use of the town whipping post. She and her neighbor Benjamin Franklin Folger agreed that it was located where the Civil

War monument now stands on upper Main Street, close to the residence of Zaccheus Macy. The occasion of the whipping—the false report of an intended Wampanoag insurrection—is dated by Obed Macy to September 1738. There is no court record of the matter, however, and if, as Mitchell believed, the post itself was removed soon after, then another was put up elsewhere. The Nantucket court continued to sentence people to whippings for decades to come.

In the time of the branding and the whipping, the Society of Friends was assuming its pervasive influence on the island. How, it has been asked, did people committed to pacifism, square their consciences with the bloody slaughter of thousands of large marine mammals for their own enrichment? How, too, it might be asked, did people who were coming to the conviction that involuntary servitude violated universal human rights manage to live with a court that mandated the brutality of the whipping post?[10]

And what about the gallows? How could this be tolerated by a community in which Quakers dominated nearly every institution? In 1835 Friend Obed Macy weighed the question of capital punishment, made some arguments against it, concluded that the topic required greater persuasive powers than he possessed, and mildly expressed the hope that the practice would be given up.

The Nantucketers had apparently been taken aback by the death sentence they had meted out to Sabo in 1704. A Quaker visitor, Thomas Story, recorded in his diary that several of them approached him in private to discuss whether there was any way that—having properly reached the verdict by jury trial and having sentenced Sabo according to the dictates of English law—they could now avoid actually hanging him. Story offered them two loopholes, and he says ambiguously that the Nantucketers took the former way. This might mean that they went ahead and hanged Sabo or that they made use of the first of Story's loopholes. Since Sabo turns up on all the variant lists of men hanged on the island, it appears that the English Nantucketers felt constrained to go through with his execution. It is significant, nonetheless, that they were troubled and sought Friend Story's thoughts on the matter.

The early abandonment of branding and the increasingly frequent practice of letting people buy their way out of whipping may reflect the Friends' scruples. But the gallows did stand, and Wampanoag men were taken there to be dropped even after the epidemic, when not many remained alive. Subsequent to the Sabo case, Nantucketers seem to have taken more readily to capital punishment. They employed Wampanoag Sam Humphrey as hangman.

Nantucketers were a practical lot, and it was obvious that branding and whipping only served to make people sullen and unproductive, while fines and restitution were meaningless when cash was absent and what had been stolen had also been consumed. Court practice was to turn the loaded docket to advantage by sentencing those convicted of crimes to periods of servitude in English households and aboard whaling vessels. The same sentencing served for instances of insurmountable debt. Those who had run up accounts entirely beyond their means to pay were made to work the debt off by uncompensated labor. The time of service was meted out in months and years, but for people over their heads in debt as well as for those convicted of serious crimes, the years of service extended before them into old age and to the grave.

"Indian debts" were a commodity to be traded, inventoried in probate, and passed on in wills. Bound servants, too, were subject to probate and inheritance. In 1762 Hannah Wyer wrote in her will, "I give unto Isaac and Mercy Chace my Indian girl." She also bequeathed to Mercy a silver chain and a quilt.

---

10. Besides conviction for theft and other similar offenses, the Nantucket court also sentenced newly delivered mothers of children born out of wedlock to be whipped. Unmarried women who found themselves pregnant faced coercion to identify the child's father, so the town at large would not have to pay for support of the child. If the woman did not come to court on her own and denounce the father of her unborn child, midwives forced her to reveal his identity during the duress of labor. Postpartum, she faced whipping unless she could pay her way out of her predicament.

Wampanoag children were bound into servitude for the debts of their father. In 1717 Richard Macy made a loan of 40 shillings to Ephraim to be repaid within two months. Written into the agreement was the proviso that if Ephraim failed to repay the money on time, his son Jacob would be bound to Macy for "whaling and fishing on this shore." Ultimately it came about that "2 young sons" of Ephraim were bound to fish on the shoals for Macy "until they are of the age of 21 years of age."

Already back in 1670 the selectmen had passed a town by-law that "If any person English or Indian shall at any time carry in any vessel any Indian servant to any English on the Island, whosoever shall carry any such person off the island without orders from his master shall be fined twenty shilling." Confinement to the island with the prospect of being bound in service to an English master for all one's young life was more than some Wampanoags could bear. In 1734 John Cheges, servant of Samuel Coffin, and Deborah Hews, servant of Richard Folger, planned their escape. When they were apprehended, they had stolen a boat, a compass, warm clothes, and a bucket of sugar for their flight from Nantucket. Both were sentenced to fifteen stripes at the whipping post and a fine. Samuel Coffin paid his servant's fine in exchange for an additional eight years of Cheges's bound service. Deborah was sentenced to an additional twelve years of service to Richard Folger and others.

The return of bound servants to households from which they had fled was certainly awkward. It is hard to imagine the dynamics of Peter Coffin's household in 1709 after his servant Ned knocked Coffin's wife down with an iron tool and then took several shots at Coffin himself. The court extended Ned's term of service to Coffin for an additional year, but who would dare to take such an attacker back into service on land? Surely the only thing to do was to keep him at sea continually with no shore leave.

The institution of servitude for debt and for crime on Nantucket gave rise to a new generation of *patrones*, English businessmen who attended trials, paid debts and fines for those convicted, and put them to work in their enterprises. One of these men was none other than Zaccheus Macy: a highly successful businessman in his own right, Nantucket politician, Quaker elder, town bonesetter, and eventually the Nantucket historian of his century. The great-grandson of one of the first English settlers to reside on the island, Zaccheus Macy was said to be the last of the settlers' descendants to speak Massachusett. Eliza Mitchell wrote that he was "the only person of that time who understood the Indian Dialect. He could converse freely with them and consequently could influence them in many ways for their good." When Jonathan Tony was convicted of breaking and entering and theft in 1760 and the court awarded twenty-five years of Tony's labor to the plaintiff, the plaintiff immediately made a deal with Zaccheus Macy to take Tony off his hands. Macy benefited from fewer than four years of Tony's service, however, before the epidemic carried him off.

Another of the men who attended court looking to take charge of the lives of Wampanoag debtors and criminals was Zaccheus Macy's contemporary, Cromwell Coffin, great-grandson of Tristram and the first of the many Cromwells in his family. By the 1740s three men—Peter Folger's great-grandson Abishai Folger, Jonathan Coffin, and Richard Coffin—were, moreover, serving as "Guardians for the Indians" in Nantucket despite the Wampanoags' protest to the General Court of Massachusetts that they did not want Folger or any other Englishmen living on the island to be in a position of authority over them.

In court records one learns of failure, destructive behavior, and social isolation. Despite Zaccheus Macy's short list of "the most Respectable Indians" and Crèvecoeur's report of literacy and strict piety among Nantucket's Wampanoags, other Nantucket sources hardly present a bright picture. Men's long absences at sea left behind on land old people, women, and children unable to cope with the heavy work of planting and harvesting. The loss of men to alcohol, drowning, and the gallows unbalanced the ratio of Wampanoag men to women, and there was no way to reconstitute Wampanoag families.[11] Christianity had imposed monogamy, and—contrary to what happened on the Cape and Vineyard—no marriages were formalized on Nantucket between the Wampanoags and the English. At the end of the 1700s, after the epidemic and after the last hanging, Wampanoag women outnumbered Wampanoag men by four to one. As for children, the 1770 probate inventory of the estate of schoolmaster Benjamin Tashama, lists fifteen chairs, silent witnesses of the school where his students had learned to read and write in Massachusett, back in the days before the epidemic.[12]

Following King Philip's War, Wampanoags on Nantucket had begun sending petitions to mainland authorities complaining that the island's sachems had deeded to the English proprietors land that they had no authority to sell. From then until the late 1750s such petitions continued to be posted off-island, expressing ever more distress. The most fully developed of the petitions made the following assertions: The English had usurped Wampanoag land and stripped the island of wood; they had evicted the Wampanoags from the land and cultivated it for themselves; they charged rent from the Wampanoags for use of their own land; and they were forcing the Wampanoags off their traditional land in Squam to live in an area, Miacomet, where corn would not grow. Moreover, the English limited the Wampanoags in how much livestock they were permitted to keep; they impounded and killed the Wampanoags' animals; and the Englishmen's animals consumed Wampanoag crops. Wampanoag houses had been knocked down, and the English threatened to demolish others. The English forced Wampanoags to take to their boats after whales, cut up those that were killed, put codfish out to dry, and butcher sheep on the Sabbath. And finally, the English prevented the Wampanoags from having their own justices.

The English selectmen rebutted the Wampanoags' petitions point by point. They said the Indians had more land for their own use than they knew what to do with; that far from taking the Wampanoags' wood, the English had allowed the Wampanoags to have the stumps the English cleared from their own land; that the deeds transferring the land from the sachems to the English settlers were all in order; that they did not run their livestock on land they did not own; that the only Wampanoag animals they had killed were sheep-killing dogs; and that rum and evil-minded non-Wampanoag agitators lay behind the complaints.

The General Court of Massachusetts was unresponsive to the petitions it received, but apparently in the 1750s a judge finally came to Nantucket, listened to all sides, and upheld the position of the English proprietors. As Obed Macy wraps up his description of the proceedings: "On this conclusion the court rose, the Indians withdrew, and, though not satisfied with the decision, were never very troublesome about it afterwards."

With only a few years left until the coming of the epidemic of 1763–64, the Wampanoag population on Nantucket had fallen to 358.

The disease—whatever it was—descended upon Miacomet like a bolt from the blue. Because it killed its victims in a matter of a few days, during which time they became jaundiced, it was described as "yellow" fever. Two hundred

11. The Hews family had a particularly hard time with the English justice system. Prior to conviction for stealing a quilt and letting his sister out of jail, Sam Hews had already taken ten stripes at the whipping post for stealing clothes and been sentenced to another whipping (not to exceed twenty stripes) for stealing linen. The year before Deborah Hews and John Cheges tried to flee Nantucket, Simon Hews was convicted of theft, sentenced to twenty stripes at the whipping post, and bound for four years' service on a vessel. Before the four years were up, Simon was again convicted of theft, took a whipping of fifteen stripes, and was bound for an additional four years' service, this time to a fellow Wampanoag. Decades later, having survived the epidemic, he died on the gallows according to Obed Macy. Comparing the various lists of men hanged, it appears that in addition to Sabo and Simon Hews, others included Finch, Joe Noby (probably Nobynash), Happy Comfort, John Comfort, Joel Elisa, Henry Jude, and Nathan Quibby. The lists of ten include Tom Ichabod, but his name also appears on the list of people who perished in the epidemic.

12. A century after they were devised, Benjamin Tashama still employed John Eliot's educational methods. That Eliot's teaching materials remained extant on the island is confirmed by Crèvecoeur. Writing about Nantucket in the eighteenth century, he stated, "the Bible and a few school tracts, both in the Nattic [Massachusett] and English languages, constituted their most numerous libraries." In 1917 the boulder that had marked the site of Benjamin Tashama's house and school near Bean Hill on the Milestone Road was moved to the grounds of the Nantucket Historical Association's Fair Street Museum.

twenty-two Wampanoags died, while the English remained unaffected.[13] The apparently little attention most English Nantucketers paid to what was happening seems callous until one looks further into the historical record. There one sees, as did Hector St. John de Crèvecoeur at the time, that epidemic disease with huge mortality among indigenous populations was the rule rather than the exception wherever Europeans had set themselves down near or among them. Isolated though Nantucket had been before its active maritime economy evolved in the 1700s, the sort of epidemic that had emptied the coastal mainland was overdue in Nantucket. By the time Experience Mayhew wrote in the 1720s about the deaths of godly Wampanoags, the Vineyard had already suffered badly.[14] In 1753 the native minister of Mashpee, Solomon Briant, lost all eleven of his children to an epidemic there. In 1759 an infectious disease said to have been brought back by Nipmuck men serving in the English army spread through Natick, lasted for three months, and killed twenty people.

As for Nantucket, the island had grown less salubrious for everyone in the 1700s. The private record of deaths among the English Nantucketers maintained by Isaac Coffin notes that between 1753 and 1756 sixty-nine English people had died, fifty-five of whom were children. Then, in 1759–60, eighty-eight English Nantucketers died, sixty-nine of them children. Diphtheria had reached the island in 1741, small pox and measles in 1759. In 1765 thirty-two English children died, while in 1768, the toll of infant mortality was thirty-six. The big families of the settlers that had built the English population for four generations were now being relentlessly culled.

In Miacomet, where the "Indian sickness" struck all ages, there was hardly anyone left to care for the sick, much less to mourn. According to a later account, Richard Mitchell found two starving children vainly trying to wake their dead parents, begging to be fed. The English feared to go to see what was happening to their Wampanoag neighbors. Physician Benjamin Tupper, who was also sheriff, warned of contagion comparable to the bubonic plague that had ravaged Europe, and stayed away. Most of the townspeople heeded his example and did likewise.

Eliza Mitchell claims that Zaccheus Macy was one of the few exceptions. Throughout the epidemic, she says, he had his own sheep slaughtered and boiled down into nourishing mutton broth, which he daily delivered to a place at the edge of Miacomet village where anyone ambulatory could fetch it back to feed the sick and the survivors. Richard Mitchell went further and carried food straight into the homes of the stricken.

The compassionate efforts of these two Quaker men seem to cast Dr. Tupper in a bad light, but it is worth remembering that Macy was himself a medical practitioner with particular knowledge of Wampanoag herbal medicine and that Macy and Mitchell were both speakers of Massachusett. These facts in themselves are compelling reasons why they should have been the ones to attempt to minister to the sick in Miacomet, while Tupper kept away in order not to risk becoming a conduit of infection to the residents of the English town.

The possibilities of what the sickness might have been, how it had arrived, and how it was transmitted among the people of Miacomet have been exhaustively examined. In the end, we cannot know for sure what it was, only what it did. From Nantucket it spread to the Wampanoags of Martha's Vineyard, where fifty-two people were infected and twenty-nine died. A Wampanoag woman from Nantucket and a man from Mashpee who had the misfortune to visit Nantucket in the

13. Never before or since have the living on Nantucket had to arrange burial for 222 people in the course of a half a year, and to dispose of personal effects and housing that might still harbor a deadly infectious agent. A modern comparison would be the deadly outbreak caused by the Ebola virus in Kikwit, Zaire, in 1995. In spite of modern medical management, that epidemic killed 245 people and caused anxiety around the globe.

14. Between the Mayhews' arrival in 1642 and the end of the century, the Martha's Vineyard Wampanoag population fell by a third, from an estimated 1,500 to 1,000. By the winter of 1763–64, when Nantucket's population of 358 was reduced in a matter of months to 136, the Vineyard's total Wampanoag population had fallen to 313. Had the full force of the epidemic struck the Vineyard, the consequence there would have been what it was on Nantucket. Instead, the population gradually grew to 360 in 1807 and 393 in 1861.

fall of 1763 carried the disease to Mashpee, where there were fatalities as well. Nonetheless, the virulence of the disease in Miacomet seems to have decreased with time and distance.

When it was over, according to Zaccheus Macy, there were only 136 Nantucket Wampanoags left. In Miacomet village thirty-four who had been sick recovered, and thirty-six escaped infection altogether. The disease that had traveled from Nantucket to the Vineyard and to Mashpee had not spread out across the island of Nantucket. All eight Wampanoags who lived in Madaket were uninfected. Ironically, being in service to the English proved to be the greatest saver of life. The eighteen men who were safely at sea during the epidemic and the forty Wampanoags who were living as servants in English households were unscathed. Records of deeds, wills, and probate inventories provide us with the names of about half the survivors and the eventual death dates of about a third of them. Two children born after the epidemic eventually came to be reckoned as the last Nantucket Indians.

Mark Corduda relocated to Chappaquiddick, and Sam Robin moved with his wife and child to Mashpee. Wampanoag seamen went back to work. A few years later, aboard the whaling schooner *Sally*, two of them—Peleg Titus and Isaac Jeffrey—died at the hands of another, Nathan Quibby. While they were locked up together in Nantucket's jail, Quibby turned on his shipmate John Charles and killed him too. Convicted of multiple murders, Quibby went to the gallows in Nantucket.

Who could think of marrying anyone among the dwindling group of survivors? Thankful Micah married Seneca Boston, whose parents were both Africans. According to her brother-in-law, many of the other survivors also found spouses in the African community. In a corner of Newtown, a village situated between the English town of Sherburne and the now all-but-defunct village of Miacomet, Wampanoags and Africans began merging into a new community of people of color in a neighborhood that came to be called New Guinea.

Despite the universal agreement of English Nantucketers and such off-islander observers as Crèvecoeur that rum had been the agent of destruction, the seeds of annihilation had been sown before alcohol became readily available to the island's native people. The ecological system of which they had been a functioning part was radically altered from the moment English livestock were brought over from Martha's Vineyard to graze on Nantucket's sandplain grasses. The subsequent fencing off of parts of the island, restriction of access to natural resources, stripping of trees and ground cover, and the gradual hemming-in of the Wampanoags made it impossible to subsist as they had. At the same time, they were denied the possibility of full adaptation to the new lifeways that had been introduced to the island. Their exclusion was a product of the appropriation of more and more of the island's resources by the English and of the profound mutual cultural incomprehensions that existed between the indigenous people and the newcomers. With only their labor left to sell, the Nantucket Wampanoags could not compete in the developing money economy. In the first half of the 1700s, as the rapidly increasing English population grew prosperous from the evolving whaling industry, the difference between the material circumstances of the English proprietors and that of the descendants of the ancient proprietors precipitated a crisis. From the beginning of English habitation on the island, rum had always been present for the taking. With the passing decades, access to food, money, and personal freedom became ever more desperate issues for the Wampanoags. And then the "Indian sickness" delivered the coup de grâce.

Elegies

The end of Nantucket's own indigenous people was oft-heralded. In 1790 Zaccheus Macy compiled a list of seventeen vessels in which he had owned shares, concluding with the comment, "Now all gone and worn out excepting the sloop Friendship and the schooner Dianne and all the Indians

*Abram Quary, long considered Nantucket's "last Indian,"
was born at Miacomet in 1769 and died on Nov. 25, 1854.*

*Dorcas Esop, born in 1776, survived Abram Quary by six weeks, living
until January 12, 1855. The last of her husbands was Thomas Honorable.*

excepting old Peter Micah and old Isaac Tashama, and myself almost 77 years old and cannot expect to stay much longer."[15] Two years later he admitted that there were a few more than just the two old men: four men, in fact, and sixteen women. Fifteen years after that James Freeman wrote, "At present there are only two Indian men and six Indian women left on the island."

Obed Macy believed that with the 1822 death of Abigail Jethro, a descendant of the sachem Nickanoose through his son Joshua Jethro, the offspring of Nantucket's ancient proprietors had come to an end. Of her ancestors' experience with his own he wrote a devastating summation: "…they [the Wampanoags] opened to them [the English settlers] their stores, bestowed upon them their lands, treated them with unfailing kindness, acknowledged their superiority, tasted their poison, and died. Their only misfortune was their connection with Christians, and their only crime, the imitation of their manners."

Then Abram Quary, who lived until 1854, became celebrated as the "last Nantucket Indian," memorialized by his 1851 portrait in the Nantucket Atheneum as a solitary, pensive hermit sitting barefoot by the fireplace of his house. As an old man he supported himself by pit-steaming quahogs for visitors and weaving baskets for sale. Hezekiah Pinkham, Sarah P. Bunker's father, once bought a basket from him and painted his initials "HP" on it. In the Atheneum portrait an almost identical basket, filled with berries, is on the table next to Quary and through the window one glimpses the harbor where he went clamming at low tide. By the early 1850s the age of photography had arrived, and we have another image of Abram Quary, in which he returns the camera's unblinking stare with his own grave, penetrating gaze.

But was he "the last"? There is a photograph as well of Dorcas Honorable, who outlived Quary by several weeks. The way Quary had passed the last years of his life, however—living alone and

15. A contributor to the *Nantucket Inquirer* (April 1, 1853) misunderstood how Zaccheus Macy referred to himself after Peter Micah and Isaac Tashama, and—writing of Macy's bone-setting practice—described him as "a Sagamore or Indian Chief" and concluded, "This honest, worthy Indian, died in November 1797, at the advanced age of 84 years, a remarkable instance of native ingenuity and humanity."

carrying on traditional foodways and crafts that he made available to the public—appealed to the sensibilities of nineteenth-century people as appropriate to "the last of his race." By contrast, Dorcas Honorable, as her mother before her, had worked as a domestic servant in Nantucket households. The 1830 census shows Dorcas living at home in New Guinea with Thomas Honorable, the last of her several husbands. She was a Baptist in life and received burial from the Baptist Church at death. [16]

— Martha's Vineyard Historical Association

Born on Martha's Vineyard in 1882, Charles Vanderhoop of the Aquinnah Wampanoags served as assistant keeper at Sankaty Head Lighthouse in 1912 and again in 1919 before returning home to serve as keeper of Gay Head Light-house from 1920 to 1933.

Were Abram Quary and Dorcas Honorable then, finally, the last?[17] After their deaths Wampanoags from the Vineyard and Cape Cod came to live on Nantucket from time to time. A report to the governor of Massachusetts "Concerning the Indians of the Commonwealth" listed two large families—the Dennisons of Herring Pond and the Amoses of Mashpee—resident on Nantucket in 1859. Charles Vanderhoop of Aquinnah was assistant lighthouse keeper at Sankaty Light for a year beginning in 1912 and came back in 1919 for another year's service before going home to be keeper of Gay Head Light.

As recently as 1952 the *Inquirer and Mirror* ran a photo of "Mrs. Ruth West Coombs of Nantucket, known as Princess Red Feather among her people, and a descendant of Massasoit of the Wampanoag Tribe." Her husband, Darius Coombs of Mashpee, was a descendant of Hiacoomes.

What is more, back in 1822, the year of Abigail Jethro's passing, Essex Boston—born the son of African slaves on Nantucket—had joined with others in Nantucket's New Guinea community to write that "We hereby certify that there are among the coloured people of this place

— Louis S. Davidson photograph, NHA

In the 1950s Ruth (West) Coombs (right) made public appearances and sang in concert in the persona of Princess Red Feather to promote Wampanoag history and culture.

remains of the Nantucket Indians, and that nearly every family in our village are partly descended from the original inhabitants of this and neighboring places." As we shall see, members of the Boston family would identify with Nantucket's indigenous heritage as well as with their African roots for decades to come.

There is a way, however, in which Abram Quary and Dorcas Honorable were truly the last. At the age of 93 Mrs. R. H. Sturgis of Mashpee recalled visiting Abram Quary when she was about fifteen years old and that he could "speak Indian." Solitary as he and Dorcas became in their old age, the spoken language of their ancestors survived only as long as they did. They were the last fluent speakers of Massachusett on Nantucket, and their deaths took their language—the language of the care-worn Massachusett Bibles—forever from the island.

In the 1830s the phrenology craze reached Nantucket. It had its roots in Vienna and gained a worldwide following for the notion that characteristics such as acquisitiveness, combativeness,

16. Eliza Mitchell, who pasted a photo of Dorcas into her manuscript of "Reminiscences," wrote Dorcas's story as she understood it down the sides and across the page below it: "She was daughter of Sarah Tashma. Sarah was the last Indian female and a daughter of the famous Preacher and Teacher who lived before my time. Sarah was called Manta in Miriam Coffin, or the Whale Fishery. Imbert probably the father of Daucas./Sarah was a true Indian but was never known to smile after her visit from Imbert. I remember her well as she worked for my mother when I was very young. Been dead about 70 years or more./Dawcus lived many years in the family of Capt' John Cartwright. 6 feet tall, a noble woman of her Tribe, always kept aloof from bad company, lived to be over eighty." Mitchell's memories of Dorcas and her mother were intermixed with bits from Joseph Hart's 1834 novel and a fictionalized story about Sarah Tashama that had been printed in the *Nantucket Inquirer* in 1833. There probably was no Imbert, and the phrase about Sarah's never smiling again originally had to do with her surviving the epidemic of 1763–64.

17. Two marriages were recorded for Abram Quary: to Abigail Dingle in 1793 and to Fanny Hall in 1810. It appears that before marrying Thomas Honorable in 1820, Dorcas had been married four times previously, the first time as a teenager in 1792.

generosity, amorousness, and even religiosity, could be directly mapped onto bumps and indentations on the external surface of the skull. A labeled phrenological chart was developed and widely distributed. Undergoing a phrenological "reading" of one's own head at the hands of a self-proclaimed expert became something of a party game—rather like having one's fortune told—but public examination of skulls carried more cachet. Available skulls were inevitably those of disenfranchised individuals with no one to object on their behalf—typically criminals, the indigent, and aboriginal peoples, whose graves were looted in the name of science.[18]

As soon as the Nantucket Atheneum opened, a phrenological lecture series that apparently had been going on in another venue was moved to the Atheneum. On March 25, 1835, the eighth lecture in the series was announced in the *Inquirer*, and the April 1 issue carried a notice for the ninth lecture.

Mary Cushman, visiting the island that April, wrote a letter to her mother about social activities on the island. After a long day's outing, she reported, "We were engaged to go to a Phren'l society this evening, but I was too tired and stupid, so the gentlemen went without us. R. just came in from there to get two skulls (which he found Saturday afternoon in exhuming from the Indian burying place) to carry back."

By 1846, the burial place of the epidemic victims had been so thoroughly mined by phrenological enthusiasts that Charles Dyer wrote in his diary, "One mile from town is the old Indian burial where many graves have been dug over to get the skulls. Some of the other bones are left in the ground but too much decayed to be worth bringing away." The looters had, however, missed a few skulls after all, and it was one of those whose backhoe-assisted emergence in 1987 led to the recognition and protection of the site.

Marker placed at Miacomet cemetery after its rediscovery in 1987.

An account in the *Inquirer and Mirror* of the burials found by Albert Folger in 1882, just up the street from Sarah P. Bunker's home, reports that "Relic hunters are eager for pieces of the bones." It was an improvement on this that David Nevins turned over the remains from his property to the Nantucket Historical Association, but in retrospect it is painful to learn that a skull was placed on exhibit. How, indeed, would Sarah P. have felt if the foundation hole of a summer mansion had intruded on the Old North Cemetery where her father was laid to rest, and Hezekiah's venerable skull had ended up on public view?

By contrast, in 1987, when the Miacomet cemetery was once again disturbed, work was stopped, construction plans were revised, the cemetery was fenced and marked, and Wampanoags came from the Cape and the Vineyard to rededicate it. Then, in 1996, the Nantucket Historical Association transferred the human remains in its collection, fifteen sets in all, to the Commission on Indian Affairs for reburial in the earth from which they had come to light. Their return followed a strange odyssey through twentieth-century Nantucket, a world as alien to their people's imaginations as the spirit world of the Wampanoag powwows is to ours.

18. Not all Nantucketers were taken in by phrenology. A series of columns on the philosophy of science printed in the *Inquirer* beginning on January 10 and signed only "M." (William Mitchell or his daughter Maria?) took issue with the notion that external contours could tell anything at all about the brain within for the simple fact that the sinuses occupy space inside the skull and thereby disrupt any one-to-one relationship of the surface of the brain to the exterior surface of the skull. In the January 10 column M. also pointed out that it follows logically from the notion that an individual's social behavior is foreordained by the physical properties of his or her brain and skull that criminals must be exonerated of their misdeeds on the grounds that they have no control over their behavior.

CHAPTER TWO

African Nantucketers

Vestiges

*I*f the story of Nantucket's ancient proprietors, the Wampanoags, is one of dispossession, the story of the African Nantucketers is one of acquisition. Before the English settlers arrived, the sachems and their people had been in full occupation of the island, but in the course of a century they lost almost all their land and then almost all of them lost their lives.

The Africans who were brought to the island during that century so fatal to the Wampanoags had lost everything but their lives upon being taken into slavery. The survivors of the Atlantic crossing started from nothing. Arriving on Nantucket, they had no property, no personal freedom, not even their own names. The men were called by classical and biblical names: Cato, Pompey, Seneca, Nero, Moses, Jonas, Ishmael, and—ironically—Caesar and Prince. Women were given such servants' names as Hagar, Patience, Phebe, Phyllis, Rose, and Maria.

As the ancient proprietors' fortunes declined, the Africans on Nantucket acquired freedom, surnames, and families. Ultimately they gained admission to all the public schools. By then they had become entrepreneurs as well as household help, laborers, and mariners, and in the process

This 1821 town map shows the row of windmills that once stood on the hills west of New Guinea, "Negro Hall," a burying ground, and the Newtown Gate.

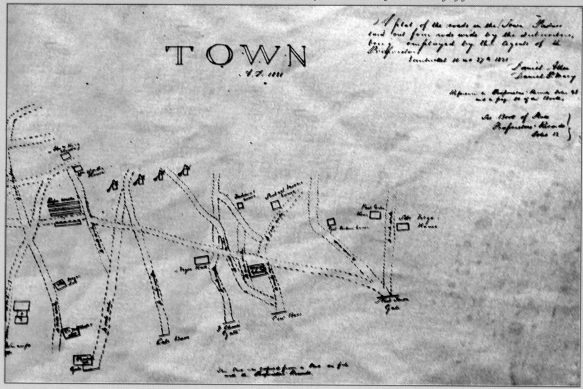

they had put together a neighborhood of their own. Buying and consolidating land, they built dwelling houses, stores, a school, churches, boarding houses, workshops, barber shops, and a dance hall.

All that survives today of the Wampanoag village of Miacomet is its burial ground. Less than a mile away the African neighborhood, too, has its cemetery. The difference is stark. The interments at Miacomet took place in the course of a few months under crisis conditions. There are no individual markers, no discernible family groups. For a long time it was lost completely. In "the Burying Ground that belongs to the Black People or people of Colour," tucked in behind Mill Hill Park and viewable from the windows of the island's hospital, there are family plots where succeeding generations have joined their forebears as recently as 1999 when Mattie Pina was laid to rest beside her mother after a lifetime that spanned an entire century.

Downhill from the last remaining windmill, at the confluence of streets known as Five Corners,

stands the African Meeting House, which was built in the 1820s to house a school and church and to provide a public meeting space for the African Nantucketer community. There are vestiges of the African presence throughout the town. But just as with Nantucket's Wampanoags, the descendants of Nantucket's original African families are no longer to be found on the island.

From Africa to Nantucket

On Nantucket there is disbelief that slavery ever existed on the island, since the word "slave" is all but absent from local court and probate records and even from deeds of manumission, where the word "servant" is used euphemistically. Slavery is generally thought of as a Southern plantation phenomenon; moreover, the local Quaker community had an old and distinguished abolitionist history. As for the African community that established itself on the southern edge of town, popular wisdom has it that its inhabitants came to the

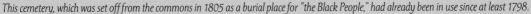

This cemetery, which was set off from the commons in 1805 as a burial place for "the Black People," had already been in use since at least 1798.

59

island on whaling ships, their numbers augmented by fugitive slaves who found on Quaker Nantucket refuge and protection.

These beliefs have a basis in fact, but Nantucket history is deeper and more complex. English families first settled on Nantucket in 1659, and for the next fifty years there was little organized religion on the island among anyone but the "praying Indians." The influence of the Society of Friends, with its intolerance of involuntary lifelong servitude, is a phenomenon that evolved in the 1700s, and the documented cases of fugitive slaves resident on Nantucket are from the 1800s.

Between 1659 and the late 1700s, some Nantucketers—including Quakers—owned slaves, who appear in the records with single slave names. The first documented is a man called Africa, who had the good fortune to be manumitted in the opening decade of the 1700s. The next is a sadder case. In 1715 Jockey, identified only as a "Negro," drowned in the harbor along with four Wampanoags as they were trying to board a sloop from a sinking fishing boat.

Africans brought to the island as servants did not come voluntarily, and their Nantucket-born children were born into slavery. In 1716 Stephen Hussey willed one African each to his "beloved wife Martha," his son Silvanus, and his daughter Theodorata. Martha Hussey was to receive "a Negro woman named Sarah," Silvanus "a Negro boy named Mark," and Theodorata "a Negro girl named Dorothy."

Four years later James Coffin sought to pass ownership of an African woman through two beneficiaries, writing in his testament that, "I will that Hagar my Negro servant shall dwell with and serve my Daughter Mary Gardner during her natural life and after her decease I give my servant to my son John Coffin." Sixty-five years after James Coffin wrote his will the Nantucket selectmen voted that "the Negro Woman Hagar be considered as one of the Town Poor."

African slaves appear in estate inventories, grouped with household goods, livestock, and tools. Like the other inventoried items, they have money values placed on them. The inventory of Jonathan Pinkham's estate in 1735, for instance, lists: "a bedstead 24 [pounds sterling] / *Sambo* 20 / 1/3 of a tenant saw 13 / a farrow hog 30 / a sow hog 25." The 1740 estate inventory of Samuel Barker lists his slaves immediately after his stock of gingerbread. The youngest of them, a "Negro Child," was valued at five pounds, the same as the gingerbread. The adults were worth a great deal more. Thomas Brock—investor in sloops, a wharf, and a tryhouse—left a huge estate upon his death in 1750. In the probate inventory, listed between a tablecloth valued at one pound six shillings and a "Schooner Main [sail] and Jib" valued at ten pounds, is an unnamed "Negro woman" worth one hundred twenty pounds.

Roots

In 1710 an old man who lived on Centre Street took stock of his life and his estate and made a decision. William Gayer had been born into the gentry of Devonshire, the same west country from which the Coffins had sprung and had come to Nantucket to build a fortune, as they had. Upon arrival he married into the Starbuck family, and in the course of the 1670s he and his wife had three children, Dorcas, Damaris, and William Jr. As a young man William Jr. was sent back to England to marry a cousin and hold together a Gayer family estate there. Dorcas and Damaris had made good matches on the island, Dorcas marrying a Starbuck cousin and Damaris marrying a Coffin. But loneliness was lurking around the corner for their father. Just when his three children were grown and settled, his wife died. He tried marriage again with the widowed mother-in-law of Peter Coffin, but his second wife died too, and now in the house he had bought for his family he had lived for a long time in the company of just his housekeeper and his manservant.

With William Jr. gone to England with no prospect of return, who was to manage this Nantucket estate that now included the house, a barn, tryworks, a garden, land on the edge of town, sheep commons, livestock, and part of the island of Muskeget? William Gayer took up his pen and wrote his last will and testament.

He left a share of Nantucket commons and the privileges that accompanied it to William Jr. "if my said son shall ever come hither again." He left one eighth share of the Nantucket land he had from his father-in-law and half of his Muskeget land to each of his daughters. Then he divided the rest of his property in half and gave it in life rights to "Africa, a negro once my servant" and to Patience Poot "my housekeeper."[1] Within the divided house (the east chamber, half the lean-to, and half the barn to Africa; the west chamber, garret, and half the lean-to as well as half the barn and tryhouse to Patience Poot), almost as an afterthought he left unspecified space to his daughter Damaris "if she should come hither to live." The livestock Gayer bequeathed to Africa and Poot totaled sixty sheep, one horse, one cow, and commonage on which to graze them.

Gayer had confidence in his daughters to carry out his unconventional wishes, for he designated them joint executrices of his estate.

With Gayer's death, Africa was a free man endowed with housing, livestock, and productive land. Subsequently he appears from time to time in town records as an entrepreneur and weaver, identified as "a free Negro." When he died, he had not written a will, and the town ordered an inventory of his estate. The value is listed at 102 pounds, 16 shillings, 11 pence, and the inventory lists a variety of possessions, including books, three guns, pewter plates, weaving materials, yarn, and cloth. There were more than thirty creditors to be paid, and a couple of men owed Africa money at the time of his death. It appears from court and probate records that part of Africa's business involved buying from, and making loans to, Wampanoags.

A year before his death he had taken one to court over a bad debt and won the case.[2]

Town records show that Africa was an active businessman and that he outlived William Gayer by eighteen years. There is no evidence that he had a family of his own. In 1721 Africa sold his dwelling house to George Hussey, perhaps to raise collateral for a business venture or to pay off a debt. By 1723 he had money available to buy the house back. Selling one's home is not the act of a family man. That Africa made no will before he died also suggests he had no one to provide for, and the probate inventory doesn't mention survivors. On the other hand, William Gayer had sixteen grandchildren on Nantucket whom he had passed over in favor of his servants.

William Gayer's daughter Damaris survived her husband Nathaniel Coffin by over forty years. Back in 1723, when he died, she had signed and certified the inventory of his very substantial estate, which included the following items and their values: "George Negro 50 [pounds]; Phyllis 42; Sabina 15." Although Africa was free, slave-owning in the family continued.[3]

William Gayer had not been a member of the Society of Friends, but his daughter Dorcas was First Clerk of the Women's Meeting. Her sister Damaris did not "come into meeting" until after her husband's death. Only then would she have experienced religious persuasion to free George, Phyllis, and Sabina. In 1716 an English Quaker, John Farmer, had visited American Quaker communities, including Nantucket, speaking against slavery. Farmer's position was denounced on both sides of the Atlantic, and in time he was disowned by the Quakers. Nantucket Friends, nonetheless, found themselves in agreement and became the first Quaker Monthly Meeting in the world

1. In the Massachusett language pootop means "whale," and Nantucket usage shortened it to poot. From Gayer's housekeeper's surname it would appear that she was a Wampanoag. But there are no other Nantucket Wampanoags documented with Poot as a surname. There are no Nantucket records of anyone named Poot, or Root for that matter. Patience was a common given name for Wampanoag and African women.

2. Africa owed Isaac Corduda's estate money in 1721; in 1726 Africa was accused of selling rum illegally; in 1727 he won a bad-debt suit against a man known only as Ephraim.

3. A Coffin family thread connects several Nantucket slave owners, coincidentally or otherwise. William Gayer married Peter Coffin's widowed mother-in-law, and he owned Africa as a slave. When his son-in-law Nathaniel Coffin died, his estate included three African slaves. Damaris and Nathaniel Coffin's son Benjamin only manumitted his slaves in 1775. William Swain married Peter Coffin's daughter, and he owned a pair of African slaves and their children. James Coffin was also a slave owner.

to declare that it was "not agreeable to Truth for Friends to purchase slaves and keep them for a term of life." In the winter of 1729–30, in his house, which still stands in a hawthorn grove south of Madaket Road, Elihu Coleman wrote a tract in which he raised and refuted one-by-one the conventional justifications for slavery. Published in 1733, Coleman's arguments were not immediately convincing to all other Friends, neither those in Newport, the site of the New England Yearly Meeting, nor even in Nantucket. In both places slaves continued to be owned by Friends for more than another half century, and in Rhode Island some Quakers amassed fortunes through the slave trade.

The Nantucket Meeting, nonetheless, did not back down from its radical position, and in the course of the 1700s Nantucket's slaves were manumitted, albeit with glacial slowness. When Damaris Coffin wrote her own will in 1764, she left to her surviving children and grandchildren land, 240 sheep, sheep commons, and her personal effects. At her death her estate did not include slaves, indentured servants, or "Indian debts."

Trees

From roots in slavery sprang Nantucket family trees bearing (among others) the surnames Barlow, Boston, Dyer, Pompey, Sampson, and Summons. Just as the descendants of the original English proprietors were the elite of white Sherburne (the name the town bore throughout the time slavery existed on the island), the descendants of slaves brought to Nantucket in the 1700s constituted the first families of the African-Nantucketer community of New Guinea. In the published vital records for Nantucket to 1850 (births, marriages, and deaths compiled from many different sources),

the English family surnames that occupy the most pages are Coffin, Gardner, Swain, Folger, and Macy.[4] African Nantucketers' births and deaths are under-recorded in the surviving vital records, but marriage intentions are better documented. In them, the three surnames occurring most often are Boston, Pompey, and Summons.[5] In Nantucket land deeds and probate records the relative frequencies of the names are directly proportional to their frequencies in the marriage records. There is no doubt that within their community those three African-Nantucketer families occupied a position corresponding to that of the white Coffins, Gardners, Swains, Folgers, and Macys in theirs.

The Boston family was much the largest and seems to have intermarried with just about every other African-Nantucketer family. The Pompey family was nearly as big and equally influential. Among other multigeneration families were the Williams family, the Warren family, the Gardner family, the Bears family, and the Maxcy family.[6]

"Maxcy" is a variant spelling of Macy. Since Maxcy's Pond is at the site of the seventeenth-century English settlement, it is almost certainly named for the white Macy family.[7] In the old New Guinea area, on the other hand, Warren Street, which connects lower Pleasant Street with Orange Street, probably was named for the black Warren family rather than the white Warrens. Williams Street and Bear Street, which run parallel to Warren Street, were probably named for the black Williams and Bears families. Cato Lane, which originally led to one of the cow gates on the south edge of town, bears the name of black landowner Cato Cary, who purchased land "southward and westward of the Wind Mills" in 1774.

Early Nantucket marriage records for people identified as "blacks" or "Negroes" typically give

---

4. The Coffins occupy 248 pages, the Gardners 159 pages, the Swains 122 pages, the Folgers 110 pages and the Macys 106 pages. A second tier is constituted of Bunkers and Colemans (78 pages each) and Husseys (75 pages). The Starbucks (48 pages), Chases (44 pages), Worths (42 pages), and Pinkhams (39 pages) make up a third tier.

5. If the various spellings Summons, Simmons, and Simons are combined.

6. Keziah (Coffin) Fanning wrote in her diary for August, 2, 1799: " Took tea at Maxcy's, he lives in New Town in his own house."

7. Maxcy's Pond was formerly called Wyers Pond because the house lot of settler Nathaniel Wyer (d. 1681) adjoined the west side of the pond, but by 1809 it appears on a town map as Maxcy's Pond.

only single names, a potent identifying flag of slavery. In the mid-1700s one finds records of unions between couples where one or both of the parties have but a single name: Bristol married Rose in 1751; Rose and her two sons, one of them named Bristol for his father, were still in slavery on the eve of the American Revolution. The Nantucket Historical Association holds a document of manumission signed by their owner Benjamin Coffin in 1775.

Nancy married Robin in 1754; Pegg married Toby in 1755; Cesar married Ann Ichabod (a Wampanoag) in 1763; Timit married Bash Twina in 1766; and Pompey married Viner (Lavinia) in 1767.

Even as slavery ended on the island, some marriage partners were still recorded with but a single name: Cato married Violet in 1774; Prince married Patience Tompum in 1776; Mike married Sarah Cote in 1788. An early union between two people with two names each occurred in 1758, when Ruth Jones and Cuffy Fortune were married, but it is not until around 1770 that the records show most African Nantucketers as having both given name and surname.

One source of surnames was the custom of adopting a father's slave name as the family name. The progenitors of the Boston family were slaves of William Swain. Between 1739 and 1760 Boston and Maria increased Swain's holdings by producing eight children born into slavery. Toward the end of his long life, Swain gradually freed the family. He freed Boston in 1751 and then in 1760 he formalized the manumission of Boston, Maria, and their infant child. Their other seven children were freed one by one over the 1760s and into the 1770s, until a 1773 court case involving one of their sons, Prince Boston, provided the impetus for the end of slavery on Nantucket.[8]

The year after gaining his freedom, their son Seneca married Thankful Micah, whose surname implies that she was a Wampanoag survivor of the epidemic. Seneca and Thankful proudly named their first-born child Freeborn Boston. Fifteen years later their next-to-last child, Absalom, was born. Although Seneca and Thankful invested their hopes first and foremost in Freeborn, it was in Absalom that their heritages came together to produce a Nantucket businessman, community leader, and significant figure in the racial integration of the island's public schools.

The Pompeys were another Nantucket family that adopted its progenitor's slave name as a surname. The earliest Pompey (locally pronounced "Pompy") had been a slave of Ebenezer Gardner, who manumitted him in his 1741 will. When, after a half century of freedom, he died in 1791, the selectmen directed Peregrine Folger to make a coffin for "Old Pompey" at town expense. Another Pompey was a blacksmith and adopted the name Pompey Nailor.[9] Pompey Nailor's sons, however, chose to be George and John Pompey rather than George and John Nailor. The prolific Pompey family brought forth businessman Edward Pompey, whose 1848 estate inventory showed a well-stocked store, shares held in the schooner *Highland*, and an impressive collection of books. Edward Pompey served as the Nantucket subscription agent for William Lloyd Garrison's newspaper *The Liberator*, and he was an active abolitionist during Nantucket's turbulent 1840s.

For a man who made nails on an anvil to take Nailor as a surname was in line with a common practice among Africans as they were freed from slavery. Other Nantucket family names derived from professions include Barber, Painter, Dyer, Draper, Farmer, and Cooper.

For a century and a half, to the mid-1800s, the children of African Nantucketers married one another in typical island pattern to create intertwined genealogies, surnames sometimes being bestowed as given names in order to recognize

---

8. Prince Boston's brother Silas remained in slavery for another year. In 1775 Benjamin Coffin manumitted his slave Rose and her sons Bristol and Benjamin. The legal end of slavery in Massachusetts came in 1783, after the American Revolution.

9. There are death records for two nearly contemporaneous Pompeys in the 1700s. "Old Pompy" died in 1791. Pompey Nailor's death at age 78 was recorded in 1796.

both sides of a child's parentage. In particular, the names Freeborn and Freeman wend their way through the town records.

African Nantucketers also shared some family names with English settler families. There were both white and black Barneys, Bunkers, Carys, Eastons, Gardners, Macys/Maxcys, Warrens, Whippeys, Winslows, and Wrights. Octogenarian Robin Brock, who was living in the household of Jeffrey Summons in 1810, had been a slave of Thomas Brock. According to Thomas Brock's 1750 will, "my Negro man Robin" was to be free when he attained the age of thirty, about five years from the date of the will. This list of surnames shared by white and black Nantucketers only partially overlaps the known slave-owning families of Nantucket: the Barkers, Brocks, Carys, Coffins, Folgers, Gardners, Gayers, Husseys, Pinkhams, Swains, Worths, and Wyers.

A black Tabitha Coffin appears in published marriage intentions at the end of 1769, but this is a transcription error for Tabitha Cuff, whose name was correctly recorded when she married Essex Boston at the beginning of 1770. Much later, in 1835 William Coffin, a young "coloured man," died of tuberculosis. Before the 1763–64 epidemic two Nantucket Wampanoags used the name Coffin, and in 1830 the name of a Mashpee Wampanoag veteran of the American Revolution who died on Nantucket is recorded as Obed Coffin. In 1850 among the transient seamen aboard Nantucket whalers there was one Cape Verdean using the name Coffin and six nonwhite Coffins from the Hawaiian Islands. Otherwise, on Nantucket people of color did not use that surname.

That there were few or no black Coffins, Folgers, Swains, Pinkhams, Husseys, etc., may have to do with objections from the white families. The black whaling captain and merchant Paul Cuffe was born on Nantucket's neighbor island Cuttyhunk of an African father and a Wampanoag mother. As a slave, his father Kofi (a day-name in the language of the Ashanti people

of West Africa) had been owned by Quaker Ebenezer Slocum. In 1742 Kofi was sold to Ebenezer's nephew John Slocum. Upon attaining his freedom, he called himself Cuffe Slocum, and his children began to use Slocum as a surname. According to family history, the English Slocum family objected, and Cuffe Slocum's children switched to using Cuffe as a surname. It is easy to imagine the lineage-proud Coffins doing the same on Nantucket and the Macys ceding the Maxcy spelling and pronunciation of their name to a black family, possibly to distinguish former slaves from former owners.

The Gardners, on the other hand, apparently found no difficulty with the fact that for a while in the 1700s a white Daniel Gardner and a younger black Daniel Gardner shared the island. There were both white and black Easton and Warren families.

White Barneys, especially Jonathan Barney and his wife Abiel (Coffin) Barney, had ongoing real estate dealings with African Nantucketers in the early 1800s. By the mid-1800s Jonathan and Abiel's son Nathaniel and his wife Eliza had become ardent abolitionists and integrationists. During the 1840s, when Nathaniel Barney was a member of the school committee, and Eliza Barney was an officer of the Women's Anti-Slavery Society, they and likeminded Nantucketers were the targets of insinuation in letters to the editors of the local newspaper, the *Nantucket Inquirer*, that they sought "amalgamation" of the races first through school integration and ultimately through intermarriage.

As for the Whippeys, they had no distaste for amalgamation. White David Whippey famously forsook Quaker Nantucket for life in Pacific island society. His entry in the *Barney Genealogical Record* states that he was born in 1801, married "a native of the Feege Islands," and died in his adopted home in 1875. New Zealand-born William Whippey, probably half-Maori, came to Nantucket, married Maria Ross, daughter of Africa-born James Ross, operated a sailors' boarding house for Pacific islanders, and fathered at least three children before dying of tuberculosis at the end of the 1840s.

Amalgamation was a fact of life on the island. By 1850, when the federal census began to divide the nonwhite population into black and mulatto, one in seven nonwhite people on Nantucket was classified as mulatto rather than black. This included the teenaged children of the Barber family, whose head of household was a black man with an Irish wife.

The unions from which Nantucket's mixed-race population sprang do not appear in the island's marriage records, however, because in 1786, three years after abolishing slavery, the Massachusetts legislature enacted an antimiscegenation law that remained in effect until 1843. This "Act for the Solemnization of Marriage" prohibited anyone from joining in marriage "any white person with any negro, Indian or mulatto, under penalty of 50 pounds and all such marriages shall be absolutely null and void."

In defiance of the diminishingly small pool of legitimate marriage partners circumscribed by state law, the African-Nantucketer population grew both by natural increase and by absorbing outsiders. Early unions, in particular, were blessed with a multitude of children. In less than a decade of marriage, for instance, Tobias and Falla Boston produced twins Mary and Priscilla in 1768, Phebe in 1771, Lucy in 1774, and Prince in 1777. Young Prince was named for his uncle Prince Boston, who had obtained his freedom from slavery four years before his nephew's birth.

The 1850 federal census not only categorized residents by race, it also recorded place of birth. For that year we find that Nantucket's nonwhite population included people from mainland Massachusetts, Rhode Island, Connecticut, New Jersey, New York, Pennsylvania, Maryland, Washington, D.C., Virginia, South Carolina, and Louisiana. Three were from Nova Scotia, where former slaves who had served with the British army against the colonists had been settled after the American Revolution. In 1850 there were still Nantucket residents who had been born in

– Jay Avila illustration

Africans enslaved in New England in the seventeenth and eighteenth centuries had been taken from the west coast of Africa.

Africa. One was Lucinda "Lucy" (Gordon) Cooper, second wife of onetime fugitive slave Arthur Cooper, and the other was James Ross, father of Maria (Ross) Whippey and of Eunice Ross, in whose name the public schools had just been racially integrated.

The greatest number of nonwhite off-islanders came to Nantucket from New York, but nearly as many came from the slave states. In the Grantham family the husband was Virginia-born, while his wife had been born in Maryland. Their two young children had been born in Massachusetts. Both adults were illiterate and had probably escaped from slavery.

New Guinea

By the late 1700s an independent community had formed between the harbor and Popsquatchet Hills, where a rank of windmills stood. Within what had been laid out in 1726 as the West Monomoy lots, the area where the African community established itself came to be known as New Guinea. Nearby was and still is Angola Street. Both "Guinea" and "Angola" reflect the West African origin of the village's residents.

At the far southeast was the Newtown Gate, through which people passed out of town onto the sheep commons, and outside the Newtown Gate lay Gallows Field, the site of executions in the 1700s.[10] South toward the ocean shore lay Miacomet valley, to which Nantucket's Wampanoags had been displaced from other parts of the island by the burgeoning English population and its livestock. New Guinea's situation made it a natural meeting place for Africans and Wampanoags, and alliances between the two peoples were formed through business transactions and marriages.

With the decimation of Miacomet village by the winter epidemic of 1763–64, solitary Wampanoags merged into the New Guinea community. One of them was schoolmaster Benjamin Tashama. Another, it seems, was Thankful Micah.

The Wampanoag heritage of residents of New Guinea was recognized not only by Essex Boston in 1822 but by people engaged in the struggle over the public schools in 1844. In that year the integrationists attempted to force the town to go on record that it truly did "mean to deprive any child having *any appreciable mixture of Negro or Indian blood*, of the privilege of attending any schools where there are white children."

As house servants, African men and women had lived in white Nantucket households. Writing about the Cary house on Upper Main Street, Eliza Mitchell recorded Betsey Cary's description of living arrangements and permitted entertainment for the household servants:

"Now, they [the Carys] were the owners of a number of slaves and cared for them as if they were house servants. The attic had several sleeping rooms and finished fireplaces, where the servants could go after their day's work was over and have all the fun they wanted in a reasonable way. They

Betsey Cary described the lives of the servants who lived in the garret of the Cary family's house at 117 Main Street.

had instruments of music, fiddle, banjo, etc., etc., and sometimes they were allowed to have a sort of picnic and then parch'd corn and molasses and they lived quite as contented and happy in their way as one can imagine. I think I never saw such large locks & keys as some I remember of seeing in my young days in that house."[11]

This vivid description of slave life on Nantucket is compromised by the fact that the Cary house was not built until after slavery had come to an end on the island. Either the people living in the attic of that house were employees rather than slaves, or the attic life, fiddling, banjo playing, and corn-popping took place in the house the Carys occupied prior to building the one that stands to this day at 117 Main Street. To be fair, the chilling comment about big locks and keys that follows directly on the description of how the Carys' house servants lived is the second or third mention of household security in the account and may not have been intended to imply that the servants were locked into their upstairs quarters.

Evidence that the Carys owned slaves in the 1700s is to be found in the Nantucket records. In 1774 Cato, a "free Negro," purchased land with a house and rights to a well in the area near the

---

10. In the Nantucket Registry of Deeds there is a 1799 list of street names compiled by Isaac Coffin, Nantucket's Principal Assessor, which includes Angola Street and describes New Guinea as "the Negro Town or Negro Village at the Southward and Eastward of the Wind Mills." In this 1799 compilation, York Street, Warren Street, and Bear Street are also already in existence. Pleasant Street is said to run "to the Southward and Eastward to the Newtown Gate." Coffin also writes that "All the Blacks are situated and live in New Guinea who live at the Southward and Eastward of the four Windmills in the Negro Town or Village, New Guiney, Negro Town Village or Negro Hill."

11. Eliza Mitchell writes that this information was given to her by Betsey Cary in 1845. Betsey (Swain) Cary had married into the Cary family in 1798, and her son-in-law later acquired the Cary house on Main Street for himself and Betsey Cary's daughter, also called Betsey.

windmills. The prior owners had been Josiah Barker and Christopher Starbuck, but Cato bought his homestead free and clear from Edward Cary, ropemaker, within the month that Edward Cary freed him. In 1781 Cato Cary, having assumed his former owner's surname, married Hannah Panchame, a Wampanoag survivor of the epidemic of 1763-64.

Gainful Employment on the Seas

For single persons, couples, and growing families alike, the issue for former slaves living in New Guinea was how to integrate themselves into Nantucket's economy. They could no more survive on subsistence farming alone than the Wampanoags before them. Families needed income to survive. Owners had sent slaves whaling, and these voyages provided access to skills and knowledge that would serve the first free black whalers and their descendants for at least a century to come. In the labor vacuum created by the epidemic, black men—enslaved and free alike—replaced Wampanoag men at the oars of whaleboats. By 1807, according to James Freeman, "The larger whalemen have three boats and twenty-one men, of whom nine are commonly blacks; and the smaller, two boats and sixteen men, of whom seven are black." Freeman went on to express his opinion about this change:

> …the Indians having disappeared, negros are now substituted in their place. Seamen of color are more submissive than the whites; but as they are more addicted to frolicking, it is difficult to get them aboard the ship, when it is about to sail, and to keep them aboard, after it has arrived. The negroes, though they are to be prized for their habits of obedience, are not as intelligent as the Indians; and none of them attain the rank of endsman.

It was the practice of signing slaves onto whaling crews that ultimately brought slavery to its end on the island. When William Swain freed Boston, Maria, and their youngest child, he put their older children on a schedule for manumission. Tobias, the eldest, was to be freed at age twenty-five. The rest—from Essex, the next to eldest, to George, the next-to-youngest—had to each continue in slavery until reaching the age of twenty-eight. In other words, their most productive working years belonged to Swain, and only thereafter would they be free to go out on their own.

The Swain family sent one of the brothers, Prince—born in 1750 and scheduled to be freed in 1778—whaling on the sloop *Friendship* in 1772.[12] When the *Friendship* returned to Nantucket, Captain Elisha Folger paid Prince's lay (his share in the profits of the voyage) directly to Prince. William Swain had died, having choked to death on a piece of meat at age 82. His son John Swain, nonetheless, sued to recover Prince's wages, but a jury concluded that Prince could keep what he had earned. Prince then successfully petitioned for immediate freedom, five years before William Swain's deed of manumission provided for it.

This 1773 court case does not mark the absolute end of slavery in Nantucket. Silas Boston worked out a deal with the Swain family to go whaling for them one more time in exchange for his freedom in 1774, the same year that Edward Cary manumitted Cato. In 1775 Quaker Benjamin Coffin was still delaying manumission of his three slaves, Rose and her sons Bristol and Benjamin, when the Nantucket Meeting came close to disowning him over the issue. In 1791 another case was in court over the lay of Moses, who had belonged to the Tolman family. The voyage in question had taken place back in 1775, when it appears that Moses was still enslaved. Contrary to the decision in the Prince Boston case, and even after Massachusetts had abolished slavery, the Nantucket court retroactively awarded his earnings to the Tolmans.

And still slavery continued to cast its shadow across the sea to Nantucket. In 1796 Dr. Benjamin Tupper's grandson, also named Benjamin, wrote a

---

12. Quaker historian Zaccheus Macy was a shareholder in the sloop *Friendship*. Just as he derived whaling profits from indentured Wampanoag labor, he also benefited from African slave labor.

letter from Paris to his mother in Nantucket, sending warm greetings to their good friends the Carys and announcing, "I have bought a large ship of five hundred tons, and she sails this day for the West Indies.…I own one half the ship. She carries five hundred negroes. If she arrives safe, I shall have money enough to come home and live with my friends, which I should like, although I like France very much."

The maritime career of Cuffe Slocum's son Paul Cuffe was bracketed by the American Revolution and the War of 1812, both of which had profound economic repercussions for American whaling. While still a very young man during the Revolution, Paul Cuffe began making daring runs around the English blockade to provision Nantucket. As Lamont Thomas describes these exploits in his biography of Cuffe, "He …finally succeeded in making Nantucket his first maritime market." Cuffe developed a close working relationship with Nantucket Quaker businessman William Rotch Sr., whose son William Jr. had been born in 1759, the same year as Cuffe. The mutual esteem of the Rotches and Paul Cuffe was instrumental in Cuffe's successful application for admission into the Westport Meeting of the Society of Friends.

After the Revolution Paul Cuffe and his Wampanoag brother-in-law Thomas Wainer began building a major whaling and mercantile business in Westport (near Dartmouth and not far from New Bedford). They captained their own ships, working by preference with nonwhite crews and whenever possible with close relatives. With their income they purchased agricultural land and they built more ships. Cuffe became an outstanding figure in early United States commerce and politics and in the movement to return former slaves to Africa. He also was a generous donor to the Westport Meeting of the Society of Friends. The War of 1812 disrupted whaling and commerce once again and with them Cuffe's plans for economic development in West Africa. After the war's conclusion there was insufficient time to realize his long-held ambitions before he died in 1817.

Absalom Boston, Master Mariner

Absalom Boston, born in 1785, was a quarter century younger than Paul Cuffe. When he boarded the ship *Thomas* to go whaling around Cape Horn in 1809, he was already a seasoned mariner, twenty-four years old and recently married. He was also literate. While other men signed the *Thomas*'s crew list with marks, he signed on with the same elegant signature that appears on subsequent documents throughout his life.

In years to come Absalom Boston's literacy not only advanced his career, it had broad influence within New Guinea and beyond. White Anna Gardner, who was to become school teacher to a younger generation of New Guinea's children and then to children of former slaves in the South during and after the Civil War, wrote of how Boston introduced her to William Lloyd Garrison's abolitionist paper *The Liberator* when she was eighteen years old: "Absalom Boston, a colored man who had lived in Grandfather Macy's family to do outdoor work, and who had become quite domesticated there, frequently came to see Mother. He brought the 'Liberator' for her to read. I at once subscribed for it—his name and mine coming out in the paper as the only subscribers from Nantucket."

By any measure Absalom Boston enjoyed success in life well beyond that attained by his neighbors in New Guinea, but the course of his public success was punctuated by private losses. His brother Freeborn and his father Seneca died almost simultaneously in 1809. Thankful, his mother, was unable to manage on her own. In the 1810 census she is listed as 56 years old and living in a household headed by Freeborn's widow Mary (Summons) Boston. By the time Seneca's estate was finally settled two years later, Thankful was described as insane. Mary contracted to care for her mother-in-law for life in exchange for the dwelling house that would have been Thankful's.

During the forced inactivity imposed on Nantucket by the War of 1812 (which was not concluded until early 1815), the residents of New Guinea shared the misery of interrupted income, inadequate food, and insufficient fuel during a period of unusual cold.[13] Absalom lost his first wife, Mary, and was left with a motherless young son. In 1814 he married the widow Phebe Spriggins, their marriage being recorded in the South Congregational Church (now the Unitarian Universalist Church). Not only did Phebe look after little Charles, but she and Absalom had three children together—Henry, Caroline, and an infant who died unnamed.

Absalom returned to whaling after the war, joining the crew of the ship *Independence*, but he was looking for opportunities ashore. In 1820 he successfully applied for a license to keep a public house. He also continued to engage in real estate transactions, a practice he had begun in 1812, trading on his inherited assets, and actively buying and selling land. With the capital he raised, he was in a position to make mortgage loans to other members of the New Guinea community and was becoming an influential figure. In 1822 he finally sailed as captain of the ship *Industry* with an all-black crew on a voyage to the Atlantic whaling grounds.

While a grand emulation of those of Paul Cuffe, the voyage was not a financial success. The *Industry* returned with only seventy barrels of oil, and the ship itself was auctioned for expenses. Absalom did not take command of another vessel but involved himself with community and business matters on land.

In 1826 his second wife was gravely ill. In order to stay at home, he signed a contract for driving cows on a daily basis from May through October. Phebe died in August, and once again there were children who needed to be looked after. Instead of going to sea, Absalom bought a quarter share of the lay of another seaman who joined the crew of the *Independence* as it set out for the Pacific whal-

— Nantucket Historical Association

Whaling captain and businessman Absalom Boston was the son and grandson of African slaves held by Nantucketer William Swain.

ing grounds. Fortunately for Absalom and his children, Hannah Cook of Dartmouth became his wife within the year. She and Absalom lived out the remainder of their lives together, adding five more children to their family.[14]

When the whaleship *Loper* of Nantucket set out in 1829 with a black crew under white Captain Obed Starbuck, Absalom Boston again stayed on land. Upon the *Loper*'s return in the fall of 1830 from a highly lucrative voyage, he and his New Guinea neighbor Samuel Harris mounted horses to lead the jubilant crew in a triumphal parade through town. The post-voyage banquet was replete with toasts, the gist of which was that scoffers had said it couldn't be done, but it was time for the naysayers to concede. The *Loper*'s crew had

13. A public soup kitchen was set up in the winter of 1814-15. In February the temperature dropped to a record low of 11 degrees below zero. Because of particulate matter in the atmosphere from a volcanic eruption far away, 1816 was the infamous "year of no summer" with frost every month of the year, and the following year saw a snow storm on June 17. Obed Macy recorded in his journal that the temperature dropped to –11 degrees on February 1 and that on June 11 there was "a heavy white frost and ice as thick as the blade of a knife." The war was over, but life continued very bleak on the island. It was at this time that David Whippey left Nantucket permanently to live in Fiji.

14. Hannah Cook was in some manner related to Paul Cuffe, whose son and daughter both married into the Dartmouth Cook family. In Nantucket the brothers Nathaniel and William Borden married Deborah Cook of Dartmouth and Lucretia Cuffe respectively. Nathaniel and Deborah moved to New Bedford soon after they were married. In 1850 fifty-seven-year-old Mary Cuffe was living in Absalom Boston's household. Absalom Boston's marriage connections to the Cuffe family are yet to be fully documented.

brought back "greasy luck" in the form of 2,280 barrels of oil and done so in record time.

The whaling industry had recovered from the War of 1812 and was booming on Nantucket. Absalom's sons Charles (born to Mary) and Henry (born to Phebe) saw their future on the sea. Like their father before them, both appear in records as "mariner," but neither lived to achieve Absalom's rank of "master mariner."

With the deaths of Charles and Henry as young men, the only child surviving from Absalom's first two marriages was Caroline, who married James Clough in 1839. From his marriage to Hannah Cook there was first-born Phebe Ann, and then the boys Absalom, Oliver, and Thomas, all born in the 1830s, and finally Sarah, who was born in 1841. Little Absalom and Sarah both died, leaving Phebe Ann, Oliver, and Thomas as Absalom's and Hannah's hope for the years to come. They were diligent in their efforts to secure a bright future for their growing children.

Other Maritime Careers

Most New Guinea men at sea derived their income from whaling, working on coastal freight schooners, or fishing. But there were other possibilities. Prince Boston's brothers Peter and Silas went out as seamen on privateers in the 1770s and early 1780s. Serving together on the gunship *Hazard*, they were part of an unsuccessful attempt by the Continental Navy to seize a British fort in Maine and ended up walking from the Maine woods all the way back to Boston. On the basis of this, they both applied for pensions as sailors of the Revolution. By the time Peter was in his early thirties, he was back on land, married to Rhoda Jolly (whose mother was a Mashpee Wampanoag), and on his way to being a father of four.

Absalom and Hannah Boston's son Oliver emulated his great-uncle Peter by enlisting in the Union Navy during the Civil War. After his discharge in 1864, he continued a civilian maritime career from New Bedford.

Military service was a route to productive citizenship for Peter and Oliver Boston, but it also offered opportunities to stray. At the beginning of the 1860s, when Nantucket was in deep economic depression, Charles Godfrey Jr., son of one of the founding members of Nantucket's African Baptist Church, enlisted in the Union Navy. The previous year he had married a Nantucket woman. A year into his hitch he married a second woman in New Bedford and managed to conceal his bigamy for decades. Eventually he disappeared from his first family. After the requisite seven years, his Nantucket wife successfully petitioned to have him declared dead, and only thereafter, when she applied to the Navy for a widow's pension, did it come to light that Charles Godfrey was still alive.

Landlubbers

The most commonly listed occupation of New Guinea men was mariner, but many African-Nantucketer women and men found work on land. In legal documents and censuses men are commonly identified as laborers, but usually individuals so identified are elsewhere shown to engage in some more specific line of work as well, such as trading, trucking, or occasional whaling. In a court deposition Arthur Cooper, one of the founding members of Nantucket's Zion Methodist Episcopal Church, is described as a laborer. In a document filed in the Nantucket Registry of Deeds, Cooper testified that he served as the shipping agent who had signed under-aged John Robinson, Jr. on board the whaleship *Three Brothers* without the knowledge of his father. (The boy was beaten and verbally abused on the voyage and finally left the ship. He refused to return, and his father sued for his lay.)

At some point in their lives, most African Nantucketers worked for a while as domestic servants. Children and young adolescents were sent to live and learn in white households. Anna Gardner wrote of how Absalom Boston had formed a lasting bond with her mother from the time when he had lived with her grandfather Francis Macy's family. Since there were no public schools in Nantucket at that time, it was probably the Macys who fostered young Absalom's reading skills and handsome penmanship.

The 1800 census reports forty-three nonwhite people in white households. About the same number were live-in domestics in 1810. Not all were young. Some, it appears, had never left their former owners. An 1800 census shows six black people living with the aged Joseph Barker and his wife Elizabeth. The Barkers were both around seventy years old, and the ages of five of the people living with them ranged from forty to sixty years. The one young person in the household was a fifteen-year-old called Prince.

The Cary family also continued to enjoy the services of African Nantucketers. In 1810 Phillis Hero, age forty-five, and her six-year-old son Fariud were living with the elderly Edward Carys, while William Hero (no age given) was living in the home of Richard and Margaret Cary. Clearly the tradition of live-in help for the Carys survived the end of slavery on Nantucket.

Day labor and domestic service were by no means the only occupations of the residents of New Guinea. Mahalah Collins, daughter of Peter and Rhoda Boston, took in washing, while Sally Dennison, wife of trader and mariner James Dennison, was a seamstress. Phebe Lucas worked as a domestic, but she specialized in nursing.

Venus Peters is unique in being described in a legal document as a "plebian." In March of 1793 she took a man identified as "Nicholas Portugue" to court, but the case was continued to October. Venus died in April, however, so her suit didn't come up again, and we can never know the substance of her complaint against Nicholas. Since she hadn't written a will, a probate inventory was made of her belongings, which were anything but plebian. She owned bedsteads, several changes of household linen, a half dozen cups and saucers, white plates, and a milk pot. Her wardrobe included dresses, skirts, a pair of "green stays," a black satin cloak, bonnet, and gloves. In her possession at the time of her death was a two-year-old IOU from Nicholas Portugue for "eighteen pounds [sterling] on Demand." Also left behind was Henrietta, "a Minor and Orphan Daughter of Venus Peters." The court appointed Josiah

Sampson as guardian to Henrietta. If "Josiah" was actually Uriah, then Henrietta was placed in a New Guinea household. Uriah Sampson, identified in an 1785 debt dispute as a mulatto "now resident at Sherborn," had married into the Pompey family. In 1833 Henrietta James was laid to rest in the cemetery behind Mill Hill. If she was the daughter of Venus Peters, she had lived, married, and died in a village smaller than today's Siasconset, a place where gossip about Venus's black satin cloak, green stays, and white plates must have been daily currency for a lifetime.

New Guinea supported more than a dozen men identified as traders and merchants, including Absalom Boston and Edward Pompey, who both owned and operated stores. Stephen Pompey was specifically a grocer, William Harris was a "victualler" and William Simmons was a baker. Numbers of households took in boarders, and a few people, again Absalom Boston among them, ran boarding houses or inns.

The community also benefited from land-based work directly supported by the maritime industry. On the 1821 map prepared by Daniel Allen and Daniel P. Macy one can see ropewalks located on the site of present-day Prospect Hill Cemetery. Among the residents of New Guinea identified as ropemakers are Cato Cary in the late 1700s and John Sip in the early 1800s. Joseph Painter was a blockmaker, and, in addition to Pompey Nailor, Simon Borden was a blacksmith. Charles Godfrey Jr. and Sampson Pompey were coopers.

Just as African Nantucketers followed the Wampanoags into whaling, they also took up weaving, as the Wampanoags had done before. Africa is an early case. Later Seneca Boston became a weaver as well. His brother Essex took up the craft of shoemaking once practiced by Peter Folger's son Eleazar.

A profession that seems over-represented among New Guinea residents is barbering. More men are identified as barbers or hairdressers than as taking in boarders. Aboard ship the jobs of cook and steward had become almost exclusively the domain of African Americans. Correspondingly, on shore barbering was considered an appropriate profession for African-American men, and within African-American communities, it was invested with more prestige than work at sea. All of Absalom Boston's adult sons followed the sea except Thomas, the youngest, who was trained as a barber.

Young Thomas also had music lessons, and he used music as an entrée into a society he yearned to be part of. In 1895 the writer of a memoir submitted to the editor of the *Inquirer and Mirror* recalled dances in New Guinea for which music was provided by fiddler Harry Wheeler. Thomas Boston, on the other hand, played his violin at parties and dances in white Nantucket households, and ultimately it was through music rather than barbering that he supported himself and his wife.

Notable among members of the Boston family through several generations is their readiness to diversify their work and their investments. Seneca Boston was both a mariner and a weaver, while his brother Essex made shoes. Absalom Boston worked his way up from mariner to ship captain while operating a store and an inn. Moreover, both Essex and his nephew Absalom were identified as "yeomen," which means that they farmed their own land. On Nantucket Thomas Boston barbered and entertained with his violin. Later, he worked in a bookstore and auction house in Boston, as a portrait photographer in Westport, then in a bank in Washington, D.C. He worked in a laundry when he had to, and he gave music lessons on the side. Rarely did a Boston have all his eggs in one basket.

If there was one single occupation ashore that can be said to have rivaled whaling for residents of New Guinea, that would be the buying and selling of real estate. The 1850 census lists thirty heads of household with real estate ranging in value from under a hundred dollars up to a thousand dollars, that being Absalom Boston's second

house, outbuildings, store, mowing lot, and garden. The property values are much more modest than those held by Nantucket's wealthiest white families. Merchant Philip Folger, for example, owned real estate valued at $14,000.[15] On the other hand, proportionally more New Guinea residents than whites owned bits of real estate above and beyond their dwelling houses, and they were very active in buying and selling them. Prior to 1850 over a hundred and fifty transactions involving land in New Guinea are recorded in the Nantucket books of deeds. Unlike the Wampanoag deeds, which nearly always mark the passing of land into the hands of the English settlers, the New Guinea deeds involve African-Nantucketer men and women buying land from white Nantucketers, circulating it among themselves, and only occasionally selling it to white buyers.

Population

In 1790 there were seventy-six people, about equal numbers of men and women, living in their own households in New Guinea and another thirty-four living in white households for a total of 110. By 1800 the number of people classified as nonwhite had risen to 228. Another decade later the total was 300, with 192 living in their own households. Then the censuses appear to record a decline in nonwhite population even as Nantucket's total population was in a period of rapid growth. This must be the effect of underreporting, however, because in 1840 a nonwhite population of 576 was recorded.

At this point a significant imbalance had developed in the community. Of the 576 residents counted in the census, 429 were male and only 147 female. Some were children of course, so there were relatively few adult women in a context that had become very much a man's world. By 1850, after fire had devastated downtown Nantucket and many island men, black and white, had departed

15. The next largest real estate holdings in 1850 were those of Thomas Macy, merchant, $13,000; William Hadwen and Charles C. Coffin, merchants, $12,000 each; John W. Barrett, merchant, $10,500; Edward W. Gardner, merchant, $10,000; John H. Shaw, oil manufacturer, $10,000; George Easton, farmer, $10,000; George C. Gardner, farmer, $9,000; George Starbuck, merchant, $8,500; Matthew Starbuck, merchant, $7,000; and Tristram Starbuck, farmer, $2,000. But wealthier than all these men was Elizabeth Starbuck, whose commercial real estate was valued at $15,500.

for the California gold fields, the male population of New Guinea had fallen to 251, but there were only 91 women and girls of all ages. The continuing departure of men throughout the next decade reversed the proportions, leaving only 53 men and boys in New Guinea to 73 women and girls.[16]

The total population of Nantucket from 1790 had risen from a bit over 4,600 to a high of close to 10,000 in 1840, before it plunged back to just over 6,000 in 1860. It would continue to fall in years to come to around 3,000, which is what the island's population had been just after the epidemic of 1763–64. A whole century passed before the year-round population began to grow again. By then no descendants of the Bostons, the Pompeys, or their neighbors had lived on the island for decades.

Troubles

Despite the aspirations of old established families—white and black—to a quiet, orderly life, whaling made the town a place of too many loosely connected young men. Through most of the 1700s a sort of rough frontier behavior afflicted the island despite the pacific influence of the Society of Friends. The courts were clogged with cases involving thefts and assaults lubricated by improbable quantities of rum. The jail was always full, and the whipping post and the gallows were in use. Before the epidemic, Wampanoags were disproportionately represented in criminal and civil proceedings, but the children and grandchildren of the English settlers got into trouble too. English women were frequently caught illicitly selling rum, cider, and beer from their homes, and were increasingly brought to court for bearing children out of wedlock. In March 1757 Mary Johnson was so charged, "with this aggrevation that it is of a mixt blood of the negro."

Meanwhile English men brawled indoors and out, and some married couples were often before the magistrates. Particularly flagrant were Stephen Pease and his wife, who were repeatedly in court for selling rum to Wampanoags.

In 1714 Isaac Coleman accused Stephen Pease of invading his home and beating him. Pease was convicted of breach of the peace and was sentenced to being whipped or paying a fine, plus court costs and damages awarded to Coleman. Three years later, when a constable went to Stephen Pease's house with a warrant to search for illegal liquor, Pease "took an ax in his hand and swore he would cleave him down if he came on to search his house." The house was searched anyhow, and an eighty-one-gallon cask of rum was seized.

The next year John Harper and William Percy teamed up with Wampanoag Andrew Bone to steal a fishing boat. They were also sentenced to whipping as well as indentured service to the boat owner.

In 1759 Tom Jesper of Sherburne accused Nathan Gershom of Martha's Vineyard of a knife attack that left him half-scalped.

Women and men kept arriving from off-island uninvited, apparently seeking to part returning seamen from their lays.[17] A couple named Boyle was repeatedly accused of illegal liquor sales. A man named McMurphy from New Hampshire was evicted from the island, but Joseph and Molly Quinn managed to establish a boarding house in Newtown by the early 1760s. According to one account, it was a Wampanoag washerwoman working there who first contracted the "Indian sickness" and carried it to Miacomet in 1763. Molly Quinn was said to have been the sole non-Wampanoag to have been infected, although—unlike most of the Wampanoags—she recovered. Later she denied that she had ever been sick.

16. A list of nearly 600 transient mariners serving on Nantucket ships attached to the 1850 census shows that roughly one in four crew members was nonwhite. Most were African Americans or Pacific islanders. Few were from Cape Verde or the West Indies. Whether or in what numbers these men boarded on shore when their ships were in port in Nantucket is not recorded.

17. Between 1760 and 1763 the following people who had come "to reside here which may be of bad consequences to the town if not removed" included Elizabeth Hutchinson, a widow from Chilmark, and her three daughters, Jane, Katherine, and Hannah; Moses Blanchard, wife and child of Falmouth; Mary Gibson of Boston; Zubia Nickerson, single woman, of Chatham; Thomas James of Newport, R.I.; Zebdoyis Fish of Boston; John Wood of Newport; Thomas Chase and wife and child of Tisbury; William Kent, wife, and child of Yarmouth; Elizabeth Merrifield, a single woman, of Wells, Maine; John Colefox of "some town in the colony of Connecticut"; Joseph Coffin, wife and family of Newberry, Mass.; Clother Prier of Connecticut; Joseph and Timothy Jackson of Boston; Samuel Barrett of Boston ("we are not in want of any such tradesman in this town"); James McMurphy of Newfield, New Hampshire; George Cade of Boston; Elias Cotton and family of Boston; and Joseph Glasier of Boston.

At the same time that the Quinns were operating their establishment, Benjamin Clark was in court for keeping "a disorderly house" where "youths both males and females" held "frollicks… contrary to the orders of their parents and masters." Clark did not deny that there was frolicking in his house at night but promised the court to keep better order.

In 1807 Freeman had said that the African Nantucketers who had replaced the Wampanoags in the whaling industry were given to frolicking, which made it difficult to get them aboard ship and keep them there.

In March 1811 Abigail "Nabby" Gurrell was brought before the grand jury for running an "Ill-governed and Disorderly House" in her dwelling where she admitted people, both black and white, at night as well as in the daytime for tippling, carousing, and general misbehavior "to the great Damage and Common Nuisance of all the subjects of the Commonwealth." She also sold hard liquor without a license.

At least one black entrepreneur brought entertainment away from the waterfront. In the early 1800s, John Pompey built a dance hall in New Guinea. On the 1821 map of the area there is a large building labeled "Negro Hall," which may be it. The dance hall appears three times in the town records for 1823, when John Pompey mortgaged it.

Beginning in the mid-1700s the town's selectmen attempted to control businesses catering to single mariners by deporting people suspected of coming to set up or work in such establishments and by licensing the public houses that were permitted to operate. Applicants for liquor licenses were required to put up a bond against damage and disturbance caused by their patrons. Between 1750 and 1760, the annual number of license applications rose to thirty, and those licenses were not just for retailing liquor but also for sale of coffee and tea to paying customers. No record of John Pompey seeking a license has come to light. Absalom Boston did apply for and receive

a license in 1822, despite a letter to the editor of the *Nantucket Inquirer* from "A Citizen" inquiring "how many inn holders and retailers of Spiritous liquors there are in this Town, and to whom the houses of those kept by Negroes belong."

Until late in the 1700s there were very few "free Negroes" on the island,[18] and discipline of slaves was the direct responsibility of their owners. Accordingly, few black men and women appeared in court. In 1726, sixteen years after his manumission, Africa was accused by a Wampanoag of selling him liquor. Africa initially denied the charge but then gave in and paid the fine. In the same year Silvanus Hussey brought Primus, "his Negro," to court, accusing him of conspiring with some Wampanoags to steal fifty pounds of meat. Primus was sentenced to a whipping and jailed until the sentence could be carried out. Then he went back to Hussey, who returned to court in 1730 accusing Moses Pomet of "beating his Negro and abusing him very much to the endangerment of his life."

As the 1700s wound down, so did cases of debt, theft, and assault. The Wampanoags, who had once monopolized the courts, had ceased to be a presence, and either the recently freed African Nantucketers were uncommonly law-abiding, or they settled matters among themselves. This is not to say that New Guinea was crime-free or that its residents were hindered in seeking redress when they wanted and needed to. The court heard the 1796 complaint of black Isaac Barlow, who had been attacked and beaten by white Elisha Folger while at sea on the ship *Olive Branch* (of all names!). Awhile later John Carter, also black, filed a complaint that John Brown assaulted him twice during the year 1803 while they were aboard the ship *Edward*, once while in Concepción Bay in South America and again half a year later while at sea in the Pacific.

The Fenix family was ill-starred. George Fenix was called to court in 1799 for wife-beating, and his wife Jenny Fenix was repeatedly in court for theft. In 1804 she was sentenced to be whipped

---

18. Africa, James, Jonas, Cato, and Pompey appear in eighteenth-century records as "free Negroes." Ishmael was freed in 1718 and Boston in 1751.

for breaking and entering, and in 1822 she stood accused, along with another woman, of robbing an inebriated off-islander. Then there was Dorcas Mingo, who was charged with repeated assaults on other women. In 1804 Essex Boston testified as a witness against her. In 1804 Jeremiah Virginia broke windows in a man's house and beat him up. When two constables arrived on the scene, Michael Antonia got into a fight with them as he attempted to help Virginia get away.

In 1811 came another case of broken windows and worse. One March day Abiah Gordon, Joseph Capee, William Pompey, and Stephen Williams, "Black men, mariners," went on a rampage. They set upon Daniel Gardner, a black householder in New Guinea, beat him with a stone, and "did wound and bruise him, the said Daniel, so that he raised a great quantity of blood and other injuries and wounds to him." They broke the windows of Gardner's house and also unhinged the door. The same day the same gang attacked John Sip, rope-maker, and broke his collar bone.

Social Institutions

Such disturbances must have exasperated the solid citizens of New Guinea, but a long time passed before they turned to the political process for community improvement. It was not until 1839 that anyone from the neighborhood sought to run for public office. Predictably, the first to put himself forward as candidate for the board of selectmen was Absalom Boston. Just as predictably, no one voted for him.

African Nantucketers were unencumbered by *patrones* of the sort who had interposed themselves between the Wampanoags and the English population. There was no one to compare with the Guardians for the Indians, such as Gideon Hawley in Mashpee or Abishai Folger, Jonathan Coffin, and Richard Coffin on Nantucket in the 1740s. As slaves the Africans had been owned. Because of their sojourn in white households, they did not require the services of interpreters or translators

once they and their children were free. The one arena for paternalism might have been religion, but Puritan days were long over in New England, and Nantucket's Quakers were not evangelical. The people of New Guinea organized their own churches.

Intimations of racial segregation in the local white churches are in some cases ambiguous. A Quaker writing under the name of "thy Friend" to the *Islander* on January 16, 1841, to protest the proposal to close the Atheneum to "persons of color" asked rhetorically whether there were not designated Negro seats or Negro pews in "your Christian churches." But there is no ambiguity whatsoever to the letter from Harriet Peirce and Eliza Barney to the trustees of the North Congregational Church declining the use of that church for meetings of the Women's Anti-Slavery Society after the Society and the church had been unable to reach an agreement about admission of black people.[19]

Absalom Boston's marriage to Phebe Spriggins in 1814 is recorded in the church book of the Second Congregational Church, which had separated from the First (North) Congregational Church in 1809. Although the Second Congregational Church building came to be known as the South Church, it was not located far enough south to be even on the edge of New Guinea.

In late summer of 1821 the *Nantucket Inquirer* reported that the "coloured people of this Island" had formed a society for worship with its own room and its own black leadership. A month later Lorenzo Dow, a visiting preacher, came to the island and spoke outdoors in fields for several days to large gatherings. A Sabbath school was organized for black children, and the following year it was held again, admitting thirty for an hour of religious and moral instruction one afternoon a week. On January 3, 1825, the *Nantucket Inquirer* carried the following announcement: "*African Church*. An edifice at Newtown for the purpose of accommodating the coloured population will be

---

19. This letter was published in the *Islander* on January 1, 1841, but had been written some years earlier.

consecrated as a house of worship tomorrow afternoon at 2 o'clock. Seats will be provided for those who choose to attend. Sermon by their preacher, Mr. Lake. A contribution will be taken up after service to be appropriated towards defraying the expenses of completing the house." Serving as trustees of the African Baptist Society in the mid-1820s were Peter Boston, Absalom Boston, Michael DeLuce, and Charles Godfrey.

Nearly a decade after the formation of the African Baptist Society, in May of 1831, New Guinea residents "on this Island, far from the Churches to which some of us formerly belonged" called upon Seth Emmers of Martha's Vineyard and Edmund Harris of Hyannis to assist in organization of the African Baptist Church. Constituent members who signed the charter for the new church were John Barber (whose wife was Irish), Charles Godfrey, Sr. (a trustee of the Society), Charlotte (Boston) Groves, Priscilla Thompson, Mary Marsh, Sarah Dennison, Rhoda Boston, Hannah Boston, and Sara DeLuce.[20] Notable about this group is the preponderance of women (three of them the wives of the trustees of the Society) and the absence of the names of their husbands.

This regrouping was fraught with tension. Three months after the signing of the charter, former trustees of the Society—Absalom Boston, Michael DeLuce, and Charles Godfrey (who seems to have been on both sides of the issue)—were accused of breaking the lock of the church building and keeping the plaintiffs from "the use, possession and improvement of said church." The complainants were the trustees of the reorganized church: George W. Summons, John Marsh, Thomas Cooper, Philip Tyler, William Harris, Daniel Valentine, and John Peters. A letter from Jeffrey Summons to the *Nantucket Inquirer* about a funeral that took place shortly before the alleged break-in mentions "two of the pretended Trustees, who now have the school house in their possession." The substance of the embarrassing disagreement, which must have made for spirited debates within the Boston and DeLuce households, is nowhere made clear.

In 1832 a second church—the Zion Church—was established. Bristol Wright, Arthur Cooper, and John Cooper received a piece of land from James Ross for the purpose of "building an African Methodist Episcopal Church."

Arthur Cooper, a fugitive from slavery in Virginia, had arrived in Nantucket with his family in 1820. Two years later an agent for his former owner came to the island to recover him and to claim Cooper's free-born Massachusetts wife and children as well. Nantucket Quakers foiled the attempt and hid the Coopers in the home of Anna Gardner's parents. Local interference with the agent and his two deputies at the time (reported in the *Nantucket Inquirer* on October 22, 1822), the subsequent legal actions, and the ensuing public debate focused Nantucket's attention on the problems of a nation in which some states had abolished slavery while others continued and protected it. As for Anna Gardner, her intense childhood impression of the fear in which the Coopers lived while hiding in her family's house was a formative experience that set her on her way to a lifetime devoted to abolitionism, equal rights, and education for African Americans.

Another Nantucket churchman began his life in slavery in Virginia. The Reverend James Crawford was the son of a Virginia plantation owner and one of his slaves, Mary, who ended her days living in Nantucket with her son. James Crawford escaped from Virginia by going to sea on a merchant ship, which he managed to leave in the North. He began a life of freedom in Providence, Rhode Island, where—largely self-educated—he succeeded in being licensed as a Methodist minister. In 1848, during a visit to Nantucket, he agreed to serve as pastor to the local African Baptist Church. Moving to the island with him were his South Carolina-born wife Ann, their young daughter Juliana, who had been born in Rhode Island, and his mother Mary, who—at age 70 and

20. The African Baptist Church reorganized again in 1848, when the members were encouraged by the Ecclesiastical Council overseeing the reorganization to rename themselves "The Pleasant Street Baptist Church."

suffering from dementia—had been released from slavery to the care of her son.

Ann's younger sister Dianna and Dianna's daughter Cornelia were enslaved in North Carolina. In order to collect funds to free his sister-in-law and niece, James Crawford traveled extensively throughout the northern states and Canada, dramatically recounting his own life experiences. Then, at great risk to himself, he traveled south into the slave states, passing as a white man, bought Dianna and Cornelia, and brought them to freedom in 1858. Ann Crawford had died, and James and Dianna married, but this second marriage was brief. Both Dianna and Crawford's mother Mary died in 1860. Eight years later he married the widow Rebecca Elaw Pierce, daughter of Zilpha Elaw, a noted black Methodist preacher. James Crawford gave forty years of deeply appreciated service to both the African Baptist Church and the Summer Street Baptist Church, neither of which had the resources to pay a living wage to a clergyman. Not surprisingly, the Rev. Mr. Crawford supported his family as a barber.

As can be seen from his photo, it would have been difficult to identify James Crawford as "black," a fact upon which he staked his freedom when entering the slave states to redeem his sister-in-law and niece. Generations of involuntary childbearing by enslaved women like his mother Mary and her mother before her had so attenuated their African genetic heritage that their children and grandchildren were different in appearance from many northern "free Negroes." Jeffrey Bolster, writing about black seamen in Southern ports in the 1800s, remarks, "Free dark young men from the North stood out in the lower South––not only because of their speech, but because most local free blacks were either mulattos or older people manumitted after they became enfeebled."

In 1850 the old Fugitive Slave Act of 1793 was strengthened and threatened people like the Coopers and the Crawfords living in free states. Another set of laws created in the 1830s threatened the livelihoods of free blacks. Once these laws were in place, the career of Paul Cuffe could not be

In 1822 Nantucket Quakers hid fugitive slave Arthur Cooper and his family from an agent seeking to return him to his former owner. Later he became an elder of the Zion A. M. E. Church in Nantucket.

replicated by other ambitious black men. Captain Absalom Boston and Captain Edward Pompey, both of whom had begun their careers on the sea, showed foresight in diversifying their investments on shore in Nantucket. Had they continued to go to sea, they would have placed their freedom and their lives at risk.

In the 1700s and early 1800s, black seamen both free and enslaved (an example being Prince Boston before and after his manumission from the Swains) took to the water in great numbers. Whaling, coastal freighting, and working the high seas on merchant ships all provided employment and cosmopolitan contacts unavailable on shore. This put slave owners in a bind. On the one hand, they could earn money by putting their slaves to work on vessels, but on the other hand, they stood to either lose the men in free ports or to have them return home with news of how other black men had achieved their freedom. Slave uprisings in the Caribbean struck fear to the hearts of slave owners in Southern ports.

Former slave James Crawford passed as white on a trip into the slave states to rescue his sister-in-law and her daughter. Arthur Brock recalled Crawford as having "wonderful brown hair, and the merriest blue eyes and dimples, and that large, humorous, lovely mouth that spoke evil of no man."

In the 1820s, printed informational leaflets were being carried south by black seamen appealing to Southern blacks, few of whom could actually read, to resist slavery. States reacted by passing Negro Seamen's Acts to prevent contact between black seamen and black slaves on shore. South Carolina began imprisoning free black crewmen. The state of Georgia followed by placing a forty-day quarantine on any vessel that arrived in a Georgia port with black crew members aboard. Since no ship could afford forty days in port, captains were discouraged from signing black men on for voyages that would put in at Savannah. During the 1830s North Carolina and Florida followed South Carolina's lead. Florida's legislature banned all free blacks from coming there on pain of imprisonment. The states with ports on the Gulf of Mexico were slower to adopt restrictions, but by the end of the 1830s Alabama's ports were closed, and finally Louisiana fell in line, too, radically affecting cosmopolitan New Orleans. In the meantime the ports throughout the Spanish Caribbean closed to black seamen, and all free people of color were prohibited from landing in Cuba or Puerto Rico.

In some states the new laws went much further than requiring captains to keep their black crew members aboard ship while in port. Louisiana's Negro Seamen's Act required captains to surrender their black crew members to be held in jail onshore for the duration of their ships' stay in port, and captains were required to pay for their men's maintenance while they were detained. Soon New Orleans jails were filled to the bursting point with black seamen, especially cooks and stewards, living in horrible conditions and compelled to work in chain gangs building Louisiana roads.

This may account for the otherwise inexplicable tragedy that befell the family of Daniel Gardner in New Guinea. News made its way slowly in the 1800s, returning to Nantucket by letter or word of mouth passed from ship to ship. So it was that in 1837 widowed Anstris Gardner learned of the loss of three of her sons. Nathaniel, age 30, had died whaling "some time past, round Cape Horn." This was the loss to which Nantucketers black and white steeled themselves when their men left to go whaling. But Oliver Gardner, age 26, and his brother Joseph, age 24, had died "sometime past in New Orleans." At about the same time 36-year-old David Forting of Nantucket had died in New Orleans of "fever," and a while earlier James Sims had died there too. Perhaps they were all victims of yellow fever, to which blacks were mistakenly believed to be immune. Perhaps they had run afoul of the law in Louisiana.

The lower South was a profoundly dangerous place for free black men. The year after the Gardner boys lost their lives, Isaac Wright of New York was advertised for sale as a slave in Mississippi. On the eve of the Civil War, some coastal Georgians claimed they were within their rights to sell into slavery any free blacks who entered their waters. Official representatives from northern states who went south to arbitrate for the release of imprisoned black seamen were unsuccessful.

Black captains in the tradition of Paul Cuffe, Absalom Boston, and Edward Pompey were doubly affected by Southern laws. They could not enter Southern ports with black crews, and from 1821 they themselves were prohibited from commanding vessels. The U.S. Attorney General ruled in that year that free blacks in Virginia were not citizens of the United States and by extension this meant no free blacks were qualified under federal law to command vessels engaged in either coastal or overseas trade. Until it was finally overturned by Abraham Lincoln's attorney general, this ruling was most often honored in the breach, but it made black captains extremely vulnerable. The Cuffe family enterprises collapsed. Under the circumstances, it is no wonder that Absalom Boston did not captain any more ships after the voyage of the *Industry* in 1822.

In 1852 the Louisiana law was changed so that free black crew members were no longer taken ashore but were confined to their ships under the custody of their own captains. This was less expensive and had the advantage of making desertion very difficult. Through the years of legal restrictions, however, black crew members had become a liability to ship owners and captains, and they never recovered the opportunities seamanship had once offered them.

In Nantucket opportunity was already crumbling in any case. Intensive whaling had reduced the number of whales to be found, no matter how far across the oceans the island's whalers ranged. The oil-soaked business district and wharves suffered two fires, one in 1838 and a second, vastly more devastating one in 1846. Lacking the protection of jetties and without regular dredging, access to the harbor was blocked by the sandbar that continuously builds along the north shore. As a port, Nantucket was losing out to the deep-water harbor of New Bedford.

Ashore no one seemed to foresee impending disaster. The quiet, earnest consensus and simple living of Quaker Nantucket had given way to some ostentatious living on Main Street and Orange Street, and Nantucketers of all persuasions engaged in stormy public debates. Not least, the Quakers fell completely out of consensus, dividing into a number of rival meetings, each actively disowning whomever they disagreed with, until ultimately they had alienated all their own young and entered into a period of suspension that lasted into the next century.

Newspapers, particularly the long-lived *Nantucket Inquirer,* provided a public forum for opinions expressed in deluges of letters to the editor. Annual town meetings and other public meetings were also venues for debate, and the establishment of the Nantucket Atheneum in 1834 provided a place for members to borrow books and to hear off-island speakers on a great range of topics. When the original Atheneum building was leveled in the fire of 1846, it was the first to be rebuilt, opening just six months after it had gone up in flames with all its books and its irreplaceable collection of "curiosities" brought back on Nantucket ships from all the world's oceans.

The Nantucket Atheneum had not been founded as a public library, and its membership could exclude whomever they chose. The early 1840s witnessed the height of debate about national abolition of slavery and local integration of the Nantucket public schools, with hardening of opinion on both sides. Opposition to a three-day antislavery meeting taking place at the Atheneum in August 1842 turned riotous on the first day. Fearing damage to the building, the trustees denied the organizers the right to continue meeting there, and the abolitionists had to scramble to find another place. The Atheneum closed its doors to African Nantucketers and did not reopen to them for two years.[21]

There were alternatives for African Nantucketers. Obed Barney had already made

---

21. In December 1845 Nathaniel Barney wrote a letter to Samuel Rodman about the closing of the New Bedford Lyceum to African Americans, "Our Atheneum for a time was alike proscriptive, and even more so, inasmuch as no coloured person was free to attend any meeting there, for, I think something like two years. During this time I absented myself from the Institution, I refused my support to it, either by tax or otherwise….The proprietors, however, saw the wrong and they magnanimously acknowledged it, by throwing the doors wide open to all." Obed Barney, who provided space for an alternative reading room, was Nathaniel's brother.

room upstairs over his store for a free anti-slavery library and reading room. A committee of New Guinea residents was appointed to oversee its operation consisting of Pennsylvania-born William Morris and William Harris; William Harris's Massachusetts-born son William H. Harris (a barber); and New Guinea's fiddler, Henry T. "Harry" Wheeler. On January 16, 1841, the men signed a letter of thanks to everyone who had contributed to setting up the reading room and published it in the *Nantucket Inquirer*.

A reading public was developing in New Guinea, served by the antislavery library and also by Edward Pompey, who offered copies of William Lloyd Garrison's *Thoughts on African Colonization* for sale as well as subscriptions to *The Liberator*. When he died in 1848, his estate inventory included an impressive list of books. It is possible that they were those that had been made available to patrons of the library/reading room above Obed Barney's store. Among the more than twenty different titles, there were books about religion, law, slavery, American history and geography, English grammar and literature, biographies, bookkeeping, and human health. There were three copies of the biography of Frederick Douglass and one of the *Narrative of William Brown*, which had been published just the year before, in 1847. William Wells Brown, born into slavery, had been active in the cause of abolition since 1836 and had been hired in 1847 as a Massachusetts Anti-Slavery Society lecture agent. Edward Pompey's book collection was absolutely up to date.

That there was a book on human health also points to New Guinea concerns. A Health Society was formed. At dances held twice a month, presided over by Trillania Pompey, Edward Pompey's sister-in-law, the society distributed information and promoted public health—a serious issue in the community as it suffered from tuberculosis and other infectious diseases.

Another New Guinea organization was the African Society, whose 1829 Independence Day observance, dinner, and procession was reported in the July 18 issue of the *Nantucket Inquirer*.

The African School and Meeting House

On March 26, 1825, Jeffrey Summons conveyed for the token price of $10.50 a piece of land "in Newtown on Pleasant Street in West Monomoy Shares" to the "Trustees of the School Fund for the Coloured People" provided that the trustees would build and maintain a schoolhouse there "and a school to be kept in it forever."

This was not the first school in New Guinea. Historian Obed Macy recorded in his journal that in December 1819 "The cry of Fire alarmed the Town at 10 o'clock in the night, which proved to be Rhoda Harris' house at Newtown, which took fire in the School room."

For thirty years Nantucket had been out of compliance with a Massachusetts law mandating free public schools. Quaker families were uninterested in having their children educated together with non-Quaker children. Non-Quaker families who could pay depended on private schools, and there was considerable reliance on home schooling. For children of some indigent families charitable organizations such as the Fragment Society provided clothing and basic education. Nonetheless, a town-appointed committee had identified three hundred children for whom none of these alternatives was providing even the most basic of primary education. Probably many of them were children of New Guinea, but it is important to understand that in 1820 African-Nantucketer children were not excluded from Nantucket's public schools. There simply were no public schools.

A year prior to the town committee report about unschooled children, Samuel Jenks had moved to the island, where—some years later—he married Martha Coffin. Martha was a descendant of the first English settler families. She was as patrician as one could be in the Quaker-dominated white community, and she was active in the Fragment Society. In 1821 Martha's husband-to-be bought the *Nantucket Inquirer* and launched a campaign for free public schooling on Nantucket. Such a school system was finally established in 1827, and Samuel Jenks was elected to the Nantucket school committee.

By then New Guinea already had its own neighborhood school. The time was overdue for public education, and African Nantucketers had taken the initiative ahead of the Town of Nantucket.

Their school was underfunded from the start. Nantucket Town's appropriation "in part support of the African school" was $75 per year to begin with but later was reduced to $60.[22] Between 1825 and 1829 three different men held the post of schoolmaster, one of them a missionary circuit teacher who spent a month each at a number of schools on the Cape and islands and otherwise left the school in the hands of a Miss Thomson. Minister Jacob Perry, the first black schoolmaster at the African School, announced in May of 1829 that he would have to give up the job because he could not live on the salary. Nonetheless, he was the speaker that summer at the Fourth of July exercises.

The construction of the African Meeting House on the corner of York and Pleasant Streets that housed the African School apparently began before Jeffrey Summons formally deeded the land to the trustees. At the time of the January 3, 1825, announcement of its consecration, it was at least framed, although acknowledged to be unfinished. An 1829 letter to the editor of the *Nantucket Inquirer* refers to school being conducted in "the African meeting house in this town." An 1831 letter to the editor from Jeffrey Summons speaks of "the African School house and Meeting house."

Two different late nineteenth-century sources describe Jeffrey Summons as a Quaker. Betsey Cary's account of the house at 117 Main Street contains the statement "In the mansion that I have described, there yet remains on some panes of glass in the back part of one of the rooms names written with diamond. One is Jeff Summons, who was a colored servant. I remember him well as a good old Quaker. Another is Richard Cary, who was a son of Edward [Cary]."[23] Summons's act of selling the land to the school trustees for "so low a price...to save the expense of another deed" is cer-

tainly in line with Quaker thrift. Membership in the Society of Friends is also consistent with books being part of Jeffrey Summons's probate inventory. Yet despite owning books, he signed the deed of land to the school trustees with a mark rather than a signature, and he and his wife signed other deeds that way as well. Only when she signed the settlement of her husband's estate after his death did Martha Summons sign her own name.

Sometimes illiterate people possess books they are unable to read, and that might be the case with Jeffrey Summons's two Bibles and three other books, but it is hard to reconcile illiteracy with Summons's role as executor of John Gordon's will in 1831 or his eloquent letter to the *Nantucket Inquirer* on September 17, 1831, describing Gordon's difficult funeral arrangements.

What else can be learned from census records and deeds of sale is that Jeffrey Summons was born around 1756 and that beginning in 1798 he actively bought and sold land. He married twice. His first wife's name was Nancy, and after her death he married a Mashpee Wampanoag woman named Martha Dartmouth who outlived him. He died in 1832 leaving a rather large estate that included, along with his books, two silver watches, silver shoe buckles, four walking canes, quite a lot of clothing and furniture (including a looking glass, bedsteads, and a feather bed), "sundry tools," livestock, meat, grain, and fifteen chairs.

Summons, benefactor of the African School, is an enigmatic character. He seems to have come out of slavery, probably to the Cary family, but unlike the younger Absalom Boston and Edward Pompey—whose occupations as mariners, traders, and storekeepers are well documented— Summons appears to have simply had his wealth rather than working for it. At death it was distributed to his widow, surviving children, and grandson. When his son George died just two years after his father, the two silver watches were part of his estate.

22. The Polpis School, which then had an enrollment equal to that of the African School, received only $20 per year.

23. An 1895 memoir of prominent residents of New Guinea also refers to "the Old Quaker Jeff," but I have found no documentary evidence of Jeffrey Summons belonging to any Quaker Meeting.

Cyrus Peirce and Public Education

Throughout much of the twentieth century Nantucket had a "north school" and a "south school." The proper name of the north school was Academy Hill School and that of the south school, on Atlantic Avenue not far from the African Meeting House, was Cyrus Peirce School. Students at both schools had only the vaguest idea, if any at all, of who Cyrus Peirce was and why the school bore his name.

Two years before the outbreak of the War of 1812, Cyrus Peirce—newly graduated from Harvard College—had come to Nantucket to teach in a private academy. When the war began, he left the island, not to fight but to pursue theological studies. As soon as the war ended, he returned to the island to teach for another three years. Then he departed again to begin his deferred preaching career.

In the prewar years of the early 1800s when corporal punishment was the rule in boys' schools, Cyrus Peirce was unconventional in his approach to education. He sought the cooperation of his students through positive expectations rather than the threat of pain and humiliation. Upon his return in 1815, he began teaching girls and boys together, in the spirit of Quaker education. The following year, he married one of his students, Harriet Coffin, sister of Martha Coffin, future wife of newspaperman Samuel Jenks. Although the Peirces left Nantucket in 1818, just when Samuel Jenks arrived on the island, they continued in contact with the island through family connections, which eventually included Samuel and Martha Jenks.

Throughout the next dozen years, Cyrus Peirce gradually came to the conclusion that teaching, rather than preaching, was his vocation. He left the ministry and gained more experience in an off-island school before he finally accepted the call to resume teaching in Nantucket. By the time he returned, he had developed an educational methodology that completely rejected corporal punishment, and he shared his principles and techniques with Harriet. For six years the couple managed a large private academy on Nantucket, assisted by other personally trained assistants, one of whom was Maria Mitchell.

At the same time that he was directing the private school, Cyrus Peirce, like his brother-in-law Jenks (both members of Nantucket's Union Lodge), was working for the development

The African Meeting House in the 1880s. It was built in the mid 1820s to house both a school and a church.

of Nantucket's fledgling public school system. Following his plan it was organized into four levels: primary, intermediate, grammar, and—ultimately—high school. In May of 1837, right after his fellow Masons had voted to rent their meeting hall to Peirce to use as a schoolroom, he gave up his private school position to become principal of the new Nantucket High School.

Peirce's efforts had a number of unintended consequences. First, the enthusiasm for public schools that he and Jenks promoted from their influential positions within the community led to the collapse of most of Nantucket's private schools with the exception of the privately endowed Coffin School, which was also founded in 1827. Second, after only two years as principal of Nantucket High School, he was called off-island by the newly created Massachusetts Board of Education to serve as principal of the first normal school in North America and to oversee modern teacher training. Like his protégée Maria Mitchell, Cyrus Peirce in death was laid to rest in Nantucket's Prospect Hill Cemetery, but in life his professional career had taken him away from the island's students once again and forever.

Yet another consequence of Cyrus Peirce's organization of a high school on Nantucket was the racial integration of Nantucket's schools. Recounting Peirce's life work, the Rev. Samuel May wrote:

> The private schools were, to a considerable extent, relinquished; and the children of all classes came together, as they were able, to enjoy alike the common bounty, —of all classes except that which had always been subjected to the greatest disadvantages, and therefore needed assistance and encouragement the most. The colored inhabitants of the town were not allowed to send their children into the public Grammar Schools; but a provision was made to educate them by themselves. Against this decision, Mr. Peirce remonstrated and contended, with his wonted earnestness and determination. But the "prejudice against color" was too mighty for his appeals to prevail.

Cyrus Peirce may have been defeated by conservative forces in the town—not least of whom was his brother-in-law Jenks—but a decade before May's words were published in 1857, Nantucket's schools had been integrated and black students admitted to all levels of the school system. This had been accomplished through unremitting public pressure from two sources: white abolitionists in Nantucket and their off-island allies on the one hand, and on the other eloquent voices and determined action arising from within the African-Nantucketer community. It was the town's refusal to admit to higher education two daughters of New Guinea that proved to be the tippoint in the struggle for integration.

As everywhere, the notion of separate but equal education was popular in the white community but impracticable. Just as it short-changed female students and female teachers, so it short-changed African Americans. On Nantucket, while Cyrus Peirce was building public school facilities with "improved desks and seats, effective ventilators, better text-books, and…the services of well-qualified teachers," as many as fifty children in New Guinea studied together in the single room of the African Meeting House, where—due to poor salary—there was a high rate of teacher turnover. One black man served for a short time as teacher, as did several white men.

One of the white male teachers was Cyrus Peirce's fellow Mason Wilson Rawson, whose career and community involvement mirrored that of Absalom Boston to a remarkable degree. Both were master mariners, although Rawson captained coastal freighters rather than whaling ships. On land Rawson, like Boston, operated an inn. While Boston was trustee of the African Baptist Society, Rawson was a deacon of the First Congregational Church (the North Church). Rawson was characterized as an "enthusiastic Mason," and he may have been the member to initiate the decision on the part of the lodge to donate its chandelier to the African Church in 1837.

Often, however, the teachers at the African School were white women, who in the 1800s were considered unqualified to teach advanced topics. Consequently they were paid less, and the education they imparted was considered inferior. In the first years of the African School's existence Miss Thomson took over teaching from circuit-teacher Frederick Baylies, who had a number of schools to look after, and had her contract extended throughout the year. Eliza Bailey, daughter of Nabby Gurrell, the woman whose disorderly house catering to a biracial clientele had been censured in 1811, began teaching at the African School in 1834, but two years later epilepsy made it impossible for her to continue.[24] Then Anna Gardner took over and taught for four years. While teaching in New Guinea, Gardner herself attended the new Nantucket High School. At the same time, she prepared Eunice Ross, the youngest child of James and Mary Ross, for entrance to high school.

In 1840 Eunice Ross was examined by the Nantucket school committee and found qualified for admittance. When Eunice was barred from the high school because of race, Anna Gardner resigned her teaching position at the African School and dedicated herself to antislavery and equal-rights activism. An interim woman teacher was appointed, and then in the spring a new advertisement for a teacher for the African School was published, this time stipulating that only male candidates would be considered.

While Anna Gardner was still teaching at the African School, it was reported that the trustees of the African Meeting House were unwilling to continue renting it to the town for use as a school building. It was deemed necessary to erect or purchase another building. Six hundred and sixty dollars was set aside for the African School the following year in a category that also included "fitting" other schools and purchasing books and stationery. Whether the school was moved to a different building at this time is unclear.

The prospect of moving into a better building coincided with Eunice Ross's exclusion from the high school and Anna Gardner's resignation from teaching. When African Nantucketers refused to send their children to the school (whether it was old or new), accusations of ingratitude were leveled at New Guinea parents who would not take advantage of "the School they [the school committee] established at their door" and "the ample provision made by the town in the premises." Samuel Jenks, in his capacity as member of the school board, delivered himself of the opinion that the African School had offered the children of New Guinea real advantages: "a convenient location; an able instructor; and so few pupils (about 30) that consequently, each commanded more of the attention and services of the teacher."

During the first half of the 1840s Nantucket witnessed simmering, sometimes explosive public debate about school integration on-island and abolition of slavery off-island. In 1842 cobblestones and eggs were thrown at abolitionists meeting in the Atheneum. The composition of the school board teetered back and forth between integrationists and segregationists. Town meetings erupted in scathing proposals and counterproposals. Black children were admitted into schools with white students and then, after a while, pulled from their classes and returned to the African School, a painfully humiliating experience.

Through it all, white writers peppered the editors of the newspapers with opinion pieces, some of them inflammatory. A frequent contributor to the *Nantucket Inquirer* writing under the name "Fair Play" argued that the school committee had been obliged to refuse Eunice Ross admission to the high school because her presence would have been fatally disruptive of school order. The letter asserted that "there is a difference of color; there is a difference of odor," and concluded by saying, "We say that the presence of coloured children is as obnoxious to us, and even more so to some of us, than the presence of contagious disease. Some dislike canker-rash, measles, whooping cough, and other contagious diseases more than they do coloured children, others dislike the coloured children the most....Whatever is so obnoxious to a large portion of parents and children as to

24. Eliza Bailey died in 1841 at the age of 29. Her headstone in Prospect Hill Cemetery identifies her as a teacher in the African School.

threaten the dissolution of the schools ought to be excluded in 'self defense,' that this exclusion is '*in maintenance* not in *derogation* of the equal rights of education.'"

The New Guinea community would have none of it. Already in 1842 in an address to the school board published in both the *Nantucket Inquirer* and the *Islander*, they had taken the position that their children were being denied access to the full range of education available to white children—access guaranteed to all as a constitutional right. In a four-level system (primary, intermediate, grammar, and high school) only primary and intermediate education had been offered at the African School. Students there did not receive even grammar-school-level instruction, much less admission to high school. In the latter part of 1844, when African-Nantucketer parents boycotted the African School, some white families withdrew their children from the public schools in solidarity with them.

Legal counsel was sought but offered no route to forcing the town to desegregate its schools. Finally, in 1845 a pair of petitions was directed to the Massachusetts State House. The first, on behalf of "between thirty and forty children who are deprived of their right to equal education…for no other reason, but…*color*" was signed by Edward Pompey and over a hundred other residents of New Guinea, including Absalom Boston, Arthur Cooper, and several of Eunice Ross's relatives. The second petition was signed just by Eunice Ross, who had been waiting five years to begin high school. On March 25, 1845, both houses passed House Bill 45, guaranteeing equal education to all students and permitting parents to sue their towns for damages if their children were excluded.

The town of Nantucket, which had remained out of compliance with the 1789 mandate for free public education for so long, was not ready to comply with the new law. The name of the African School was changed to the York Street Grammar School, and—with a male teacher—it was expected to meet state standards for offering equal education.

The new law, however, offered parents recourse that they had previously lacked, and the person who stepped forward to avail himself of it was Absalom Boston. During the years since Eunice Ross had taken the high school entrance exam, Absalom's and Hannah's daughter Phebe Ann had exhausted the resources of the African School and was ready to move on. When Phebe Ann was denied admission to higher education, as Eunice Ross had been, her father brought suit on her behalf. As a result, on September 3, 1845, a special town meeting was called to try to decide what course to take "in relation to an action brought by Phebe Ann Boston, by her father and next friend, for depriving her of the advantages of Public School instruction."

The town ducked the issue by referring it to the school committee, and a stalemate ensued. Delays held up the Boston case in court, while the black boycott of the African School, now called the York Street Grammar School, stretched on and on. Nantucket voters finally resolved the issue once and for all by voting out the conservative school board members, including Samuel Jenks, and voting in a completely new one that set about integrating the schools during the year 1846–47.

Absalom Boston dropped his suit against the town. He had once run for the board of selectmen with no success, and he had also run for the school board with the same result. In 1844 Wesley Berry of New Guinea rose in town meeting to speak in favor of school integration, and two years later he ran for the board of selectmen. Although he did not win election either, it was no longer unthinkable that African Nantucketers would have a voice in Nantucket politics.

In 1849, less than four years after her father had moved heaven and earth to secure her all the education she wanted or needed, Phebe Ann Boston fell victim to a fatal case of dysentery. Absalom and Hannah didn't survive their daughter by many more years. Absalom died in 1855 just short of his seventieth birthday, and Hannah soon followed. Of all the children born to Absalom Boston, only Caroline, Oliver, and Thomas remained, and the two young men left Nantucket, never to return.

Unmarried, unemployed, and rather solitary, Eunice Ross lived until 1895, finding her pleasure in French literature. Her sister Sarah worked as a domestic servant all her adult life. When Sarah died in 1896, she was laid to rest beside Eunice, and twin headstones mark their graves. Other Rosses benefited from Nantucket's public education. A hand-written note on an 1895 newspaper clipping identifies an otherwise unnamed Nantucket-connected black clergyman in Florida as the Reverend J. Gardner Ross, born on Nantucket and an 1877 graduate of Newton Theological Seminary. Grandnephew of Eunice Ross, J. Gardner Ross was born in the mid 1840s, during the struggle for school integration.

The African-Nantucketer community had taken giant strides in the course of a century, and especially during the two decades between the opening of the African School and the integration of all the public schools. Beginning in slavery, succeeding generations had become landowners, diversified their employment, established businesses, developed a literate middle class with its own social institutions, and successfully claimed its place within the Nantucket community, not on its margins. Just when all this had been achieved, Nantucket's maritime economy collapsed, and within a decade of African Nantucketers' greatest victory—the integration of the schools—the community dissolved, leaving its accomplishments behind along with its dead interred in their cemetery downhill from the windmills.

Ills

From the Nantucket death records, including the dates on headstones in the cemetery, a sense of longevity is perceived within the African community on Nantucket. In 1796 Pompey Nailor died at the age of 78. In 1815 Ruth Forting died at the age of 89; Cato Barlow at 76 in 1816. In 1819 Rebecca Pompey, aged 70, died; 1821 took Violet Arnold, 75, and Betsey Arnold, 82. Absalom Boston's

brother-in-law Michael Douglass, "a Cape di Verde Portuguese Negro" drowned in a Nantucket pond in 1836 at age 70. Douglass's wife Mary Douglass had preceded him in death two years earlier at age 66. When Lucy Cooper, born in Africa and brought to Nantucket via Newport, Rhode Island, died "of general debility" in 1866, she was reportedly a centenarian.

Nonetheless, New Guinea was not always a comfortable nor a healthy place to live. Despite its residents' industriousness, poverty was their close companion. Mary Eliza Starbuck, who lived on Pleasant Street not far from the edge of New Guinea writes that during a period of her childhood "there was a group of people on the outskirts of the town who used to send their children out with baskets, begging for 'cold pieces.'"

The ancient Hagar was not the only black person certified as one of the town poor. In 1819 four African Nantucketers were among those at the poorhouse, while eleven of the 109 households receiving town aid were headed by New Guinea widows. After the town established a "poor farm" in Quaise in 1822, eight black people moved there. They were not, by any means, proportionally overrepresented at these institutions, where most of the recipients of the town's support were white, but there was dreadful humiliation attached to being in need. Of the poor in the alms house Obed Macy wrote in his journal in 1822 that they were "miserably provided for; it is represented that they are nasty & wicked, etc., etc." He adds some historical perspective on the punitive attitude of the town toward indigent people: "Somewhere about 1796 it was concluded that all who wanted supplies from the town must come and reside at the work house (so called). This plan by midwinter came near to starving some of the poor to death, for rather than take their families and go to the work house, they would suffer."

There were always "childhood diseases" such as measles and whooping cough to contend with. Children also died of something recorded as "canker." Dysentery could and did turn deadly, carrying off Phebe Ann Boston before she could enjoy the fruits of her public school education. And there had come another killer. Among the people of New Guinea the first recorded death from tuberculosis, which went by the names of "consumption" and "lung fever," occurred in 1834. From then on, hardly a year went by without at least one documented tuberculosis death. Some years three or four people died of it. Insidiously, the disease crept through families, carrying off members at intervals.

Isaac Barlow died of it in 1835, his wife Annie two years later. Eight years after that Sarah Barlow, by then thirty years old, died of it, too. In 1842, the Valentine family lost 66-year-old Mary and eight-year-old Ann.

The Boston family was particularly hard hit. Tuberculosis began to plow its destructive swath through the family in 1834. That year Peter and Rhoda's daughter Priscilla Quinn died of it, and then Absalom's oldest son Charles and his young wife died. On one day—September 15, 1838—Freeborn Boston's son William and William's niece Harriet both died. Eight years after Priscilla Quinn's death, her husband Frederick succumbed to the disease, and then Absalom's son Henry, and Priscilla's mother Rhoda.

The residents of New Guinea, whose families had grown rapidly in the late 1700s, could hardly be faulted for feeling that their houses had been infected by an insidious agent, one more slow-acting than what had destroyed Miacomet in the previous century but equally deadly. When the center of Nantucket town burned to the ground in 1846 and the news of gold in California exerted its mighty pull on Nantucket's men in 1849, what wonder is it that the houses of New Guinea emptied as swiftly as the tide running out?

From New Guinea to the Outback

The 1860 census shows vacant houses in New Guinea. One that was still occupied was where Patience Cooper lived. She was approaching her fiftieth birthday, and although she was twice married, she had been alone for nearly a decade, living in the house she had inherited from her mother. The 1860 census describes her as a mulatto woman who worked as a domestic. It also places a value on her piece of real estate double what it had been a decade earlier, despite the fact that many houses in its vicinity had been abandoned.

Four hundred yards away on Silver Street, just around the corner from Orange Street, Phebe Fuller, a white woman in her sixties, operated a shop in one room of her home. She may have begun to suffer from forgetfulness. According to a sworn deposition to the court by Trillania Pompey, Mrs. Fuller "displayed a difficulty remembering the proper names of colored people with whom she came in contact often."

On a night in late November of 1860, Phebe Fuller was found brutally beaten in her blood-spattered living room. Her skull had been fractured with a whalebone fid, which her attacker had left behind on the living room floor. For nearly two weeks she passed back and forth between unconsciousness and lucidity before she died from her injuries.

During intervals of consciousness, she told different stories about her assailant. When first asked she said it was Patience Cooper. A while later she said it was a white man she had never seen before. On a third occasion she gave a detailed account of Patience Cooper coming to see her about a bill and then hitting her with something wrapped in a white handkerchief.

Patience Cooper was arrested. She admitted that she had seen Phebe Fuller in her shop that day and that she had been carrying a soup bone wrapped in a napkin, but she steadfastly insisted that she had not bludgeoned her neighbor.

After Phebe Fuller died, Patience Cooper was indicted for murder, later emended to manslaughter, and a jury found her guilty; a retrial had the same outcome, and she was sentenced to ten years of confinement in the Nantucket House of Correction. Finding imprisonment unbearable, she eventually made a confession, stating that she and Phebe Fuller had argued over a bill, and she had been so provoked by Mrs. Fuller's language that she hit the elderly woman in the face, but no blood had been spilled. When she left the shop, she said, Mrs. Fuller was standing leaning against the shop counter.

In 1871 Patience was transferred to the Bristol House of Correction in New Bedford to complete her term. Finally released in 1873, she returned to Nantucket and lived on until 1885. Once a robust, active, independent woman, she had grown old and debilitated during her long confinement, and she passed her last years in the town asylum.

In retrospect, Patience Cooper's confession appears to exonerate her. The attack on Phebe Fuller took place in her living room, not in her shop, and it was executed with such violence that the victim could not have been left standing. The weapon, a spike for separating strands of a rope, was a seaman's tool, and a cash drawer ajar in the shop suggests a motive. Phebe Fuller having sustained severe head injuries, it is plausible that her last clear memory would be of an argument that had taken place earlier in the day. Little wonder if she believed that Patience Cooper had struck her suddenly from behind with her napkin-wrapped soup bone.

After a long time, murder had again been committed on Nantucket, and once again the person on trial was a person of color. But times had changed since Sabo and his successors had passed through the Newtown Gate to the gallows. Some Nantucketers felt ten years' imprisonment was scandalously light punishment for murder. Others were convinced that Patience Cooper had been unfairly deprived of her freedom. But against the violent background of the Civil War and in spite of the declining influence of the Society of Friends, Nantucket had ceased to exercise capital punishment.

The 1860s were the sunset years of both the Quakers and the African Nantucketers on the island. Patience Cooper lived in a recently emptied neighborhood, and the remaining descendants of the families who had once owned slaves also lived surrounded by vacant houses.

The population, recently at an all-time high, was in free fall. Where had everyone gone?[25]

When she confessed to having slapped her white neighbor, Patience had said it right out. She had brought disgrace on her family, she said, and on her "dear brother in Australia."

He was not the only one to have gone to the ends of the earth. By the 1860s William West had reestablished himself in Nelson, New Zealand. William had come to Nantucket from Philadelphia and married Sophia Godfrey in 1845. It was a promising match. Young Sophy Godfrey, according to a memoir published in 1895, had been the belle of many a New Guinea ball, and William was a barber with a shop on Main Street.

The Great Fire of 1846 left New Guinea untouched, but it destroyed every business on Main Street from Straight Wharf right up to the Pacific Bank. William and Sophia had to start over again. On April 17, 1849, William left Sophia with her parents and took sail for California. By 1852 she had gone to San Francisco to join him, but five years later William moved on again, this time to Nelson, New Zealand, where he operated a barber shop and a tobacco shop for the rest of his life. After another sojourn with her parents in Nantucket, Sophia once again set out after her husband. When William died in late 1891, a throng of Nelson residents attended his funeral, despite bad weather, because of the "innumerable" kind deeds he had done over the years. His Nelson obituary in *The Colonist* was reprinted in Nantucket's *Inquirer and Mirror* with the added information that Sophia had survived him. She lived on in Nelson until 1900, and when she died, she was buried beside William, there on another island as far away from Nantucket as it is possible to go on this globe.

Leaving New Guinea

Death kept some of New Guinea's residents from even beginning the exodus. A walk through the cemetery recalls the community that once was. Clustered together near the southeast corner

25. The 1860 census shows over a hundred unoccupied houses located throughout the town of Nantucket.

are the graves of Absalom's children—Sarah, Charles, and Absalom Jr.—and of their aunt Mary Douglass. Phebe Ann's last resting place is a bit apart from them, as is Henry's. There, too, are the graves of dance-hall owner John Pompey and his wife Hannah. By the time Charles Godfrey Sr. was buried west of the Bostons, his daughter Sophia was living in New Zealand. Out in the middle, in a fenced enclosure, lies fugitive slave Arthur Cooper flanked by his first wife Mary, who had been born free, and his second wife Lucy, who had been taken from Africa as a child. The Reverend James Crawford, his mother Mary, his three wives, and his daughter Juliana share another enclosure. Captain Edward Pompey lies to the south of the enclosed family plots and Eunice Ross to the west.

Most of the young and the healthy had left the island, seeking new ways in new places to support themselves and their families. Nantucket's economic collapse left them few alternatives, and African Nantucketers must have been more than content to leave behind a place where they had been recently subjected to so much disrespect. In town meeting and in letters to the *Nantucket Inquirer,* it had been insinuated that black children in integrated schools might infect white children with diseases (a fear easy to internalize in the face of so much tuberculosis and of Phebe Ann Boston's death). Teachers at the African School, Anna Gardner among them, had been lavishly praised for their efforts to "improve the condition of this class of children" and in "elevating a race," as though educating the children of New Guinea was a Herculean task. A great deal of disgust had been publicly expressed not only at the thought of "amalgamation" but even at the prospect of sitting next to a black person. The Atheneum had closed its doors to African Nantucketers, and the North Congregational Church had offered to make its premises available for meetings of the Women's Anti-Slavery Society only on condition that no black people attend. Even if economic survival had not been the issue, African Nantucketers—having just come through all this—had little reason for nostalgic attachment to their island home.

William H. Harris Jr. had served with his father on the committee in charge of the antislavery library and reading room, and in 1842 he was chairman of the committee that demanded that the town integrate its public schools. In the course of the 1840s he and his wife Phebe became the parents of four children who might have attended those schools, but despite William's 1848 election as deacon of the African Baptist Church and although Phebe was expecting their fifth child, they decided to leave the island far behind them. In 1849 they were halfway across the Pacific when Phebe's pregnancy reached term. She died after giving birth to a daughter in Hawai'i. The Harrises baptized the baby Phebe Ann, a name that seems to have spelled doom to those who bore it. Phebe Ann Harris, having miraculously survived her mother's death, died two months short of her eleventh birthday and her father soon followed her in death.

There had been earlier trailblazers to faraway lands. Before 1800, when slavery had just ended on Nantucket, Thomas Gardner chose to exercise his freedom by leaving the island. In Newburyport, Massachusetts, he married the daughter of Tobias Wornton and his wife. Africaborn Tobias had been taken into slavery and given the slave-name Bacchus. By serving in the Revolutionary Army and fighting at the Battle of Bunker Hill, he had won his freedom at about the same time that African Nantucketers had completely achieved theirs. His wife was "an Indian of this country" bound in service to an English family. Their granddaughter Nancy was born in Newburyport in 1799. Just months after Nancy's birth, Thomas Gardner died, and Nancy grew up with an Africa-born stepfather and many half-brothers and -sisters.

Thomas Gardner had not traveled far from the island before tuberculosis ended his life, but his daughter became one of the most cosmopolitan and activist of the descendants of the African Nantucketers. After a difficult and poverty-stricken childhood and adolescence in and around Gloucester and Salem, Nancy literally met her prince. He was a black seaman named Nero Prince, an eminent member of Boston's African-American community and a founding member of the first black Masonic lodge in America. Nero Prince met and married Nancy while he was home in Boston from a sojourn in St. Petersburg, Russia, and after their wedding, he carried her back with him to the czarist court. Throughout the 1820s she learned foreign languages, sewed exquisite baby clothes for the czarina, and took notes on daily life and grand state occasions in Russia.

When Nero Prince's health began to decline, they decided to return to the United States. Nancy Prince left Russia first, while her husband remained behind to conclude his obligations. To her grief, he died before he could rejoin her.

A childless widow, Nancy Prince threw herself into religious and social work within Boston's African-American community, and then she turned her attention to the people of Jamaica. During the 1840s she worked diligently, although with indifferent success, to raise money to found a women's vocational school there to help Jamaican women achieve economic independence. Among the people she turned to for assistance in fund-raising was Nantucket-born Lucretia (Coffin) Mott.

Returning to Boston from a discouraging stay in Jamaica, Nancy Prince continued work in abolitionism and women's rights, gave public lectures about life in Russia, was a speaker at the 1854 Women's Rights Convention in Philadelphia, and published her autobiography, which was sufficiently popular to go through three editions. (The Nantucket Atheneum holds a rare first edition in its nineteenth-century collection.) In accomplishments she was a sister in good standing to the white Nantucketer abolitionists Lucretia Mott, Anna Gardner, Harriet Coffin Peirce, and Eliza Barney, and among them she was without question the most far-traveled.

Some African Nantucketers put the whole globe between themselves and Nantucket. Others joined white Nantucketers going to California, where opportunity seemed to abound. Still others left the island, but did not leave New England,

and some went only as far as a community on Cape Cod that had much in common with New Guinea—namely Mashpee.

California constituted the middle distance, between the most distant destinations on the one hand and New England mainland towns on the other. San Francisco had been a staging area for William and Sophia West while they gathered themselves for crossing the Pacific. For the Berry family San Francisco became as much a symbol of tragedy as New Orleans had for Daniel Gardner's family.

The Berry brothers had come to Nantucket from Maryland by way of New Jersey around 1830 and married into the New Guinea community. Lewis Berry married Freeborn and Mary Boston's daughter Eliza, and his younger brother Wesley married the widow Mary Marsh, who had been one of the signers of the 1831 reorganization papers of the African Baptist Church.

Wesley kept a sailors' boarding house in New Guinea and devoted great effort to antislavery and equal-rights work. He appears as one of the signers of the 1842 resolution that threw down the gauntlet before the Nantucket school committee, demanding integration of the public schools. In 1846 he ran for the board of selectmen. Having adopted the island as his home, he never left it, dying on-island in 1883. In his will he conferred on his widow a life-right in his estate. Then, since they were childless, it was to pass on to his wife's nieces and their children should they have any. Otherwise, upon Mary's death, he named the town of Nantucket as his beneficiary.

Lewis Berry, a whitewasher by trade, would probably have done well to follow his brother's example of remaining island-bound. Instead, he went to California in 1852, and his sons Lewis Jr. and Isaac joined him there, while his wife Eliza and their two daughters remained on Nantucket. During Lewis's first three years in San Francisco he accumulated more capital than the total value placed on Absalom Boston's Nantucket estate in 1855. Then he lost everything and had to start over. Once again he prospered, and like Absalom

The New Guinea neighborhood and Angola Street below the sole remaining windmill in 1881.
Beyond the windmill lies the cemetery that was set off for "the black people or people of color" in 1805. – Spinner Collection

Boston, was in a position to lend out substantial sums of money. Having been sexton of the Zion Church of Nantucket, he continued as a material supporter of the Zion Church in San Francisco.

Lewis Berry passed his seventieth birthday in San Francisco, and then in 1875, violence struck him in the way it had stricken Phebe Fuller. One day he was found dead in bed, bludgeoned to death in the early-morning hours by his thirty-three-year-old son Isaac, who was described as insane. Two years later his son died in Stockton, California. According to the censuses, Lewis's widow Eliza had been living alone since 1860, and so she lived until her death on Nantucket in 1883, more than thirty years after her husband had left the island.

Others fared better in California. In addition to Sophia (Godfrey) West, a number of other members of the Godfrey family—Joseph, Edward, and Nathaniel—gave it a try. Joseph had relocated to California in 1856, just before William and Sophia moved on. Working as a steward and a waiter, he eventually became a saloonkeeper. He married in California and eventually was widowed

there. Edward Godfrey, widowed on Nantucket, moved to San Francisco in 1862 and found a new wife. Nathaniel Godfrey left his half-Irish wife Rebecca and their children in Nantucket and in 1860 was living the life of a bachelor miner. Somehow Rebecca managed to get the family to California, and ultimately they had eight children in all. Rebecca survived Nathaniel. In 1896 she was a widow living alone in San Francisco.

Joseph and Edward Godfrey were lucky to find wives in California. The ratio of marriageable women to men there in the 1850s was even more skewed than it had been in New Guinea. Unattached women were at a premium and greatly appreciated. Perhaps this is why middle-aged Peggy Skinneman liquidated her Nantucket estate and departed the island for California, where she lived out the rest of her life.

In contrast to the adventurers who went to California and beyond, some African Nantucketers moved just a little way off. The community of Mashpee was a special case. To understand the attraction of that nearby town on the Cape in the mid 1800s, one needs to look back nearly a hundred years to the dissolution of a distinct Wampanoag community on Nantucket. During Puritan times Mashpee was a closed Wampanoag praying town. Coincident with the epidemic in Nantucket, a legislative act in 1763 opened Mashpee to nonwhites from elsewhere, making it possible for the first time for them to be taken in and made proprietors of the town. Between 1765 and 1776, the number of Mashpee households increased from 73 to 81. In Gideon Hawley's records of births, deaths, marriages, and "removals," it is recorded that at least one Nantucket Wampanoag family, that of Sam Robin, contributed to Mashpee's growth.

At that time other survivors from Miacomet married into New Guinea. The Wampanoag school teacher Benjamin Tashama, having been widowed in the epidemic, married Jenny Richards, a black woman. They had a New Guinea house that can be seen on the 1821 town map situated north of the burial ground. By the time the map was made, the house had been for decades in the hands of Benjamin's daughter Sarah Esop, who had sold her grandfather's house in Miacomet and lived in her father's New Guinea house with her daughter Dorcas. Dorcas over the years married several men in New Guinea, the last of them being Thomas Honorable, and she ended her days as Dorcas Honorable, the very last of Nantucket's "last Indians."

Essex Boston's description of the New Guinea community as "coloured" is significant. The people living there were not simply "black" in the sense of being of African descent. They were of mixed race— people of color—and one of the major strands from which the community was woven was the Wampanoag strand as witnessed by Wampanoag/African marriages recorded in Nantucket after 1763. The marriages of Seneca Boston to Thankful Micah and of Benjamin Tashama to Jenny Richards are only two of the three dozen or more recorded unions of people from Nantucket Wampanoag families with African Nantucketers. Additionally there were marriages between African Nantucketers and people with the names Pocnet and Couit, who

probably had come to the island from Mashpee. It is certain that Martha Dartmouth and Mehitabel Keeter had come from Mashpee to marry on the island. Rhoda (Jolly) Boston's mother was also from Mashpee.

As for the Mingos, who could say if they were Wampanoags or Africans? Early Nantucket records identify Mingos as the former, and later records record Mingos as "black." As the people of Mashpee learned over time, so too on Nantucket an individual's ethnic/racial identification could change from census to census. Abram Quary was counted as black in the 1830 census, and Dorcas Honorable was recorded as a mulatto woman in the 1850 census.

Although New Guinea was considered African and Mashpee was considered Indian, their constituencies were much the same. In these two towns (as throughout New England after the seventeenth century) being African or Indian became ultimately a matter of self-identification, a personal matter of which strand in one's heritage was given allegiance.

In any case, Mashpee Wampanoags were comfortable in New Guinea, and Nantucket's African Nantucketers were comfortable in Mashpee. Marriages between Nantucket men and Mashpee women such as those between Jeffrey Summons and Mary Dartmouth and Peter Boston and Rhoda Jolly created bonds between families in the two locations and, in the case of Mashpee, conferred the right to proprietorship. When Nantucket fell into bottomless depression in the 1850s, Mashpee offered a haven for some, such as Mashpee-born Phebe Ann Weeden and Nantucket-born Benjamin Pompey. Phebe Ann later died on Nantucket, while their son died in Mashpee, but both were buried in the Mashpee churchyard, and the name Pompey continued in Mashpee through two sons born there to Benjamin and his wife Rose. Censuses show the way the Mashpee population grew as the Nantucket population crashed. Nonetheless, despite the depression two large Wampanoag families from Cape Cod were residing on Nantucket in 1857: the Dennisons from Herring Pond and the Amoses from Mashpee.

During the years leading up to and through the Civil War, prejudice against African Americans hardened, as can be seen locally from letters to the *Nantucket Inquirer* during the struggle to integrate Nantucket's schools. Simultaneously a romantic nostalgia for the "vanishing Indian" developed. Under the circumstances, self-identification as "Indian" became attractive to some sons of New Guinea. Absalom Boston's sons Oliver and Thomas had a Nantucket Wampanoag grandmother, but it was through their mother, Hannah Cook, that they enrolled in the Dartmouth tribe. When the young men left Nantucket after their parents' deaths, they had more opportunity to experiment with their identities than they ever had on the island, where genealogies were known in details back in all directions for a hundred or more years.

Oliver Boston's documented career history is straightforward. He was born in 1836, and—although not yet twenty years old—was already identified as a mariner when his father died. Oliver and Thomas took up residence in their mother's hometown of Westport, near New Bedford. Oliver continued to be employed as a mariner, and in 1862 he married a New Bedford woman. During the Civil War he served in the Union Navy for a year. After his discharge he lived for a while in Boston before returning to New Bedford, where he died at age 36, leaving no children.

Thomas Boston's life was much longer, and it was filled with twists and turns. He was, by several descriptions, very light-skinned, fastidious about his appearance, and florid of speech—not at all suited to life at sea. Instead he was trained as a barber, an elite profession among African Americans. Moreover, he played the violin. Mary Eliza Starbuck later wrote of Thomas that "He was a violinist, and he was so anxious to be with white people that he would offer to play without pay at balls and parties in private houses." Both Starbuck and her contemporary Joseph Farnham agreed that despite his father's high status in New Guinea, Thomas was unreconciled to being an African American. Farnham said that Thomas "was a

dandy but not a fop" who regretted bitterly that he wasn't white. Mary Starbuck goes a little further, reporting that "we had been told that he often said that he would gladly be skinned if he could only be white."

Early in the spring of 1857, the same year he was listed as a Dartmouth Indian by race and a daguerreotypist by profession, resident in Westport, Massachusetts, Universalist minister Phebe Hanaford wrote in her Nantucket diary: "Thomas Boston, a colored young man, was in this afternoon to bid us goodby. He awoke my sympathies for his race. He is now in Phillips, Sampson & Co. store in Boston and has won their respect. Would that all his race were free!" Thomas would probably have cringed at her sentiments. We might wonder how he could be in two or three places at once, pursuing two different occupations, all the while being black by birth and upbringing in Nantucket and Indian by registration in Westport. In hindsight, the contradictions reflect stress fractures in Thomas Boston's psyche.

In October 1869 the *Inquirer and Mirror* printed a description of Thomas Boston's lavish wedding to Anna Wilson, daughter of a cashier at the Freedman's Savings and Trust Company main office in Washington, D.C. The wedding reception was held at the home of the father of the bride, and the guest list was celebrity studded. Thomas Boston was described as Assistant Cashier at the Freedmen's Bank and leader of a Washington, D.C., dance band. The *Inquirer and Mirror* noted that he was the son of Captain Absalom Boston and a product of the Nantucket public schools, concluding on the self-congratulatory note that Thomas's "success in life has been owing to the liberal system of education here, which gave all alike, black or white, an opportunity to profit by it if so disposed."

In later documentation, it is specifically denied that Thomas Boston had been a cashier at Freedmen's. Instead, he is described as a clerk. A critical article that was printed in newspapers in both Savannah and Washington in 1871 described Boston as "young, airy, dressed in the height of fashion, and the color of Java coffee" and went on to assert that "Daddy Wilson and Brother Boston are mere figure-heads kept there in dumb show by cunning fellows who work the machinery from behind the scenes and are filling their own pockets." It was also reported that both men lived well beyond their means.

Three years later, despite bringing Frederick Douglass on board as president to restore patrons' confidence, the bank—eaten away from within by massive corruption—collapsed. With few exceptions, all the embezzlement and bad loans had been the work of white officers of the bank. One of those exceptions was Thomas Boston, who had emptied the account of an illiterate depositor of nearly a thousand dollars of savings. Testimony that the "little failure in 1874 did more to rob the Negro of hope and to rob him of faith in banks than any other occurrence that has happened since he landed in Jamestown" would have broken Absalom Boston's heart.

Dismissed from a bank that had already closed its doors, Thomas Boston moved from his prestigious address in Washington to a more modest one and went to work in a laundry. By 1877 he was no longer listed in the Washington directory.

Anna Boston did not separate from her disgraced husband. From 1883 to 1893 she and Thomas lived in Chicago, where Thomas patched together a living by playing and teaching music and by working as clerk and salesman. In 1883 a favorable review of a piano recital he gave in Cleveland, Ohio, appeared in the *Cleveland Gazette*. Some years later his name turns up again on a list of dignitaries at a Masonic convention in Springfield, Illinois. Sometime before 1926, Thomas died and left the widowed Anna living in Illinois.

Benajah Boston Jr. was second cousin to Oliver and Thomas. His grandfather Peter was brother to their grandfather Seneca. Both Benajah Sr. and his father Peter before him had served in the U.S. Navy, so it is hardly surprising that Benajah Jr. followed the same course. After gaining experience on whaling ships out of Nantucket beginning at the age of seventeen, Benajah Jr. enlisted in the Navy and served during the Civil War. When a list of Nantucket men eligible for state militia service in 1864 was made up, he was unavailable by virtue of being "at sea." Nantucket heard nothing more of Benajah for half a century. Then early in 1916, a ten-verse poem about retirement from the sea appeared in the *Inquirer and Mirror*. It began:

> Neptune, I bid you a long farewell.
>   And as I did not drown
> I have come to Snug Harbor in peace to dwell
>   And have got both anchors down.

The poem came from a rest home for old sailors on Staten Island, New York, and the author was Benajah Boston.

In a lengthy interview granted to the *Inquirer and Mirror* from temporary quarters in Providence the octogenarian Boston claimed to be "a full-blooded Indian." Through his grandmother Rhoda (Jolly) Boston he traced a line of Mashpee Wampanoag descent, but unlike his cousins Oliver and Thomas, Benajah Jr. does not appear in the 1859 Earle Report list of Indians of the Commonwealth of Massachusetts. Nonetheless, he too at some point had decided that an Indian identity was preferable to an African one.

In the course of the interview he brought Nantucketers up to date on his long and eventful life on whalers, in the Navy, and in the merchant marine, where he served until past sixty years of age. He told of having his leg broken by a whale on his first voyage and how the captain had him strapped to a stanchion while setting the bone with a weight and pulley. He told of fifty-month cruises and of being at sea in gales and hurricanes, of military service and defecting from the Navy at the end of the Civil War. In his poem, he described shipboard brutality, beatings, robbery, and being "twice in my life shanghaied." What is remarkable about the interview and the poem is how well spoken Benajah Boston was for a man who had gone to sea at seventeen and worked at sea until he was past sixty. He must have been a good man in a gam.

In 1896 he had finally come ashore, married, and even applied for a pension from the Navy, which he received despite his irregular departure. Now past eighty and a widower with two monthly support checks, he had "decided to pull up anchor and sail for New Bedford, where I would tie up during the rest of the voyage of life."

He didn't tie up in New Bedford, however. Ten years after his interview, past the age of ninety, he died in Rock Island, Illinois, where he had gone to live with his cousin Thomas's widow.

Back on Nantucket, Eliza King, "the oldest colored person and woman on the island" died in 1902 just short of her ninety-fifth birthday. She was the oldest child of Arthur and Mary Cooper, one of the children who had been hidden in Anna Gardner's family home in 1822, and the last surviving member of her family. Her obituary concludes: "She was buried Wednesday from the little church at the corner of York and Pleasant Streets, within a stone's throw of the little home in which she so long dwelt." The church would not be serving the neighborhood much longer. The last service was held in the African Meeting House in 1910, and two years later its last custodian, Edgar Wilkes, turned the key in its lock for the last time. A long hiatus ensued until the building was restored and reopened to the public in 1999.

The closing of the African Meeting House did not mark the end of an African presence on Nantucket. After the descendants of Nantucket's first people of color had departed, their place was taken by Cape Verdeans who settled in the old neighborhood but, as Catholics, did not take over the old black churches.

The Cape Verdeans had come as labor for commercial cranberry growing, a new economic enterprise on Nantucket. The real replacement for the lost maritime industry was, however, the summer trade. As wealthy families sought refuge on Nantucket from the summer heat in American cities, they brought along African-American cooks, maids, and chauffeurs to staff their households. Numbers of those domestics saw opportunity in Nantucket and managed to stay, some in New Guinea and others in a new settlement "under the Bank" in 'Sconset—a neighborhood that came to be called Codfish Park.

House on Angola Street in the 1890s. In the 1790s this one-street neighborhood was called Allentown.

Part II
From Other Ocean Islands

Ships anchored off the volcanic coast of
Fayal, Azores, circa 1890   *Spinner Collection*

Far-Away Neighbor Islands

When Sarah P. Bunker's gifted young neighbor Gulielma Folger was urged to apply to study at Vassar College under the tutelage of her relative, Maria Mitchell, she asked why she should go to the mainland when there were still places on Nantucket she hadn't seen yet.

Gulielma was atypical. Although island childhoods are often idyllic and retirement to an island a comfort, midlife can be a daily contention with limits on space, company, privacy, resources, and opportunity. Islands by their nature block the impulse to run free and far, unless under sail.

When people leave their native islands in search of better lives, they often migrate to other islands. Many of them have a comfort level with island living that is not so easy to acquire later in life.

Nantucket's English settlers had sojourned awhile on the New England mainland before moving offshore, but they were aware of having come from a large island separated from the European continent by an oftentimes turbulent channel. They brought with them the on-island/off-island dichotomy.

In time they were joined by other islanders, migrants who came over the seas to Nantucket from Ireland, the Azores, the Cape Verde archipelago, and most recently from Jamaica. Among the first to become a visible presence in Nantucket in the 1800s were young men who arrived from the heart of the Pacific.

A whaleship at anchor in Kealakekua Bay, Hawai'i. In the autumn of 1819 the whaleships Balaena of New Bedford and Equator of Nantucket arrived in Hawai'i and immediately took a whale in the waters off the big island of Hawai'i. The painting is by whaler-artist Benjamin Russell, with Caleb Purrington, 1845, from their 1500-foot panorama, "Whaling Voyage Round the World."

New Bedford Whaling Museum

CHAPTER THREE

Canackas

Mele kanikau, "Mourning Chant in Honor of the
kūpuna kāne Who Passed Away in Nantucket"

Composed by Noelani Arista, Ikaika Hussey, and Lehuanani Yim, 2001

Aloha ʻino! ua make ʻē, ko kākou kūpuna kāne	Alas, our *kūpuna kāne* have already died
Hele hoʻi ʻole mai i Hawaiʻi	Gone never to return to Hawaiʻi
Aloha e nā manu lele mai ka pūnana mai	Farewell, birds that have flown from the nest
Lele manu heu i ka ʻāina ʻē	Young men that have flown to a foreign land
Mai nā pali kū nihinihi	From the jagged cliffs
Nā kula kāhelahela	And the expansive flat lands
A me ka ʻehu kai.	And the ocean sea mist.
Kēia mau kāne i holo i ka ʻāina ʻē	These men who traveled in foreign lands
Holo hoʻi ʻole mai	Gone, never to return,
Nā hoa paio o ke koholā…	Adversaries of the whale…

During the century after the first English settlers came to Nantucket, European exploration of the Pacific got under way, first in the South Pacific and then ranging northward. It was in January 1778 that Captain James Cook found Kauaʻi, the northwesternmost of the island chain that came to be called the Sandwich Islands and later the Hawaiian Islands. In time the harbors of Honolulu and Lahaina became as familiar to Nantucket whalers as Madaket and Polpis harbors are to Nantucket scallopers today.

The explorers of the 1700s found the Pacific Ocean to be full of islands, most of them inhabited. A thousand years previously, Polynesian voyagers had found their way to Kauaʻi, Niʻihau, Oʻahu, Molokaʻi, Maui, Lānaʻi, Kahoʻolawe, and the youngest of the islands—the big island of Hawaiʻi. They had come by a circuitous route—across the Pacific Ocean to Tahiti and the Marquesas, then north to the Hawaiian Islands, while others traveled southwest to New Zealand.

The long voyage north had been relatively recent, and the memory of return voyages to Tahiti were still preserved in Hawaiian chants. The language of the people Captain Cook encountered on Kauaʻi had so little diverged from that spoken far to the south that knowledge of Tahitian served as a first means of communication between the English and Native Hawaiians.

Despite some facility in communication, things soon went badly in the first encounters between Native Hawaiians and the English explorers, and people died in the ensuing conflict. One of those killed was Captain Cook.

This inauspicious beginning heralded much more fighting to come throughout the Hawaiian Islands. These islands had a two-class social structure—the ordinary working people and the rulers, the *aliʻi*. Each island or district supported its own aristocrats headed by a local chief. In the decades after Cook happened upon Kauaʻi, the ambitious rival chiefs Kamehameha of the island of Hawaiʻi, and Kahekili of Maui became deadlocked in efforts to extend their control across the islands.

Until then, warfare between chiefs had been carried on with spears, slung stones, and hand-to-hand combat, but in the wake of Captain Cook came long-distance traders with no scruples about providing the Native Hawaiians with whatever they wanted in exchange for fresh food and water. The introduction of steel blades, cannon, and firearms changed the nature of the conflict. As both Kamehameha and Kahekili acquired ships, guns, and European strategists, warfare escalated in intensity. Kamehameha's military victory in 1795 unified the islands under his rule, but the tumultuous rush of social change could not be turned aside.

Orphaned by violence, a Native Hawaiian boy signed aboard a New England ship that went to Canton, China, and then on to New York and finally to New Haven, Connecticut, where in 1809 he turned up on the Yale University campus. Taken in, he survived nine years in New England, during which time he mastered English, underwent conversion to Christianity, and was baptized.

Inspired by the young man, whom they called Henry Obookiah, the Boston-based American Board of Commissioners for Foreign Missions founded the Foreign Mission School in Cornwall, Connecticut. In the decade of its existence, it prepared forty-three Native Americans, twenty Native Hawaiians, a number of other Pacific islanders, and two Chinese to return to their people as missionaries. In that context, Henry studied Hebrew and Latin and practiced translating the Old Testament into his own language, an exercise he said he found easier to do from Hebrew than from English. Mainly he was employed in devising a writing system for the language of Hawai'i, and creating a grammar, dictionary, and spelling book, all of which have since been lost.

One of the words in the dictionary was *kanaka*, which means 'person.'

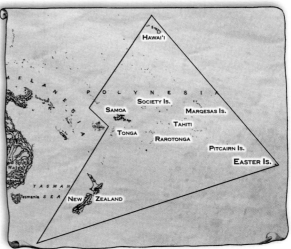

– Jay Avila illustration

The Hawaiian Islands, called the Sandwich Islands by Nantucket whalers, are at the apex of the "Polynesian Triangle" of Pacific islands.

Henry Obookiah did not live to return to his native island, but his example inspired the First Company of Congregational Missionaries to the Sandwich Islands, men and women who sailed aboard the ship *Thaddeus* from Boston in October 1819. They were soon followed by more missionary families, who established churches throughout the Hawaiian islands—places of resort in years to come not only for Native Hawaiians but for the seagoing families of Nantucket whaling captains.[1]

The traffic was not all one-way from New England to the Pacific. Following the course of Henry Obookiah, Native Hawaiians and other Pacific islanders, collectively known as "Canackas," continued to come ashore at New England whaling ports.

In 1822 the *Nantucket Inquirer* reprinted a letter written from Nantucket to the *New York Christian Herald* urging the establishment of a seamen's bethel in Nantucket. The article mentioned in passing "three *Heathen Youth*, who had previously belonged to our Sabbath School" who had set sail on a three-year voyage aboard a Nantucket whaling ship, in the course of which they would

---

1. Mary Buckingham Gulick died on December 12, 2001, in Nantucket. Her great-grandfather, John Thomas Gulick, was born on Kau'ai in 1832, son of Peter Johnson Gulick and Fanny Hinckley (Thomas) Gulick, a missionary couple who went to Hawai'i in 1827. Descendants of Peter and Fanny Gulick served as missionaries in Japan, China, Mongolia, and Micronesia. John Thomas Gulick and Addison Gulick, Mary Gulick's grandfather and father, were distinguished evolutionary biologists.

be educated and prepared "to carry the Gospel to their countrymen of the islands of the Pacific Ocean." Another letter writer, who signed himself "Ferret," expressed his opinion that the onboard schooling of these boys would not be the curriculum of the Cornwall School but would instead consist of practical lessons in whaling.

The following week the *Nantucket Inquirer* carried a front-page story announcing the resumption of a Sabbath School in "the South part of town" attended by "about thirty coloured youths" and the opening of one by the First Congregational Society with seven Native Hawaiians among 120 admitted scholars.

Ferret was back in the *Nantucket Inquirer* on May 9 with an extract from another letter, purportedly from Nantucket, that had been published off-island, this time in the *Boston Recorder*. The letter stated, "Not many years ago there resided here [on Nantucket] twenty Society and Sandwich Islanders, who on stated evenings when it was clear, assembled in the streets, erected ensigns of idolatry, and in frantick orgies" worshiped their own deities, unrestrained by any townspeople. Ferret contended that the Pacific islanders alluded to in the article were engaged in child's play, and that they had been left alone because, "the idea that they were practicing religious rites never entered the heads of those who witnessed their innocent frolics." He suggested readers let "all nations walk in their own ways" and wondered "why so much pains should be taken to represent this place [Nantucket] as a nest of people involved in heathen darkness and suffering for want of missionaries."

The same issue of the *Nantucket Inquirer* carried a report on the transformation of Hawaiian society and the Hawaiian economy. It claimed that the frequent visits of American and English ships had turned Native Hawaiians from their own customs to imitation of what they observed among the officers and crews of the foreign ships, and that this process had been accelerated through the efforts of the recently arrived Congregational missionary families, who had already established a school to teach reading and writing. According

— Jay Avila illustration

Captain Cook first arrived on the island of Kau'I in 1778. Honolulu and Lahaina were the two Hawaiian ports frequented by Nantucket whaleships in the 1800s.

to the correspondent, twenty-eight foreign vessels had stopped in the Hawaiian Islands in the past year, and the Hawaiians themselves now had ten square-rigged vessels of their own plus a number of sloops and schooners with which they carried on active interisland commerce. One of their ships had sailed with a Native Hawaiian crew under a white captain all the way to Kamchatka to trade salt for dried salmon. The writer concluded with the news that "On the south side of the Island of Oʻahu is one of the most commodious harbors in the world: no wind or waves ever enter there to endanger the safety of a vessel. There can be obtained refreshments of every kind, and a ship be repaired if needed—for this last year it has been a resort for all the Whale ships cruising in the northern latitudes, for refreshments and supplies."

And so Honolulu would remain for a long time to come—a place for on-shore rest and recreation, a source of fresh provisions, and a recruiting ground for crew members who sometimes "came here in one of our Whaling Ships from Round Cape Horn," as did one "Sandwich Island Indian" who had the misfortune to die on Nantucket in 1837.

As far as residents of Nantucket were concerned, Canacka meant 'male Pacific islander,' for whaling ships brought only young men, "single mariners," halfway around the world. In 1825 the *Nantucket Inquirer* estimated "more than fifty natives of the South Sea Islands employed on board whaleships belonging to this port…many are now on the island." During their time ashore they needed lodgings, and New Zealand-born William Whippey saw a business opportunity in providing for them. The sign for his "Canacka Boarding-House" is preserved in the collection of the Nantucket Historical Association.

In 1824 the Nantucket whaleship *Oeno* departed for a voyage around Cape Horn. Because a sandbar blocked passage of heavy ships in and out of the harbor, the *Oeno* sailed first to the Vineyard to be loaded for the outward voyage. The crew that signed on was made up in equal parts of white Nantucketers, "strangers" (what Nantucketers called anyone from "away"), and people of color. One of the people of color was a member of the Wampanoag Corduda family, certainly from the Vineyard, because there were no longer any Cordudas living on Nantucket. Another was "Henry Artooi," a Native Hawaiian. Perhaps he had been living in a New Guinea boarding house, or possibly he joined the crew on the Vineyard. Whatever the case, Henry Artooi (probably Akui) had been born in the Hawaiian Islands and ended

his days in Fiji, as did all but one member of the ship's crew. Far out across the Pacific their ship was wrecked on Vatoa, or Turtle Island as it was then known, and after a while they were attacked by Fijians. Only Nantucket-born William Cary returned to tell what happened to the men of the *Oeno*. In his account, Cary set out inland in search of a safe hiding place. A Native Hawaiian crew member—Henry Artooi without question since he was the only one—followed along behind him for a bit and then turned back to the beach to meet whatever awaited him there. He was the last crew member Cary ever saw alive.

To Nantucketers, Canackas were not only male but black. A list of mariners attached to the 1850 federal census for Nantucket has three racial categories: white, black, and mulatto. Crew members on Nantucket ships that year from Hawai'i, included ten men identified as white, six as mulatto, and the remaining twenty-eight as black. Among the nonwhite Hawaiian crew members were one bearing the surname Swain, two Owens, and six Coffins. Four used Canacka as a surname, six used Maui, and one used Oahu.

Hawai'i, circa 1880. Whalers made port in Hawai'i to replenish supplies and overhaul their ships.

In 2001 Native Hawaiian visitors chanted mele kanikau *for men from Pacific islands who died and were buried on Nantucket during whaling days.*

In 1850 crew members on Nantucket ships from the Society Islands (including Tahiti) were evenly divided, five white and five black. All seven who had signed on from the Friendly Islands (including three who used "Rarotonga" as a surname) were categorized as black, as were one crew member each from the Marquesas and Navigator's Islands and John Buttista (Juan Bautista) from Java.

As black men, Pacific islanders ashore on Nantucket lived in New Guinea. An 1830 local census of Nantucket reports two young men named Jack and Harry (no ages given) living in the household of John and Elizabeth Gordon. Their names are followed by the letter "A" for 'alien' and the notation "Sandwich Islands." At the end of February 1832, a man described as a Canacka was found dead under Coffin's barn on the North Shore. The dead man had come on a "whaleship from around Cape Horn," was a free man, and had lived "in Negro Town New Guinea." Perhaps this was the bitter end of Jack or Harry.

Four years later a 21-year old Canacka died in New Guinea, and another at the town asylum. The next year, another expired at the end of February, in this case a 35-year-old man who had come to

Nantucket on a whaling ship. A man called John President and identified as a Canacka was taken to the town asylum, where his death was recorded on the first day of August, 1840. In 1844 yet another died, in this case of tuberculosis at age 25. Twenty-four-year-old Joseph Dix, born in Hawai'i, but not identified as a Canacka, died in 1843 of tuberculosis, as did James Swain, in 1844, and 31-year-old, Hawai'i-born Thomas Clay in 1848. The same year, Hawai'i-born John Smith died in Nantucket of typhus.

In all, six identified Pacific islanders and four more seamen born in Hawai'i, are known to have died in Nantucket between 1832 and 1848. All across the Pacific, people of their parents' and grandparents' generations believed that, at death, their souls detached from their bodies, traveled to jumping-off places on their islands' coasts, and from there, in the company of other souls, set off over the sea to the land of the dead. Was there such a launching place for solitary souls cut loose on freezing-cold, faraway Nantucket? We have no way to know if other Hawaiian seamen were present to chant a *mele kanikau*, a mourning song, to encourage and comfort them on their way.

CHAPTER FOUR

Irish

MACK'S SMOKE SHOP

We're going to America next week.
— Richard Mack

By 1820 Pacific islanders had dispersed over the world's oceans and found their way as far as Nantucket. The chain of consequences that led to their arrival had begun with the introduction of long-distance maritime commerce and fire-arms to their home islands. A quarter century later, another massive dispersal from an island brought a new population to Nantucket's shores, the Irish.

Once again the driving force of the migration was a foreign introduction, in this case the potato, a Peruvian plant that crossed the Atlantic and first arrived in Ireland in the late 1500s. The Irish subsistence crops up to then had been oats and barley, grains of limited nutritional value. The Irish soil and climate produced bumper crops of the highly nutritious potato, which in turn supported explosive human population growth.

Despite oppressive and economically destructive English rule in Ireland, the population tripled between the beginning of the 1700s and 1845. With over eight million inhabitants, the carrying capacity of the island had been pushed to the brink, as the whole world would learn when a plant disease crossed the Atlantic and caught up with the potato in Europe. In 1845 it destroyed not just part of Ireland's sustaining food crop, but most of it. The following year it happened again. English governmental policies exacerbated the disaster. A million people perished from starvation and disease in Ireland, and more than another million fled—some to England, others to Australia, but most to Canada and the United States.

In Nantucket there had been precursors to the potato-famine refugees. As early as the mid 1700s, people with Irish names appear in town records. In 1743 Eleanor Boyle was accused of selling rum to Wampanoags. The court found that she had no license "to justify her in said sale of…rum, which is contrary to the peace…and to a law of this province."

Four years later Henry Fitzgerald married a Nantucket wife and started a family that carried through many generations on the island. In the 1860s one of his descendants took a strong interest in the murder trial, conviction, and subsequent confession of African Nantucketer Patience Cooper.

Among at least a half dozen people listed for expulsion from Sherburne in 1763 for having taken up residence without permission was James McMurphy, who had come to the island from Newfield, New Hampshire. His presence, like that of other people sent packing by the selectmen, was deemed to be of potentially "bad consequences to the town if not removed." Yet James Murphy of Ireland, whether the same man or another, managed to settle in Sherburne and raise a family before dying on-island in 1775. His descendants appear in Nantucket genealogical records as late as 1905.

The "Indian sickness" that struck the island in the fall of 1763 was believed to have spread to the Miacomet Wampanoag community from the Newtown boarding house of Joseph and Molly Quinn. Writing of the catastrophe thirty-five years later, Christopher Starbuck remarked, "What is further very wonderful is that it should not spread among the white people, except with this Irish woman Molly Quin." Molly Quinn, for her part, denied that she had ever been sick, but Nantucketers seem to have been determined to lay the blame for the epidemic on the Irish. Stories that first appeared decades after the fact traced the infection to bodies washed ashore from an Irish plague ship and to infected Irish clothing brought ashore to be laundered.

By 1850 ninety Irish women and fifty-five Irish men were resident on the island. Although flight from the potato famine was at its height at the time, many of the Irish on Nantucket had left home in advance of the great emigration. Eight families had Massachusetts-born children who had already reached their teens by 1850.

The disproportion of women to men reflects the work available. In 1850 half of the Irish women on Nantucket were working as live-in domestics. As on the mainland, so too on the island Irish maids had become a status symbol in wealthy households. Nantucket's most prosperous families—those that employed cooks, maids, and laundresses—were slow in coming to terms with the island's economic depression and kept right on hiring servants.

African Nantucketers, however, were leaving as the Irish arrived. Already in 1840 one of the local newspapers carried an advertisement for "girls and women needed for house duties." Over the next ten years the number of black women and girls living on Nantucket dropped from 147 to 91. Nantucket families accustomed to being served by black domestics filled the growing void with Irish women.

Although a few came as seasoned housekeepers in their forties, most of the Irish women in service, whether called Bridget or Catherine or Mary, were in their late teens or twenties and single. In 1850 one in five could not read or write. About the same rate of illiteracy occurred among the Irish-born men and married women living on the island at the time.

Among the men were a mason, a cooper, a shoe-maker, and a ropemaker. A few worked on ships or fishing boats, and more worked on island farms, but by far the largest number were employed as unskilled laborers at a time when Nantucket's labor needs were diminishing. For men there was no local demand comparable to that for women.

Despite the departure of many black men from Nantucket, the gender imbalance in New Guinea persisted. In 1850 there were 251 men and boys living there and only 91 women and girls. On the other hand, there were half again as many Irish women as Irish men on-island, and most of them were young and single. The Massachusetts law declaring all marriages between whites and nonwhites invalid had been repealed in 1843, opening the way for African-Nantucketer men and Irish women to marry. Rebecca Godfrey, born in Massachusetts of an Irish mother, became the wife of Nathaniel Godfrey, son of one of New Guinea's prominent black families. Their first child was born in 1852. By 1860 the family had left Nantucket.

Elizabeth Ann Barber, born in Ireland, entered into an interracial marriage before the law against such unions was dropped. Her husband, John Barber, had been born in Pennsylvania and moved to Nantucket in the 1820s. Between 1832 and 1836 John and Elizabeth Ann had three children. Then on January 26, 1839, Elizabeth Ann gave birth to triplets, only the second such birth in Nantucket's recorded history up to that time. The babies, given the names Shadrach, Meshach, and Abednego, died in infancy. All the surviving Barber children were categorized as mulatto by the 1850 federal census. In 1850 the eldest, 18-year-old John Jr., was employed as a mason. In 1855 the Barbers had one more child, but Elizabeth Ann was widowed soon after, and by 1870 she and the children had all left the island. Only the grave markers of John Barber and their daughter Sarah Ann are still to be found in the cemetery behind Mill Hill as reminders of the family's residence here.

Between 1866 and 1878 seven daughters were born to William Owen, categorized as mulatto, and his Irish wife Julia. The 1870 census identified Annie and Carrie Owen as white, but the 1880 census categorized them and their sisters Lizzie, Martha, Charlotte, and the twins Priscilla and Winnie as mulatto.

New Guinea was home to a number of other interracial families in the 1860s and 1870s. One was the Snow family. Thomas Snow, white liquor-store owner, and his wife Lucretia had three children classified as mulatto by the 1860 census. Their live-in domestic servant was white and male. Also in the neighborhood lived Calcutta-born William Porte, his wife Christina, and their five children, all classified as mulatto.

The Nantucket school committee had once simply distinguished white children from children of African and Wampanoag heritage. By integrating public education in the late 1840s it had spared itself the dilemma of the greater ethnic diversity present in the latter half of the 1800s. The neighborhood name "New Guinea" was losing its significance, and sometime after 1858 the street leading from the Five Corners intersection to Surfside Road was renamed Atlantic Avenue. Angola Street faded from memory to the point that eventually a mispainted sign reading "Angora Street" was placed on a nearby lane and allowed to stand for decades uncorrected as to location and spelling.

Housing left vacant by the exodus of African-Nantucketer families was taken over by Irish families, who became neighbors of black families even if they did not become kin by marriage. In 1850 George and Bridget Flood were living in New Guinea with their four Massachusetts-born children, and so were the widow Mary McNellis and her four teen-aged children. William and Mary Warren also lived in the neighborhood with their Ireland-born daughter and her three younger Massachusetts-born siblings.

By 1860 at least four Nantucket farms were Irish-owned and operated. Ten years later two more Ireland-born men had purchased farms. Michael Nevins had a knack for building capital and growing a family. In 1870 he and his wife Catherine had six children at home, and among the Irish living on Nantucket the sum of the value of his real estate and personal estate was exceeded only by that of a wealthy cooper named Samuel King. The ultimate legacy Michael and Catherine Nevins left to Nantucket was not monetary, however, but musical, through the instrument of their descendants, the Flanagan family.

In 1952, Charles Flanagan returned to Nantucket from service in the Korean War to teach English, bookkeeping, and music at Nantucket High School and to direct the choir at his church. Ruth Ann Murphy brought a trained singing voice to their marriage, and their four children, Daniel,

Charles Flanagan, Sr. and Ruth Ann Flanagan with their children and grandchildren in performance at Nantucket's Unitarian Church, July 2000. Proceeds from the concert benefited a memorial scholarship for Charles Flanagan, Jr., who died in 1989.

Catherine, Elizabeth, and Charles Jr., grew up singing harmony at home, on trips, in church, at the hospital, the Homestead, and Our Island Home, at fairs and receptions—wherever Nantucket people gathered in expectation of hearing their voices. Eventually a third generation of musical Flanagans and Stovers joined in. Over the years Charles Flanagan emerged as a model of island philanthropy, active in multiple service organizations and described as "part of the soul of this community." Daughter Catherine Flanagan Stover became Nantucket's town clerk in 1998 and as justice of the peace has performed countless weddings at lighthouses, on beaches, and in gardens all over the island.

Members of other Irish immigrant families would also follow the course from hard farm labor to prosperity to positions of community responsibility. Back in 1870 dairyman Robert Mooney and his wife Julia were closing in on the Nevins family with five Massachusetts-born children and an estate value of just fifty dollars short of theirs. In the course of three generations they contributed to Nantucket a police chief of seventeen years' service, Lawrence F. Mooney, and then attorney/law-maker Robert F. Mooney.

A family of McNamaras arrived in Nantucket between 1850 and 1860. They reported their surname as Mack on the 1860 federal census, tried to go back to McNamara ten years later, but subsequently reverted to Mack. Mary Mack was an octogenarian when they all emigrated from Ireland. Ann Mack was in her forties and had a grown daughter with her. Ellen Mack, nearly thirty and still single, immediately found work as a live-in servant for one of the Starbuck families on Main Street. Thomas and Dennis Mack contributed to the support of the family by working as day laborers. Only the youngest members of the family

— Courtesy of the Mack family
Richard Mack, son of Irish immigrants Thomas and Margaret Mack.

could read and write. By 1870, Mary Mack and Thomas's wife Sarah had died, and the other Macks had moved on. Thomas, father of two young children, remarried, and by 1886 Margaret Mack, also born in Ireland, had given birth to ten children. One of them, Robert Mack, served as one of Nantucket's town assessors and then as registrar of probate in the 1920s. His youngest brother, Richard Mack, operated a newspaper and tobacco shop on Main Street until he fell victim to the 1918 influenza pandemic.

Richard Mack's nephew and namesake served on Nantucket Lightship 112 and later worked to bring the retired vessel to Nantucket, where for a number of years she was a colorful feature of the waterfront. Richard and Kay Mack's sons Daniel and Jerry currently serve on the Nantucket police force.

Barnard Collins and Rosanna Riley were in their teens when the potato famine struck. They fled and married on Nantucket. Rosanna was not yet twenty when the first of their nine children was born. Their daughter Agnes, born in 1857, married Robert Mooney Jr., Nantucket-born son of Robert and Julia Mooney. Her younger sister Emma, born in 1861, married into the Macy family, linking the Irish immigrants with the "descended Nantucketers." The son of Clinton and Emma Macy was Huram Macy, a renowned builder during the economic reawakening of Nantucket as a summer resort.

John Killen, brought to the United States from Ireland at age five, spent the first part of his adult life operating coastal schooners. At age 55 he appears in the 1900 census as a dealer in coal, wood, and grain. Two years later he built an ice plant on Nantucket and acquired most of North

Shortly after this photograph of Richard Mack's Smoke Shop was taken, its proprietor fell victim to the 1918 influenza pandemic.

Courtesy of the Mack family

Wharf and Straight Wharf. Late in his long and prosperous life he turned to public service and died in office as a member of the Nantucket board of selectmen in 1927.

Bridget Hatch arrived in the United States as a teenager in 1880 and became a naturalized citizen eight years later. In early middle age she was widowed. Sometime after 1900 she brought her children to Nantucket, rented a house, and set about supporting her family as an "ice cream caterer." By 1920 she was proprietor of her own ice cream parlor.

In the teeth of profound economic depression Nantucket had nonetheless offered opportunities to some hard-working, ambitious immigrants. There was only so much productive farm land available on the island, however, and with the passing of years fewer Nantucket families could afford live-in servants. As opportunity diminished, the Irish who had come to the island began to move on. Despite ongoing new arrivals, the total Irish-born population dropped from a high of 146 in 1860 to the 90s, then the 70s, and then the 50s. In 1910 there were equal numbers of Ireland-born and Canada-born people living on Nantucket, although some of the latter were the children of potato-famine refugees who had originally sailed to Canada. By 1920, the number of Canada-born residents of Nantucket had surpassed the number of the Ireland-born.

Irish families living on Nantucket before the mid 1800s did so without benefit of Catholic clergy. From the middle of the 1800s to the end of the century the island's Catholics were served by mainland priests who made periodic visits by boat. It was not until 1897 that the island had a resident priest and a church. For a century and a half, beginning in 1849, the priests serving Nantucket were almost without exception Irish Americans.

In the 1980s and early 1990s a new wave of Irish workers arrived. Once again they were mainly young and single, but unlike the potato-famine refugees, they came with the expectation (shared by the United States Immigration and Naturalization Service) that they would take on short-term work, save their wages, and return to Ireland. The Northeast was dealing with labor shortages by filling jobs with Irish citizens on work visas.

For a century Nantucket's tourist season had extended from Memorial Day at the end of May to Labor Day at the beginning of September. Schools, colleges, and universities did not go back into session until after Labor Day, and students were readily available to work as "summer help"— waitresses, chambermaids, dishwashers, clerks, landscapers, baby sitters, and camp counselors. Then, at about the time Nantucket businesses succeeded in extending the tourist season in both directions—from late April to early December, schools moved their opening dates to late August in order to finish the fall term before Christmas. As a result of those changes, students got out of school too late and went back to school too early to meet Nantucket employers' needs. The Irish labor pool that was staffing mainland hospitals and tending its bars was not bound to the North American school year and offered a solution. Soon Irish flags began fluttering all over the island where young Irish men and women were renting rooms in Nantucket homes or crowding into rented houses for the extended tourist season. For the better part of a decade they provided most of the island's basic services and much of its off-hours entertainment.

It was inevitable that through marriage and through business opportunities some Irish workers—an estimated three hundred by the year 2000—would become permanent residents of Nantucket and begin their families here. On July 13, 1999, the Nantucket Cottage Hospital recorded the birth of Cían Eamon O'Mahony, son of Gillian Dwyer and Michael O'Mahony of Nantucket. All the grandparents were in Cork, Ireland.

As the year 2000 approached, the Irish domestic economy began an expansion that was dubbed "the Celtic tiger," and it was no longer necessary for its citizens to work overseas. The Irish presence once again receded on Nantucket, yielding to seasonal workers from Jamaica.

Chapter Five

From the Azores and Cape Verde Archipelagos

There are four groups of islands in the Atlantic Ocean off the coast of Portugal and Africa. From north to south they are the Azores Islands; Madeira, with its companions Porto Santo and Las Desertas; the Canary Islands; and the Cape Verde archipelago. All entered recorded history in the 1400s when Portuguese, Spanish, and Italian mariners put them on their maps and began using them as staging areas for further exploration. The Canary Islands, crucially important to the voyages of Christopher Columbus, came under Spanish rule in 1479, while the Azores, Madeira, and the Cape Verde archipelago were retained by Portugal.

Like the Portuguese explorers of previous centuries, Nantucket whalers of the 1700s and 1800s used the Azores and the Cape Verde islands as stopping points on their voyages, picking up provisions and crew members before sailing on. Eventually some Azorean and Cape Verdean mariners landed on Nantucket and stayed. Later, economic pressures on their home islands sent Azoreans and Cape Verdeans to southern New England, where their concentration forged new

— Jay Avila illustration

Atlantic islands that have sent population to Nantucket: Ireland, the Azores, the Cape Verde archipelago, and Jamaica.

connections among Providence, New Bedford, Fall River, and the communities of the Cape and islands. The *Boston Globe* reported on July 16, 2000, that "Forty percent of the southeastern Massachusetts population is of Portuguese and Cape Verdean backgrounds."

Resident Azorean and Cape Verdean families contributed to Nantucket's already cosmopolitan

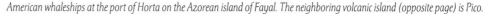

American whaleships at the port of Horta on the Azorean island of Fayal. The neighboring volcanic island (opposite page) is Pico.

mix the new elements of Portuguese language and culture—especially Portuguese foods—as well as the Catholicism they shared with the Irish who settled on the island.

Azoreans

It is said that always being in sight of the ocean gives Azoreans a vital sense of the possibility of going somewhere.

—Tides of Migration

Come July, Nantucket yards are adrift with blue hydrangeas. Meanwhile, more than two thousand miles east across the Atlantic Ocean, the mountain slopes of the Azores Islands are drenched with the blue of wild-growing hydrangeas.

The Azores archipelago consists of three groups of islands between seven and eight hundred miles west of the Portuguese coast. No other North Atlantic islands lie so far from the European mainland, and to seafaring Nantucketers they were known as the Western Islands. The easternmost islands are Saint Michael (São Miguel) and Santa Maria. The central group includes Fayal (Faial), Pico, Saint George (São Jorge), Terceira, and Graciosa. To the northwest lie Flores and Corvo.

Like the Hawaiian Islands, the Azores are the summits of volcanoes thrust up from a geological hotspot. Situated on the west side of the undersea Mid-Atlantic Ridge, Flores and Corvo are old and inactive, but earthquakes and eruptions shake the islands to the east, and from time to time new vol-

— Jay Avila illustration

The Azores, known to Nantucket whalers as the Western Islands. Horta on the island of Fayal was port of call for Nantucket whaleships. Ponta Delgada became the point of embarkation for emigration to the United States.

canic cones break the surface of the sea only to be eroded away by surf. Pico is in no danger of such obliteration, however. Its cone rises nearly eight thousand feet above sea level, a towering landmark for ships seeking the islands.

The islands were uninhabited when the Portuguese discovered them. Settlement began on Santa Maria in 1432, then on Saint Michael in 1444. Terceira was the third island discovered and settled. By the end of the century, all the islands were occupied. Most of the early settlers—including a few Moors, Jews, and enslaved Africans—came from Portugal, but settlers were also recruited from Flanders, and it is believed that some Bretons settled on St. Michael.

Painting by Russell and Purrington, 1845, New Bedford Whaling Museum

Saint Michael, the largest island, came to support the greatest population despite having its capital buried by a volcanic eruption in 1522. Within a dozen years of that catastrophe, the inhabitants of the Azores had been subsumed into a Catholic diocese under the archbishop of Lisbon, and throughout their history the Azoreans have been dedicated participants in *festas*, community celebrations of dates in the annual liturgical calendar, especially the Feast of the Holy Ghost in June.

Offering fresh food and water, the islands became an ocean crossroads. Christopher Columbus, returning from his 1492 voyage across the Atlantic, made his first stop in the Azores on his way to reporting his discovery to King Ferdinand and Queen Isabella. Six years later, Vasco da Gama put in at Terceira on his return voyage from India. During the 1500s and early 1600s, while Portugal was under Spanish rule, convoys of treasure ships from Mexico and the Caribbean rendezvoused in the Azores on their way to Spain. Their presence attracted pirates, especially during the time of England's Queen Elizabeth I, but the Azoreans were not intimidated into turning their backs on the sea. Instead, they

expanded their economy by boldly fishing and whaling off their shores.

In the Azores archipelago it is never cold and seldom hot. Throughout the winter it rains every other day. In the summer a weather system, the Azores High, moves up from the south, bringing dry nor'easters. The islands would have been paradisiacal were it not for the spewing volcanoes, marauding pirates, surplus population, and attendant poverty. In time, as in every place with large families living on limited agricultural land, many adolescents and young adults could find no means of support, and they set out across the Atlantic, seeking opportunity elsewhere.

Sharing a mild maritime climate with the Azores, Nantucket eventually proved to be a hospitable place for hydrangeas to take root. Despite differences in language, culture, and religion, it was also an attractive destination for transplanted Azoreans.

Marriages between Portuguese men and local women are documented before 1800. Around 1770 Anthony Swazey (Antonio Soares), "a Portuguese," married a Martha's Vineyard woman named Jerusha. They had at least eight children, and at some point the family moved from Edgartown

Horta, Fayal, in the 1880s. Whaleships would routinely anchor in Horta's bay for provisions and to recruit crew members.

to Nantucket, where Manuel Swazey married Elizabeth Bassett in 1795, Abigail Swazey married David Lumbert in 1797, and Charlotte Swazey married Portuguese Thomas Ray. Sons Henry and Seth appear in Nantucket death records. When Anthony Swazey died in Nantucket's asylum for the indigent in 1835, he was eighty-two years old.

In 1796, John Sylvia Sr. married Susan Coffin, and twenty-one years later their son, John Jr., married Elizabeth Marshall, also of Nantucket. In 1831, John Lewis, "a Portuguese," married Maria Gibbs of Nantucket, who was soon left a widow when John was "killed by a whale, from the Ship *Baltic*, William Chadwick, master, round Cape Horn." A year later she married another Portuguese husband. None of those Portuguese early arrivals are specifically identified as from any one of the islands of the Azores, but by the middle of the nineteenth century the federal census and Nantucket vital records had become more precise.

The rule was Azorean men marrying Nantucket women, but there was at least one exception. According to the *Eliza Starbuck Barney Genealogical Record*, Henry and Theodate Starbuck's son James B. Starbuck, born in 1819, married Maria C. Silvia of Fayal. The couple's twin daughters Ann Maria and Emeline also appear in the *Barney Record*. James Starbuck lived until 1862, and Maria survived him until 1875.

In 1850 there were twenty-seven Azores-born men resident on Nantucket. All but five had Massachusetts-born wives and some were approaching their twentieth wedding anniversaries. Most of their families were large, with seven or eight children at home. Forty-five more men from the Azores were serving on Nantucket whaleships. Two of the Azorean men living on land were identified as nonwhite as were five of the men onboard ships. The 1850 federal census categorized the other sixty-five Azoreans as white.

Some men anglicized their Portuguese surnames, turning Dias into Day, Reis into either Ray or King, Leial into Lee, Mello into Miller, Pereira into Perry. Moreover, they used English versions of their given names: Joseph, John, Edward, Andrew,

Lawrence, William. Some had taken Nantucket surnames; in 1850 there were two Azorean Coffins, a Mayhew, a Swain, and a Worth. In time there were also Azorean families using the names Gardner, Macy, and Starbuck. By far the most common names

– Nantucket Historical Association
Ferdinand Sylvaro weaves a Nantucket lightship basket.

in use in Nantucket were, however, combinations of Manuel, Joseph, Antone, Francis, and Sylvia: Manuel Sylvia, Joseph Antone, Joseph Francis, Francis Joseph, Antone Sylvia, and so on. The most striking name recorded in 1850 was Joe Citizen, a twenty-five-year-old seaman from Fayal.

The men had been Catholics when they came to Nantucket, an island without resident priests where the first Mass was not celebrated until 1849. That their Nantucket wives had not been raised as Catholics and their children were growing up outside the church appears to have been a matter of indifference. In 1843 the pastor of the Congregational Church married Joseph Sylvaro of St. George and Phebe Ann Fisher of Nantucket. In 1864 Enos Sylvaro of St. George married Joseph and Phebe Ann's daughter Ellen. Also joined in matrimony by a Congregational pastor, they raised a family of six in a tiny house on North Centre Street, just half a block downhill from Sarah P. Bunker's home. The lightship baskets made by their son Ferdinand Sylvaro have become collector's items featured in Nantucket's Lightship Basket Museum.

In the early 1850s the potato blight that had driven so many Irish into emigration affected the Azores, where potatoes were also a staple crop. Beginning at about the same time, two other plant diseases wiped out the Azorean vineyards and orange groves. By 1860, while the overall population of Nantucket was dropping sharply, the number of Azorean immigrants to Nantucket had nearly doubled. The same number of Azorean men had Massachusetts-born wives as ten years earlier, but now four Azorean couples and two Azorean single mothers were living on the island. Unmarried sisters, daughters, and boarders accounted for seven more Azores-born women.

John Francis Sylvia was the last operator of the one mill remaining on Mill Hill.

The majority of the men were mariners: forty-year-old John Pease was a master mariner; George Enos, mariner from Flores, left the sea in 1855 to take over operation of Swain's Mill from Jared Gardner. Nine years later he sold the mill to Captain John Murray of Graciosa, who soon resold it to John Francis Sylvia, a miller from Fayal. Sylvia, who managed to keep on grinding corn for another twenty-six years, was romanticized as "The Last Miller" and was the subject of works by a number of artists.

Sylvia bequeathed the mill to his brother and a nephew in Fayal. Uninterested in taking over its operation, they engaged fellow Azorean John Murray Jr. as their agent to sell the mill at auction, where it was purchased for the Nantucket Historical Association. As a historic property since 1898, the Old Mill has been the very symbol of Nantucket's English history despite having been in Azorean hands during its last half century of private ownership.

In the late 1800s operating a windmill on Nantucket was an anachronism. The most common onshore line of work was day labor and farm labor. By 1860 three Azorean men had acquired farms of their own, and Joseph T. Sylvia of Fayal was a gardener with real estate of about the same value as a small farm. He and his Massachusetts-born wife had six children, the four oldest in school. Two couples operated boarding houses, one man owned a liquor store, and one was a grocer. Two Azorean women did tailoring and dressmaking. Maria Starbuck was a milliner. Like the Irish who had taken up residence on Nantucket, the Azoreans were filling in for departed Nantucketers, with one striking difference. Azorean woman did not work as domestic servants.

Ten years later the number of Nantucket residents who had been born in the Azores had fallen, but the number of their Nantucket-born children and grandchildren was growing, making the Azorean community a substantial one within the greater community of Nantucket. The majority of Azores-born men were still considered mariners, but it was an aging population. More than half of them were past fifty years old and probably no longer went to sea. Azorean mariner George Folger was eighty-four years old. Joseph Francis, fifty-eight, and formerly a mariner, had turned to fishing. Francis Thomas, fifty, recently arrived with his family from the Azores, was also fishing with his seventeen-year-old son Manuel. Joseph Sylvaro had become a gardener. Joseph Enos, whose wife Sarah was Irish, was a cooper. Two men in their late sixties candidly admitted that they no longer had any occupation at all. Among the Azorean women, three were engaged in tailoring and dressmaking.

The census records are inconsistent between reporting specific island of origin or simply "Western Islands," but the town death records generally record the home island of the deceased as well as the names of both parents. Insofar as islands are reported, Fayal seems to have contributed the most immigrants to Nantucket in the early years, when its harbor at Horta was port of call for whaleships. St. Michael took over in later years with the institution of regular packet-boat service to New Bedford from its port of Ponta Delgada. Pico and Flores also contributed substantially, followed by St. George, Terceira, and Santa Maria. Tiny Corvo appears in the records only as the home of Francis Colha, who married Catrina de Gezers of Flores. The couple's daughter Filomena settled on Nantucket.

Around 1870 a family had arrived from Graciosa, changing its name to Murray somewhere along the way. (According to J. Butler Folger the

Cutting in a whale alongside the schooner Abby Bradford while moored at Straight Wharf, 1870.

Murrays originally had the surname Santos and wanted to change it to Macy, but the Nantucket Macy family objected.) Throughout the 1860s John Murray Sr. had captained the whaling schooner *Abbie Bradford* out of Nantucket and done a bit of buying and selling of shares in the vessel while maintaining a young son on Graciosa. In 1869 he took the *Abbie Bradford* on one last voyage, which was described as a "plum pudding voyage."(Herman Melville defined a plum pudding voyage was a short one limited to the North Atlantic.) Having decided to retire to Nantucket, Captain Murray picked up his son John Jr. from Graciosa and brought him to the United States.

Settled on Nantucket, Captain Murray, his son, and his Graciosa-born daughter-in-law, Anna, took up the grocery business. The young Murrays soon were sworn in as naturalized citizens, the grocery store on Orange Street became an exemplar of Nantucket entrepreneurship, and the Murrays grew influential within the Azorean community and beyond.

In the meantime a second Azorean cooper had taken up residence on Nantucket. "Mariner" had become obsolete as a profession, replaced by "seaman" and "sailor." A few more men were fishing and farming. Two more had married Irish women. The number of Azores-born residents of Nantucket was holding steady.

In 1873 the Portuguese government tightened its requirements for army service. No longer was it possible to avoid conscription by paying a fee for a substitute. Young Azorean men had little desire to spend years as Portuguese soldiers, and they took every opportunity to flee. The government saw the consequences and changed its policy to permit young men to emigrate if they posted a deposit guaranteeing their return for future army service, but the change came too late. Men, boys, and whole families had boarded ships in Ponta Delgada and sailed for the United States.

Between 1880 and 1900, a fresh influx of Azoreans nearly doubled the number on Nantucket. One of them, sixty-five-year-old Peter L. Sylvia, gave his profession as "whaler." His Massachusetts-born son was listed as "boatman." Some of the newcomers were even older than Peter Sylvia. John and Mary da Costa had come to the United States in 1892 when they were both seventy. Despite their age, they bought a house on Nantucket and made a home for their son-in-law and two small grandchildren.

In addition to the old whaler and his son the boatman, one man was identified as a seaman and another as a sailor. Most of the men working on the water were fishermen, however. Their numbers were equaled by men working as day laborers, including eighty-six-year-old Francis Sylvia, who had once been a mariner. Only one Azorean farmer remained, but there were three grocers, a pair of carpenters, a cobbler, a cook, and a steward. An Azorean woman was running a boarding house.

There was another Murray on-island—Philip Murray, also of Graciosa, who was working at the time of the census as a day laborer. And there were now other Azorean grocers besides the Murrays. One of them was Manuel Mendonça, who had first come to the United States at the age of twelve as mess boy on a whaling ship. He met and married his Azores-born wife Louisa in New Bedford, and the couple had two Nantucket-born children, John and Mary, who would both grow up to be educators. When Mary Mendonça retired from teaching sixth grade at Nantucket's Academy Hill School in

1955, she had served the Nantucket public schools for thirty-nine years.

John Mendonça was recruited as a scholarship student at Exeter by his friend and classmate J. Butler Folger, a thoroughly "descended Nantucketer." From preparatory school he entered the Harvard class of 1922, while Folger went to Dartmouth College and then stayed on to teach Spanish and Portuguese at his *alma mater*. After graduation from Harvard, John Mendonça taught in the New York public schools until retirement, when he returned to Nantucket and became well known as Nantucket's oldest scallop fisherman. His love of life on the water was matched by a love of storytelling.

In 1910, Nantucket's Azores-born population had doubled again. It now numbered over 160 out of a total island population of fewer than three thousand. Thirty of the Azorean immigrants were using the name Sylvia or Silvia. Seven of the Sylvias were named Joseph, five Antone, and five Mary. There were two Manuels and two Isabellas. There were also eight Araujos (two named Beatrice), four Rays, and four Souzas with all their

Nantucket-born children. Public-school teachers and the town clerk must have been hard-pressed to keep track of the many newcomers with so much duplication of names.

Commenting on Nantucket's early assimilation of Azoreans, John Mendonça remarked, "I imagine those who came first and married Nantucket girls, their names have been changed to something else. Joe Starbuck and his father on Silver Street, well, they were Portuguese. Now where they got the name Starbuck from I don't know, because I never knew what their original name was. Yes, they took a Nantucket name." J. Butler Folger gave other examples, "Ellenwood Folger in 'Sconset was no Folger at all. Eldred Gardner told me that Captain Frank Gardner 'gave my grandfather his name.' I had always thought of Eldred as a scion of the Gardner clan and doubtless related to my grandmother, who was Sara Emily Gardner. Genie Brooks's grandmother, the wife of old Captain Clisby, out here at Surfside, was half-Portuguese."

With the marriage of Enos and Ellen Sylvaro's daughter Elizabeth to Edgar Ramsdell (son of

Among the 1911 Academy Hill School seventh grade class were John Mendonça (front row, first left), J. Butler Folger (front row, first right), and Ellen Ramsdell (second row, fifth from left).

Warren Ramsdell, for whom Warren's Landing on Madaket Harbor was named) an on-island Azorean family was joined to an old-time Nantucket one. Their daughter Ellen Ramsdell was born in 1898, the same year as John Mendonça. Graduating from Nantucket's Coffin School in 1917, she went on to the New England Conservatory of Music. Then, like John and his sister Mary, she became a teacher, serving the Nantucket public schools as music director for decades. A faithful Episcopalian, she was also organist for Nantucket's St. Paul's Episcopal Church.

During the early days, when Azorean whalemen had married Nantucket women and then left on long voyages to the Pacific whaling grounds, their children grew up speaking English in a New England cultural environment. They became, at least to people outside their immediate families, indistinguishable from their mothers' descended-Nantucketer relatives. The arrival of Azorean women, however, slowed the rapid assimilation of the earlier years. During the last decades of the 1800s, Azores-born couples raised their children in more traditional Portuguese Catholic households that fostered the intergenerational use of the Portuguese language. Nantucket-born John and Mary Mendonça spoke Portuguese with their parents and grandmother, their cousins, and their boarder, fisherman Jacinth Leial.

John Mendonça's friend J. Butler Folger aspired to speak Portuguese, too, and he developed conversational skills with Nantucket-born Carrie and Emily Miller and their sister Mary Almeida. He wrote, "The Miller girls told me to come and talk with them evenings if I wanted to practice. I used to go down twice a week. Mary Almeida was always there. Carrie and Emily would come in from the movies and we would talk about everything, including neighborhood gossip. I would leave the house with my sides aching from the fun and wit that Carrie especially evoked. Her description in Portuguese with an occasional admixture of English of Izzy Swain's sister's wedding or Irving Hatch selling gasoline were some of the funniest recollections that I still treasure."

The Nantucket Azorean community's strengthened sense of Portuguese identity was most public at the 1895 dedication of Alfonso Hall. Houses along the way were illuminated, and fireworks were set off as members of the Portuguese United Benevolent Association and the Nantucket selectmen, led by the Nantucket Brass Band, made their way from Orange Street to the hall. More fireworks greeted their arrival. The hall itself was decorated with Portuguese and American flags, and the portraits of George Washington and King Alfonso I of Portugal hung side by side. The program began with the Portuguese national anthem, and in the course of the evening Lewis Marshall "delivered an address in Portuguese overflowing with patriotic affection for his native land and grateful allegiance to the country of his adoption from which he had received such substantial benefit since he landed penniless on its shore."

The chairman of the board of selectmen reciprocated by welcoming the Portuguese citizens to

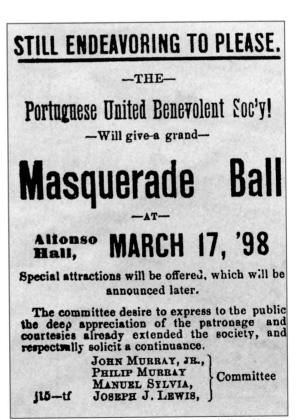

Nantucket Historical Association

citizenship and complimenting them on their fine social hall. Another member of the board of the selectmen told of having acquired the Portuguese language as a child from crew members on his father's ship and jocularly warned the audience that he still understood it. Arthur Gardner, "in behalf of the native Nantucketers," expressed gratitude for the entertainment and praise for "their Portuguese friends." The evening concluded with Portuguese dances featuring the *chamarrita* accompanied by singing, followed by American dances to Barrett's Orchestra. This had all been accomplished before Nantucket Catholics and their missionary priest had received permission from the bishop of Providence to build a church on the island.

The Benevolent Association used Alfonso Hall to raise money with events such as the "grand masquerade ball" advertised in the *Inquirer and Mirror* for March 17, 1898. Money also flowed in from the auction of food at the annual Feast of the Holy Ghost held each June at the hall. The celebration featured Portuguese and American flags, a silver crown, processions of children dressed in white, and the cooperation of many men from Nantucket's Azorean community.

Captain John Murray and his son John Murray Jr. had been instrumental in organizing Nantucket's Azoreans, building Alfonso Hall and sponsoring the celebrations there. When Captain Murray died in 1899, his obituary stated that he "was a highly esteemed citizen, and his funeral…was very largely attended, many citizens, including the members of the Portuguese United Benevolent Association, accompanying the funeral cortege on foot, and the flags at Alfonso hall were displayed at half-mast." John Murray Jr. survived his father by two decades. When he died, his funeral services were held at his Orange Street home, and he was interred in Prospect Hill Cemetery with full Masonic rites. Members of the four organizations to which he had belonged— Union Lodge F. & A. M., the United Benevolent Association, the John B. Chace Engine Company No. 4, and the Portuguese Fraternity of the United

States—served as pallbearers, and "as a mark of respect, the stores on Orange Street were closed during the hour of funeral services."

Feasts, dances, weddings, and funerals brought Azorean families together and drew their New Bedford and Fairhaven relatives to the island, as did hog-butchering and sausage-making. John Mendonça conveyed the flavor of these family gatherings in the following story:

Portuguese used to make what they called mor-cela. It's a blood sausage, you know. They cut up onions and—oh, I don't remember—pieces of fat. I don't remember what used to go into that stuff. They'd scour out the entrails of the pig, you know, and fill it full of that stuff. They'd have a big wash boiler there, [and] they'd have a stick across the top. They'd hang them on there and put them in that, you know. Then they would keep a long time if you kept them in a cool place. Well, my aunt was making those, and my mother was down helping, and it came—oh, I guess it was getting late—and my mother said, "Look, you kids go to bed." So my three cousins and I went to bed upstairs. And they were all sleeping in the same room. There was one, two, three beds. So I said, There's no bed up there for me!" So my mother said, "Well, it won't hurt you. You're young. Sleep on the floor." So my aunt came upstairs and I remember she spread a quilt—you know, one of those down quilts folded in two—down on the floor for me.

The Nantucket kitchens of Azorean wives were rich with the aromas of baking sweet bread, kale soup on the back burner, *linguiça* sausage sizzling in frying pans. In Azorean kitchen gardens grew garlic and tomatoes in abundance. Hydrangeas, roses, and geraniums appeared in yards. The most widely accepted and emulated Portuguese gift to Nantucket has been flower gardens. When Ellen Ramsdell died at the age of 93, her obituary told of her life's passions: "Second only to her love of music was her love of horticulture. For decades her garden was a visiting point on walking tours of the island."

Gardening was more than an avocation. In her garden Ellen Ramsdell built the Garden Gate Gift Shop where she offered garden-related items and preserves made with her home-grown fruits and vegetables. Joseph Viera, who came to Nantucket from St. Michael when he was twelve years old, operated his own gardening business for twenty years before his death in 1967 and was an active member of the Nantucket Grange.

In the summer of 2001, Nantucket lost another Azorean gardener, Philip Marks, Sr. Born in New Bedford in 1909 to parents who soon went back to St. Michael, he returned to the United States as a teenager to live with relatives on Nantucket. In the midst of the Depression years, he married Mary Macy, and the couple raised six children on a small farm on the south edge of town, across the street from Alfonso Hall. Although he worked for four decades at the island's power plant and also as a baker, his devotion was to gardening, and he maintained an impressive flower and vegetable garden on his property until his death at age 91.

According to his son John, Manuel Mendonça's heart was never in the grocery business. It had been his wife Louisa who had insisted that he give up whaling, but his heart had never been in that either. Like most Azorean men, what he really yearned to be was a farmer, but circumstances prevented the realization of his dream.

Eugene Perry was a whaleman who came ashore to run a business on Nantucket. He had been born on St. Michael in 1870, emigrated to Boston as a teenager, and arrived in Nantucket in 1891. Soon he was recruited by a New Bedford company that operated arctic whaling ships out of San Francisco. The *Inquirer and Mirror* reported his safe return from one such voyage on the ship *William Baylies* in 1904, a successful voyage despite the *Baylies* losing three whaleboats, becoming stranded by low water in one port, and having part of its crew desert in another. Five years later he was serving on the *Baylies* again when she was crushed in arctic ice off the Russian coast. The crew spent days camped out on the ice under makeshift shelter until they were picked up by another whaler and taken safely to Nome, Alaska. This was not the end of Eugene Perry's adventures at sea, however. Gold was discovered in the Yukon, and he immediately

– Courtesy of Catherine Flanagan Stover

The Perry family from St. Michael, the Azores, photographed in New Bedford in 1905. Nantucket-born Catherine Theresa Perry stands between her grandparents Michael and Mary Perreira.

shipped as an engineer on a vessel carrying miners and their supplies from San Francisco to Alaska.

When he finally returned to Nantucket, Perry operated a string of businesses: a tobacco shop in 1910, a poolroom in 1920, a fleet of fishing boats, and eventually the Dreamland movie theater, which he operated until his death in 1947. His wife was Annie Nevins, daughter of Catherine and Michael Nevins, and their marriage was yet another union of a Portuguese husband and an Irish wife.

Over the years the Azores had enriched Nantucket. In their home harbors, the Azores islands had provisioned Nantucket ships with fresh water and food. From the islands Nantucket had received expert boatsmen, husbands, hydrangeas, *morcela* and *linguiça,* music and dancing, and more. Nantucket had reciprocated with employment, land, wives, free public education, and more. In the early days of all-male immigration, Nantucket had simply absorbed Azoreans. In the later days of mass immigration, Portuguese ethnic solidarity had been tolerated, sometimes celebrated, on Nantucket.

During the years leading up to World War I there was a change in American attitudes toward all the nation's ethnic minorities—immigrants and their American-born offspring. Postwar quotas put the brakes on immigration. The foreign-born already resident in the United States were pressed hard to break ties with "the old country," and speaking any language other than

English was discouraged.[1] Schools, including those on Nantucket, initiated Americanization classes. Through the 1920s, prudent "foreigners" kept their heads down and their mouths shut. And then the Depression struck.

The Azores still had one more contribution to make to Nantucket—a newspaperman who cultivated democracy with the passion that other Azoreans brought to cultivating roses. The Nantucket political establishment didn't see him coming and was still teetering off-balance when he left. Some Nantucketers were exasperated by him and wished he would go away. Many others were admiring friends. Hardly anyone was indifferent to what appeared in the pages of the *Town Crier*, whose owner/editor was dedicated to exposing every worm in the venerable fabric of Nantucket. In the nineteenth century there had been Joe Citizen. In the twentieth century there was Joe Indio.

Joseph Indio was born on St. Michael in 1911 of an Azorean father and a Brazilian mother. The family moved to New Bedford, where he and his sister and brothers grew up bilingual. In high school he added three more Romance languages to his native Portuguese—Latin, Spanish, and French—accelerating through four years of French in three. In 1930 he completed New Bedford High School's college-preparatory curriculum and graduated with distinction. He had emerged from school into the Depression, however, with no resources to continue his education at a college or university. Instead, he went to work for New Bedford's *Evening Standard*, initially working without pay to prove himself to his future employer. In 1932 the newspaper assigned him to Nantucket, where he worked as a reporter for a decade, becoming adept at camera work and using airplanes to chase news stories at sea. During that time he married Nantucket-born Constance Heighton, whose parents, originally from Nova Scotia, had come to farm in Polpis.

In 1942, as the war years descended on the United States, Joseph Indio became a naturalized citizen and moved on to a position covering the Massachusetts State House for United Press International. The following year he entered the U.S. Army and for three years served in the Counter Intelligence Corps and in Military Intelligence. At UPI and in his army service his language skills were an asset. For his work on undercover assignments, the army awarded him the equivalent of the Bronze Star, noting his careful attention to accuracy and his investigative and writing abilities. At the end of the war he would take these well-honed talents back to journalism.

— Nantucket Historical Association

Joseph Indio looks over a copy of the Town Crier *in August 1956.*

Upon discharge from the army he gained more experience writing newscasts for radio station WHDH in Boston, while he and his wife were planning their return to Nantucket as founders of a weekly newspaper to compete with the island's venerable weekly, the *Inquirer and Mirror*. The name they chose for their paper was the *Town Crier*, a name appropriate to its mission to bring to readers' attention the way business-as-usual was conducted on the island. In the sixteen years of its existence the small newspaper campaigned against the Steamship Authority's unprofitable service to New Bedford; for the erection of a modern high school; for open meetings; and against bigotry, prejudice, ignorance, and injustice. Many an ox was gored, and many an indignant complaint called in, all to little avail.

---

1. In 1917 Congress imposed a literacy requirement on immigrants. According to the 1920 federal census, at least a third of Nantucket's Azores-born population were illiterate and would have been prevented from entering the country under the new restriction. Then, in 1921, an immigration quota system known as the Three Percent Law was enacted, which reduced the number of permitted immigrants from all of Portugal to all parts of the United States to just 2,500 people a year. Three years later, even more restrictive legislation was passed, ending Azorean immigration to Nantucket.

In 1938, the editor-in-chief of the *Standard-Times* had written, "Joe is a fine reporter, and one of the best things about him is that he stands as firmly as a rock when the going gets hardest." In his wife Connie, he had found a kindred spirit. The Indios were attractive, personable, activist journalists who refused to be intimidated. For ongoing coverage of the Steamship Authority's business, the *Town Crier* was nominated for a Pulitzer Prize in 1960. Commendations also came from all quarters for the *Town Crier*'s saturation coverage of Nantucket catastrophes, among them the collision of the ships *Andrea Doria* and *Stockholm* and the 1958 Northeast Airlines plane crash in which twenty-five people lost their lives.

The *Town Crier* was a small operation in which everyone, including one of Sarah P. Bunker's great-great-grandsons, pitched in at nearly every job as needed. Publication of the summertime guide *Nantucket Holiday* brought in revenue to augment subscriptions and advertising. Getting the newspaper out on time each week was both exhilarating and consuming, and sixteen years into the enterprise, Joseph Indio's health began to fail. The 1963 sale of the business, complete with *Nantucket Holiday*, to the publisher of the *Inquirer and Mirror* took Nantucketers by surprise. Letters, some from long-time antagonists, poured in to the Indios expressing shock and sadness. Consensus was that competition had improved the *Inquirer and Mirror* and that the *Town Crier*'s passionate editorial voice had benefited Nantucket. Henry Beetle Hough, editor/publisher of the *Vineyard Gazette*, wrote, "I'd like you both to know how sad I am about the end of the road for the *Town Crier*. It was a gallant venture and through its exciting years you have much to be proud of. There are not many strongly individualistic papers left."

The words of praise were welcome, but Joseph Indio had wearied of the good fight. He had once advised his friend Jim Geggis, "Cynicism has a place in our makeup, particularly in news work, but it cannot replace faith in the future, even when the walls are crumbling." Now, as the walls

of his own future began to give way, he had done all he could do or wanted to do for Nantucket.

After the sale of the business and some European travel, he began drafting a personal memoir of the *Town Crier* and its Nantucket battles, but he laid the manuscript aside unfinished. As unyielding to terminal illness as he had been to public criticism, he took an off-island position at Southeastern Massachusetts Technical Institute, did some work in public relations, and became a licensed real estate dealer. Before he died in a New Bedford Hospital in 1968, he expressed his desire not to be buried on Nantucket, and so he was laid to rest in St. John's Cemetery in New Bedford. A man who reflexively trusted and acted on the courage of his convictions, he had given Nantucket's pot a mighty stir.

Cape Verdeans

We have been here for so many years.
— Viola (Cabral) Howard

Buffeted by dry winds blowing off the Sahara, the desert islands of the Cape Verde archipelago are seldom green. They derive their name from Africa's westernmost point of land, a 'Green Cape' that juts out from the Senegal coast three hundred miles to the southeast. Seven hundred miles off to the southwest lies the coast of Brazil, and more than three thousand miles to the northwest are Massachusetts and Rhode Island, places important to Cape Verdean economic history.

The northern, windward islands are San Antonio (Santo Antão), Saint Vincent (São Vicente), Santa Luzia, Saint Nicholas (São Nicolau), Sal, and Boavista. The southern, leeward group includes the major islands of Maio; Santiago (São Tiago), with the capital city of Praia; Fogo; and Brava.

Most of the Cape Verdeans who relocated to Nantucket came from the leeward islands, particularly from Fogo and Brava. No matter which island had been their home, as immigrants they were collectively referred to as "Bravas."

People from Fogo had, in fact, moved to Brava repeatedly, blurring the distinction between Bravans and Fogoans. Although much the larger of the two islands, Fogo (*fire* in Portuguese) is a single, active volcano rising from the sea. Over the centuries, residents living on its steep slopes and farming inside its crater have periodically fled for their lives and crowded onto little Brava. An eruption in 1680 turned the summit into a lighted beacon visible from far at sea, earning the island its name. Eruptions continued throughout the New England whaling era: in 1785, 1799, 1847, 1852, and 1857. Whaleships putting in to Brava's bay of Faja d'Água for supplies found many men ready and willing to sign on as crew members. They had left everything behind on smoldering Fogo and were prepared to sail away from Brava, even as far as New England.

When the Cape Verde islands were sighted and then charted in the mid 1400s, they were uninhabited, and with their scant rainfall and thin soil they did not offer good prospects for cultivation. Nonetheless, Portugal dispatched administrators, farmers, convicts, political exiles, and "New Christians" (Sephardic Jews who had been forced to convert to Christianity) to render the islands productive.

Today there are Jewish cemeteries on several of the islands of the Cape Verde archipelago, including Brava, but these date not from the early peopling of the islands, but from the 1820s, when some of the few remaining Sephardic Jews of Portugal sought political refuge in the islands, and from the 1850s, when Jewish men from Morocco and Gibralter arrived to work in the leather trade.

– Jay Avila illustration

The Cape Verde archipelago. During whaling days Nantucket ships picked up additional crew from the islands of Fogo and Brava, islands that were later the main source of immigration to southern New England.

In the early days, it was this improvised population sent from Europe that organized the clearing of the land for sugar and cotton plantations. Enslaved Africans were imported to do the hard field labor. African slaves were also brought to process salt on the islands of Sal (Portuguese for *salt*) and Maio, to spin and weave cotton grown on the new plantations, and to gather indigo and other dyestuffs that grew on the islands.

In the long run, the islands could not be agriculturally self-sufficient. Too little of the land was arable, and periodic droughts wiped

Fogo's volcanic eruptions in the mid-1800s made it a natural beacon guiding New England whaleships to nearby Brava.

Painting by Russell and Purrington, 1845, New Bedford Whaling Museum

out crops, livestock, and significant percentages of the human population as well. Nor could the export of dyestuffs, salt, and salted fish support the residents of the islands. Profits derived overwhelmingly from the slave trade.

In the 1500s and early 1600s, the "raw" slaves brought to the Cape Verde islands for re-export came mainly from the Upper Guinea coast. Later, an increasing number were brought from Angola. These facts were reflected by names of places in Nantucket—New Guinea and Angola Street—long before Cape Verdean families came to live in the neighborhood.

In a "seasoning" process, slaves were baptized as Catholics with Christian names and were introduced to the work they would be doing in the future. Most were destined to be sent on, but some were retained for local work, especially women and men of the Wolof people, who were valued for their skill in spinning and weaving. The labor of these specialists produced textiles known as *panos*, which were used by the Portuguese as currency for purchasing yet more slaves on the African mainland.

Very soon a racially mixed population—offspring of the small number of European men resident on the islands and enslaved women—emerged as the majority population on the islands. Within a century from the first arrivals, more than two-thirds of the population was of mixed African and European ancestry, with another quarter of African ancestry, and those proportions have remained more or less the same ever since.[2] The population of Brava is exceptional in this. Despite its good harbors, which proved so attractive to New England whalers, Brava was not a station in the slave trade. With fewer Africans present, admixture with the descendants of Portuguese settlers—many of them from the Azores and Madeira—has been noticeably less.

Unrelenting pressure to self-identify as Portuguese was a permanent condition for those who remained in the Cape Verde islands. For Cape Verde's mixed-race population, thinking, speaking, and believing oneself Portuguese was the route to freedom and even to personal profit from the slave trade. Within a generation, those *Crioulos* became middlemen in the trade both on the islands and on the African coast.[3] Meanwhile, West African languages and culture survived as substrata that distinguished Cape Verdeans from other Portuguese.

Nowhere has this been more evident than in the language of the archipelago. The local language, also called *Crioulo*, has been thought of generally as an imperfect, Africanized form of Portuguese. It is as incomprehensible to speakers of other varieties of Portuguese as Jamaican Creole English is to English speakers, and for good reason. Cape Verdean Creole Portuguese and Jamaican Creole English are not simply extreme nonstandard varieties of Portuguese and English, respectively; they are separate languages. Cape Verdean Creole shares most of its words with Portuguese, but not only are they pronounced differently, and not only is the language spoken with a very different rhythm, but the grammar is also different from Portuguese. The same can be said of Jamaican Creole with respect to English. Although they got their words from different languages, Cape Verdean Creole and Jamaican Creole are more like each other in how they put sentences together than they are like the languages from which their words have come. Whether this is because of their common African roots or because of the nature of creole languages worldwide is a matter of debate among people who study them; but in any case, Crioulo—the home language of most Cape Verdeans—is not substandard Portuguese. It is a creation of the people of the archipelago that at once defines their

---

2. This is in marked contrast to Nantucket, where the entire "colored" community of mixed Wampanoag, African, and white ancestry in the second half of the 1700s and on into the 1800s remained in the hundreds while the English population grew to a peak of nearly 10,000.

3. *Crioulo* is the Portuguese word corresponding to English "creole." Its original meaning in Spanish and Portuguese seems to have been 'someone of Iberian heritage born overseas.' In practice it has come to be synonymous with *mestizo*, meaning someone of mixed racial heritage.

Cape Verdean identity and poses an obstacle to communication with speakers of Portuguese from other islands such as the Azores. On Nantucket this noncommunication between Azoreans and Cape Verdeans was as significant as their shared Portuguese culture and Catholic religion.

The first Nantucket resident identified as Cape Verdean is Michael Douglass, who, despite his Scottish-sounding name, is described as "a Cape di Verde Portuguese Negro." Born in the mid-1760s, he took up residence in Nantucket when he was around forty years old, about the time a man would hope to be able to retire from work at sea. He does not appear in the 1800 census but is in censuses from 1810 through 1830. In 1809, he married Sally Smith of Nantucket, and they appear together in the 1810 census, but it seems he lost his wife soon after, because in 1811 he married Mary Boston. Subsequently their names come up in records of the Boston family's real-estate dealings. For a while their household grew, although it is not clear who the people were who shared their home. By 1830 Michael and Mary Douglass, both in their 60s, were living alone again.

Three decades younger than Michael Douglass, José da Silva was born on Brava in 1794. Sworn in before the Nantucket Court of Common Pleas in late October 1824, he was the first Cape Verdean to be naturalized as a citizen of the United States. Da Silva is described in the court documents as "an Alien, being a free white person and citizen or subject of the Kingdom of Portugal, but now a resident of Nantucket." Over time in Nantucket, "da Silva" changed to Sylvia.

Two years before assuming U.S. citizenship, Joseph Sylvia had married a Nantucket widow, Mary Lyon, the mother of a young daughter, Rebecca. In the course of the 1820s Mary and Joseph had three children together. The family of six appears in the 1830 federal census for Nantucket. Mary died in 1847, and there are no Nantucket marriage or death records for daughter Elizabeth or for Joseph Jr., suggesting that after their mother's death they left the island. Middle daughter Delphina remained on Nantucket, however. She married, had four children, and lived until 1907.

There may have been other men making their homes in New Guinea with whom Michael Douglass could reminisce in Crioulo about the Cape Verdean archipelago. A couple of men named DeGross and a man named DeVert married African-Nantucketer wives even before Douglass married for the first time. The 1810 census identifies Manuel Antonia as black, and beginning in 1820, federal and local censuses register the New Guinea household of Michael DeLuce through two decades. Michael DeLuce was one of the trustees of the African Baptist Society at its inception in the 1820s, and his wife Sara signed the charter of the reorganized African Baptist Church in 1831. Nowhere are the DeGrosses, DeVert, Antonia, or DeLuce identified as Cape Verdean, and we know no more about how they came to Nantucket than we know how Michael Douglass arrived or how he came by his name. That they were all single men who, with the exception of Antonia, found wives in Nantucket's African community suggests that they came to the island as "single mariners," a category that does not appear on the census forms until decades later.[4]

However they came to be living on Nantucket, they may have all counted themselves lucky. On March 9, 1833, the *Nantucket Inquirer* printed an account of the horrific toll being taken by the drought and famine then afflicting the islands of the Cape Verde archipelago. The brig *Emma* had been sent from Philadelphia with a cargo of food for the famine victims. A passenger aboard the relief ship reported that as they made their first landfall at the windward island of San Antonio, men who appeared to be living skeletons rowed out to beg them to stop and sell them some food. When they learned that the ship had come to give them food, people onshore attempted to raise a cheer of

4. As early as 1775 there were people identified as Portuguese living in New Guinea. In that year Abraham Williams of Sandwich reported to Colonel Nathaniel Freeman in Watertown that there had been "a considerable riot and affray there between the negroes and Portuguese on the one side and the inhabitants on the other, in consequence whereof many of our Indians and Molattoes are come off."

thanks, but the only sound they could manage was a groan. The desperation on San Antonio, wrote the *Nantucket Inquirer*'s correspondent, "was beyond the power of tongue or pen to describe."

Whichever island Michael Douglass had left so long ago, news of the situation on San Antonio in 1833 must have struck to the heart of the aging Cape Verdean. If, over the years on Nantucket, he had harbored the thought that in his lifetime he might revisit the place from which he had set out, that hope was now extinguished.

In 1834 Mary Douglass died, and two years later Michael followed, a solitary man who drowned at age seventy. The name Michael Douglass had never rested comfortably on his shoulders, or perhaps on his tongue. Over the decades of his life on the island Nantucketers had understood it and written it many ways: Mike, Micah, Michael and Douglas, Duglass—even Guglas. On Mary's headstone, placed among the Boston family graves, she is identified as the wife of Mikel Dauglass. No grave marker is to be found for her husband.

Elsewhere in the cemetery is a broken stone for Peter Antone, born at St. Anthony (San Antonio). The date is obscured, but the initials C.V., for Cape Verde, are still discernible. Other markers in the cemetery bear Portuguese names, but they are from a later time. The censuses of 1850 and 1860 show almost no Cape Verdeans living in New Guinea. In 1850 Joseph Antonio, a single mariner, was there, and by 1860, Joseph Lewis, another black Cape Verdean mariner had established a household with his Pennsylvania-born wife and Massachusetts-born children. At some point, too, mariner John Bravo, born in 1796 and considered white, had settled on Nantucket, where he died at age 75, never having found himself a wife.

The list of transient seamen attached to the 1850 federal census lists a total of 76 men of Portuguese nationality serving on Nantucket ships. Of those, only eleven were from Cape Verde. Two were from Saint Nicholas and one from San Antonio. The home islands of the other eight are not identified. Four were classified as black, and

the rest were not racially categorized. This runs contrary to accepted wisdom that Nantucket whaling ships were largely crewed by Cape Verdeans. By 1850 Nantucket whaling was in decline, while the New Bedford whale fishery continued strong for some time to come and afforded Cape Verdean seamen a way out of their islands' desperate circumstances.

The 1860 federal census shows only one Cape Verdean resident on Nantucket, fifty-one-year-old Joseph Lewis. Lewis had been away from his homeland a long time. He had taken an African-American wife, and the oldest of their children, all born in Massachusetts, was already eighteen years old. In the course of a decade Lewis accumulated significant real estate holdings in New Guinea, but by 1870 he had died, and his widow Julia, their son Joseph Jr., and their daughter Emma (perhaps named in honor of the relief ship sent from Philadelphia in 1833) were living-in with a white family. In 1900 Joseph Jr. and Emma had reached middle age still unmarried and were sharing a household. Julia survived to nearly the end of the century and Emma died in 1917. Both women were buried in the cemetery behind Mill Hill. After his father's death, Joseph Lewis Jr. had gone to sea, but in his later years, while living nearby on York Street, he served the Nantucket Historical Association as one of the custodians of the Old Mill. A newspaper article about the owners and subsequent custodians of the mill described Joseph Lewis as a veteran whaleman.

After Joseph Lewis Sr., nobody Cape Verde-born appears in Nantucket censuses until 1910. In mid-April of that year 110 Cape Verdeans were resident on the island. Of them, a dozen had been in the United States less than a year, and three had arrived since January.

Theirs must have been an exotic presence on Nantucket, where the African-American population had fallen to twenty-nine. Some of them had names to trip the Nantucket tongue—names such as Hermenegildo Rodericks, Roamo Araujo, Liberto Santos, Remicho Gomes, and Sabana Viera. There is no doubt the Cape Verdeans confounded local ideas about color. In the race column of the census sheets the enumerators categorized them as "B" for black. Subsequently someone went through and overwrote each "B" with "W" for white.

The newcomers were for the most part in their twenties or thirties and single. More than half were unable to read and write and a third did not yet speak English. Men outnumbered women by well over two-to-one, but there were, nonetheless, fifteen married couples, including a half dozen in which one spouse was not Cape Verdean. Among them, these families had twenty children under the age of fifteen. Many of the single men lived in shanties on the large commercial cranberry bog under development north of the road to 'Sconset, next to Gibbs's Pond. Some, including two single mothers with their children, lived in the village of 'Sconset, and a dozen Cape Verdeans lived on North Wharf. Nearly everyone was renting or boarding. Only two couples owned houses on the island.

In mid-April, when they were counted for the census, the cranberry-bog workers were setting out new plants. Over the summer they would weed, and in the fall they could look ahead to working their way through the bog on their knees, the women harvesting the fruit by hand while the men worked with wooden cranberry scoops.

Millard Freeborn, whose grandfather was one of Nantucket's earliest commercial cranberry growers, wrote, "I well remember the days when the cranberry pickers used to come and harvest what was then a great crop of cranberries, requiring eighty pickers and some times as many as a hundred, each day. Uncle Asa Coffin…was the one who kept the tally of the number of quarts gathered by each picker. Two cents per quart was the price paid the pickers, and my father was the boss of the job. I can see him now as he stalked up and down the line of pickers, making them come back and pick all the berries they had skipped for the rule was to pick them *all*."

Work went on in all sorts of weather out on the bog, where there was no shelter or protection. In 1913 twenty-eight-year-old Ben Lopes was struck by lightning and died.

Crowded housing was universal on the cranberry bogs. There are seven men outside the shanty in this 1911 photograph from Crocker's Bog on the mainland, but inside there were bunks for twelve.

Lewis W. Hine photograph, Library of Congress

It was hard work that made one either love or hate the business. For every person for whom the very sight of cranberries off the job—much less the taste of the berries—was unendurable, there was another who wanted nothing more than to own a bog of his own. One of the people counted by the 1910 census was Peter Tavares. At the time he was twenty-three years old, single, illiterate, and as yet unable to speak English. In time he married and became an independent farmer and bog owner in Polpis. Late in life, after his Santiago-born wife Johanna died in Nantucket, he sold his land and returned to Cape Verde.

Not all Cape Verdeans resident on Nantucket worked the bogs, however. In 1910, Cape Verde-born Annibal Martin was at the Muskeget Lifesaving Station. He had arrived in the United States at the age of fifteen, and thirteen years later he had not yet been naturalized. Apparently this was not an obstacle in the Life-Saving Service; quite a number of Nantucket's lighthouse keepers and telegraphers were also aliens. By age twenty-eight Martin had a white Massachusetts-born wife and a three-year-old daughter Evelyn, and they, too, were living on Muskeget. The 1910 census categorized Martin and Evelyn as mulattos. Ten years later, the Martins had moved to Fair Street, and there were five children, all of whom—from Evelyn, the oldest, to the youngest, a little girl named Blanche—were categorized as white, although their father continued to be categorized as mulatto. Still not naturalized, Annibal Martin was supporting his family by working as a harbor fisherman.

Like emigrants from many other countries, most Cape Verdeans had not come to the United States with the intention of staying permanently. Their aim was to accumulate enough capital from their labor to purchase land on their home islands to which they could eventually retire. In the meantime, they went back to visit whenever they could, and even when they could not go themselves, they sent back all sorts of American goods to their families. To connect the emigrants to their homes, enterprising seamen among them purchased old sailing vessels, often retired whaleships, and operated them across the vast stretch of sea between New England ports and the Cape Verde archipelago. Those vessels, known as packets, continued to make round trips as late as the 1960s.

Harvesting cranberries on Nantucket, circa 1940. At one time the commercial bog off Milestone Road was the world's largest.

Their cargoes included all sorts of goods for the benefit of family members left behind and for the construction of future retirement homes, including cedar shingles that imparted a Nantucket look to the far-off Cape Verde islands. A memorial to the packet trade that brought workers to New England and carried the fruits of their labor back home is the restored schooner *Ernestina* which puts in to Nantucket from time to time as she carries an educational program about Cape Verdean history along the New England coast.

In 1910 three of the Cape Verdeans living on North Wharf had left the labor of cranberry cultivation. Joseph Gomes had gone to work for Holland-born florist Hermanus Voorneveld, while his brother Frank worked in the coal yard and their younger brother Remicho was doing odd jobs. Frank had been the first to arrive in the United States from Fogo in 1902, and Joseph had joined him the following year. Remicho was just twenty years old when he left home for America in 1908. Over the next five years their sisters Pauline and Isabel and their young half-brother Peter came to Nantucket, too, and they all lived together in an upstairs apartment on North Wharf. Joseph was known as a quiet person who still did not speak English after more than a dozen years of life and work in the United States.

During the summer of 1915, Joseph Gomes worked at a Nantucket golf course. On the evening of August 1, home from a long, hot day of work, Joseph was in a strange mood, and after Frank had gone to sleep, he began to beat their sister Pauline.

Luther Rose, a cranberry bog worker who lived in the apartment below, called out to Joseph to leave his sister alone. Shortly before midnight Joseph went down to Luther's apartment, and hit him on the head with a wooden club. In the dark Luther attempted to defend himself with what came to hand and stabbed his attacker with a pair of scissors. As a crowd gathered, Joseph Gomes bled to death where he had fallen.

Witnesses, including Gomes's sisters and Julia Pina, agreed that Joseph Gomes had been behaving irrationally and had attacked Luther Rose without provocation. An autopsy revealed no evidence of alcohol, and speculation was that heat stroke was the precipitating cause of the incident.

The reporter for the *Inquirer and Mirror* wrote sympathetically of the painfully injured Luther Rose and the bereaved Gomes family, but he opened his piece by harking back to the murder of Phebe Fuller a half-century earlier, pointedly identifying Patience Cooper, the woman convicted of that crime, as "a Negro." He then went on to say that investigation of the circumstances of Gomes's death

Vessels at anchor in Brava, Cape Verde Islands, circa 1910. A crowd of people is gathered at the dock. Packet ships commanded by Cape Verdean captains actively transported people and goods between the islands and New England.

was difficult because everyone involved was "Brava Portuguese and unable to speak intelligible English."

In court Rose was found to have acted in self-defense. He left the bogs to become a fisherman, and in 1938, at the age of seventy-two, he was living alone on Orange Street, still a fisherman. Apparently the stigma of having killed his fellow Cape Verdean isolated him for life. As a child, Arline Bartlett lived near Luther Rose's tiny house and had been warned to beware of him, because he was a murderer. She recalled him, nonetheless, as a gentle elderly man with a shambling walk who responded courteously to greetings.

The Gomes siblings weathered the storm and stayed on in Nantucket too. Five years after their family tragedy, Frank had married, and he and his wife named their infant son Joseph. Pauline, Isabel, and Peter married on Nantucket, too. Only Remicho remained single. They all finished their days on the island, far from their birth island of Fogo.

The year after Joseph Gomes died, Elsie Clews Parsons came to Nantucket to collect Cape Verdean folklore. One of America's first anthropologists, she was famous for her landmark studies of the pueblo culture of the American Southwest and of the Zapotecs of Oaxaca, Mexico.

Parsons's early work on Cape Verdean and Caribbean folklore is less well known. In 1915 Franz Boas, one of the founders of American anthropology, had appointed her associate editor for African-American folklore at the *Journal of American Folk-Lore*. She soon found a wealth of material and also a skilled colleague among Cape Verdeans living in Newport. Fogo-born Gregorio Teixeira da Silva was a laborer with connections in the factories and on the docks in Providence, Fall River, and New Bedford as well as in Newport. Together, Parsons and da Silva found people to talk to in churches, factories, tenements—even in alleys—and especially in the homes of other people who had been born on Fogo.

What Parsons liked best was collecting riddles. A person with an uncommon propensity for roughing it, she found getting out of the cities and going to the cranberry-bog shanties invigorating,

as—in fact—some Cape Verdeans themselves did. Parsons, however, was a wealthy woman who could return home to great comfort whenever she pleased. Reality for Cape Verdean workers was quite otherwise. As Sarah P. Bunker's great-granddaughter observed, "I know out to the bogs here ten or a dozen would live in a twelve-by-fourteen-foot shack, and the bog owners paid them next to nothing, then sold them their food and took out for their rent, and when the end of the month came, they had nothing." The 1910 census bears out her description of crowded living quarters. That year on the new bog there were families living together, couples sharing space with unrelated people, and groups of seven or eight men living together. One twenty-two-year-old man was listed as head of household for eighteen other men.

While engaged in fieldwork, Elsie Clews Parsons shared the pleasure of the Cape Verdeans in getting together to pose riddles and to tell traditional folktales. Her happy anticipation of taking a boat out to Nantucket with da Silva and collecting folklore on the island was, however, dashed. After the two of them had made a difficult six-mile buggy ride from town to the cranberry bog "through long stretches of sand or swamp," the boss insisted that the men there had no stories to tell and sent them away. It was, she said, "our most signal defeat." The following day, Parsons and da Silva had better luck in "a sunny little yard" in town, where people were more relaxed and open. Parsons remained unaware of the trauma the Nantucket Cape Verdean community had recently experienced or that the boss at the bog may have been fending off the prying public curious about Luther Rose and his coworkers.

Although Parsons could participate in asking and answering riddles in Portuguese and Crioulo, her ability to understand and write down Crioulo was limited. In collecting stories, she had to depend on da Silva to make on-the-spot translations into English and later to recreate the original stories from his notes. She regarded the work they did together a joint project, and it was both a personal and a professional loss when da Silva died in 1919.

Parsons forged on with publication of what they had done, first producing an article about Cape Verdean beliefs and practices in 1921, and then in 1923 bringing out a two-volume compilation of the stories, proverbs, songs, and riddles they had collected. She dedicated the volumes to Gregorio Teixeira da Silva, her "interpreter and teacher."

Cranberry cultivation did not live up to expectations on Nantucket, and by 1920 the number of Cape Verdeans and their American-born children resident on Nantucket had fallen to seventy-two. In the meantime, the number of home-owning families had risen to nine. Eighteen people, three generations of one family, were living in a single household on Washington Street; living at home with them, John and Elsie Fernandes had four unmarried children, three married daughters, three sons-in-law, and six grandchildren.

Migrant travel from place to place around southern New England to harvest strawberries, blueberries, and cranberries brought together Cape Verdeans who otherwise might never have met. The circle of on- and off-island marriages and friendships widened, and a great deal of visiting between Nantucket and the mainland has always been the rule. This moving back and forth has made the Cape Verdean community on Nantucket a fluid one. Only ten or a dozen of the people in the 1910 and 1920 censuses lived out their lives on Nantucket. Most Cape Verdeans listed in those censuses left Nantucket and were replaced by others coming from the Cape and the New Bedford area.

Former Nantucket dockmaster Joe Lopes was brought by his parents to Nantucket from New Bedford at the beginning of the Depression when he was seven years old, while New Bedford-born Augusto ("Augie") Ramos, eventual owner of a construction company and Nantucket selectman, arrived on his own at age seventeen. The late Jareaseh St. Jean had come to the island at age ten to live with her aunt after her mother's death. For

— Nantucket Historical Association

George Gebo (far left) photographed with other World War I veterans on the steps of Nantucket's Methodist Church in November 1919.

her dedicated volunteer work after her retirement from nursing she was named Senior Citizen of the Year 2001 by the Nantucket Council on Aging.

After 1920 many of the new arrivals in Nantucket were Massachusetts-born children of Cape Verdeans. The postwar restrictive quotas had nearly stopped the flow of new immigrants from the archipelago to the United States, a flow that did not resume until the 1970s.[5] From the Nantucket town records can be seen the result—an aging and diminishing population. Before 1950, Cape Verde-born people who died on Nantucket were for the most part in their 50s and 60s. After 1950, the Cape Verde-born who died were in their 70s and 80s. Annie Gebo—widow of Luther Gebo, mother of six, grandmother of fourteen, great-grandmother of fifteen—lived to the age of 100 and was featured in the *Inquirer and Mirror* twice: on her ninety-sixth birthday in 1967 and three years later on her ninety-ninth.

Both times the *Inquirer and Mirror* revealed a geographical confusion pervasive among non-Portuguese Nantucketers. In 1967 the newspaper reported, "Mrs. Gebo was born in the Cape Verde Islands, Azores, on January 20, 1871, and came to this country in 1891 when she was 20. She took up

---

5. In the decade from 1910 to 1920 over 18,000 Cape Verdeans emigrated to the United States. After a law was passed in 1917 prohibiting illiterate would-be immigrants from entering the United States and following the imposition of immigration quotas, the number dropped precipitously. In the course of a quarter century beginning in 1927, fewer than 2,000 documented emigrants managed to leave the Cape Verde archipelago for the United States. Nantucket has not attracted recent Cape Verdean immigrants to Massachusetts. The work niche they might have filled on the island has been taken over by Jamaican contract workers.

her residence here in 1911, which means she has been living here for fifty-six years." Three years later, the error reappeared uncorrected: "She was born in the Cape Verde Islands, Azores, and has lived in Nantucket since 1911."

The confusion goes both ways. In 1899 Captain John Murray's obituary in the *Inquirer and Mirror* stated that he "was a native of the Cape de Verde islands," although he and his son, John Murray Jr., had both been born on the island of Graciosa in the Azores. The following week the newspaper printed a correction regretting "that an error on our part as to the place of his nativity should have caused his friends annoyance."

To this day Nantucketers are prone to saying they know of someone from one island group and then naming an island in the other.

In view of their different histories and their profoundly different languages, it is hardly surprising that this confusion has injured the pride of Cape Verdeans and annoyed Azoreans—on Nantucket and off-island as well. More potent than geographical ignorance has been racial stigma. Azoreans have dreaded the assumption that they share any African heritage with Cape Verdeans. They make much of the Flemish and the putative Breton background of the Azorean population without acknowledging that among the early settlers of the Azores were also some Sephardic Jews, Iberian Muslims, and African slaves.

When the first Portuguese Congress in America convened at Harvard University in early June of 1973 and passed a resolution demanding official recognition of Portuguese Americans as a minority, the resolution contained a nondiscriminatory racial clause "to unify a community that has been long divided." The *Boston Globe* went on to report: "Some immigrants from Portugal and the Azores don't like to consider Cape Verde immigrants—part of Portugal's African holdings—as Portuguese." Arnaldo Cruz, a member of the steering committee of the Cambridge Organization of Portuguese-Americans, was quoted as saying, "Portuguese here will be welcome—whether they are black or white—if they want to join us."

For Cape Verdeans before and since 1973, the resolution and the statement by Cruz have been contradicted by their unrelenting experience of racism. Back in 1856 *Harper's New Monthly Magazine* printed an unsigned essay entitled "The 'Gees." In it Herman Melville describes the humiliating treatment of men from Fogo aboard Nantucket and New Bedford whaleships. He invents a fictional Nantucketer, "Captain Hosea Kean," who chooses the crewmen he ships from Fogo by bursting into their homes in the dead of night to take them by surprise. He also describes the role of a "'Gee jockey" in weeding out potential troublemakers: "For notwithstanding the general docility of the 'Gee when green, it may be otherwise with him when ripe. Discreet captains won't have such a 'Gee. 'Away with that ripe 'Gee!' they cry; 'that smart 'Gee; that knowing 'Gee! Green 'Gees for me!'" Melville concludes that one needn't go to Fogo to observe a 'Gee first hand, because they "are occasionally to be encountered in our seaports, but more particularly in Nantucket and New Bedford." People to be met in these ports, however,

When Josefino Lopes Cabral and Maria Gibian Roderiques were married in Nantucket, their wedding party included Frank Correia, Florence Roderick, Isabella Mendes, Dorothy Burgo, Elizabeth Mendes, and Isabella Burgo.

are "sophisticated 'Gees, and hence liable to be taken for naturalized citizens badly sunburnt."

One might take this as satire ultimately sympathetic to exploited and abused Cape Verdean seamen were it not for the relish with which Melville describes Cape Verdeans as the "amalgamated generation" descended from Portuguese convicts and "an aboriginal race of negroes, ranking pretty high in incivility and rather low in stature and morals," further debased by the siphoning off of the most fit to serve as cannon fodder in Portugal's wars. This is just the beginning of a humorously intended defamatory catalogue characterizing Cape Verdeans' physical stature, hair, skin color, teeth, diet, intellect, and seamanship.

Such odious humor could hardly be published these days, but it was common fare in the 1800s and well into the 1900s. Cape Verdeans on Nantucket had to live with it and deal with it on an everyday basis. John Mendonça told a story of an occasion on which scornful racism proved costly to the steamship line:

> There was a Captain Neves who owned his own business and ran a packet between the Cape Verde Islands and New Bedford. He was the man who was on the steamer with me that time old Captain Fishback was on the bridge. That was a terribly foggy day, and this Captain Neves said to me, "You know, if he keeps running on this course for another five minutes, he's going to be on the rocks." He said, "Go up and tell him." So I said, "Why don't you tell him, Captain?" He said, "I'm colored." He said, "I can't tell him anything." So I went up and told the captain. The captain said, "Who sent that message?" "Captain Neves." (I can't say what he said on a tape recording.) "Go tell that G-D Negro (He didn't use that word.) to mind his own business." Five minutes later he had crashed on the rocks with the old steamship Martha's Vineyard.

When Josefino (Lopes) Cabral and Maria (Gibian) Roderiques were married on Nantucket on July 28, 1928, their attendants included best man, maid of honor, bridesmaids, and a flower girl, but permission to have their wedding in St. Mary's church was denied, and they had to settle for being married in the rectory. The elegant Cabral wedding portrait was finally published in the *Inquirer and Mirror* more than a half century after it took place.

Through the first half of the twentieth century, Nantucket newspaper reporting continued what can at best be described as a patronizing attitude toward Cape Verdeans, as illustrated in the coverage of Nantucket's original "underground man."

In December of 1998 the chief topic of conversation on Nantucket was the discovery of a commodious, well-appointed chamber constructed below ground in a pine grove on land owned by the Boy Scouts. Non-Cape Verdean Tom Johnson was said to have occupied it for a decade, and many islanders admired his ingenuity in living so comfortably for so long without detection. Health inspector Richard Ray described the dug-out as "a marvel of craftsmanship" but cited it for health-code violations, and it was demolished.

Johnson was not the first to go underground, however. In 1932 Nantucket police located the subterranean distillery of Joseph Garcia in a pine grove between the Milestone Road and Polpis Road. It was at least the equal of Johnson's later construction. The wood-lined main chamber contained a kerosene stove, a wash boiler and copper coils for distillation, three hogsheads of fermenting mash, and a hundred

Chinese laundryman Wing Gee Der with a group of Cape Verdeans, circa 1940. Standing left to right: Josefino Cabral, a relative of the Cosmo family visiting from Martha's Vineyard, Dominga (Fernandes) Cosmo, and Frances Fernandes. Right front: Alfred Moniz.

gallons of finished product ready for delivery. A trap door let down from the chamber into a thirty-foot well tapping into a spring that supplied water to the nearby Mooney farm duck pond.

Nantucketers of the early 1930s were as admiring of Garcia's still as Nantucketers of the late 1990s were of Tom Johnson's domicile. According to the *Inquirer and Mirror*, "The outfit, just as the officers discovered it, would have been worth visiting and inspecting by the general public, even for a small admission fee." But just as Johnson's underground home was condemned and destroyed, so in the interest of public safety was the hidden still denied its potential as a paying attraction. "Owing to the fact that the cave might possibly be stumbled upon by someone out in quest of berries, or that some Boy Scout or child might accidentally come across it, the police officers decided that the place should be destroyed at once. So Sergeant Mooney and Officer Henderson went out Tuesday evening equipped with axes and shovels and demolished the whole thing."

With the demolition of the still ended a profitable enterprise for Cape Verdean entrepreneur Garcia, whose name was only revealed in the last sentence of the news story. Up to that point he had been identified as a "Brava Portuguese," "the Brava," "an ignorant Brava," "the man," and "the fellow." The *Inquirer and Mirror* report concluded: "The Brava? Oh, he was placed under arrest, brought before Judge Fitz-Randolph, fined $100, declared he did not have the money, and has gone to the House of Correction at New Bedford to ponder over the situation. His name is Joseph Garcia and he has been there before."

Until quite late in the century most Cape Verdeans were excluded from positions in which they would meet the public; instead they were relegated to invisible and even inaudible jobs. Working as a telephone operator was considered excellent employment for a woman between high school and marriage, but according to Cape Verdeans, a young woman who applied encountered resistance even though she was Nantucket-born, educated in the Nantucket schools, and indistinguishable in speech

from her classmates. Cape Verdean women seeking employment were instead relegated to cleaning and cooking. They recall compensation for janitorial work ranging from twenty-five cents an hour at the Maria Mitchell Association to a dollar an hour at the Nantucket Historical Association's Whaling Museum. Without island-wide public transportation, they walked from their homes far south of Main Street to jobs in places as distant as Cliff Road. One of the most positive social changes of the last quarter of the century was the emergence of Cape Verdean women and men as professionals in businesses, health care, and politics.

In 1989, one hundred and fifty years after Absalom Boston first presented himself as a candidate for public office, Cape Verdean Augusto Ramos succeeded in his bid to be elected to the Nantucket board of selectmen, the first nonwhite to hold that office. His resignation from the board soon after his election remains open to conflicting interpretations, but it is undeniable that the town has been the better for electing him and vindicating its Cape Verdean community.

With doors shut to them for decades and many opportunities out of reach, Nantucket's Cape Verdeans actively looked out for themselves. With the *joie de vivre* that was so appealing to Elsie Clews Parsons, they kept traditional music and food—especially the Cape Verdean rice-and-beans dish called *jag*—central to their celebrations. Departing from the saints' day calendar of feasts observed in the archipelago, celebrations in the United States came to be centered on Thanksgiving and Christmas. The long Thanksgiving holiday gave families the opportunity to hold reunions large and small. In 1990, 160 members of the Correia family sat down to dinner together in the Knights of Columbus Hall, the old Alfonso Hall originally built by the Azoreans. Nantucket-born sisters Edith (Correia) Perry and Elizabeth (Correia) Campbell presided as the eldest members of the family, surrounded by younger relatives who had come from as far away as Texas and from as near as next door. Yvonne Barrows was quoted as saying, "Everyone looked alike. You knew who everyone was just by looking at them. It was all family, no intruders.… We'd talk about who got married first, how they lived, how they would cook, how they all sang Christmas carols, and helped name each other's children."

For Cape Verdean men fishing and hunting have been a source of great pleasure. In an interview Viola (Cabral) Howard and Pauline (Cabral) Singleton told about their father and his friends: "They knew the waters. Here on the island most of them are fishermen or scallopers, or they love to go out surf fishing or fishing on their boats, 'cause it's just handed down. Their friends or uncles or the older ones, they just enjoyed it so much, and that's their thing. When the bass are running or the bluefish are running or the scallops. If they catch anything, they come home, cook up all the deer meat and jag, sit around the table and talk. My father was a hunter. He had friends from sixty years old down to maybe twenty, because they loved him so. He taught them how to hunt. I remember Thanksgiving Day, that was the day to go out hunting. We would eat dinner about three o'clock. We'd have about twenty-five, thirty that went out hunting. And at Christmas we'd have venison, rabbit. We'd have duck, all the game, just about, and we loved it. It was delicious. It brings back a lot of memories. They're getting old now. They took a couple of years off, but they went out this year and enjoyed it, and we enjoyed it as well. They had some good times hunting. Very close and just enjoyed each other's company."

In December 2001, when the Cape and Islands public radio station was searching for Nantucket Christmas traditions, Cape Verdean Christmas caroling was clearly the most distinctive and also the least generally known. Viola Howard and Pauline Singleton recalled a Christmas in the early 1970s when they could not get together the full complement of singers and musicians from years past. That year they carried a record player from house to house to play old 78 rpm records of Cape Verdean *canta reis,* which they accompanied on a guitar. "People were so happy to hear them again," they said. "It was the last time we did it, thirty years ago."

As the Christmas caroling tradition passed into abeyance, a summer celebration took its place. In July 1988 the recently formed Sons and Daughters of Arquipelago de Cabo Verde held the first of a series of annual festivals featuring Cape Verdean food and music. Guest of honor at the first Cape Verde Heritage Festival was Consul-General Alirio Vincente Silva of the Republic of Cape Verde, who made a public presentation in the Unitarian Church. The next afternoon a Cape Verdean story hour was held at the Nantucket Atheneum, and in the evening there was yet another public event at the Nantucket Whaling Museum. The third day of the festival was given over to music and a feast at the Knights of Columbus Hall. The Nantucket Cape Verdean festivals continued for seven years, attracting hundreds of Cape Verdean visitors from southeastern New England until finally the burden of organizational work and cooking overwhelmed the local organization.

The Nantucket chapter of the Sons and Daughters of Arquipelago de Cabo Verde suspended the festivals after 1994, but its members continued to advance its originally stated aims: "To revive interest in Cape Verde culture; assist Cape Verdeans in developing a greater sense of ethnic and national pride; and assist in providing Cape Verdeans with a growth-oriented environment that promotes a real spirit of togetherness/individual initiative/personal pride for all people."

The primary focus of the organization's initiative has been public education. Cape Verdeans' experience with the Nantucket schools has not been an actively negative one, but over the years they have had to deal with low expectations on the part of teachers and administrators and the channeling of Cape Verdean students away from college preparatory courses into vocational tracks.

The Cape Verdean cranberry-bog workers recruited to Nantucket in the first two decades of the twentieth century came from an environment in which anything beyond the most basic education was unavailable. For speakers of Crioulo, moreover, Portuguese—the language of formal education—was a language as foreign as English.

As a result, more than half arrived in Nantucket unable to read or write. Even those who were literate were for the most part able to read only in Portuguese. Working long, hard hours on the bogs, they had little time for learning English, and they were handicapped in helping their children with school work. It is not surprising that of thirty-one children in "special classes" in 1930-32, half came from homes in which English was probably not spoken. One appears to have been Hungarian, and another Swedish, but fourteen had Portuguese names.

Between 1920 and 1925 the Nantucket public schools offered Americanization classes to the parents of these children, and the classes were popular with both Cape Verdean and Azorean men. About twenty-five enrolled in evening classes each year, progressing through a program of reading and writing English that included dictation and practice in letter writing plus arithmetic and geography. After that they moved on to courses in United States history and government required for taking out citizenship papers.

In 1924, women's names appear for the first time on the enrollment list, but none are Portuguese. This does not mean that Cape Verdean women did not have English classes, however. A report for the year 1921 remarks that men's class attendance declined during good fishing weather when they were busy dredging and opening scallops, and that women met for classes in their homes, because after supper, when the evening classes were held, they were busy with their families.

The Sons and Daughters organization has striven to advance this hard-earned basic education among Nantucket's Cape Verdeans by presenting annual scholarships at Nantucket High School graduation. True to their goal of encouraging individual initiative and personal pride *for all people*, they have not limited scholarship eligibility to students of Cape Verdean descent. Two of three Sons and Daughters scholarships awarded in 2001 went to non-Cape Verdeans. The third went to Falynne Correia, Cape Verdean and president of that year's graduating class. Falynne also took

– Larry Cronin photograph   – Nantucket Historical Association

Augusto Ramos and his horse Prince. Ramos was elected to the the Nantucket board of selectmen in 1989. At right, class president Falynne Correia on graduation day at Nantucket High School, 2001.

part in the Nantucket Junior Miss pageant in the fall of 2000, receiving scholarship awards in three categories. On graduation night she received a Sons and Daughters scholarship plus additional ones, making a total of six scholarships from Nantucket organizations to help her on her way through college.

In an *Inquirer and Mirror* article about a visit of the *Ernestina* to Nantucket in June 2001, James Duarte and Augusto Ramos lamented the fading of Cape Verdean culture from Nantucket. Ramos is quoted as saying, "The ethnicity is gone. The kids don't know what it's about any more." Duarte added, "Today's kids don't grow up the way we did and it's too bad. Now some of these kids don't even know their cousins." Where were the young hands to help with the festivals and—in time—to take over? Falynne Correia agreed that there is a division between generations and described a situation in which young Cape Verdeans simply do not know which island their great-grandparents came from, but she felt strongly that the older Cape Verdeans are mistaken in thinking the youngest Cape Verdeans have no interest in their heritage. Studying Portuguese, writing essays about Cape Verdean history, and making a trip to the islands with a grandparent would be the very first steps in the process of answering the question, "Who are we?" and coming to think of herself as Cape Verdean—not African-American, not simply of mixed race, but as a person with a distinct heritage.

CHAPTER SIX

Jamaicans

Nantucket is not America. Noooo, Nantucket is NOT America!

— Jamaican man's voice heard
from within the Jared Coffin House

Nantucket is not at all like Jamaica either. At first glance it seems that the two islands have little in common and, prior to the 1990s, few points of contact.

As Herman Melville so aptly described it, Nantucket is "an elbow of sand" in the ocean, and a chilly ocean at that. Jamaica's mountains and rich, fertile valleys, on the other hand, bask in Caribbean warmth ninety miles south of Cuba. Wampanoags continued to live on Nantucket for a century after the arrival of English settlers, while Jamaica's Arawaks had perished before the English came. Since the mid 1600s Nantucket has had many more Euro-Americans than African Americans, while the reverse has been overwhelmingly true for Jamaica. There, Africa-born slaves and their Jamaica-born descendants labored in the sugar-cane fields of the north and west and the coffee plantations of the east, while a small population of free blacks and people of mixed race (known in Jamaica as "colored") lived in towns, mainly in Kingston on the south coast.

The number of enslaved persons in Nantucket in the 1700s was small both in absolute numbers and as a percentage of the total island population. Boston and Maria with their eight children in William Swain's household appear to set a record. A slave sent whaling, as Prince Boston was, might be the only man on board who was not free, and it appears—at least in that case—that the master of the vessel made no distinction between enslaved and free crew members. In Jamaica, on the other hand, white estate owners—fewer than ten percent of the population—held almost all the rest of the

inhabitants of the island in servitude. There were domestic slaves in the great houses, and slaves were overseers and skilled laborers on the estates, but most of Jamaica's slaves labored in the fields in work gangs of from 50 to as many as 600 men and women. They lived in slave villages, raised food to augment the salted fish provided by the estate owners, and were generally denied the benefits of marriage and established family life.

– Frances Karttunen photograph
The Jamaican flag flies at St. Paul's rectory on August 26, 2002.

On guard against rebellion, plantation managers made every effort to prevent the arrival of news from outside. The planters were for the most part hostile to Christian missionary work among their slaves, whether by European representatives of the Moravian, Baptist, or Wesleyan Methodist churches or by African-American preachers who began traveling to Jamaica after the American Revolution.

Throughout the 1700s, as Nantucket's maritime economy expanded, Quaker principles dictated sober living and avoidance of ostentation. By contrast, during that century, as Jamaica became England's most important asset in the Caribbean, that island's planters engaged in building what today's Nantucketers would recognize as trophy houses on their estates, and the extravagance of their lifestyle was the talk of London. In 1763, the year of Nantucket's "Indian sickness," Jamaica produced more sugar than all the other British West Indian islands together. That sugar was the product of a system of forced labor like nothing ever known on Nantucket.

In the extreme circumstances of Jamaica's plantations, enslaved Africans and their Jamaica-born descendants created from sources at hand a distinctive way of life and a language—Jamaican Creole English. Survivals of various West African ways of doing things and talking about them melded with observed European lifeways and English words for talking about them. Dancing continued to pervade life as it had in Africa. At Christmas celebrations, slaves danced to drums and also danced formal quadrilles and gavottes to violin accompaniment. Jamaican Creole English put English vocabulary together with profoundly un-English sentence rhythm and sentence structure.

Although similar developments took place on the islands of the Cape Verde archipelago, nothing like this particular creative process was initiated on Nantucket. Only in recent years has Jamaican Creole English been brought to Nantucket—by Jamaican workers on seasonal work visas. Unlike Cape Verdean Creole Portuguese, which most Nantucketers have rarely if ever heard, Jamaican Creole English is now ubiquitous, to be encountered on the island even in the dead of a Nantucket winter.

Despite their geographical and social differences, Nantucket and Jamaica share long parallel histories. Replacing the Spanish who had earlier occupied the island, the English established themselves in Jamaica in 1655, and the first English settlers arrived on Nantucket in 1659. Contact with Europeans led to the demise of both islands' indigenous populations—the Wampanoags on Nantucket and the Arawaks of Jamaica. English settlers on Nantucket were threatened by the proximity of King Philip's War, while the English in Jamaica were at risk from the Maroons—former African slaves of the Spanish who had established themselves in the mountainous interior of the island.

During Jamaica's long history as an English colony, free black and colored (mixed race) Jamaicans lived in the cities on the south coast, while most of the island's population labored as slaves on sugar plantations in the north and west of the island and on coffee plantations in the east. Nantucketer Jared Coffin carried on business in Kingston and Morant Bay in 1796.

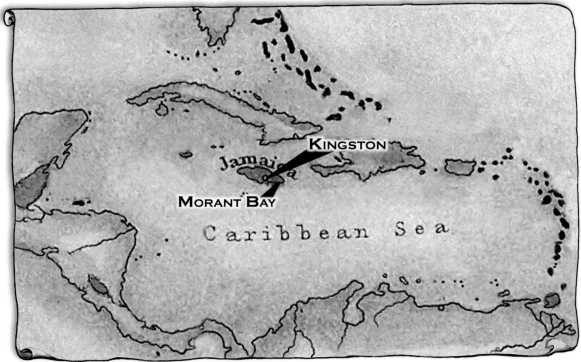

Before the vast expansion of sugar-cane cultivation, the early English settlers in Jamaica had small numbers of African slaves and some indentured whites working for them, just as in Nantucket a number of English families had obtained a few African slaves and put some of them to work on whaling vessels together with indentured Wampanoags. In time, by different routes and in vastly different numbers to be sure, the island-born descendants of Africans achieved freedom on both islands and set about demanding equality as landowners, farmers, and entrepreneurs.

Throughout the 1700s and into the early 1800s religion played a central role in the social history of both Nantucket and Jamaica, and education for African children arrived on both islands at about the same time. In 1826, within a year of the opening of Nantucket's African School under the aegis of the African Baptist Society, the Baptist school in Kingston, Jamaica, built a new schoolhouse and took on the education of sixty-five students. In both African schools the subjects taught were basic literacy followed by history and grammar.

These parallel developments went on independently of direct contact between the islands. During the 1700s they had little contact. Fenced off from the Atlantic Ocean by the islands of Cuba, the Bahamas, Hispaniola, and Puerto Rico, Jamaica was not a convenient provisioning place for ships working the Atlantic whaling grounds. Nor did Jamaica—unlike the ocean islands where Nantucket whalers regularly made port—offer the opportunity to pick up crew replacements. Prior to 1838 the vast majority of the Jamaican work force was not free to ship out.

Nonetheless, in 1796 a Nantucket merchant named Jared Coffin[1] was operating out of Jamaica. In a series of letters written that year from Kingston and nearby Morant Bay, Coffin documented his trade in candles, lumber, and rum and contemplated expanding his business into iron and cowhides.

At the time when Coffin was operating in Jamaica, Nantucket's black Gardner family was a generation away from producing another remarkable and little-known connection between the islands. The 1790 census shows Thomas Gardner living on Nantucket. Shortly after the census was taken, Thomas left the island, married the daughter of an Africa-born former slave in Newburyport, Massachusetts, and had a daughter. Nancy Gardner, granddaughter of an African and daughter of an African Nantucketer, was born free in 1799, when the total number of free Africans in all of Massachusetts numbered about 500, many of them living on Nantucket.

From a difficult childhood in Salem, Nancy was sent out to work without schooling, but through her church in Boston and through her marriage to Nero Prince, she became a woman of the world. Her life played out on a global scale—in Salem and Boston; then in St. Petersburg, Russia; and then in Jamaica, with stops in New Orleans, Philadelphia, and New York along the way.

During the 1820s, while Nancy Prince was living in the czarist court, speaking French and doing needlework, Jamaican society was undergoing a profound change, a change that can be traced back in part to the 1733 publication of Nantucket Quaker Elihu Coleman's antislavery tract. It was not until 1761 that the London Yearly Meeting followed Coleman's declaration against slavery, but once the London meeting stated that any Friend engaged in the slave trade should be disowned, their abolitionist persuasion spread beyond the Religious Society of Friends, and "within a decade it was the received wisdom of the educated, including the political nation, that slavery was morally and philosophically condemned."

Facing a myriad of obstacles as they labored to bring Jamaica's slaves into the fold of orthodox Protestantism, missionaries in Jamaica—Baptist and Methodist in particular—brought with them the European enlightenment notions of the equality of all humankind and the moral repugnance

1. This merchant is not the Jared Coffin (1784–1860) who built two mansions in Nantucket—one now known as Moors End and the other the Jared Coffin House. Nor were the two Jareds father and son.

of slavery. Although they sought to convince their congregations of the rewards of being faithful and obedient servants, they could not help but convey the welcome message that slavery must end and all people be free.

The 1831 rebellion was rightly perceived by the estate owners to be of a different nature from previous uprisings in which slaves sought to escape from the English plantation system. This time the aim was to fundamentally change Jamaican society in such a way that all people formerly enslaved would be free. In fact, they considered themselves already free.

The rebellion was put down by force in a matter of weeks, and retaliation against both slaves and missionaries was severe. Black Jamaicans were executed by the hundreds, unbalancing the gender ratio among the slaves to just ninety-two men to every hundred women within a year of the uprising. Only military intervention saved missionaries from lynch mobs. Some sailed to England with firsthand reports of what had happened. In spite of opposition by Jamaican estate owners to Parliament and the Colonial Council, expelled missionaries carried the day in England, and on August 1, 1834, the slaves throughout the British West Indies were emancipated.

Childless and widowed after a decade of life in Russia, Nancy Prince turned her attention to Jamaica in 1840, having responded to a recruitment lecture she attended in Boston. She wrote, "I was sensible that I was very limited in education [but] I hoped that I might aid in some small degree to raise up and encourage the emancipated inhabitants and teach the young children to read and work, to fear God, and put their faith in the Savior." For support in her efforts to establish a vocational training school for Jamaican women, she turned to Nantucket-born Lucretia (Coffin) Mott and her associates in Philadelphia. Due to inadequate capital and difficulties with Jamaican officials, the project was not successful. Nancy Prince's life, already replete with loss, was made the harder by frustration of her best intentions, but as she tells it in her autobiography, she had made a grand attempt.

Self-published in Boston in 1850, the *Narrative of the Life and Travels of Mrs. Nancy Prince* was a success as abolitionism heated up in the northern states in the years prior to the Civil War, and her book went through two more editions in 1853 and 1856. A copy of the first edition made its way to the Nantucket Atheneum and is still there.

In the 1850s another link was forged between Nantucket and Jamaica. South Carolina-born Ann (Williams) Crawford, wife of the Reverend James Crawford, had two sisters, one of whom married abolitionist Henry Highland Garnet. Like James Crawford, H. H. Garnet had been born into slavery, escaped to the North, and become a clergyman. In the 1850s he experienced a call to missionary work and took his family to Jamaica.

On March 13, 1858, the *Weekly Mirror* of Nantucket reported the safe arrival in Nantucket of Ann's other sister, Dianna, and her daughter—heroically redeemed from slavery by James Crawford. In relating how this had come about, Crawford began with his brother-in-law and sister-in-law, the Garnets, deciding to offer themselves in service to the newly emancipated Jamaicans. Soon after arriving there, they received terrible news:

On hearing that they were Americans, a gentleman stepped up and inquired their pedigree, and on learning that Mrs. Garnet was of Charleston, S.C., and a member of the Williams family, he informed her of the sad condition of her youngest sister, Dianna, and her daughter Cornelia, who had fallen into the hands of one John N. Maffit of schooner Galveston, in the American Coast Survey, and he had offered them for sale.

H. H. Garnet immediately sent word from Jamaica to James Crawford in Nantucket, and a group of island residents, described by Crawford as "distinguished gentlemen of Nantucket," set about negotiating for Dianna's release. John Maffit replied that Dianna's and Cornelia's freedom could be bought for $1,900. A short time later Maffit sent a second letter reporting that he had concluded the sale of Cornelia, and that he anticipated selling Dianna within a month. From their two islands the brothers-in-law both appealed to Quakers in

England to help raise the sum to ransom Dianna and then to purchase Cornelia. With funds in hand, James Crawford—passing as white—traveled into the slave states, "managed to assume the character of a master, and having procured his niece, started for home. But he was in constant fear of being taken, and more than once his suspicions were aroused, supposing that plans were being devised to place him for violation of the laws of the state."

Crawford and Garnet lived on into the 1880s. With his missionary days in Jamaica behind him, Garnet was posted as United States minister to Liberia but died shortly after arrival in Monrovia. Crawford outlived Ann and Dianna, served the African Baptist Church on Nantucket for forty years, and died on the island.

By 1848 Nantucket's whaling industry had pitched into a decline from which it never recovered. Simultaneously, the sugar industry declined in Jamaica, partly because of tariff revisions, but also because Jamaica's freedmen refused to return to working for low wages in the service of their former masters. To fill the labor shortage, the planters recruited indentured laborers from India and China. In the meantime, formerly enslaved Jamaicans, experienced in raising their own food and marketing their surplus, sought to acquire their own land for small, independent farms.

Searching for new ways out of profound economic depression, Nantucketers looked to commercial cranberry cultivation as one promising new revenue source. Jamaica, dealing with declining income from sugar, was receptive to investment in large-scale banana growing by the Boston Fruit Company. In the long run, neither cranberries nor bananas could sustain the two islands' economies, but they played a part in diversification of those economies. Nantucket's cranberry industry was ultimately stopped in its tracks by off-island overplanting. Lethal enemies to Jamaican banana plantations were European trade policies and a blight known as "Panama disease."

Just as Nantucket's inhabitants responded to unemployment in the 1850s by leaving the island in great numbers, so eventually did Jamaicans respond to poverty, population pressures, and lack of opportunity at home by emigration to Cuba, mainland Central America, the United States, Canada, and England. Eventually political events in some of those destinations and immigration restrictions to others turned the flow from outright relocation to seasonal migration on short-term work visas reissued from year to year.

In the second half of the 1800s as their neighbors left for the mainland, for California and beyond, the Nantucketers who stayed behind found their most lucrative asset to be their open spaces, cool sea breezes, and beaches lapped by clean ocean water. Nantucket women began renting rooms in their houses and serving meals to summer visitors. No longer employed in whaling, Nantucket men worked on the steamboats and operated large catboats for parties of holiday-makers. Massive wooden hotels sprang up around the island with horse-car and train service to transport guests from Steamboat Wharf to their lodgings and back again. Money was to be made by selling lightship baskets and ice cream to tourists, transporting visitors around the island, taking them out on the water, and generally entertaining them.

To Nantucket in the 1880s came Charles and Rachel Grant. How and where they had met and married is a mystery, as Charles had been born in Kingston, Jamaica, and Rachel Saco's birthplace was Winslow, Maine. However their union came about, they were in their early thirties when they arrived in Nantucket with sufficient capital to open a saloon. Life on the island was not easy for them. In 1885 their eight-month-old son Frederick died and was buried in the cemetery behind Mill Hill. They had another son, Charles Jr., in 1888, and a third, Willie, the next year, but Willie didn't survive to see his fifth birthday. He died of diphtheria and was laid to rest beside Frederick in 1894. Three years later, Charles Grant Sr. was buried in the Grant family plot. He was only forty-three years old.

Rachel and Charles Jr. were on their own, living in the house on Coon Street that Rachel

Charles Grant whose father was born in Jamaica, was Nantucket's fish warden from the mid-1930s to the mid-1940s.

Grant owned free and clear of any mortgage. Rachel took in a Connecticut-born foster child, Josephine Lawrence, who was four years younger than Charles, and sent both children to school. Josephine was one of the witnesses when the Reverend P. B. Covell married young Charles and Blanche Hawkins of Boston in 1912, but by 1920 Charles had been widowed and was living alone with his mother and fishing for a living.

Georgia-born Ruth Jones worked as a maid, dividing her years between Nantucket in the summers and Greenwich, Connecticut, in the winters. In the summer of 1933, she married Charles Grant, who was by then middle-aged. Shortly thereafter Charles was appointed Nantucket's fish warden, in which capacity he served until six months before his death in 1948. He only outlived his mother Rachel by three years, but Ruth lived on until 1985. With her burial—one of the most recent in the two-century-old cemetery—the family group was complete. All the Grant family graves are marked with handsome headstones. Their house on Coon Street, said to have been the repository for furnishings of the African Meeting House after its closure in 1912, was sold, and Nantucket memories of this Jamaican-American family began to slip away.

At the opening of the twenty-first century Jamaican seasonal workers have become a visible and an especially audible presence on Nantucket.

Jamaican Creole English flows between check-out aisles in the grocery stores, rollicks about restaurant kitchens, echoes in hotel corridors, and ricochets through shuttle buses. For local naturalists, the arrival of Jamaican voices in April foretells the imminent passage of migratory birds following the same route from the Caribbean to New England. When Nantucket's tourist season ends, the seasonal workers hurry home. But every year—despite the dark, damp, and chilly weather and despite visa restrictions—some Jamaicans winter over on Nantucket, and babies are born on Nantucket with all their grandparents in Kingston.

The Jamaican presence on Nantucket began in 1989 and gathered force in the 1990s after Hurricane Gilbert wrought havoc in the Caribbean and just as the tide of Irish workers in the United States began to run out. For Nantucket businesses Jamaican seasonal workers have been a godsend like no other. Experienced from work at home in what has come to be called the "hospitality industry," they can arrive early and stay late, as college students cannot. From about a hundred people contracted to work on the island at the beginning of the 1990s, the number rose to between five and six hundred a year in the course of the decade. Although Jamaican women are more visible in their employment than men, the numbers of men and women coming to work on the island are about equal.

Beginning in 2004, a cap on the number of visas issued to foreign seasonal workers has been enforced, threatening Nantucket with loss of Jamaican employees who had become regular annual returnees to the island. Employers and employees are united in opposition to this disruption of their established working relationship and are making every effort to get around the visa restrictions.

A century and a half after Nancy (Gardner) Prince went to Jamaica on behalf of Jamaican women, Jamaican women and men began using Thomas Gardner's home island as a resource. His daughter would have been surprised and gratified by this unexpected turn of history.

Part III
Nantucket and the World's People

AROUND THE HORN   PITCAIRN 14,300 MI.
SAMOA 15,000 MI.
N.ZEALAND 15,800 MI.
N
Y
200 MILES
HONG KONG 10,453 MI.
VALPARAISO 5,335 MILES
TAHITI 14,650 MI.
W
MACKINAC ISL. 1,05
MELBOURNE 11,253 MILES
DAYTONA BEACH 1,282 MILES
ICELAND 24
BUENOS AYRES 6,914 MILES
GARDINER'S CORNER
POLE 2740
'SCONSET 7½ MILES
S
"THAR BLOWS"
N
BERMUDA 690 MI.   WAUWINET 9 MI.
NANTUCKET
PERRIN GALLERY
CAPE TOWN 11,033 MILES
HALIFAX 486 MI
LONDON 3,612 MILES
CAPE VERDE ISL. 3,200
PARIS 3,746 MILES
BERLIN 4,185 MI.
MOSCOW 5,335 MILES
BOMBAY 9534 MI.
E
SPAIN
CALCUTTA 11,124 MILES
ROME 4,654 MI.
3,000 MILES

**Compass rose created by H. Marshall Gardiner at the intersection of
Main Street and Washington Street.** *– Nantucket Historical Association/Spinner Collection*

We and Thee

Nantucket's English settler families were not the first inhabitants of the island, nor has there ever been a time when their progeny, the "descended Nantucketers," were the only residents. Sarah P. Bunker, who serves as the *leitmotif* for these Nantucketers, lived in a house built hard by a Wampanoag burial site and inherited a basket made for her father by Abram Quary, Nantucket's "last Indian." When she was a girl, her father—a sea captain in the China trade—was in the habit of receiving crewmen and foreigners at home, and he employed live-in "help" to assist with the care and upkeep of what was known grandly as "the Pinkham estate."

Years later, in the straitened circumstances of her widowhood, Sarah P. supported the household by nursing injured, sick, and dying people of "all sorts" as Nantucket's bone-setter Zaccheus Macy had done a century earlier. As she lived out the last decade of her life in her upstairs room, what reached her ears from downstairs day in, day out was the incomprehensible conversation of her granddaughter-in-law's relatives from Finland. Sarah P. knew full well that on Nantucket there were strangers to be found wherever one turned, not just in sailors boarding houses and the servants quarters of descended Nantucketers' houses.

While Nantucketers in general have partitioned the world geographically into on-island and off-island, Quaker Nantucketers sorted the world's population into two kinds: themselves and everyone else. Everyone else—Bostonian and Bantu, Presbyterian and Portuguese, Maori and Methodist, Freemason and Finn—constituted the "world's people." As early-eighteenth-century Quaker tolerance hardened into nineteenth-century rigidity, Nantucket's Friends began to exclude each other, expelling people from Meeting for marrying among the world's people, for socializing with them, for imitating their fashions. However would the shades of departed Quakers judge the Nantucketers of the twenty-first century?[1]

From 1725 until 1850 the descended Nantucketers, a great many of whom were also birthright Quakers, constituted the overwhelming majority of the island's population, but during the mass immigration period of 1850–1920 Nantucket was right in step with the rest of the United States. In

---

1. Worldly practices proscribed by the Religious Society of Friends ranged from "attending a place of music and dancing" to vaccination against smallpox. Ultimately, factions of the remaining Friends mutually disowned one another, forming competing Meetings. An informational marker formerly in the Quaker cemetery at the corner of Madaket Road and Quaker Road stated that in the Orthodox Quaker view, the members of the Hicksite Meeting were "heretical Friends." Scientist Maria Mitchell and social activist Anna Gardner, both raised in Quaker families and imbued to the core with Quaker principles, sought their spiritual home elsewhere, in the Unitarian Church. As Quakerism in Nantucket imploded, the island's churches in general found their membership rolls expanding with ex-Friends.

Nantucket waterfront from Brant Point, 1895.

1910 fifteen percent of the population of the United States was foreign born. By 1920, fourteen percent of the Nantucket population was foreign-born. Back in 1830, when the island's population was recorded as 7,310, roughly four percent were classified as nonwhite. After a century of dramatic fluctuations, the population in 1930 stood at 3,678, with Cape Verdeans and African Americans together accounting for about seven and a half percent.

The Depression years of the 1930s and the prewar days of the early 1940s were uncharacteristically static. Few children who entered the Nantucket public schools in the 1940s had not been born on the island even if their parents or grandparents had come from "off." The second half of the twentieth century was, however, a period of great population growth. By the close of the century, "Where are you from?" had become a standard conversational opening gambit, and descended Nantucketers began to seem and feel exotic.

Nantucket men (and some captains' families) who went to sea in whaling days had observed firsthand the world's geography and the variety of the world's people. Pacific islanders, Asians, Africans, and the great panoply of peoples known as *mulattos* and *mestizos* held no mystery for them. Even the Nantucketers who stayed at home—Sarah P. Bunker and her young neighbor Gulielma Folger, for example—knew a great deal about the world's

people, because despite the selectmen's efforts to deport the uninvited, they have always been coming to the island.

In general, the new Nantucketers of the twentieth century have not converged in a particular part of town. Ethnicity has not determined the churches or the social organizations they have joined. There have been Armenian Congregationalists, Norwegian Catholics, Jewish Episcopalians, and Italian Jews who have also been Masons, Red Men, Oddfellows, or—most recently—Rotarians. While stereotyping has become nigh impossible, quick assimilation has also meant Nantucketers have never quite gotten to know where some of their neighbors (or their own grandparents) came from or what forces pushed them across the sea to this small island where they put down new roots. In this, we are all more insular than we should be.

Scandinavian, Dutch, and Latvian fishermen have not yet been recognized in Nantucket's public history, nor have Armenian rug merchants, Greek grocers, or Jewish restaurateurs. Even so, Nantucketers born in the twentieth century grew up with all of these and more. The current surge of East Europeans, Central Americans, and Southeast Asians finding employment on Nantucket comes on top of centuries of international migration to the island. Here are some of their stories.

Spinner Collection

CHAPTER SEVEN

From the Far Antipodes

China

Forty years after the last execution on Nantucket, there was another death by hanging on the island. It happened in 1809—the same year that a desperately displaced Native Hawaiian boy is said to have been found weeping in desolation on the Yale University campus. That year a Chinese man known as Quak Te, thinking himself abandoned on Nantucket, succumbed to despair and took his own life.

In consideration of the fact that "Quak Te, of Nantucket, a Black man deceased, having while he lived, and at the time of his decease, Goods, Chattels, Rights, or Credits in the county aforesaid, lately died intestate," Judge of Probate Isaac Coffin ordered an inventory of what had been found in his room. The inventory identified Quak Te as a mariner and placed a total value of $72.67 on his belongings, $41.60 of this being in cash held by the deceased. He was also in possession of a sleeping bag and a very large wardrobe. Among the clothes listed in the inventory were four pairs of "Nankeen trousers" and three "Nankeen jackets," a "China coat" and a pair of black pantaloons, three waistcoats, a greatcoat, and more. This was not what would be found in the sea chest of an ordinary seaman.

Who was poor Quak Te, and how had he come to such a sad end on a November day in Nantucket?

In 1807, Chinese merchant Punqua Wingchong and his servant had come to Nantucket on the ship *Favorite*, a vessel owned by a consortium of Nantucket ship owners. Among the Nantucketers entertaining Punqua Wingchong was Keziah (Coffin) Fanning, who described her guest as "a Chinaman that came with Mr. Whitney last fall from Canton. He is a merchant there. He is the color of our native whites."

Relations between the United States and England had been deteriorating, and while Punqua Wingchong and his servant were visiting Nantucket, President Thomas Jefferson imposed a foreign trade embargo that blocked them from returning to Canton. After a long, frustrating stay on Nantucket, the merchant traveled to New York to appeal to John Jacob Astor to help him get home. Astor prevailed upon President Jefferson to allow a ship with cargo to sail for Canton in the summer of 1808, and Punqua Wingchong took passage home aboard her.

But what about Punqua Wingchong's servant? Apparently he was left behind on Nantucket to look out for his master's wardrobe until his return. That return was long delayed, however. It was only after the War of 1812 that Punqua Wingchong returned to the island, not once, but twice. On his second visit, in 1818, he stayed with Betsey Cary, and left his name in her lodging book.

It was all too late for Quak Te. He had waited for his master for over a year, frugally rationing out the cash he had been left for board and lodging. Then, as late autumn darkness enshrouded a Quaker town apprehensive of war, Quak Te had found his abandonment on Nantucket unendurable and made his exit by hanging himself in his rented room.

Decades passed after Punqua Wingchong's stay at Betsey Cary's lodging house before any Chinese again resided on the island. With the end of the China trade and the collapse of Nantucket whaling, there was no reason to come. But as Nantucket became a summering place for well-to-do city dwellers, demand for services of all sorts arose. The summer people required others to do their cooking, gardening, caddying, housekeeping, and laundry. Nantucket's Azorean, Cape Verdean, and African-American families assumed these services, but there remained, nonetheless, a niche for Chinese laundrymen.

The aging Chinese men who hand-washed and pressed the clothing and household linens of the nation's well-to-do had been brought to the United States as contract workers to lay railroad tracks from coast to coast. Through their labor an overland alternative to the long voyage by ship came into being, and wooden ships—many from Nantucket—were abandoned to rot in west-coast harbors. In a sense, the Chinese laborers, having done their part, were left to rot as well.

The snowballing volume of Chinese immigration and the decrepit conditions of the urban Chinatowns that sprang up around the country alarmed United States voters and lawmakers, and in 1882 the Chinese Exclusion Act was passed, cutting off further immigration. Chinese men in the United States were prevented from bringing their wives and children to join them, and—having sent most of their earnings back to China—they did not have the means to go home. As a result, the populations of Chinatowns remained overwhelmingly male (twenty-seven men for every Chinese woman in 1890, still four men for every woman in 1930). The two sources of employment for stranded Chinese men were laundries and restaurants. Because they required less initial investment, laundries became ubiquitous.

In 1900, the Chinese laundry on Nantucket's Main Street was operated by two men who had come to the United States a decade before the passage of the Chinese Exclusion Act. Middle-aged Lee Wah and his elderly employee Han Leung lived on the premises, washing and ironing day and night. Ten years later they had passed on the business to a younger man, Charles Leung, who had arrived in the country just a year before Chinese immigration was stopped. Until 1919 Leung operated the Canton Laundry in the building presently occupied by Murray's Liquor Store. In the spring of 1920, Henry and Mabel Rosen expanded their housewares store to occupy the whole building, and Leung moved his business up the street.

CHINESE FOOD
At NO. 4 MAIN STREET
Carry out
Monday, Thursday and Saturday
FRIED CHICKEN
And CHOP SUEY
dec 10-3mos.

Inquirer and Mirror, December 10, 1938.

By 1930 the Chinese laundry had moved to a rented building at the foot of Main Street, now operated by Hot Chin and Harry Der. They told the census enumerator that both of them had been born in California of Chinese parents about a decade after the Chinese Exclusion Act came into force. Eight years later the Canton Laundry was being run by Wing Gee Der and Wing Jaa, who were also offering take-out Chinese food three evenings a week. With them was Wing Gee Der's son, Ning Der, who had arrived a year earlier from Canton and been enrolled in the Academy Hill School. Legislation in the 1930s had finally permitted limited immigration from China to resume, reuniting separated family members.

At the age of fifteen Ning Der was placed in the second-grade classroom at the Academy Hill School. By the fall of 1938—having been tutored in English by the pastor of Nantucket's Summer Street Baptist Church, the Reverend N. Bradford Rogers, and by Mrs. Rogers—he had advanced to the fifth grade, and from there he moved at the normal rate of one class a year through his sophomore year in high school.

At the time, woodworking classes for boys were held at the Coffin School. During a class change that involved going from one school to the other, Ning Der suffered a potentially catastrophic injury described in a news story headlined, "Nantucket's Chinese Boy 'Ning' Will Not Lose His Eyesight:"

An unfortunate accident occurred on Monday afternoon when Ning Der, the popular little Chinese youth, was struck in the right eye by a wooden disk, thrown by a careless boy. The accident occurred while a class was en route between the Coffin School and Academy Hill school. The wooden disc, scaled through the air, shot off at an angle and struck Ning Der squarely in the eye.

For a time it was thought that the youth would lose the eye. Dr. George A. Folger, School Physician, after an examination at the Hospital, 'phoned an eye specialist in Boston, making arrangements for Ning's transfer to the Memorial Hospital in that city. On Tuesday, the injured boy was placed in a police car, which had been detailed to rush him to Boston. As soon as the boat reached Woods Hole, the car sped over the roads with Officer Wendell Howes at the wheel.

The latest information received indicates that Ning's eyesight will be saved. This is cheering news, as the alert little Chinese boy has been virtually adopted by Nantucketers, and his happy personality and never-failing courtesy have attracted the attention of summer visitors, also. His father, Gee Der Wing, operates the Canton Laundry, at the foot of Main Street.

Despite the description of him as a "little" boy, Ning Der was in his teens at the time. His classmates recall him as a slight, graceful boy who enjoyed playing basketball at Bennett Hall. They also recall his engaging personality.

While in the Nantucket public schools Ning Der constructed a model of Nantucket's Unitarian Church. Completed in 1939, when its maker was seventeen years old, the large model with its turkey-egg dome was stored out of sight for many years but is now exhibited in the rear of the church itself. The informational text with it quotes one of his teachers as saying, "Ning was never satisfied with halfway measures. He went to the church and recorded its dimensions; he counted the rows of shingles in the walls and the number of shingles in a row; he counted the panes in the windows." His translation of these meticulous observations into a precise scale model produced a community treasure.

Ning Der and his model of the Unitarian Church.

In 1942, as World War II raged, Wing Gee Der found his own opportunity to serve the community. In late May of that year forty-two men were rescued on the open sea south of the island. Their vessel, the S.S. *Poseidon*, had been torpedoed by a German submarine in the vicinity of Bermuda, and they had drifted in two lifeboats all the way to Nantucket. Nantucket boatsmen—recently recruited as a civil patrol—brought them ashore. Upon landing, the men were taken to Bennett Hall, which functioned not only as a basketball court, but also as a community meeting hall and emergency shelter. Of the forty-two rescued crewmen, thirteen were Chinese, and Wing Gee Der was called upon to serve as their interpreter.

1943–44 was the last school year Ning Der was registered in Nantucket High School. By then the grandfather of the little three-generation family was in failing health, and they gave up the Canton Laundry in Nantucket to move to Boston's Tremont Street. Gradually other members of the family—Ning Der's mother and a brother and sister—arrived from Canton and Hong Kong to join them. Ning Der found wartime work in Boston as a radio engineer and married Ada Clark, a young woman he met through his former English tutors, the Reverend and Mrs. Rogers. After the war the couple moved to Bernardston, Massachusetts, where Ning Der was employed as custodian at two public schools until an accident in 1968 took his life at age 47.

If Ning Der had stayed with his Nantucket High School class, he would have been twenty-three years old at graduation. After his departure the Nantucket schools saw no more Chinese children for quite a while.

India

The entrepreneurial Porte family was descended from Calcutta-born William Porte, who came to Nantucket as a seaman and later was employed as a cook on the steamboats serving the island. Classified as "black" in the 1850 census, he had married the widow Christina Newell, whose parents—Ezekiel Pompey and Lydia (Corrington)

Pompey—had been scions of Nantucket's original New Guinea families. By 1850 William and Christina Porte had acquired real estate of substantial value and were taking in boarders. They were also two of the thirty charter members of the Pleasant Street Baptist Church, a reorganization of the African Baptist Society under the recently arrived Reverend James Crawford. In 1852 William Porte took over as church clerk.

Death carried off the men and boys in the family, leaving the women on their own. "Our little brother" Crawford Porte died as an infant in 1860, the first to be laid to rest in the family plot. Two years later Louis Philippe Newell, Christina's son by her first marriage, died six months short of his twentieth birthday and was buried next to Crawford. His half brother, William Porte Jr., succumbed to tuberculosis at age twenty-three and was buried beside Louis Philippe. William Porte Sr. himself only lived to the age of fifty-three.

After William Sr.'s death in 1866, Lydia moved in with Christina and her surviving children and lived with them until her death in 1880. She had been born in 1797, and in her life had witnessed the rise and the decline of Nantucket's original African community. Her daughter Christina Porte lived on until 1895, and in the last year of her life was photographed in front of the family house on Atlantic Avenue.

The business sense of the Portes passed on to William's and Christina's daughters. Ellen, Emma, and Ida Porte advertised themselves as coatmakers, dressmakers, and "tailoresses." In time Ida became a chiropodist, and the unmarried women were joint owners and operators of a beauty shop.

There was another Porte daughter. Philena "Lena" Porte, the eldest, was mother of three children—Lottie, Christine, and Lincoln. Lena was unmarried and, unlike her business-minded younger sisters, she had no stated occupation. She and her children lived with her mother just past Five Corners, where Pleasant Street bisects the old New Guinea neighborhood, and she is thought to have worked as a domestic servant in the opulent Hadwen House at the other end of Pleasant Street, at the corner of Main Street—then and now the most elegant address in town.

The 1900 census lists the birthplace of Christine's and Lincoln's father as "unknown." By then their grandmother Christina had died, Lena and Lottie were missing from the census, and young Christine and Lincoln were living with their aunts. There are no headstones for Lena and Lottie in the family plot, so it would appear that they had left the island, never to return.

Following her aunts' example, Christine remained unmarried and was employed early on as a housekeeper and store clerk, later as a physician's bookkeeper. At age 21 Lincoln Porte went to work for the post office, retiring after forty years of service interrupted only by World War I.

Over the years, a reclassification of the Portes took place, demonstrating to what extent race has been a social construct in Nantucket as everywhere else. To begin with, not only was Christina Porte, descendant of African slaves, considered black, but so was her Calcutta-born husband. For

that matter, the people boarding in their New Guinea household were all classified as black, too. Nonetheless, in 1870 the Portes' five surviving children were all considered "mulatto," according to the federal census of that year. Ten years later Lena, Ellen, and Emma Porte were classified as black once again, while their sister Ida remained classified as mulatto, and Lena's daughter Lottie was classified as white. Coming forward to 1920, the census enumerator of that year overwrote what appears to be IN (for "Indian") with W for all the surviving Portes. Ten years later, Lincoln Porte was considered unambiguously white for the purposes of the federal census, and so he remained until his death at age 86.

As the Porte women died—Ellen in 1912 at age fifty-nine, Christine in 1935 at age fifty-three, Emma in 1949 at age ninety-three, and Ida in 1961 at age ninety-eight—they were buried with their family members in the "colored" cemetery behind Mill Hill. Only Lincoln, who as a young man had moved away from the New Guinea neighbor-

Christina Porte in front of the Porte family's house at 5 Atlantic Avenue circa 1895.

Nantucket Historical Association

hood and bought a house on Lowell Place, lies elsewhere, buried with his Irish-American wife in Prospect Hill Cemetery.

When Lincoln Porte married the widow Ellen Snell, he adopted her young son George. George Snell's children recall Lincoln Porte as a kind grandfather, perhaps doting all the more on his grandchildren because he himself had been motherless by the time he was six years old and fatherless all his life. Because of the pall of illegitimacy that he still perceived as hanging over him, he stipulated in his will that his funeral should not be public.

Apparently it was the stigma of birth out of wedlock rather than of race that caused Lincoln Porte to avoid publicity. His wife was reportedly discomfited by the very existence of his aunts and sister, but his adopted son and grandchildren took it in stride that he came from a black family. With their profound genealogical preoccupation, descended Nantucketers—Sarah P. Bunker's great-granddaughter among them—shared the knowledge and considered it a curiosity. People who knew Lincoln Porte at work or through the many men's social and service organizations to which he belonged never thought of this grandson of an African Nantucketer and a mariner from India as anything but white.

The Philippines

As early as the 1860s crewmen aboard the South Shoals Lightship passed their time weaving baskets. A distinctive style evolved that apparently owed much to the craft of coopers, whose barrel- and cask-making techniques were adapted for creating sturdy baskets with staves, hoops, and wooden bottoms. These baskets were both esthetically pleasing and nearly indestructible. They ranged from diminutive single-egg baskets to capacious laundry baskets, and there was considerable latitude for inventiveness in form and materials. Handles varied with size and intended use. Sewing baskets sometimes had wooden or woven lids.

When they left the lightship, men brought their basket molds, tools, and talents home and continued the craft on land. In the latter half of the nineteenth century, as Nantucket was shifting from a maritime economy to summer tourism,

Employees of the Nantucket Post Office in 1925. Lincoln Porte is third from right, seated behind a pile of mail.

Courtesy of the Mack family

lightship baskets—selling for a few dollars apiece—became an item in curio shops, especially those on or adjacent to Centre Street's "Petticoat Row."[2]

Nantucket's basket makers were men—mostly retired mariners or their sons and grandsons—but artist Elizabeth Rebecca "Lizzie" Coffin, one of the guiding lights in the redirection of Nantucket's Coffin School, sought to open the craft to women. In 1895 a girls club named the Goldenrod Literary and Debating Society had been founded on the island. In 1903 Lizzie Coffin secured financial support from the town to offer a basketry course for members of the Goldenrod Society, and she herself took winter lessons in making the classic rattan baskets.

Founded in 1827 to provide private education and nautical training to the sons of the descended Nantucketers, the Coffin School had run out of students and exhausted its endowment by the end of the century, and it closed in 1898. Lizzie Coffin formulated a new industrial purpose and coeducational curriculum for the institution, which reopened in 1903 as an adjunct to the Nantucket public schools. The new Coffin School offered day and evening classes in mechanical drawing, woodworking, and metalworking for boys and men, sewing for girls, and basketry for women. Over the winter of 1904-05, Nantucket women working with a woman instructor produced over 150 baskets—not only rattan lightship baskets, but some made from local materials, including beach grass, and with a variety of weaving and decorating techniques. Most of the baskets were sold the following summer. Coffin believed that this was the beginning of a rising new cottage industry that would ensure income to Nantucket women, but after that first year nothing more seems to have come of it. All the renowned basket makers whose names and products later became so important to collectors continued to be local men. Despite Lizzie Coffin's optimism, significant change in the traditional basket business would

not come until after World War II with the arrival on-island of the Reyes family.

José Formoso Reyes was born in 1902 in the rural northwest of the Philippine island of Luzon. Like most Filipinos, his parents were of mixed heritage: Malayan, Chinese, and Spanish. The education of both his parents was limited to what was available locally, but his self-educated father's devotion to Bible studies had led him well beyond the school basics.

In their small town José faced the same educational limitations that his parents had. At best it was possible to go as far as the second year of high school. There was no way to acquire professional training without leaving home.

Born in the first years of United States colonial rule in the Philippines, José Reyes made his way out into the greater world. At age twenty-two he was able to go to Portland, Oregon, where he graduated from high school and was admitted to Reed College to prepare for a teaching career. Reed's first Asian graduate, he received a scholarship for further education, which he applied to a master's degree program at the Harvard School of Education, completing his studies in 1932.

During his college years, he had met Mary Elizabeth "Betty" Ham, daughter of a Yankee family relocated to the Pacific Northwest. Her family returned to New England after Betty's sophomore year at Reed, but with José's arrival in Cambridge, Massachusetts, the young couple reunited and married. After receiving his master's degree, José returned to the Philippines seeking a teaching position. Betty soon followed her husband, and their children were born in the Philippines.

The years of the Reyes children's births coincided with the transition of the Philippines from a colony under American civilian governors to a commonwealth with its own constitution and democratically elected Filipino president. But these heady times in which men like José Reyes could help build their country's infrastructure were gravely endangered.

2. Late-nineteenth-century newspaper advertisements for and photographs of shops offering "rattan baskets" or "lightship baskets" include Mrs. Folger's Shell Shop; Phoebe Clisby's Shop; and Jacob Abajian's Oriental Bazaar on Petticoat Row. Chenoweth's Ye Olde Curiosity Shoppe just around the corner also offered them for sale.

José Reyes in his workshop in the 1950s.

Life on Nantucket was not to be easy, however. In a cold climate money was needed for heating oil as well as electricity and running water. The garden could not feed the family through the long winters, and the growing children had many needs.

With a master's degree from the Harvard School of Education and years of teaching experience in the Philippines, José had reason to expect that he would be hired to teach in Nantucket High School. Instead, he found himself working as a house painter, while Betty and the children picked berries and made jams and jellies to sell. José returned alone to the Philippines for over a year to settle matters there. During his absence and for years after, Betty—who was a registered nurse—worked shifts at the Nantucket Cottage Hospital while caring for the family. Their daughter Francina went to work early to help out and to earn money to pay for her own nurse's training.

The experience of immigrants leaving behind professional careers to work at low-paying unskilled jobs in the United States is nothing new and continues unabated, but it is a situation that everyone seeks to escape as quickly as possible. With teaching not an option, José Reyes turned to basket weaving, a craft with which he was familiar from his childhood in rural Ilocos Sur. Mentored by aging Nantucket basketmaker Mitchell Ray, José set to making his own rattan baskets. Adding experimental covers and lids to baskets of various shapes, he created women's handbags. The handbag design that proved unimaginably commercial had a lid that replicated the construction of the bottom of the basket, with weaving radiating out from a central disk.

It was probably because of the decorations on the lids—simple ebony or ivory whales on wood to begin with and then ever more personalized plaques and carvings—that the handbags became first a fad and then an industry involving the whole Reyes family. Waiting lists for custom-made baskets grew from months-long to years-long. New sizes and shapes appeared with ivory fittings, while lid decorations became ever more elaborate. A collector's trade in Reyes baskets developed, and the rest is history.

In 1942 Japanese forces occupied the Philippines, and the United States Army withdrew. José, who had fought with the Philippine Scouts in the holding battles against the Japanese on the Bataan Peninsula, managed to make his way home and move Betty and the children away from Manila. Nonetheless, the family barely survived a strafing attack and came close to starvation before General Douglas MacArthur was able to make good his promise to return and liberate the Philippines.

In 1945 the Reyes family arrived in the United States, and in time José was granted citizenship. While they were recovering from the trauma of their recent experience, Betty Reyes's mother arranged a Nantucket summer vacation for the family, and they decided to stay. After renting in various locations, they bought a house on the edge of the old New Guinea neighborhood. The York Street house was greatly in need of repair, but it was roomy and had a backyard with space for growing vegetables. The giant leaves of Betty's rhubarb patch resembled a piece of Philippine jungle transplanted to New England.

Baskets engaged and rewarded the Reyes family in a way that high-school teaching never could have. Moreover, the popularity of the Reyes baskets as status symbols and collector's pieces has incubated an islandwide basket-making industry of just the sort Lizzie Coffin had imagined so many years before. In the year 2000 there were dozens of men and women making baskets for sale in shops and many more Nantucketers making them as a hobby. Spin-off industries are the crafting of fittings and decorations for basket lids and the weaving of tiny golden baskets to be incorporated into jewelry. In all their forms, the baskets have become so sought after and so high-priced that imitations have flooded gift shops on-island and off, and a guild, the Nantucket Lightship Basket Makers and Merchants Association, has been formed to authenticate genuine Nantucket-made baskets.

In his Nantucket life, José Reyes was an enthusiastic joiner. Although his father Eugenio had been a Methodist, José joined Nantucket's Congregational Church, where he belonged to the men's club and sang in the choir.[3] He was, moreover, a Rotarian and a 32nd degree Mason. He also worked with Cub Scouts and Boy Scouts on the island, and although he never taught in the Nantucket schools, he was active in the Parent/Teacher Association.

José Reyes died on Nantucket in December 1980. In 2001 Paul Reyes donated his father's workshop to the recently established Lightship Basket Museum, where it has been reassembled in the museum building on Union Street, just blocks from its original York Street home.

Thailand

Lightship baskets have figured in the highly diversified entrepreneurism of Chin Manasmontri, the founder and for some time the sole member of Nantucket's Thai community. Born in Bangkok in 1951, Chin grew up with disadvantages that have hobbled vast numbers of children in that place and time. His mother was Thai, but his father was Chinese, and throughout history ethnic Chinese in Southeast Asia have been the targets of much the same sort of prejudice that Jews have experienced in Europe and the Americas.

According to an interview he gave to *Nantucket Magazine* in 1994, Chin's father deserted the family while Chin was still a small child, and by age twelve he was a factory laborer contributing to the support of his family by working for pennies a day. In the Viet Nam war era, it was not difficult to find an opportunity. As a young man working as an agent for an Air Force officer who sought to set up an export business on the side, Chin made himself so indispensable that his employer sent him to the United States to attend school and improve his command of English. Chin made a visit to Nantucket with no expectation of staying, but two decades later he was still on the island. Sarah P. Bunker's great-granddaughter, a Nantucket restaurant proprietor, was one of his early supporters.

Beginning with landscaping and restaurant-kitchen work, Chin launched his own small business empire on the island, culminating in a restaurant/workshop/residence complex at the end of a street named Chin's Way. It was a unique place where one could in principle enjoy a meal with a bottle of Thai beer, buy a ready-made lightship basket, and have a chair reupholstered all at the same time.

To make the lightship baskets, carry on the upholstery business, and staff the restaurant, Chin brought members of his family from Thailand, nine of them in all, and another fourteen Thai workers to Nantucket. Like Chin, a number of his employees were children of ethnically mixed marriages who would have been stigmatized had they gone on living anywhere in Southeast Asia. Among the employees whose resettlement in Nantucket he sponsored, five were children of Thai mothers and American servicemen.

After a quarter of a century on the island Chin himself returned to Thailand, taking his capital and his business experience with him.

---

3. This is the same church that had once offered Sunday School instruction to young whalemen from the Pacific islands temporarily resident on Nantucket.

Lightship baskets had been one revenue source in Nantucket, but he had hit upon another craft, one that had remained unexploited for more than a century. Chin looked beyond baskets and saw sailors' valentines as the next compelling item for collectors of Nantucketiana.

Sailors' valentines are boxed arrangements of shells that returning seamen brought home to Nantucket as gifts for mothers, sisters, wives, and prospective brides. At least one has made its way into the permanent collection of the Nantucket Historical Association. Contrary to local lore, seamen did not personally collect shells in the course of their voyages and pass shipboard hours assembling them into elaborate representations of floral bouquets. In the nineteenth century, sailors' valentines were made by residents of Barbados, Trinidad, and St. Lucia for sale to men aboard ships stopping at their islands.

Today, newly crafted sailors' valentines are ubiquitous in Nantucket shops and galleries, and a good proportion of them bear Chin's signature. They are now produced in Bangkok and exported to Nantucket, where they represent the latest of his far-flung enterprises.

For several years after his arrival in Nantucket, Chin and his extended family were the only Thai residents of the island, but by the time he returned to his native land, about ten other families had established themselves on the island and founded a cluster of Thai businesses. One of them, the Lucky Express convenience store, is locally famous for its record of selling winning lottery tickets to Nantucketers.

Nantucket's New Year's baby of 1995 was Wisima Samantha Nipatnantaporn, daughter of Thai residents of the island who found their own way to Nantucket. Patama Thairatana, Samantha's mother, came to Nantucket for a summer job after graduating from college in Houston, Texas, in 1987. Her intention was to use her earnings for a plane ticket home to Thailand, but instead she became a year-round resident. Six years later she and Viroj Nipatnantaporn had a business together and started a Nantucket family of their own.

Japan

In the 1890s the village of Siasconset became home to what was known as "the Actors' Colony." Fleeing from the summer heat of New York City, theater folk took refuge in the oceanside village that Edward Underhill, its most indefatigable developer and promoter, advertised as ever cool and salubrious. ("'Sconset has the coolest and purest air…'Sconset has no noise; no mosquitoes; no malaria.") In a 1904 photo album of the village and its exotic residents, a man in a white jacket identified only as "Japanese servant" appears twice, once lighting a cigarette for playwright Harry Woodruff and again serving tea to Woodruff and his guests. This unnamed man probably traveled to the island with the Woodruffs for some weeks in the summer and returned with them to the city for the fall season.

Most of a century passed before Nantucket gained a Japanese-born year-round resident with a name known to all. In 1993, years after Chin Manasmontri had introduced Nantucketers to Thai food, Yoshi Mabuchi added sushi to the island's cuisine. When Yoshi and his partner came to Nantucket, they already had a dozen years of experience operating a restaurant in eastern Connecticut, which—like Nantucket—had been without a Japanese restaurant until they opened theirs in New Haven.

Yoshi was born into wartime Japan in 1943, and like the Reyes family on the other side in World War II, his family came close to starvation during the war and in the immediate postwar years. In time, Yoshi, the youngest in the family, attended high school in Tokyo and then earned a degree in mathematics from Tokyo Science University.

To broaden his horizons Yoshi set out working his way around the world, finding short-term jobs in many places, some of them profoundly inhospitable to itinerant labor. Worldwide, one of the most likely places for an alien to find work has always been in restaurant kitchens, and by the time Yoshi, at the age of thirty-three, ended up in New York City, he was a skilled restaurant worker. In the course of less than a decade

Sushi by Yoshi has become a Nantucket institution—available in his tiny establishment across from the police station, by catering and take-out, and even from the supermarket. As a dedicated church member and supporter of local organizations, Yoshi has contributed to his adopted community in ways far beyond the culinary.

Growing up Asian on Nantucket

The new century has witnessed a phenomenon in the United States, the adoption of Chinese babies by American families. Prior to 1990 the number of adoptions from China was under fifty per year for the entire nation. By the year 2000, the annual number of adoptions from China had reached above five thousand, and virtually all the adoptees have been girls. In just a few years they have formed a cohort numbering over thirty thousand (and continuing to increase) who will move through the nation's schools together, become teenagers together, be targeted as a group by advertisers, and enter the United States job market in a wave. Nantucket will take part in this social experiment. On October 21, 1999, a headline in the *Inquirer and Mirror* read: "Adopting a new way of life: Nantucket parents hoping to adopt are looking to China." At that time four Chinese girls had already been adopted by families living on Nantucket, and there was the prospect of more.

These girls' experience will be different from Ning Der's. He was the only Chinese boy in town, living in a family of Chinese men. The island's newest Chinese residents live in non-Chinese families, but they will see each other every day at school. They will be integrated into the Nantucket community as no Chinese has been ever before in the island's history, and at the same time they will have the advantage of strength in numbers.

Besides one another, they will see children who resemble them more than the adoptees resemble their parents and most of their classmates. The 1999 article about Chinese adoptions on Nantucket mentioned that a Cambodian child was expected to arrive soon. Nantucket's Thai children, some of them already in school ahead of the Cambodian

and Chinese adoptees, are growing up in Thai families resident on-island. As languages, Chinese, Cambodian, and Thai are as unlike as can be, and the nations can hardly be said to share a common history or culture, yet as Nantucket's Asian children pass through the public schools, they will appear to most Nantucketers to constitute an identifiable, unitary group.

The children of José and Betty Reyes grew up with a Filipino father and an American mother, first in desperate wartime circumstances in the Philippines and then in a Nantucket household. Nantucketers found the Reyes children exotic and would not let it pass unremarked. In a booklet about José Reyes and his basket business, Paul Whitten wrote, "The Oriental features are quite prominent in Jose's charming and attractive daughter, Francina." Of her brothers, Whitten wrote, "The Reyes boys with their Filipino coloration and American features, along with their stalwart athletic physiques, have grown into handsome young gentlemen." Francina married one of Sarah P. Bunker's great-great-grandsons, and of their daughter Whitten observed that she "has absorbed just enough of her Filipino and American ancestry to mold her features into a beautiful doll-like child." The stereotypes of the beautiful doll and the warrior-athlete have been and remain a burden for Asian-American children. Such perceptions on the part of Nantucketers in the past imposed unwelcome self-consciousness on the Reyes children and grandchildren, and may yet prove troublesome for a new generation of children growing up on the island.

Over the years there have been, in fact, several different Asian-Nantucket childhood experiences: Ning Der as the sole Chinese student in school but living in a Chinese household; the Reyes children living in a bicultural household; Nantucket's Thai children growing up in Thai homes and going to school with other Asian children; and adopted Chinese and Cambodian children growing up in non-Asian families but seeing other Asian children in school each day. Once again, as throughout the island's history, who is a Nantucketer is being redefined.

CHAPTER EIGHT

A Song Across the Sea

Jewish Presence on Nantucket

Nantucket and Newport, Rhode Island, have a long-shared history of maritime contacts and Quakerism. It was from the New England Yearly Meeting of the Religious Society of Friends in Newport that Nantucketer Elihu Coleman had to seek approval to publish his momentous condemnation of slavery in 1733. Permission was granted even though some Newport Friends owned slaves and profited from the transatlantic slave trade. Nantucket Quakers and their Newport brethren continued at odds over slavery for decades.

Nantucket differed from Newport in another conspicuous way. A prominent feature of Newport is its Jewish cemetery and Touro Synagogue, the oldest synagogue in the United States. Newport has been the home of a Jewish community since 1658.

By contrast, from its inception in 1659 until the time of the American Revolution, Nantucket remained a closed community managed by a corporation of proprietors who struggled to prevent nonshareholders from establishing themselves on the island. Throughout the 1700s the town's selectmen expelled groups of newcomers who attempted to settle and set up businesses on-island without permission. The dominance of Quakerism on Nantucket, with its members' intent to keep apart from the world's people, strengthened the resolve of the island community to exclude "strangers."

In June 1870, Dr. John Givon, a physician born in Germany, was living on the island with his wife Mahalia, who had been born in Georgia, and their two New York-born daughters. The name Givon, which is ultimately derived from an Arabic word for 'hill,' is used as both a surname and a given name in Jewish families. At the time of the census, the Givon family was living with an elderly Nantucket couple, Zenas and Lydia Fish, who were

Newport's Touro Synagogue was dedicated in 1763, the year of Nantucket's "Indian sickness."

National Archives

also providing housing for the principal of the Coffin School, Edward B. Fox. According to the census, Josephine Givon, 16, and Felicia Givon, 10, had not attended school during the past year, implying that the family had either just arrived on the island or that they employed a private tutor for the girls. The Givons' substantial wealth, as recorded in the census, would have made for an especially comfortable life on economically depressed Nantucket, but the family does not appear in subsequent censuses.

There is no certain record of Jewish presence on Nantucket until the 1880 federal census. In that year Wendel Rothenberg—a Russian-born dry-goods merchant—was living in the Springfield House hotel. The 1890 federal census returns were destroyed in an archive fire, but Nantucket's Coffin School records for 1893–94 show young Israel Rothenberg enrolled as a student, indicating that Wendel brought his family to Nantucket and stayed for more than a decade.

By 1900 the Rothenbergs had moved on, but German-born Max and Annie Pearlstine had come with their two Massachusetts-born children to live on Nantucket. Max Pearlstine had been in the United States since 1883, but he was illiterate and had not taken any steps toward becoming a citizen. His wife Annie could read and write, however, and their children were in school. The census taker reported Max's occupation as junk dealer, a business that was undoubtedly far from lucrative for nine out of twelve months a year. By the time of the 1910 census the Pearlstines, too, had departed.

In the meantime Max Doroff, born in Odessa, Russia, had come to the island. Identified in the 1910 census as "Yiddish," he had arrived in the United States as a child in the mid-1880s and been naturalized a decade later. He found a wife in Maine, and the two of them came to Nantucket to live in rented quarters and to work. To begin with, Max Doroff did odd jobs while his wife Isabelle cooked for a family, but in the 1914 and 1919

SPECIAL NOTICE!
After April 1st the Store now occupied by the Chinese Laundry will be opened with a full line of
CROCKERY,   DISHES,   GLASSWARE,   KITCHEN WARE,   TIN WARE and FURNITURE.
WATCH PRICES COME DOWN.
ROSEN'S
Postoffice Square   Nantucket, Mass.
Where you always get bargains.

– Nantucket Historical Association

Advertisement for the opening of Rosen's store, replacing a Chinese laundry. Inquirer and Mirror, April 24, 1920.

Nantucket business directories his occupation was listed as "bootblack." So it was in the 1920 federal census, and so it remained. Despite appearing in the 1927 Nantucket business directory as proprietor of a shoe store, when Max Doroff died in Nantucket in 1950 at the age of 75, his "usual occupation" was still given as bootblack.

In the decade after the 1910 census the Doroffs had been joined on the island by Henry and Mabel Rosen from Poland and by Russian-born Emile Genesky.[1] The Rosens had both come to the United States as children in 1889 and had been naturalized in 1915. They had two Massachusetts-born children, and—like Wendel Rothenberg before him—Henry Rosen supported the family as a merchant. In 1914 he operated a clothing store on the corner of Main Street and South Water Street, and by 1919 he was also proprietor of a gro-

---

1. Despite the census information that the Rosens had come from Poland and Emile Genesky's family from Russia, their old-country origins were not so far apart. The Geneskys came from Yanaveh, a town located in the vicinity of the city of Minsk in Belarus [western or "White" Russia] not far from the Polish border.

cery store on Middle Pearl (India) Street. On April 24, 1920, the *Inquirer and Mirror* ran an advertisement announcing the opening of his store on "Postoffice Square" (Lower Main Street) offering "a full line of crockery, dishes, glassware, kitchen ware, tin ware, and furniture" in "the Store now occupied by the Chinese Laundry." Rosen had taken out a mortgage for the Main Street property, but by 1930 the family had moved off-island.

Emile Genesky, on the other hand, became an enduring player in the Nantucket business community. According to the *Inquirer and Mirror*, the Geneskys were "a pioneer Jewish family in New Bedford" where they had prospered in the clothing business, were involved in the founding of a synagogue, and belonged to "every Jewish organization in the city." Expanding the family business to Nantucket in 1908, Philip Genesky, founded the City Clothing Company ("Men's Clothing and Furnishings") on Main Street, and put his son Emile in place as proprietor, assisted by James Genesky as clerk. Emile and James lived together initially, and then Emile was on his own to run the Nantucket store.

On March 4, 1916, an emergency notice appeared on the front page of the *Inquirer and Mirror* that the City Clothing Company was being forced to vacate because the building it occupied was to be torn down within a few days. The following week Emile Genesky placed another notice that the business would move to temporary quarters in a recently vacated store on Centre Street's Petticoat Row. Most of that March 11 issue of the *Inquirer and Mirror* was given over to reports of a tremendous snowfall that had paralyzed the town. Before Genesky had even opened the door at his new location, one dyspeptic newspaper article declared the inadequate snow removal along Petticoat Row a disgrace and blamed it on "the foreign element" that had moved onto the block. Three months later, the writer of an ambivalent article listing the openings of the summer businesses remarked, "Verily Petticoat Row is becoming almost a Midway. It is certainly an attraction from one point of view." Since Armenian rug merchants Jacob Abajian and Vartan Dedeian were already established on Petticoat Row before the great snow storm of 1916, it is unclear which foreign element the newspaper writers intended to criticize.

These newspaper articles coming on the heels of an apparently unforeseen eviction from Main Street oozed hostility toward foreign-born businessmen, but Emile Genesky forged ahead. His March 11

Petticoat Row looking north from Main Street.

Emile Genesky's Toggery Shop at 62-64 Main Street (left) in the mid 1920s. — Nantucket Historical Association

notice in the *Inquirer and Mirror* mentioned that the Centre Street location would be temporary until a new building was ready for occupancy, and that promise was repeated in advertising throughout April. The new premises went up on the site of the building that had been demolished, and when his business reopened at 62-64 Main Street to an enthusiastic reception by the *Inquirer and Mirror*, it had a tonier new name, the Toggery Shop.

Brought to the United States from Russia as an infant, Emile Genesky had still not taken the final steps to becoming a citizen when, in February 1918, he was elected to the Nantucket board of selectmen and a few months later was appointed Special Justice of the newly created Nantucket District Court. Genesky served a term on the board of selectmen while making a place for himself among Nantucket's businessmen. In 1924 the *Inquirer and Mirror* wrote of him, "Since coming to Nantucket and engaging in business a number of years ago, he has been eminently successful and enjoys the respect of the entire community."

The former Hicksite Quaker Meeting House on Main Street had been moved in 1884 to Brant Point and incorporated into a sprawling wooden hotel. In 1905 the Wauwinet Tribe of Red Men, a fraternal organization that was very popular on Nantucket, bought the large building, had it rafted back across the harbor, and re-sited it on South Water Street to serve as a lodge room, dance hall, and moving-picture theater. After some years the movie operation, under the name Dreamland Moving Picture Theatre, was taken over by a partnership of Emile Genesky, John Anastos, Orison Hull, and Eugene Perry. According to their obituaries, all the partners took enthusiastic interest in the enterprise.

Opportunities for expansion continued to present themselves. Having replaced an old building between Orange Street and Fair Street with a new one to house his Toggery Shop, Genesky entered into a partnership with the Anastos brothers in 1928 to build another commercial building on the south side of Main Street. One of the old wooden buildings razed for this project had once housed the Reverend James Crawford's barbershop. The partners went on to build houses on Easton Street and nearby Harbor View Way.

After his marriage in 1924, Genesky made New Bedford his primary residence, but he continued his business activities in Nantucket and maintained a summer residence on the Cliff until his death in 1957.

Immediately upon completion of his surgical training at Massachusetts General Hospital in 1927, Jacob Fine came to Nantucket to fill in temporarily for one of the island's physicians. His intended brief service on the island extended to more than three years, and thereafter Dr. Fine returned to practice on the island during the summer months for eleven more years. Late in life he wrote and circulated a manuscript in two parts: "The Nantucket Story" and "Nantucket Personalities." In "The Nantucket Story" he locates Emile Genesky's clothing store as "directly across from Ashley's Market on the other side of Main Street, corner of Fair Street," and states that Genesky was one of fewer than five Jews on the island. Unless Dr. Fine only counted adult men and did not include himself, he undercounted.

In 1930 the town had several Jewish clothing stores. The proprietor of one was Russia-born William Kaplan, a widower whose late wife had also been born in Russia. In rented quarters, first on South Water Street and then on North Liberty Street, he shared living space with three sons, Benjamin, Donald, and Oscar; his married daughter Shirley and her husband, Louis Jones; and a grandchild. Louis Jones's mother had also been born in Russia, which may have strengthened the ties that bound this multigeneration household. Benjamin Kaplan sold clothing in his father's store, while son-in-law Louis Jones was proprietor of a shoe store.

Morris Colinsky, born in Bialystok, Poland, also operated a clothing store, assisted by young Seymour Kaplan. Unlike Wendel Rothenberg, the Pearlstines, Max Doroff, the Rosens, the Geneskys, and William Kaplan—who had all arrived in the United States in the wave of immigration of the late 1800s—Morris Colinsky had come as an adult just before World War I, applied for citizenship without delay, and been naturalized. Seymour Kaplan (who was not one of the North Liberty Street Kaplans) had been born in Massachusetts, but his father came from Grodno, Russia, not far over the border from Bialystok.

Another Jewish family, the Bilskys, operated a dry cleaning business, Beacon Cleaners and Dyers, on Union Street next to the Town Building, and Rose Bilsky offered women's ready-to-wear apparel at the Roseby Shoppe on Main Street. Shortly after the 1930 census was taken, members of the Levine family, eventual operators of the Nobby Clothes Shop on Main Street, arrived.

Paul and Minnie Levine—not relatives of the Levines on Main Street—opened a shop at 44 Centre Street. Paul Levine had been born in Poland, and like many other young men, fled from conscription into the army. Making his way to England, he apprenticed as a tailor there. In Nantucket he advertised himself specifically as a ladies' tailor, but in the depths of the Depression he also sold ready-to-wear men's clothing. An advertisement of September 9, 1950, offered "Suits made to order on short notice." It is recalled that Paul Levine would take apart a suit overnight, make a pattern from the pieces, and reassemble it for return to the owner the next day. After his death in 1955 at the age of seventy, his wife Minnie maintained her ties with the island where they had lived and worked for twenty years.

A boating accident in the summer of 1934 nearly wiped out Nantucket's Jewish business community. William Kaplan, Morris Bilsky, Hyman Levine, Max Roy, and Jack Bernstein went bluefishing with Merwin Blount, Herbert Sandsbury, and James Dennis of Nantucket aboard Captain George Studley's boat *Northern Light*. In the opening between Smith's Point and Tuckernuck a wave broke over the *Northern Light*, washing everyone but Sandsbury and Studley overboard. Studley and Sandsbury managed to pick up six of the seven men in the water, but Dennis, a sixty-eight-year old fisherman, drowned.

Among the rescued men was Hyman Levine, one of nine children born to Nathan Levine and Nellie (Cohen) Levine. Nathan and Nellie had been born in the 1860s in Poland. In 1882 they married and immigrated to the United States, where Nathan Levine began his new life as a peddler with a horse-drawn cart on the streets of New York. From there he extended his operations both south and north. The first three Levine children were born in New York, the next four in Pennsylvania, and the last two in New Bedford. Several members of the next two generations of the family came to operate businesses on Nantucket: a clothing store, a gift shop, and an art gallery.

As a whaling town, Nantucket had an attraction for the Levine siblings. New Bedford whaling had continued into the 1920s, long after the last whaling voyage left from Nantucket. Through marriage the Levines were connected to a New Bedford haberdasher who outfitted whalemen with foul-weather gear and held a share in the last square-rigged whaleship, the *Charles W. Morgan*. When Nathan Levine disowned his son Israel for marrying outside Judaism, Israel changed his name to Morgan after the ship and passed the name on to his son. Young Morgan Levine in turn married the granddaughter of a New Bedford whaling captain and became a keen collector of maritime art.

It was through family connections to William Kaplan, another of the men who narrowly escaped with his life when the rogue wave washed over the *Northern Light* in 1934, that Simon and Rose Kaufman came to Nantucket to open the Green Coffee Pot Bar and Restaurant. Its first location was on India Street (on the block then called Middle Pearl Street), but in 1936 it moved to South Water Street where "Cy's" endured as a core Nantucket institution until 1978. Now operating as the Atlantic Café, it retains the Cy's sign on the

back of the building facing Easy Street. Murals in the dining room dating from the days of the Kaufmans have also been preserved.

According to Zelda (Kaufman) Zlotin, in the introduction to her cookbook, *Once More at Cy's*, her parents came to the island from Fall River with a $600 loan from Rose Kaufman's father, Frank Cohen. The Cohens had immigrated to the United States from Russia shortly after 1900, when Rose was a toddler, establishing themselves in Sioux City, Iowa. When Rose grew to young womanhood, she was sent to Fall River, Massachusetts, to what one of her family members has described as an arranged marriage to Simon Kaufman.

Simon's father Jacob Kaufman and his wife had immigrated to Fall River from Poland. Their four sons were born and educated in Fall River, where young Simon began to learn the restaurant business. When Frank Cohen advanced Simon and Rose the capital to open their own restaurant in the depths of the Depression era, they moved to Nantucket with their two daughters and infant son and went to work. As they grew, the children

Three stalwart businesses on South Water Street. Left-to-right the Dreamland Theatre, Cy's Green Coffee Pot, and Hardy's Paints, 1965.

were put to work at the Green Coffee Pot, as were relatives who came to help at the restaurant in the summers. In time, the next generation of Kaufmans worked there too. The extended family all lived at 9 Gay Street, where for years there were minimal kitchen facilities, because family members took all their meals at the restaurant.

Simon Kaufman, proprietor of Cy's Green Coffee Pot.

Gregarious Simon Kaufman was popular among his many customers, business associates, and friends. One of the passions of his life was his membership in the Wauwinet Tribe of Red Men, which had its meeting hall upstairs in the Dreamland Theatre, next door to the Green Coffee Pot.

The Kaufmans were also noted for the broad range of their charitable contributions to island organizations. It was a sorrow to his family and to Nantucketers beyond his family when Simon Kaufman suffered a stroke in his early sixties and died a few years later.

Rose Kaufman survived her husband by twenty-one years. For thirteen of those years their daughter and son-in-law, Zelda and Milton Zlotin, operated the restaurant and Rose managed the kitchen.

Eight years before Rose's death the Kaufman family corporation, which owned Cy's Green Coffee Pot, closed its doors and sold the business. To celebrate the restaurant's long life Zelda Zlotin collected her family's recipes, menus, and Green Coffee Pot memorabilia into *Once More at Cy's* and dedicated it to her family's next generation.

Turning the pages, one sees at a glance that the Kaufmans' restaurant was not a kosher establishment or even a classic delicatessen. Although the Green Coffee Pot advertised that its meals were "served with real rye bread," lobster and shellfish dominated the menu. Baked ham and broiled pork chops shared billing with roast lamb. At one time

take-out chop suey and chow mein were also on offer. To her recipe for matzo balls, Zelda attached the note, "I learned to make these after we retired."

The Kaufmans and the Zlotins, solid members of the Nantucket community, had to contend with being identified as Jews without having a Jewish community to support them. Members of the family were aware of low-level anti-Semitism that sometimes spiked into something more overt during the 1930s and again in the 1950s. Talk around the Green Coffee Pot's bar could turn ugly, and some people did not patronize the restaurant because the owners were Jews. But as Robert Kaufman, one of the Kaufmans' grandsons, remarked, "Certain people wouldn't come into the restaurant because of who the proprietors were, and other people didn't like the patrons. There were anti-Semites who didn't come in, but not everyone who didn't come in was an anti-Semite. That's the point I want to emphasize. Some people had some good reasons for not coming in."

As World War II engulfed Europe, Nantucketers were made aware of where virulent hatred of Jews could lead. In 1942 the Nantucket Chamber of Commerce hosted a talk by a former professor of philosophy at the University of Berlin who had been forced to leave Germany in the great flight from Nazism. Dr. Fine, who had become the secretary of a group of Boston physicians preparing to resettle refugees from Germany, wrote, "On the local scene I found that pleading the cause of these victims of Nazi cruelty did reach sympathetic ears among the natives as well as the visitors."

At war's end crude prewar anti-Semitism had been dealt a blow by the revelation of the horrors of the Holocaust, but another sort of anti-Semitism took its place on Nantucket as New York office workers, many of them Jewish, began taking summer vacations on the island. In 1957 Preston Manchester, operator of the Ocean House—a hotel that was popular with the young vacationers—and the Upper Deck—a bar on Main Street—threatened to put both his businesses on the market because of "the attitude of the townspeople of Nantucket towards Jews." At the same time the New England

Regional Office of the Anti-Defamation League of B'nai B'rith took an interest in the exclusion of Jews from some organizations on the island and the obstruction Jews were encountering in attempting to purchase houses on Nantucket.

Despite these problems, Jewish families became summer residents, and a number of businessmen and retirees took up year-round residence. Gradually, Nantucket's Jewish population grew. In 1951 Morgan Levine, who as a teenager had worked in his uncle Hyman's clothing store, opened the Four Winds Gift Shop upstairs over Nantucket's last blacksmith shop. The first Passover *seder* known to have been celebrated on the island took place in the home of Morgan and Sarah Levine.

In 1983 notices for a July Sabbath service in Grange Hall were posted, and a hundred and fifty people turned out. Two hundred attended Nantucket's first Rosh Hashanah service held that year in the Congregational Church. A rabbi from Boston University came to the island with his family for three winter months to teach lessons on Judaism and the Hebrew language. At last, a Jewish congregation was established on Nantucket, with Morgan Levine serving as its first president.

Today Congregation Shirat Ha Yam 'Song of the Sea' has a permanent home in the Unitarian Church and holds services from spring into mid-autumn. Its religious education classes have been supported by the sale of "Nantucket red" *yarmulkes* (skull caps) embroidered with whales and of scrimshaw *mezuzot* carved by artist David Lazarus, whom Morgan Levine promoted as the "yiddische scrimshanderer." For *Tashlich*, people gather at Brant Point Lighthouse to cast bread on the channel.[2]

When Simon and Rose Kaufman died on Nantucket, their bodies were returned for burial to Fall River, but today Nantucket, like Newport, has a Jewish cemetery.

But what of those Newport Jews of whaling days? The Polish, Russian, and German Jews who have lived on Nantucket in the past century were *Ashkenazim*, Eastern European Jews whose Yiddish language is an offshoot of German. They became part of the great general migration to the United States and Canada that began in the late nineteenth century. The Newport Jews, who arrived in the 1600s seeking religious refuge in what became Rhode Island, were Sephardic Jews from Portugal, whose language was Spanish-based Ladino. Spain took the lead in expelling its Jews, and Portugal followed, forcing the *Sephardim* into conversions or exile. One of the places the Sephardim found to go was Newport, where they established a congregation in 1658 and dedicated Touro Synagogue in 1763.

One of the forces behind the building of Touro Synagogue was Aaron Lopez, who had been born in Portugal in 1731 and carried the name Duarte (Edward) Lopez until he and his wife Anna managed to escape the strictures of the Inquisition and depart for North America in 1752. Once in the freedom of the American colonies, the couple changed their names to Aaron and Abigail, were remarried as Jews, kept a kosher household, and observed the Sabbath and the Jewish holidays. In time the Lopez family established a very large household in Newport, and Aaron Lopez became, in the words of his biographer, a colonial American merchant prince. A decade into his new American life Lopez appealed to Sephardic communities in London, Curaçao, Suriname, and New York for funds for the construction and furnishing of the beautiful synagogue that still graces Newport today.

Nantucket was very much on the mind of Aaron Lopez, who maintained close ties with Nantucket's premier businessman William Rotch and often partnered in business enterprises with his brother Francis. Early on, Nantucket whaling assumed great importance to the far-flung and highly diversified Lopez business empire. Aaron bought spermaceti and oil from Nantucket whalemen and manufactured candles for export. His great concern was that Nantucket businessmen not begin manufacturing candles from their whale oil, but of course

2. *Mezuzot* are boxes containing lines of scripture that are mounted beside entrances to Jewish homes. *Tashlich* symbolizes the year-end casting off of sins and misdeeds with prayers for forgiveness.

they soon did. By way of competition with the Nantucketers, Lopez began building ships and had his own whalers out on voyages right up into the days of the American Revolution, when five of his whaleships were seized by the British off the Azores.

There was a dark side to the accumulation of Lopez family wealth. Around 1762 Aaron Lopez entered the slave trade, providing Jamaica not only with kosher products for Kingston's Jewish community but also African laborers for the island's plantations. In 1765, as reward for successful delivery of a consignment of slaves to Kingston, he allowed the captain and mate of one of his ships to keep a number of Africans for themselves. At the time of the American Revolution, the Lopez household in Newport included six slaves, and another six served in his father-in-law's household.

Trying to resolve the contradiction between the evident charity and tolerance manifested in the many good works of Aaron Lopez and the lack of evidence that he ever for a moment questioned the morality of trafficking in slaves, his otherwise admiring biographer could only describe Lopez as a man of his time, who—despite daily contact with Africans in his own household—never perceived them as fellow human beings.

How Lopez squared this business with his Quaker associates, the Rotches, is unknown. It must be remembered that despite the ringing denunciation of the trade by Nantucket's Friends, there were Africans held in slavery on Nantucket at the time Lopez entered the trade, and the latest known manumission of slaves on the island dates to 1775, when Friend Benjamin Coffin finally bowed to pressure to free the two-generation family living in slavery in his household.

Nantucket did not offer a home to Sephardic Jews who established themselves in Newport, but there is another Nantucket connection to the Sephardim via the Cape Verde Islands.

In 1932 Lottie DeLuz, wife of John M. Deluz, died on Nantucket. According to the death certificate, she had been born on the Cape Verdean island of Fogo in 1889 to Henry and Catherine Hebrew. "Hebrew" is an odd surname in any case,

and particularly odd to come from a Portuguese colony. Yet Cape Verde is presently in the process of recovering its Jewish heritage, seeking to understand why there are Jewish cemeteries on most of the islands, including Brava and Fogo—the two islands that contributed the most immigrants to southern New England.

Like Newport, the towns of the Cape Verde archipelago were destinations for Sephardic Jews expelled from Portugal after 1500. Richard Lobban, scholar of Cape Verdean history, writes that "The numbers expelled at this time were so great that the term 'Portuguese' almost implied those of Jewish origin." Despite Portuguese attempts to restrict their commercial activities, the Jews they had expelled to the margins of their empire became financially and culturally indispensable to Cape Verde. Among their enterprises was the African side of the trade that supplied wealthy Newport masters with their slaves.

A second pulse of immigration to the Cape Verde islands began in the 1850s, with Jewish men from Morocco and Gibraltar arriving to work in the leather trade. Unlike the nineteenth-century emigrants from Eastern Europe to North America, these men were, once again, Ladino-speaking Sephardic Jews, whose linguistic assimilation to Crioulo-speaking Cape Verde was relatively easy. The Jewish cemeteries on the islands date to this tide of migration, not back to the first settling of the islands.

Mainly men, the Jewish immigrants of the second wave married into the local population, and their children and grandchildren grew up in the Cape Verdean Creole milieu. Observance of Jewish traditions waned, but vestiges and recollections lingered. When the great migration of Cape Verdean families to New England began around 1900, it is certain that some of the immigrants were grandchildren of those Sephardic Jews who had migrated from Morocco and Gibraltar a half-century earlier. Surely Lottie (Hebrew) DeLuz was not the only person to bring a thread of the Sephardic fabric at last to Nantucket—one more melody in the Song of the Sea.

Chapter Nine

From the Old Ottoman Empire

In condemning the European slave trade of the eighteenth century, Nantucket's Elihu Coleman wrote, "Now although the Turks make slaves of those they can catch, that are not of their religion, yet (as history relates) as soon as they embrace the Mahometan religion, they are no longer kept slaves, but are quickly set free, and for the most part put to some place of preferment." In his essay Coleman favorably compared the policy of the Islamic Ottoman Empire, which—irrespective of race or ethnicity—rewarded religious conversion to Islam, with the Christian practice of his time, which imposed conversion on enslaved Africans yet nonetheless kept them in bondage.

Between the 1300s and late 1600s the Turks had expanded their rule from a small state entirely within Anatolia (present-day Turkey) to include most of the Balkan peninsula, eastern Europe as far north as Hungary and thence to the western shore of the Black Sea, Egypt, the Mediterranean coast of North Africa, and the Red Sea coast of Arabia. Their vast holdings went by the name of the Ottoman Empire, after their first sultan, Osman.

The Ottomans spread their religion—Islam—and their language—a variety of Turkish, not Arabic—throughout their empire, but they did not impose either. Still, with Turkish as the language of administration, it was in everyone's interest to be able to communicate with the empire's bureaucrats. Those who did not learn Turkish were at a practical disadvantage. Likewise, Christians and Jews were free to continue to practice their own faiths and to have their own representatives before the Ottoman government. On the other hand, the subordinate position of those who chose

Maximum expansion of the Ottoman Empire (in light gray) circa 1580.

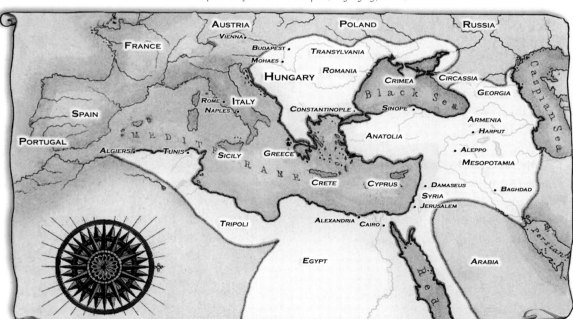

Jay Avila illustration

not to convert to Islam meant that they enjoyed fewer civil rights and paid higher taxes than their Moslem neighbors.

By the time Coleman penned his comparison of Ottoman and European forms of human bondage, the expansive power of the Ottoman Empire had been checked by alliances of European states. The first blow had been struck in the 1571 Battle of Lepanto when the Papal States of Italy and Venice together with Spain obliterated the Ottomans' naval fleet. A bit over a century later, in 1683, Austrian and Polish armies defeated an Ottoman effort to seize the city of Vienna. Over the next two centuries, as the spirit of nationalism arose among subjugated peoples, pieces of the empire broke off to become sovereign states. Finally, when—in the wake of World War I—the armed forces of several European nations occupied what was left of the empire for several years, a leader who adopted the name Kemal Atatürk led a nationalist movement that in 1923 did away entirely with the Ottoman Empire and replaced it with the Republic of Turkey.

The twilight years of the Ottoman Empire were the dawning years of Nantucket's new summer-based economy. Stores on Main Street and adjacent blocks offered curios and souvenirs to tourists and furnishings for the homes of summer residents. There was growing demand on the island for fancy fruits, candy, and ice cream as well as for amusements. Refugees from the lethal disorder of the expiring Ottoman Empire saw business opportunities and security on Nantucket and embraced them.

In the nineteenth century the first block of Centre Street as it leaves Main Street had come to be called Petticoat Row in recognition of the Nantucket women proprietors of the stores there. In the spring of 1916, however, the *Inquirer and Mirror* complained that Petticoat Row's "fame has given place to the foreign element who open

their stores only during the summer months." At that time and on past the middle of the twentieth century Petticoat Row was never without entrepreneurs from lands of the old Ottoman Empire: Prapione Abajian's New York Variety Store at 15 Centre Street (later Antoon Khouri's store); Carekin Proodian, optician and jeweler at 17 Centre; Jacob Abajian's Oriental Bazaar at 19 Centre from 1884 to 1937; Vartan Dedeian's Oriental rugs at 21 and 23 Centre; and across the street A. D. Zorub's "fancy goods" store at 14 Centre.[1]

Armenians

Armenians are neither Turks nor Arabs, and their traditional religion is not Islam. Geographically they have been favorably situated for commerce along the western reaches of the ancient Silk Road, which brought goods from Asia overland to the Mediterranean Sea and thence to all of Europe. That very location on an intercontinental trade route made them vulnerable to attack from all quarters. Over millennia, as great empires rose and fell, the Armenians were ruled by Persians, Greeks, Romans, Arabs, and Turks. From time to time an autonomous or independent Armenian state would emerge. The Armenians adopted Christianity very early, and a cleric of the church developed a specifically Armenian writing system that became a cornerstone of subsequent ethnic identity. When they were attacked by Persians in A.D. 451, the Armenians staunchly defended themselves and their Christian faith

Governance of the Armenians had been divided since the 1600s, when Persia took eastern Armenia away from the Ottomans. In the 1820s the Persian part was annexed to Russia. From that moment on, the Ottomans feared that the Armenians within their empire would declare their independence, and that Russia would

---

1. On March 16, 1935, the *Inquirer and Mirror*, in response to a query about how many women had been in business on Petticoat Row in the past seventy-five years, listed the names of twenty-four businesswomen. On March 16 the newspaper republished the list with three additions. Neither list contained the name of Prapione Abajian, proprietor of the New York Variety Store, among "the estimable ladies who have conducted establishments on Centre Street" whose names "may call to the minds of some of our readers some pleasant memories." Both lists contain the names of married women, so the fact that Prapione Abajian was the wife of Jacob Abajian, who had his own separate establishment on Petticoat Row, should not have been grounds for excluding her from the list.

support Armenian nationalism. Beginning in 1894 the Ottomans, using another of the empire's minorities—the Kurds—as henchmen, launched a two-year campaign of ethnic cleansing to rid themselves once and for all of the Armenians. The fortunate managed to flee as refugees to the far ends of the earth, where, ironically, they were often called "the Turks." Hundreds of thousands of those who did not escape in time died.

For the survivors of the killings of the 1890s and their children, more doom lay over the horizon. Turkey and Russia were on opposite sides of World War I, and once again the fear of Armenian complicity with Russia gripped the rulers of the Ottoman Empire. In 1915 they deported the Armenians living within their borders south to the desert of what is now Syria, where—deprived of shelter, food, and water—a million men, women, and children perished. In a scenario eerily like the ones played out in Bosnia and Rwanda in the 1990s, urgent reports of the killing were made by diplomats and missionaries, but the Western nations were ineffective in stopping it.

Jacob Abajian reached safety and lived a long life. He had been born in the town of Harput on October 27, 1860, and at the time of his death was approaching his seventy-seventh birthday. For fifty-three years he had been proprietor of the Oriental Bazaar on Petticoat Row, where he sold rugs, embroideries, paintings, porcelain, silver, curiosities, and island souvenirs. When he died on Nantucket in 1937, the *Inquirer and Mirror* wrote that he "held the honor of being the oldest business man in Nantucket."

Nantucketers born in the 1920s who knew the Oriental Bazaar in its last years recall the establishment as dusty, ill-kept, and redolent of a smoky fragrance that in hindsight they suspect to have been hashish. But in his heyday Jacob Abajian provided furnishings for the hotels, cottages, and summer homes being built as the island's new economy took wing. He was a master of marketing through the weekly newspaper. On August 29, 1889, five years after the Oriental Bazaar opened for business, his advertisement in the *Nantucket Journal*

offered "Japanese, Chinese, and Egyptian arts and very fine Turkish, Persian, and Afghanistan rugs, carpets, embroideries," together with attar of roses and "fine silverware from the Far East." Moreover, he promised to subsidize round-trip train fare to customers who came in from Siasconset and offered a free year's subscription to the *Nantucket Journal* to anyone spending more than a hundred dollars in his shop. Purchases would be packed and shipped "anywhere in America." Five years later, in the off-season, he placed an advertisement to notify customers well in advance that when his shop opened in May, he would offer—in addition to the carpets and silverware—"Ten principal views from 'Sconset and Nantucket, sent to the far East to be put on fine China and Porcelain." In conclusion he

Ad for Jacob Abajian's Oriental Bazaar, Nantucket Journal, 1895.

Nantucket Historical Association

states, "From Constantinople and India I have the finest and most superb curiosities ever seen in this country."

According to the *Inquirer and Mirror*'s report of his death in 1937, Jacob Abajian had come to Nantucket in the summer of 1883 and told an audience at the Congregational Church "of the persecutions of the Armenians by the Turks and of the hardships his people were obliged to endure." He was truly fortunate to have left Harput when he did. In 1895, within two years of when Abajian wrote his confident advertisement of exotic wares from his homeland, Harput was the scene of one of the opening massacres of the Armenians by the Ottoman Turks.

In 1883, the year that Jacob Abajian made his first visit to Nantucket, Carekin Proodian was born back in Harput. While he was still a boy, the Proodian family managed to leave and re-establish themselves in Massachusetts where Stephen P. Proodian and his sons carried on the family jewelry, engraving, and watch-repair business. Just as Philip Genesky had seen opportunity in Nantucket and set up his son Emile in business on Main

Street, so Stephen Proodian used Harput connections to reach out to the island. He sent young Carekin to do watch repair at Jacob Abajian's Oriental Bazaar.

Repairing watches in the summer, Carekin Proodian worked his way through South Bend Indiana College of Optics. Then he opened his own store on Petticoat Row next door to the Oriental Bazaar, advertised as a jeweler and optician, and prospered. In 1923 he married Araxy Tenazian, the daughter of an Armenian family in Cambridge, Massachusetts, who had been born before her family fled their home country. Both Carekin and Araxy were naturalized citizens of the United States. The couple bought a house on Gardner Street, which had belonged to descended Nantucketer John B. Folger and a second home in Florida, where they spent a few months each winter. Like Jacob and Prapione Abajian, the Proodians remained childless. Like Jacob Abajian, Carekin Proodian took pride in his United States citizenship and his right to vote in Nantucket. Like Emile Genesky, Lincoln Porte, and José Reyes, he found great satisfaction in being a member of a Masonic lodge.

Vartan Dedeian's sign on the gable of the building at the corner of Petticoat Row and India Street, March 1916.

For over forty years Carekin Proodian went to his store every day, including the last day of his life. One Friday in 1948 he came home from work, went to bed, and died in his sleep. Following his funeral at the Congregational Church on Centre Street, he was accorded Masonic rites at Prospect Hill Cemetery, where a large Proodian family monument was erected. He had not lived as many years as Jacob Abajian, and he had not equaled Abajian's fifty-three years in business, but for an Armenian of his generation to die of old age in his own bed was an enviable achievement.

Both Abajian and Proodian had for some years managed off-island stores in the winter—Abajian in New Bedford and Proodian in Boston—but both gave up the stores in order to become full-time residents of Nantucket.

A third Armenian merchant on Petticoat Row, Vartan Dedeian, had his primary business in Chicago and opened his Nantucket store in the summers, selling not only "a choice line of Oriental rugs," but also "antiques, old silver, household effects, furniture, &." He started in a single store on Petticoat Row and expanded to occupy two adjacent stores at 21 and 23 Centre. A large sign advertising the Dedeian business was painted on the gable of 25 Centre facing Middle Pearl (India) Street.

Apparently there was more than enough demand on Nantucket for rugs, silver, and curios to sustain two competing stores side by side on Petticoat Row. Nor were they the only stores of their kind. An undated photograph taken some time before 1916 shows a sign for Bezazian Bros. Oriental Rugs on the west bay of the Folger Block on Main Street, where H. M. Macy Dry Goods had been located in 1895. Farther downhill, the Nantucket Employment Agency at 50 Main Street offered "Nantucket Souvenirs. Oriental Rugs and China," and in 1914 the C. F. Wing home-furnishings store on the south side of Main Street offered Tyvan rugs for sale. In the heady days leading up to World War I, it seems that everyone yearned for a fine carpet and a curio collection from the lands of the old Silk Road.

Syrians

The Armenians were by no means the only Christians within the Ottoman lands. Expanding out of Anatolia, the Ottomans claimed the whole eastern Mediterranean coast including Syria, from which they were expelled only at the end of World War I. In 1918 Antoon J. Khouri was born into a large Christian family in Damascus, Syria. His older brother George left home and by 1927 had opened yet another oriental rug store on Petticoat Row, downstairs at 20 Centre Street. The rest of the Khouri family followed George to America in the 1930s, and Antoon finished his education in the Boston schools, earning a degree in accounting from Bryant and Stratton Business School while working in the family oriental rug and dry goods business.

His first visit to Nantucket came in the summer of 1939, when he exhibited his merchandise at the Sea Cliff Inn and carried it door-to-door in suitcases. The next year, as the clouds of war gathered, he entered the U. S. Army and served as a radio technician for five years.

Following World War II, Antoon Khouri returned to Nantucket and operated out of boarding houses until a vacancy occurred at 15 Centre Street, in the location that had once been Mrs. Abajian's New York Variety Store and later a shoe

Antoon Khouri's store on Petticoat Row.

Nantucket Historical Association

store. For the next thirty-five years it housed his business: Antoon J. Khouri: Linen—Lingerie—Children's Wear—Hand Made Oriental Rugs. The Khouri store offered exquisitely smocked and embroidered children's clothes, trousseau items, and table linens that became cherished heirlooms for summer residents and year-round Nantucket families alike.

Antoon Khouri and his wife Lillian (Haddad) Khouri maintained their family home in Wellesley, where he was an active member of the Church of Saint John of Damascus as well as holding membership in a veterans association and a Masonic lodge. In time they bought a summer home on Nantucket. Located behind Sarah P. Bunker's home on Cliff Road, the little house was one of Nantucket's many "barn conversions." Having once been the carriage house for Sarah P.'s family, it had been made into a cottage that the Khouris renovated for themselves and their four children. In Nantucket Antoon Khouri continued his Masonic commitment as a member of Union Lodge F. & A. M.

Since his death in 1995, members of Antoon Khouri's family—his wife and son Arthur—have maintained contact with Nantucket, expertly cleaning and repairing antique rugs for the Nantucket Historical Association and other clients.

Greeks

Greece was absorbed by the Ottoman Empire in the mid-1500s, but its inclusion was heavily contested. The Greeks achieved complete separation from Ottoman control in 1832, but independence brought no peace. The nationalism that had been simmering throughout the the Balkan region flared in the 1890s, and Greece joined in war against the Ottoman Empire. From then until the end of the empire in 1923 there was almost continual warfare to force the Ottomans out of Europe.

In those fraught times great numbers of Greeks emigrated from their home country to the United States and Canada, where they worked in textile mills and shoe factories or at whatever work they could find. Immigrants who had the good fortune to accumulate some capital operated grocery stores, bakeries, candy stores, restaurants, and other small businesses.

In Nantucket Greek-owned business had its locus on the south side of Main Street halfway uphill between Union Street and Orange Street. In 1901, at the invitation of merchant C. A. Chenoweth, George Anastos and Nicholas Kaleavas came to the island to operate a sidewalk fruit stand. At night their produce was moved into Chenoweth's "Olde Curiosity Shoppe," which was then located in a wooden building that had been erected on Main Street after Nantucket's Great Fire of 1846. When Chenoweth moved his business to Middle Pearl (India) Street, the New Bedford home-furnishings business of C. F. Wing took over the Main Street location and continued to let the fruit merchants use part of the building for night storage. By 1909 Kaleavas was proprietor of a fruit store and a "confectionery" indoors at 26 Main Street, and George Anastos was employed as a clerk there. Both were living on the premises. The next year George's younger brother John Anastos, twenty-two years old and single, came to the island to work in the retail fruit trade, and George moved to Boston to handle the wholesale side of the business.

The year 1912 brought open war between Greece and the Ottoman Empire, and John Anastos and Nicholas Kaleavas went home to Greece to fight against the Turks. Kaleavas was killed and John Anastos was wounded. Upon recovery, he continued in business with his brother George, providing fresh fruit to Nantucket. The Anastos brothers retained the business name Kaleavas for some years after taking over the store at 26 Main Street, expanding its offerings to "Choice selected Fruits, Nuts and Candies, Ice Cream and Soda, Fine Confections."

In 1920 the Anastos brothers were still renting the premises at 26 Main Street, wedged between the Masonic Block building on the corner of Main and Union Streets and the C. F. Wing Company home-furnishings store. A fire in the fall of 1925 led to the razing of the old buildings and the construction of a pair of nearly identical two-story fire-resistant commercial buildings for the Wing Company and the Anastos brothers. The side-by-side home furnishings store and fruit store held grand openings a week apart in May 1926.

Having had their own start as clerks in the fruit store, the Anastos brothers took on other Greek immigrants as employees. In 1919 Constantinos Nicoletos had been living on the premises at 26 Main Street and working as a clerk, and the 1920 federal census lists John Nicoletos boarding with John Anastos and working as a fruit salesman. Unmarried, John Nicoletos had arrived in the United States in 1899 and been naturalized. His younger brother Harry came a few years later, leaving his family behind in Varsara, Greece. Unlike John, he did not take out citizenship papers, apparently intending to return home to his family, but when his wife died during his absence, he brought his sons to join him. At some point a third brother came to Nantucket to join the family group.

In the spring of 1925 the Nicoletos brothers opened their own business on the south side of Main Street just a few doors west from the Anastos brothers. Both businesses advertised fruit, confectionery, and ice cream. The Nicoletos brothers named their business "The Modern," and when the Anastos brothers opened in their new building, they called it the "Spa." In 1927 the Nicoletos brothers announced the installation of a skylight and a new piano at their establishment.

Shortly after making these improvements at The Modern, John Nicoletos made a trip home to Greece, and while there fell seriously ill. Nonetheless, he returned to Nantucket and continued to manage the business until his death in 1931. A member of Union Lodge, whose meeting hall was just a few doors down Main Street from The Modern, he was buried with Masonic ritual.

While Harry Nicoletos's sons and yet another brother, George Nicoletos, worked in The Modern, a young Greek named Demos Ronderes assisted at the Spa and lived upstairs, sharing quarters with John Anastos, who was still unmarried.

— Mary J. Barrett photograph

Staff supper at the Spa Café in the 1950s.

Long though this bachelorhood was, however, it was not permanent. The 1938 Nantucket street list includes Greece-born housewife Athena "Anna" Anastos, twenty years younger than John. George Anastos, on the other hand, had married Lilika Popodopoulus years before. The couple resided in Boston, where their son C. George was born in 1916.[2]

C. George Anastos received his education at Boston Latin School, Harvard College, and Harvard Law School. Graduating from law school in 1941, he served in the U. S. Army Air Corps during World War II, then practiced law in Boston before moving on to the U. S. Justice Department. After additional service to federal and Massachusetts state governmental agencies, he was appointed Nantucket District Court judge, a position he held until retirement (from which he was subsequently recalled). Residing in both Nantucket and Wellesley, he involved himself deeply in community affairs.

After the repeal of prohibition in the 1930s, the family business acquired a liquor license. In 1944 the "Confectionary Spa" at 26 Main Street was still offering ice cream, sodas, pies, and candies, but also "sandwiches of all kinds, draught beer, ale." The fruit store had given way to the Spa Café at 28 Main Street, offering fish dinners, steaks, chops, lobsters, and cocktails. The side-by-side Spa complex was advertised to summer tourists as a "delightfully cool place" just three minutes from Steamboat Wharf.

2. Father and son had mirror-image names: George C. and C. George. The father's middle initial is sometimes listed as C and at other times as K, since transliteration from the Greek alphabet can go either way. It stood for Cosmo.

The wharves used by commercial fishing boats were even closer, and it became the custom for fishermen coming off the water to head directly from their boats to the Spa to drink beer. While the restaurant side held out as a place where families might still go for a reasonably priced meal, the former ice cream parlor devolved into a rough workingmen's tavern.

Late in the 1950s John Anastos retired to Greece, and at the close of 1961 the Anastos family sold the business and the building to the Nantucket Historical Trust.

Besides the businessmen on Main Street, other Greek families lived on the island. In 1931 Christy and Mary Psaradelis moved to the island from Boston and enrolled their children in school. Their son James began in the 'Sconset school and continued on through Cyrus Peirce and Academy Hill Schools to Nantucket High School, followed by his younger sisters and brother. Christy Psaradelis had been born in Tripolis, a town in the heart of the large island of Peloponnesos at the southern tip of Greece. In Boston he married Mary Melanes, daughter of a Greek father and an American mother. Their families were in the wholesale produce business in Boston, and in 'Sconset Christy carried on as a gardener and florist until his retirement in 1951. Although Mary's mother was not Greek, the Psaradelis family maintained the language, at least between Christy and Mary, so that when Nicholas Petumenos arrived on Nantucket in 1947, he sought them out for company.

Born in Laioti, near Corinth, in 1897, Nicholas Petumenos had left home for the United States as a teenager. His immigration was sponsored by an uncle who lived in the Midwest, and while still in his teens Nicholas operated his own bootblack shop in Youngstown, Ohio. Later he received training in removal of spots and stains from clothing in preparation for dry cleaning. In the mid 1940s he was married with three children and working as a garment "spotter" in Westerly, Rhode Island, when a consortium of Nantucket businessmen with plans to open a new dry cleaning plant on Nantucket met him and invited him to bring his expertise to the island.

Nicholas Petumenos spent a winter alone on-island before making a decision about moving his family from the mainland. His wife and children joined him in the summer of 1948 but left in the fall for the children to return to their mainland schools. Dryshoal Cleaners arranged for a local flight service to fly Nicholas to Connecticut every other weekend to be with his family. The next summer the family relocated permanently to Nantucket and enrolled the children in the Nantucket public schools, purchasing a spacious house next to the North Shore Restaurant. The proprietor of the North Shore was Esther Gibbs, great-granddaughter of Sarah P. Bunker. Dorothy Petumenos rented rooms to summer visitors who had no farther to go than next door for meals at the North Shore. So it was that Sarah P.'s descendants and the family of Nicholas Petumenos became long-time neighbors.

Nicholas Petumenos was the only Greek-speaker in his family or in the neighborhood, so he maintained his native language by visiting with Nantucket's other residents who had been born in Greece. Two and a half years before his death, he was called upon to put his language into service on the occasion of a maritime disaster.

In mid-December of 1976 the *Argo Merchant*, an oil tanker bound for Boston, ran aground southeast of Siasconset. Although registered in Liberia, the vessel was owned by a Greek company, commanded by a Greek captain, and manned by thirty-eight Greek crewmen.

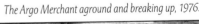

The Argo Merchant aground and breaking up, 1976.

Milton Silvia photograph, Spinner Collection

Responding to the distress call, the Coast Guard immediately lifted more than half the crew members from the ship by helicopter. After pumps failed to keep the engine room from flooding, more men were flown ashore the next day. Hopes to refloat the *Argo Merchant* came to nothing, and in less than a week the tanker broke apart, spilling the cargo of oil into the sea. A temporary security and reception area was set up for crew members taken off the *Argo Merchant* and flown to Nantucket. Serving as interpreter between the authorities and the rescued Greek seamen was seventy-nine-year-old Nicholas Petumenos.

Hungarians

Hungary came under Ottoman rule earlier than Greece and emerged from the empire earlier as well. During their expansionist period, Ottoman forces defeated the Hungarians at the Battle of Mohács in 1526. Fifteen years later the Hungarian capital of Buda fell, and over the next hundred and fifty years two-thirds of Hungary was taken into the Ottoman Empire. Another piece of it was made into a duchy under Ottoman "protection." Only the northwest remained outside the Ottoman sphere, ruled by members of the Hapsburg dynasty.

Distant linguistic cousins of the Estonians and Finns, the Hungarians (who call themselves Magyars) were neither Middle European nor Turkish of language or history. They had come from the far side of the Carpathian Mountains to the plains bordering the Danube River and into the area of Romania known as Transylvania. Around A.D. 1000, after trying unsuccessfully to push on farther into Germany and Italy, they finally settled on the vast, flat plains of present-day Hungary, became farmers, and adopted Christianity.

After the fall of Constantinople in 1453, Hungary became a frontier, exposed to attack by the Ottomans, who ultimately prevailed and began converting the Magyars' churches into mosques. It was not until nearly 1700 that the Magyar capital of Buda and the university

town of Pécs on the opposite side of the Danube (known together as Budapest) were finally rejoined to Europe. As in the case of Greece, however, emergence from the Ottoman Empire brought years of struggle for governance. The eighteenth and nineteenth centuries were rife with conflict. The twentieth century brought the devastation of two World Wars, the imposition of communist rule, and the brutal suppression of the Hungarian popular uprising of 1956.

Theresa Szabo had been born in Budapest in 1896, but she was living safely on Easton Street in Nantucket when Soviet tanks rolled through the streets of her hometown in 1956. Widow of Norwegian fisherman Hjalmar Alfred Anderson, she had been for much of her adult life the sole Hungarian among Nantucket's year-round foreign-born population.

With great prescience her father, George Szabo, had brought Theresa and her sister Margaret to the United States before the outbreak of World War I. Settling in New Jersey, they found work with wealthy families. Young Theresa was engaged first as a nanny and then as a cook by a resident of Morristown who maintained a summer home on Milk Street in Nantucket.

Teenaged Theresa married and had two children, born on the island as World War I raged over Hungary. The marriage bestowed the security of permanent United States residency, but it did not endure. In 1919 she married again. Her second husband had been a fisherman when he came from Norway, and he died a fisherman, killed in an accident at sea in 1941. Theresa was left with four children and nearly four decades of life still ahead of her on Nantucket.

In the federal censuses for Nantucket, Theresa Anderson firmly declared her nationality and first language as "Magyar," but no Magyar community existed for her on-island. Living as part of Nantucket's predominantly Norwegian community of fishing families, she had few opportunities to speak her own first language. But in that linguistic baggage so seldom opened she had brought to Nantucket a little heritage of the Ottoman

Empire. Over the course of 1500 years the Magyars had met Turkic peoples several times, sometimes on friendly terms and sometimes decidedly not. Whatever the circumstances, the Magyars always acquired some new words from the Turks. In young Theresa Szabo's vocabulary were over three hun-

– Courtesy of Grace Marshall

Theresa (Szabo) Anderson, born in Budapest, Hungary, in 1896, became part of the island's Norwegian community.

dred words borrowed more than a thousand years earlier, before the Magyars ever saw the banks of the Danube River where her home city of Budapest would someday stand. Layered on top of them were another thirty or so words from the Ottomans' language, borrowed by Theresa's ancestors in the days after their 1526 defeat at Mohács. Theresa's mother tongue was a mobile history lesson brought to the United States and finally laid to rest in Nantucket in April, 1979.

Although Theresa Anderson was the sole Hungarian among Nantucket's year-round population until after 1950, another Hungarian, also born in Budapest in 1896, began forging ties with the island in 1925 and eventually made Nantucket his home too.

This was Charles Sziklas, whose formative years were more privileged than those of young Theresa Szabo. While she was on a ship traveling to a nanny's job in New Jersey, he was concluding his college-preparatory education in Budapest and packing to go to the University of London. War, however, is an implacable leveler. World War I cut young Charles off from his country and his family and put him down in the same country where Theresa's father had placed her and her sister for safety's sake. His exile, like hers, became permanent, financed in part by the sale of family jewelry smuggled out of wartime Hungary by a priest who was a friend of the Sziklas family.

It must have been strange for a young man from Budapest to find himself in Cleveland, Ohio, attending college while Americans of his age left their classes to go to fight in Europe. Having earned a bachelor's degree from Case Western Reserve

– Louis S. Davidson photograph, NHA

Dr. Charles Sziklas, born in Budapest in 1896, became the first flying surgeon to Nantucket and Martha's Vineyard.

University, Sziklas then went to Harvard Medical School and for the next thirty years taught surgery at Boston University while practicing at many hospitals in the Greater Boston area. Most significant for Nantucketers was his pioneering work in emergency care for remote areas.

Like Dr. Fine, who began coming to Nantucket at about the same time, Dr. Sziklas brought surgical skills from Boston to Nantucket to supplement what the island's general practitioners could provide for their patients. Finding travel by steamboat or, on occasion, fishing boat from New Bedford far too slow and unreliable, he became the first flying surgeon for the islands of Nantucket and Martha's Vineyard. After a quarter century of service, he and his American wife Charlotte moved to Nantucket full time in 1956. Their son Robert had married a Nantucketer, Molly Backus, and taught science at Nantucket High School, and the elder Sziklases' move brought them closer to their grandchildren.

All the Sziklas family members took active roles in Nantucket organizations. In particular, Dr. Sziklas was influential in the establishment of the Nantucket Rotary Club and served as its president. At the age of eighty-nine he addressed the annual meeting of the Nantucket Historical Association, telling of his early days as Nantucket's flying surgeon.

Born the same year as Theresa Anderson, Dr. Sziklas outlived her by a decade. According to his obituary, he was admired as a quietly humorous man who seldom spoke of his achievements or "about his life before he came to Nantucket."

CHAPTER TEN

Continentals

Italy

The Ottomans coveted the city states of Italy but in the end had to make do with seizing outposts of Italian trade in the Mediterranean. They advanced on Venice, coming within sight of sentries watching from the bell tower in St. Mark's Square, but they did not take the Italian city closest to the border of their empire, much less Rome or any of the Papal States. Nonetheless, Ottoman naval forces and pirates operating from the North African coast constantly harassed trade and menaced coastal cities.

The name Andrea Doria is well known to Nantucketers because of the catastrophic collision of an ocean liner of that name with another liner, the *Stockholm*, off Nantucket in 1956. Ever since the massive air and sea rescue operation in July of that year, the sunken vessel lying on the ocean floor has exuded a fatal attraction for divers, more than a dozen of whom have lost their lives visiting her.

Less known to Nantucketers is the identity of the man in whose name the sunken liner had been christened. Andrea Doria was a Genoese naval commander against the Ottomans in the 1530s. A generation later, after the Ottomans seized the island of Cyprus, the Papal States, Venice, and Spain—in a rare moment of cooperation—combined forces to obliterate the massive Ottoman fleet. The Battle of Lepanto off the Greek coast in 1571 was the largest sea battle of the sixteenth century.

Frank Oddo was a person who would have known who Andrea Doria was and taken pride in him. Born in the Sicilian town of Alimena, Italy, in 1890, Oddo came to the United States in 1907. Before the age of thirty he was a naturalized citizen and a married man with three children, a business of his own, and a mortgage. He had come to the island to work for local businessman Charles

Ellis but soon went his own way. In the 1920s he operated his shoe-repair business on Main Street in the location that was subsequently taken over by the Nicoletos brothers. Then he moved to Federal Street. Advertisements for his shop appeared regularly in Nantucket newspapers and business directories until his sudden death a month short of his forty-fifth birthday.

In the depths of the Depression, Nantucket families relied on fishing and hunting to feed their families. There were shotguns in most homes, and it was not uncommon for a gun accident to take a life. Typically there was no witness, and the community could only speculate on how it could have happened. Such was the case for the Oddo family. Frank Oddo was a member of the Knights of Columbus, and the organization places a flag on his grave each Memorial Day. Of Nantucket's Knights of Columbus, he was closest in origin to Italy's two great men of the sea, Andrea Doria and Christopher Columbus.

Balancing this tragic end to a story of immigration is a cheerful story of emigration from Nantucket to Italy. The prosperous Jelleme family of Passaic, New Jersey, and Boston had a multigeneration connection to Nantucket through marriage and summer residence. An ardent sports fisherman, John Randolph Jelleme moved permanently to Nantucket in 1967 and lived here until his death at the age of ninety-five. His oldest son, Howard Jelleme, operated the Toscana construction and excavation company, whose large pieces of equipment are ubiquitous on Nantucket building sites. As much at home on the water as his father, Howard Jelleme once rowed lifeguard Jane Silva out into the rip off Great Point in a small boat to rescue two women and a child who had been carried offshore by the current.

After thirty years in business on the island, Howard Jelleme turned Toscana over to the next generation and moved to Tuscany to make wine. Returning to the island with the products of his second successful career, he has been featured at Nantucket's annual wine festival.

Spain

Frank Oddo's birthplace, the island of Sicily, only became a part of Italy in 1861. During the days of Ottoman efforts to dominate the Mediterranean Sea, the island—together with the Kingdom of Naples—was under Spanish rule.

The whaling industry acquainted Nantucketers with Latin American ports, especially those on the west coast of South America, but Spain itself remained out of the realm of Nantucket experience, and likewise there was virtually no Spanish migration to Nantucket. Morris Francis, whose surname would seem to place him among Nantucket's large Azorean population, appears in both the 1860 and 1870 federal censuses as born in Spain. A mariner, he had retired from the sea and acquired Nantucket real estate of modest value.

The presence on-island of another Spanish-born retiree, Paulino Echeverría, was recorded in the 1900 census. His wife had been born in New York, but her father was from Spain like himself. Having first come to the United States in his teens, Echeverría was still an alien forty-five years later. Over several generations the family lived in New York City and later in Morristown, New Jersey, while maintaining a summer home at 9 Cliff Road, next door to the Nevins mansion. Elderly Sarah P. Bunker was living out the last years of her life across the street at 12 Cliff Road when the Echeverrías first took up residence there. Gulielma Folger lived a few doors away.[1] According to an interview with Helen Cash, Gulielma Folger "taught German, French, Italian, Greek, and Latin and learned it all here with the help of people who came to Nantucket. Will Low's wife helped with her French accent. Mr. Echeverría helped with Spanish."

Nantucket High School only began offering Spanish as a foreign language in 1959. The family of the first teacher, Efrain Viscarolasaga, were Basque refugees from the Spanish Civil War, and the regional variety of Spanish taught was Castilian. Since then Nantucket's resident population of Spanish speakers has increased dramatically, the high school has a Spanish club, and there have been requests for such public services in Spanish as story hours at the Nantucket Atheneum's children's library. Although the speech of Spanish-speaking summer tourists may be distinctly Iberian, Nantucket's resident Spanish speakers are overwhelmingly from Latin America and speak New World Spanish.

France

As Nantucket's whaling industry struggled to rebuild itself after the devastation wrought upon it during the American Revolution, William Rotch, Quaker pacifist and merchant *extraordinaire*, negotiated the establishment of a duty-free whaling port at Dunkirk, France, in 1787. With French guarantees of freedom of religion and exemption from military service, a number of families left Nantucket direct for Dunkirk, while a larger number of Nantucket whaling captains who had been operating out of London transferred their headquarters there, creating a little Nantucket colony on French soil. Friend Benjamin Johnson, one of three traveling Quakers who visited the Dunkirk colony, wrote in his journal that he found "upwards of sixty Friends, old and young, in this place, nearly all from Nantucket and in the same business." As the French Revolution descended in all its violence, the Nantucket enterprise dissolved after just six years of existence.

Captain Thaddeus Coffin was one of the whaling captains who transferred with his family and

---

1. The road defining the edge of Nantucket's North Shore neighborhood was called North Street until well after the building of the Sea Cliff Inn in 1886–87. An amenity of the large wooden hotel, rails were laid for horse-car service from Steamboat Wharf to the inn, and the street name was changed from North Street to Cliff Road. Nantucketers persisted in using "North Street" for several decades after summer residents and patrons of the Sea Cliff Inn had taken to "Cliff Road." By the time the hotel was demolished in 1972, however, "North Street" had been forgotten, and "Cliff Road" was used by everyone.

a whaleship to Dunkirk, where his wife Ann gave birth to Thaddeus Jr. in 1789. The family managed to stay on for two years after the Rotches had fled back to England, but in 1795 Thaddeus Coffin finally "removed his family from the Republic of France," and took them to Nantucket.[2]

Young Thaddeus was just six years old when his family left France. He grew up on the island, followed in the footsteps of his father to become a master mariner, married Eliza Cartwright, and raised three children. The 1850 federal census shows one of his sons already following the sea and 67-year-old Dorcas Honorable—one of Nantucket's "last Indians"—boarding with the family. Accumulating ever more wealth with the decades, Thaddeus outlived both Eliza and Dorcas to appear in the 1870 federal census. When he died on Nantucket at the age of 87, he departed from a long life as a prosperous businessman.

Jerusha Gardner—whose father, Captain Shubael Gardner, had been instrumental in the foundation of the Dunkirk colony—was born in France twelve years after Thaddeus, and her absence from Nantucket censuses over several decades of the nineteenth century implies that it took a long time for her to settle on Nantucket, but in the last years of their lives she and Thaddeus were both residing on the island and surely had memories to share.

Lewis Imbert, a seagoing man, was born a French citizen in Marseilles around 1800 and entered the United States as a child. He was sworn in as a naturalized citizen in Nantucket in May 1825, and in the summer of 1863 he served on the trial jury that convicted Patience Cooper of manslaughter in the death of Phebe Fuller. As an octogenarian he was still living on the island when the 1880 census was taken.

Frederick Folger, a cabinetmaker some fifteen years younger than Thaddeus Coffin Jr. and five years younger than Lewis Imbert, also survived to be counted in the 1880 census. He had been born

in France, but there is no record of his taking an oath of naturalization. His wife and children were all born in Massachusetts.

Other Nantucketers born in France around the time of the existence of the Dunkirk colony were watchmaker John Smith (finally naturalized in 1839) and Hannah (Macy) Gardner (teacher Anna Gardner's mother), Eliza Macy, Deborah Baker, and Sarah Gouin. Together, they certainly constituted a group of sufficient size for a nineteenth-century social club.

In the first half of the nineteenth century, Nantucket residents of French birth had either been born in Dunkirk or come to Nantucket as mariners or both. In the latter part of the nineteenth century, as Nantucket's economy evolved away from the maritime industries, Nantucketers traveled to France for other reasons, and the world's people came to Nantucket as summer residents.

A number of Nantucket men brought home wives from France. Newly married Nantucket artist George Gardner Fish, on the other hand, took his wife Judith to Paris. They went in 1866, and during the year he spent there studying drawing and painting, their first daughter was born and named Madeleine for the church in their neighborhood. New York artist William Low came to Nantucket with his French wife Julienne. The widow Jane Turner, also born in France and a resident of New York, purchased a home on the island.

In 1860 aging Sarah Gouin was living on the island with her thirty-year-old Massachusetts-born son, Albert. As head of household, Sarah owned real estate of substantial value. Mother and son do not appear in the previous or following federal censuses, but perhaps their sojourn on Nantucket made the connection with the island that brought Paris-born Marcel Gouin to the island a half-century later.

Right after the 1900 census was taken, Marcel, a carpenter, took up residence in Siasconset with his American wife, Mary (Lowell) Gouin. In 1910

2. In 1817 Thaddeus Coffin Sr. found it necessary to renounce English citizenship and become a naturalized citizen of the Unites States of America. This suggests that he was resident abroad during the American Revolution. In his statement to the court in Nantucket, he asserts that he brought his family to Nantucket from France in 1795, remained on the island for eight years, went on a three-year whaling voyage out of England, returning in 1806, and had resided on Nantucket ever since.

– Nantucket Historical Association

The Tavern-on-the-Moors on School Street in Siasconset, 1929. The building had previously been Gouin's Livery Stable.

the Gouins, who now had two children, were still renting, but during the next decade they took out a mortgage and bought a house on New Street in 'Sconset. Marcel had also, after many years in the United States, been sworn in as a citizen, following the course of so many resident aliens who took out citizenship papers on the eve of World War I.

In the censuses and in Nantucket business directories as late as 1927, Marcel Gouin's occupation is listed as carpenter and builder, but in 1930 he emerges as a "saddle horse riding instructor," a distinctly more Gallic profession. His wife was employed as the Siasconset agent for the Martha's Vineyard Telegraph Co., with an office on Broadway. In 1930 she was operating a tearoom in the Broadway location, and later their daughter took over its management.

The Gouins' son, Marcel Jr., was born in the summer of 1900 and attended Nantucket public schools before being sent off-island to Tabor Academy, thence to a preparatory school in Annapolis, Maryland, and finally to the United States Naval Academy, where he was commissioned as an ensign in 1924. This was the beginning of a distinguished career in naval aviation, during which he was a flight instructor, commanded fighter squadrons off aircraft carriers in the Pacific in World War II, took command of an aircraft carrier, and then returned to Maryland as one of the first commanders of the Pautuxent River Flight Test

Facility. Having achieved the rank of rear admiral in 1953, Marcel Gouin retired as vice admiral the following year. Nantucket's Gouin Village is named for him, and his career is honored with a photograph and a plaque at the Nantucket Memorial Airport.

Germany

Nantucket's difficulties in retaining professionals from off-island is nothing new. The nineteenth century saw two German physicians resident on Nantucket, neither of whom stayed. In 1850 Dr. Morris Richter was living on-island with his family. He, his mother, his wife, and the oldest of their four children were all from Germany. The next two children had been born in New York, and the last child in Massachusetts. The three American-born children were all attending Nantucket schools.

With the collapse of the island's economy, the Richters joined the general exodus off-island, and over a decade passed before Dr. John Givon, also born in Germany, took Dr. Richter's place, also remaining for less than a decade.

Frederick Derby, born in Hamburg and a mariner by trade, and his Massachusetts-born wife were living with a local family in 1850. By 1860 they had three children and a house of their own. Another German mariner resident on Nantucket in 1860 was Joseph Rosenwirth, who had found himself an Irish wife in the years after the potato famine. In 1870 Frederick Olderich was still able to find work as a cooper to support himself, his Massachusetts-born wife, and his two children. A decade later, when he and his wife had six children to feed and clothe, there was no longer any demand for barrels, and Olderich was working on the wharf unloading freight and luggage.

Lewis Henry Wendell, born in Prussia, went before the court in Nantucket and took the oath of naturalization in 1851. Cast ashore from the brig *Florida* when she was wrecked off Nantucket in 1833, Wendell decided not to return to the sea. By the time of his naturalization, he had long since established himself permanently on the island with a Nantucket-born wife and daughter, whom he supported by carting freight. Enduringly concerned for fellow shipwreck victims and other needy people, he engaged in ceaseless benevolent work, and his example inspired a group of sixteen Nantucket women to form a relief organization known as the Wendell Society. The Wendellites were still in operation in the 1870s when age and ill health forced Wendell himself into retirement. Far from shunning him as a foreigner and a coof, the Nantucket community took his good works to heart. The obituary published at his death in December 1878 stated, "Throughout his long career among us, he has ever been noted for his untiring industry and sterling integrity, winning to himself hosts of friends, and commanding the respect and esteem of all." This public recognition did not prevent Eliza Barney, however, from describing Lewis Wendell in her *Genealogical Record* as "a Portuguese."

Another Prussian-born resident of Nantucket was Frederica Wilhelmina Rogers, wife of Nantucketer George Rogers. Although Frederica and George both lived into the first years of the twentieth century, the 1860 census reported Frederica as a single head of household with her two daughters—New York-born Imogene, 8, and Nantucket-born Martha, 2.

Mary Cook, only seventeen years old in 1850, was the wife of a local dry-goods merchant, and Christina Russell, thirty years of age, also had a local husband. As a very young girl Mary Mynhardt had come to the island as a servant for the cosmopolitan family of artist George Gardner Fish, whose daughter Madeleine had been born in Paris. Mary was living with the Fish family in 1870 and was still in service a decade later.

In this cohort of the foreign-born, only men sought United States citizenship. Wives shared the status of their husbands—naturalized or alien. As woman suffrage became an issue (and well before women won voting rights), foreign-born women began to seek United States citizenship for themselves. Maria Fish, wife of Nantucket farmer Fred Fish, was naturalized in 1901. In 1910, she had the company of two other German-born wives who were close to her in age, Lydia Coffin and Frieda Harvey.

Earnest Nickel came from Germany to Nantucket via Ireland, arriving with his Irish wife May and two daughters, Alwina and Violet, in 1909. In 1910 Earnest was working as a laundryman on the island and had not yet initiated the naturalization process. At some time during World War I the family moved on, leaving it unknown whether they, like so many others, sought United States citizenship during or right after the war.

By 1930 a German family, the Lubigs, had come to farm on Nantucket. Walter and Gertrude Lubig had arrived in the United States seven years earlier and wasted no time becoming naturalized citizens and buying property. Young Margery Lubig joined her brother and sister-in-law in 1928 and went to work as housekeeper for a Nantucket widower with a young child.

Frederick and Meta Schmalz had also come to the island, bringing their Pennsylvania-born son and daughters and their children's spouses along with them. Although the Schmalzes had been resident in the United States for decades, in 1930 they had just taken out citizenship papers and were yet to be sworn in. Their daughter-in-law Anna, who had arrived in the United States from Slovenia in 1921, had already completed the naturalization process.

German-born fisherman and homeowner John Stivens was living alone in 1930. He, too, had been naturalized. Automobile mechanic Paul Frank came from Germany to Nantucket via Vermont, where the first of his six children was born. Having arrived in the United States in 1909, in 1930 he had finally taken out citizenship papers. His English wife Winifred came to the United States later than her husband but had been naturalized ahead of him.

While still in his teens, Eugene Collatz gained experience working with refrigeration in the beer gardens of his hometown. His father was chief of police in Gluckstadt, a town downriver from the city of Hamburg, halfway to the coast where the Elbe River empties into the North Sea. In the wake of World War I Herman Collatz wanted his son out of Germany and away from the war clouds that still overhung Europe, so he arranged for a

At left, Frederick and Meta Schmalz and their family. Clockwise from upper left: Frederick Jr., Clara, Frieda, and Alma. At right, wedding of Eugene and Mildred Collatz, 1934. – Courtesy of the Collatz family

maternal uncle in New York to sponsor Eugene's immigration to the United States. Young Gene found work with a commercial refrigeration company and soon became a field manager. While installing a cold-storage unit for an apple orchard in Connecticut, he met the orchard manager's sister, Mildred Perun, herself a descendant of emigrants from Russia. They were married in 1934, and shortly after their wedding another refrigeration project brought them to Nantucket.

To keep fish chilled from when they were caught on the offshore fishing banks until they were brought to market, the Nantucket fishing fleet carried hundreds of pounds of ice in their holds. In 1936 work began on converting Nantucket's gas-operated ice-making plant on Island Service Wharf to electrical power, and Gene Collatz was engaged to oversee the project. When the conversion was completed, he was offered the job of managing the plant.

He and Mildred found places to rent on Hussey Street and then on Sunset Hill near the Jethro Coffin House (the "Oldest House") just across the fields behind Sarah P. Bunker's old home. Finally they settled on the corner of Atlantic Avenue and Prospect Street, downhill from the one remaining windmill and on the edge of what had once been the New Guinea neighborhood.

Work for the Island Service Company proved congenial, and the birth on-island of their children in 1937 and 1942 attached the Collatzes to Nantucket. They became permanent residents, and Gene worked for the Island Service Company and Sherburne Oil Company until his retirement as chief engineer in 1969.

Adept at repairing electrical equipment, he developed a second line of work repairing radios, record players, and eventually televisions, while

Island Service Company float in the 1938 July 4th parade. The float features the company's latest items in home refrigeration.

Mildred provided decades of substitute teaching services to the Nantucket schools.

Gene enjoyed fishing, hunting ducks, and engaging in competitive target shooting with Nantucket men at the range in Legion Hall, but when the United States entered the war, civilian shotguns were confiscated for government use, putting an end—for the time—to hunting.

For the German-born throughout the United States the war years were stressful. Skill in radio operation inevitably attracted the attention of security agencies. Gene Collatz underwent background investigation, his activities were monitored, and on occasion his son was taunted by other schoolchildren. Like many Germans and German Americans, he was rarely heard to speak German, did not seek to pass the language on to his children, and did not seek out the company of Nantucket's few other German speakers. Instead, through his work in commercial refrigeration and in his private repair service, Gene Collatz cultivated a large circle of clients and acquaintances among the residents of the island, both year-round and summer.

Switzerland and Bohemia

In 1930 a young Swiss couple, Richard and Frances Jete, were living in Siasconset, where Richard was working as an upholsterer at the Treasure Chest shop. At the time there were two other Swiss residents of the island—Frances Scharf, who lived with her husband in Seamoor Cottage in Siasconset, and Wilhelmina Hansen, whose Danish husband worked on a farm in Polpis. Rudolf Scharf, who did carpentry and operated Hathaway's Laundry, was born in the United States, but his father was German-born, and his Swiss wife listed her home language as Swiss German. The Hansens lived a modest life, with Wilhemina supplementing her husband's earnings by doing housework for a private family. Both Wilhemina Hansen and Frances Scharf had become citizens of the United States, and the newly arrived Jetes had already begun the process.

Just as Theresa Anderson had identified herself as a Magyar rather than a Hungarian on the federal census, Emily Antosch also declared her ethnicity—"Bohemian"—to the census rather than her nationality, which was problematical.

Through centuries of European history the House of Hapsburg had ruled many different ethnic groups, including both Bohemians and Magyars. Between 1867 and World War I, as a temporary solution to complicated Hapsburg dynastic problems, a dual Hapsburg monarchy ruled twin kingdoms of Austria (whose residents included Austrians, Bohemians, Czechs, Slovenians, and Poles, among others) and Hungary (including Magyars, Germans, and others). After World War I, Bohemia—with its beautiful capital city of Prague—became the western province of the newly formed nation of Czechoslovakia.

Emily Antosch had left her home before World War I and resided in New Bedford before coming to Nantucket to work as live-in housekeeper for the Wood family on Gardner Street. The dilemma she faced in identifying herself for the census enumerator was that in 1930 the Austro-Hungarian Empire was long gone, and the new entity of Czechoslovakia had been formed only after her departure. Little wonder that she declared herself Nantucket's sole Bohemian.

David Wood recalls their housekeeper's surprise that Nantucketers let perfectly good dandelions go to waste. In the spring Emily gathered them, boiled them in the Woods' kitchen, and made wine from them.

Poland and the Ukraine

Homemade dandelion wine would probably have appealed to Polish Ignatz Sikorsky and Ukrainian Nikita Carpenko, both of whom took up residence on Nantucket and were locally perceived as colorful characters.

Just as the borders of the Ottoman Empire and the Hapsburg Empire expanded, contracted, and shifted, so did those of the czarist empire of Russia. Great stretches of flat land unbroken by mountain ranges are broad highways for armies. As the Ottomans swept across the Hungarian plains, so have European powers swept back and forth across the flatlands south of the Baltic Sea. An Estonian once said that to live in those lands is to be like a bird that has built its nest on the stripe in the middle of the road.

In particular, Poland is an entity that has come and gone over the years, occupied at times by Germans, at other times by Russians. Sometimes it has subsumed the Baltic state of Lithuania to the north, and sometimes they have been separate. A person might live his whole life in one spot and be described at different times as being from Poland, Russia, Germany, or Austria.

Such was the case of Ignatz Sikorsky, whom Dr. Jacob Fine took to be a Russian. Sikorsky had come to the United States from Poland in 1910, and ten years later he was resident on Nantucket, an alien employed as a live-in servant. In 1930 he was still on Nantucket, now a naturalized citizen but still single—living alone, paying modest rent, and working as a gardener for a private family.

In his "Nantucket Personalities," Dr. Fine wrote that Sikorsky was employed by Mrs. Grace Barnes, a formerly wealthy New Yorker of reduced circumstances (although not so far down on her luck that she had to manage entirely without servants). Sikorsky, whom Barnes chose to call "Enoch," kept house for her, tended her garden, and waited on table at her dinner parties attired in "embroidered blouses she bought and insisted he wear." Fine also mentions that Sikorsky made and occasionally sold floral sculptures made of brass.

Vincent Kania and his future wife Victoria had not known each other when they were both growing up in southern Poland. He had been apprenticed to a tailor in the city of Kraków, and she had been raised in a rural village. In his early twenties he set out to find a new life in America, and a year later she fled to America to avoid an arranged marriage. They met and married in Northampton, Massachusetts, and started raising their family in New Bedford. In the mid-1920s they moved to Nantucket, where they operated Island Cleaners and Dyers on Union Street. Their advertisement in the 1927 Nantucket business directory stated, "We do Dry Cleaning in one day service. We

clean white flannel trousers in 24 hours. We also clean carpets, rugs, puffs, blankets, and furs. We do all kinds of darning, repairing, alterations and remodeling. We call at your house and deliver, on hanger, to you. Our calling and delivering is absolutely free of charge." Vincent Kania also made clothes to order, and the Kanias' oldest daughter did the bookkeeping for the business.

Although they had five Massachusetts-born children, Vincent and Victoria were still aliens when the 1930 census was taken. The family lived on Atlantic Avenue and the Kania children attended nearby Cyrus Peirce School.

The Kanias' friend on Nantucket, Stanley Ozog, married Caroline Szopa of New Bedford in 1928 and brought her to the island. Like the Kanias, they were both from southern Poland, the area around Kraków known as Galicia. Stanley Ozog had served in the U. S. Army during World War I and afterwards was employed as an electrical engineer. In this capacity he came to Nantucket to work for the Gas, Electric, and Power Company. A year into the Depression, Stanley Ozog died of a self-inflected gunshot wound in their home on Vestal Street, and his widow returned to New Bedford. Soon afterward, the Kanias, too, returned to New Bedford. When they left the island, they sold their Union Street business to Morris Bilsky, who changed the name to Beacon Cleaners and continued to advertise "White Flannel Pants cleaned like new."

The mallards that inhabit the pool fed by Consue Spring are the descendants of the pet duck of Ukrainian sculptor Nikita Carpenko, who came to Nantucket in 1930 and had his studio on the nearby lot bounded by Union Street and Spring Street. According to a short story among his papers, Carpenko—not being very knowledgeable about birds—originally called his pet "The Grand Duck Peter," but had to change the name to "The Grand Duchess Petrina" when she began laying eggs. Today a duck-crossing sign at the bend of Union Street and a wooden shelter by the spring with a quarterboard reading "Ducky" serve Petrina's countless progeny.

To Nantucketers Carpenko was as inexplicable as a character straight from the pages of Russian literature—a person of considerable talent and charm driven to act out two great stereotypes of that literature: the wounded survivor of an interrupted childhood and the sodden buffoon. It is unclear to just what extent he invented himself, and it is only possible to accept the information that appears on his death certificate as reliable because it was provided by his older sister, a sober and pious woman who joined him on Nantucket during the last years of his life. According to Luba (Carpenko) Chernitza, their parents were Andrew Carpenko and Nadezhda Kaminsky of the Ukraine. Luba was born in 1895 and Nikita in 1898, and they came of age during the Russian Revolution.

From there Nikita Carpenko takes up his own story, stating that his childhood home was Poltava, a provincial capital of central Ukraine, due north of the Black Sea. In the heart of grain and cattle country, Poltava had seen little excitement since Czar Peter the Great utterly defeated an army of far-ranging Swedish invaders there in 1709. Carpenko tells of a dreamy seven-year-old boy who, in that landlocked town, was enchanted by ships and aspired to be a sailor and shipbuilder like Peter the Great. Sent instead to the same military boarding school as his older brothers, he was spared from hazing by the other cadets because of their respect for his unique talent for building model ships.

At seventeen he was sent on to training as a cavalry officer in the czarist army, still with no prospect of going to sea. The Russian Revolution ended his prospects as a cavalry officer as well. He told a reporter that he became a pilot and did some bombing runs before fleeing the Revolution via Siberia, Manchuria, and China and thence by ship at last to Seattle. There he financed the beginning of his new American life by selling a ship model he had carried with him across Siberia and the Pacific. "From then on," he wrote, "my future was tied up in ship models. Making them and selling them."

From Seattle he moved to San Francisco, where he took art classes and had what he describes as a formative experience with a Dutch sailor and master rigger named Harry Vos. Vos, too, built model ships, and according to Carpenko, was an unsparing critic of Carpenko's efforts, claiming that he could not distinguish a cabin from a bathtub on one of Carpenko's models, slashing the rigging with a penknife, and making Carpenko do the work over until he got it right.

Responding to this mentorship, Carpenko gave himself over entirely to the art and science of model-building. Writing of himself in the third person, Carpenko said that, "he began to study, in order to learn more about the ships that he so loved. By this time, the ship models had begun to mean dreams that never came true. As he worked and learned more and more about the grace and beauty of the sailing ships, the models...took him in his imagination to strange lands. He was no longer so much interested in sea battles, but now he thought of the places where the ship had been, the strange ports, the strange cargo, the passengers as well as the sailors. He had so much love for the model ships and they meant so much to him that he now endeavored to make them as nearly lifelike as possible....There was no dry mechanical workmanship about his models...but an imaginative artistry that made the models into something alive and seaworthy."

The 1920s were a period of intense activity in Carpenko's life. In a biographical note for an exhibition brochure, he dated his departure from Russia to 1921. During his apprenticeship to Vos in San Francisco he became a naturalized citizen of the United States, and by 1930 he had crossed the country and taken up residence in Nantucket just as the Depression descended on the nation and the island.

During the hard times of the 1930s, he managed to survive by living frugally while building his reputation as a master builder of ship models.

In late spring of 1941 an exhibition of his work in Manhattan's Orrefors Gallery brought an abundance of positive publicity. Press releases described him as a specialist in American ships of 1750–1850 who dug clams during breaks from twelve-hour workdays in his Nantucket studio, where he also slept. A *New Yorker* article of May

31, 1941, expanded on the clam-digging angle to say that he located the clams with his bare toes. The May 31, 1941, issue of *Cue* also reviewed the exhibit. A model of the Hudson River packet sloop *Experiment* was commissioned for President Franklin Roosevelt.

Born in Ukraine, Nikita Carpenko was a sculptor and a long time island resident, circa 1950s.

Carpenko's model of the Nightingale.

Keeping company with Carpenko in his studio were Petrina the duck and a terrier named Lord Buckingham, both figuring in Carpenko's sketchbooks of the time. In the draft of a story, Carpenko proposes to the animals that they share their home with a princess, who turned out to be a Midwestern fellow artist named Margaret Deal. The couple married in 1944, and Peg, Nik, the duck, and the dog all appear in idyllic sketches and a Christmas card.

The couple sought to write stories together, but publishers were discouraging. In the fall of 1947 they received a letter from Adele (apparently their agent) informing them that Whittlesey House had rejected one of their coauthored stories on the grounds that the publisher did not care for animal stories for adults. She held out the promise of taking the story to other publishers while suggesting that they instead produce a children's book on ship-model building. Adele described her pitch for this potential project in which she would promote the Carpenkos as "a most attractive couple, very excellent marriage, all kinds of lessons involved, their not trying to make each other over, the contrasts, the two nationalities." This was probably the impetus for the fragmentary third-person story of Carpenko's life that appears among his papers under the title "The Dry Sea."

The marriage was not so excellent, after all, and "The Dry Sea" appears to have been abandoned. After the frenetic years of the Russian Revolution, the flight across Siberia to China, the voyage to Seattle, and then formation as an artist in San Francisco, Nantucket's slow pace during the Depression and the years of World War II proved less than healthy for a man of Carpenko's temperament. At some point he began to ravel like an old sweater. Peg divorced him.

At the end of the 1940s Carpenko had turned from model ships to sculpture. His new works, carved from whatever came to hand—broomsticks and table legs included—were mainly elongated heads reminiscent of both Modigliani's work and the *moai* of Easter Island. In the course of three years he produced over a hundred of them, exhibited his new work in New York's Guggenheim Museum, and had it featured in *Life Magazine*.

This in turn led to business correspondence with museums and galleries about rights to sell reproductions and also to private correspondence with women who aspired to be sculptors themselves. Apparently he sent invitations to them to spend summers working in his studio, growing vegetables in his garden, and selling pottery.[3] In extant letters the women answered graciously but did not come. One correspondent wrote to him on behalf of herself and another woman that "There have been times when we were on the brink of accepting your offer of room and board and no attempted seduction. (Perhaps the threat of the revitalization of your 'love parts' scares us. We have enough problems already.)" Instead it was his widowed sister Luba who came to look after him.

Her brother had become a monumental drunkard. A bottle of Emily Antosch's dandelion wine

3. Beginning in the late 1930s the *Inquirer and Mirror* carried summer advertisements for the Norwegian Pottery Shop located at "Consue at the end of Lower Union Street." The shop offered modern Finnish pottery, Danish silver and porcelain, Swedish glass, and also bronze and copper art works. Margarethe Stigum, Shirley Rei Gudmundsen and Nikita Carpenko appear together there on the 1939 and 1940 street lists, all designated as merchants.

would have been the least of it. One of Carpenko's stories opens with "Doctor Steve" emerging from a binge. "Doc's up and about again. Surely seedy and my, so thin. You'd think, wouldn't you…."

A purchaser of one of his pieces of sculpture whom Carpenko dunned for nonpayment responded with a nasty letter that reads in part, "I would like to remind you that were it not for my wife's good offices one night several summers ago, you might at this time have been banned from the island of Nantucket. As I was informed by an authority of the local government, the instance in which we became involved through our own choice was your fourth, one relatively close to the other…. We will contact you as soon as practicable to discharge the indebtedness. Until then, I hope your health remains good, and that you have not reverted to the state in which we unhappily found you."

Carpenko carved and polished a wooden head for his own memorial. On May 4, 1961, his sister found him dead in his studio. The death certificate reads "Sudden death. Presumably due to Coronary Thrombosis." His body was interred in Prospect Hill Cemetery, and over his grave a Russian cross of wood was raised. Enclosed in glass at the center of the cross was his last wooden head.

Quiet, kindly Luba, a retired registered nurse, lived on for another sixteen years tending her brother's studio and garden, and looking after the ducks before she too was laid to rest in Prospect Hill Cemetery.

At his death Nikita Carpenko had resided for over thirty years on Nantucket, longer than he had ever lived anywhere else. In time the great wooden cross on his grave rotted, sagged, and finally was removed. A man whose extravagance and prodigious appetites got him into hot water time and again, he would probably be vastly amused that his most enduring contribution to the place where he spent nearly half his life is a duck pond.

Ducks at Consue Spring.

CHAPTER ELEVEN

Fishing for a Living

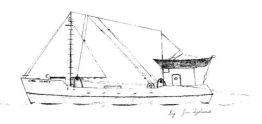

Captain Rolf Sjölund's dragger Carl Henry
drawn by his grandson James Sjölund.

The weather was the subject of conversation all the time—morning, noon, and night! Among the fishermen and the wives too. Also the price of fish on a daily basis. And where the fishing was good or bad on the fishing grounds. When the boats had to go into dry dock for painting or repair, there was always despair because of lost income. It was a hard, hard life!

—Olga Hansen

Back in the 1670s Captain John Gardner set up a Wampanoag-manned codfishing operation to meet New York's demand that Nantucket pay its taxes with barrels of fish. Whaling, which got under way at the same time, proved more profitable and absorbed the labor of all the able-bodied Wampanoag men. After the Wampanoag population crash in the mid 1700s, Africans filled the vacant spaces in the whaleboats. As Nantucket whalers traveled ever farther over the oceans, they brought back to the island crew members collected from all around the globe. A half century after the demise of that industry, the prospect of making a living from the sea once again attracted a cosmopolitan population to Nantucket.

In the 1880s dory fishing for codfish and sharks was still going on from the ocean beaches of Quidnet, Siasconset's Codfish Park, and the South Shore. For two successive days in November 1876, fifty dories put out from the South Shore, bringing back as many as three hundred fish per dory. Launching through the surf and, even worse, landing through the surf with a load of fish was dangerous business, and the dorymen blessed Captain Eugene Clisby, keeper of the Surfside Lifesaving Station, who kept a sharp eye out for

Fishermen landing a dory through the breakers.

Henry S. Wyer photograph. Nantucket Historical Association

returning boats. On March 26, 1927, the *Inquirer and Mirror* printed a letter from Leland S. Topham in which he wrote of Captain Clisby, "It was always pleasing on rough days to see the genial skipper on the beach waiting to con the dories through the breakers."

By the 1890s catboats engaged in what today would be called multitasking; in the summers they served the tourist trade with party cruises and regular transportation between the town wharves and the bathing beach, while in the winter they were used for hauling scallop dredges under sail. For deepwater swordfishing, the catboats were equipped with bowsprits from which the fish were spotted and harpooned. Later, when small gasoline engines became available, catboat owners dismasted their boats for more effective scalloping at the expense of what had once been their utilitarian grace and beauty.

In 1913 a huge bed of quahogs was discovered in the Chord of the Bay, north of the jetties. The quahogs immediately became an export item shipped to the mainland on the steamboats. That same winter a record catch of scallops was dredged up and shipped in kegs from Nantucket. In the meantime, fishing weirs set offshore were producing daily yields of mackerel, cod, pollock, bluefish, and bonita that were either sold locally or shipped in barrels to off-island markets. A fish-packing operation was established on Steamboat Wharf, setting a record on March 15, 1915, of 1,426 barrels of fish and shellfish dispatched to the mainland by steamer.

Instead of the years-long global whaling cruises of the past, the boatmen of the twentieth century either fished by the day in local waters or by the week on the fishing banks off the northeast coast. By the 1920s, the Nantucket fishing fleet included more substantial vessels than the

Dredging for bay scallops under sail, circa 1915.

dories and catboats of the past, captained and crewed by a mix of New Englanders and the foreign born. Among the latter were north Europeans and French Canadians who had come to make Nantucket their home port. These newly arrived men literally fished for a living, while some of their compatriots—women and men—worked on land, figuratively angling for a better life than what they had left behind.

Some of the fishermen and their families had emigrated from the coasts of the Baltic Sea. The longitude of their home towns was as far east as that of the inland towns of Poland, western Russia, Greece, and western Turkey whence had come the Geneskys, Kaufmans, Kanias, Bilskys, Anastoses, and Abajians—among others—of the same era. The latitude of the fishermen's home towns was well north of Nantucket's. They came from lands of ice-bound winters and summertime "white nights." They were, on the whole, a self-reliant lot.

— *Jay Avila illustration*

The Baltic countries and Fenno-Scandeinavia.

Latvians

The Baltic country of Latvia is sandwiched between Lithuania to the south and Estonia to the north, the three of them stacked on top of Poland and Belarus ("White Russia"). Finland lies north of them all—across the water from Estonia and facing west over the Gulf of Bothnia toward Sweden. During the 1800s famine was a nearly constant presence throughout the Baltic area, repeatedly inflicting starvation on its rural villages even as its cities industrialized. Yet despite what statisticians might term "excess deaths," the populations grew beyond the lands' carrying capacity for subsistence farmers and fishermen. Finland's population, for instance, tripled between 1800 and 1900. By the end of the century landlessness had reached crisis proportions. Facilitated by new railroads that made escape from the countryside possible, mass emigration from port cities on the Baltic carried thousands of working men and women away to the United States and Canada.

A half dozen Latvian families gathered in Prospect Hill Cemetery in mid-February 1920 to pay their last respects to forty-year-old Max

Egle. Since there was no Lutheran clergyman on Nantucket, his brother John Egle spoke movingly in Latvian to the assembled mourners. After presiding at his brother's graveside, John Egle himself fell gravely ill, as did his wife Alma and their daughter Erna. The three of them came close to dying but eventually recovered. Other family members did not. Within days of Max's funeral, the Latvians returned to Prospect Hill to lay to rest Katherine Duce and Max Egle's thirteen-year-old son John.

Influenza had taken three members of the intermarried Egle and Duce families in a matter of days. George Duce's wife Lena was Max's sister, and George's older brother Christopher was Katherine's husband.

They had come away from Latvia by stages, preceded by the oldest man and followed by the younger men and women. Christopher and Katherine Duce were the first. Christopher, 36 years old, arrived in the United States in 1906, and Katherine, 33, came the next year. In 1907, Max Egle, then 27, and George Duce, 25, came. The year after that, Max sent tickets to his brother John, 22, for passage to Boston from London, where the young man had arrived as a stowaway aboard a Finnish freighter. George's wife Lena got out that year with their daughter Alice, and Max's wife Pauline came with their son John. Max's future sister-in-law Alma Becker was the last to arrive in the United States in 1913. Although their immediate port of entry had been Boston, and they had quickly connected with the Latvian community in Beverly, Massachusetts, the Egles and Duces ended up in Nantucket.

In 1910 Max Egle was head of a Nantucket household that included his wife Pauline, his brother John, his sister Lena and her husband George Duce, and two four-year-olds, Alice Duce and little John Egle. That year all the men were fishing to support their families. Max, John, and George were shellfishing, and Christopher Duce, who lived apart from them, was a line fisherman.

Life on the open water was a practical skill acquired in Nantucket. The Egles had come from Tukums, a riverside town some thirty miles west of Riga, the Latvian capital. The coast of the Gulf of Riga lies at some distance from Tukums, and they had grown up in farming country.

In nineteenth-century Latvia the land was largely in the hands of absentee landlords—Baltic Germans, Poles, and Russians whose large estates were worked by Latvian sharecroppers, renters, and contract laborers. The local population was in the unyielding grasp of the estate owners, and the Latvians' alternatives were revolution at home or emigration to other lands. Russian suppression of rising nationalism in all the Baltic countries was carried out through the garrisoning of Cossack troops in cities and towns and terrorist reprisals against the small farmers and their families.

In 1978 Leeds Mitchell Jr. interviewed John Egle and wrote down his biography from school days in Latvia to old age in Nantucket. The Egle family story leading up to several members' departure from Latvia is as thrilling in its details as Nikita Carpenko's stories of the Russian Revolution and flight from the Bolsheviks. As

John Egle told it to Mitchell, his older brother Max had been subjected to a near-fatal whipping with the knout—a vicious punishment Russians used to intimidate their subjects—before he fled to America. As a teenager, John himself had been drawn into revolutionary activities, and in order to evade police interrogation he sought employment on an estate distant from Tukums. In the course of those early years he learned to speak German, Polish, and Russian in addition to his native language. Eventually, despite his best efforts to disappear, the authorities located him, and he had to take a last leave of his devastated parents and flee his home country. Members of the Latvian underground hid John Egle and a buddy in the coal hold of a Finnish freighter, and they sailed away, never to see Latvia again.

By 1910, with the exception of Christopher, the Egle and Duce men residing on Nantucket had taken out United States citizenship papers. Five years later all of them, including Christopher, had been sworn in as citizens, and so had their wives. While World War I raged on and Latvia was gaining its short-lived independence from Russia, the Latvian families in Nantucket were /expanding. By 1920 Max and Pauline had two more children, and so had George and Lena, while John and Alma had their first. All the men but John, the youngest, had given up fishing for other occupations. Christopher and George were working as house carpenters, while Max was a machinist with his own shop. Christopher and Katherine owned their home with no mortgage. George's daughter Alice had married fisherman Lambertus Lamens, who had come from Holland in 1911. The census enumerator reported that everyone from youngest to oldest spoke English.

Then disaster began to pile on disaster. When the influenza pandemic of 1918 swept through Nantucket, it had carried off newspaper vendor and tobacconist Richard Mack, son of Irish immigrants. On a return visit to Nantucket in the winter of 1920 it took out its wrath on the Latvians, killing Max Egle, his son John, and Katherine Duce.

John Egle at fifty and at one hundred years of age.

In 1927 George Duce's wife Lena died, and the next year George himself succumbed to lung cancer. After their parents' death George's and Lena's three American-born sons—Harry, Waldemar, and Arnold—went to live with their married sister Alice and her family. By then, Harry was already employed as a fisherman.

Widowed Christopher married Olga Welk, a young woman half his age, who had arrived in the United States in 1923. Compared to the five unfortunate family members who died in the 1920s, Christopher lived a long life, dying just short of his seventy-fifth birthday. In the end, however, John Egle's lifetime exceeded Christopher Duce's by a full quarter of a century.

As a young man John Egle simultaneously courted the sea and his bride Alma, whom he met among the Latvian community in Beverly. Having briefly tried working for wages on a dairy farm in Vermont and doing carpentry in Nantucket, he learned that he could earn much more by shellfishing. Investing in a boat of his own and building himself a rent-free shanty on Muskeget, he soon learned the sea in all its moods as he took his quahogs and scallops in to Steamboat Wharf and sailed in the other direction to the mainland to spend time with Alma. In the autumn of 1914 she paid a visit to Nantucket and to John's extended family, and in May of 1915 they were married. The next year Erna, the first of their children, was born.

In order to spend less time on the water and more with his growing family, John had gone to work in his brother Max's shop doing engine repair for the island's fishing fleet, while augmenting his income seasonally by operating the boats belonging to Nantucket summer residents. In the summer of 1920, months after Max's demise and his own close brush with death, he became captain of a new vessel built for Leeds Mitchell Sr., a wealthy owner of a summer home on Brant Point. For the rest of Leeds Mitchell's life and on afterward, John Egle was in what Leeds Mitchell Jr. described as "a symbiotic relationship" with the Mitchell family.

Of John and Alma Egle's three children, the eldest, Erna, married locally and remained on-island. A son, named for his father, lived only nine months. Their second daughter Wilma grew up, married, and moved to Vermont. For a while after that Alma rented rooms in their large Easton Street house, and then she and John moved into a smaller one that John built on the edge of the Lily Pond close to their daughter Erna's home. After fifty-seven years of marriage, Alma's death left John a widower.

John Egle was a man who seldom let others do for him. Like most other Nantucket family men, he hunted deer, rabbits, and pheasants to provide his household with meat during the 1930s and 1940s. He grew his own vegetables and flowers. He baked his own bread. He maintained and repaired his own boats. When he needed a house, he built one. When the walls of his house seemed bare, he painted landscapes for them. After Alma's death, he concentrated his time and attention on painting. His daughter, Erna Blair, was herself greatly admired for her ability to create unusual lamps and lamp shades. Her shop on the edge of the Lily Pond was a popular local business where she exhibited her father's work.

Over a dozen years, between the ages of 86 and 98, John Egle produced three hundred paintings, which were exhibited to acclaim locally and, in 1988, at the DeCordova Museum in Lincoln, Massachusetts. Even after the Nantucket Artists' Association honored him at age 97 for his accomplishments, he continued on robustly until his death at 101, by then the holder of Nantucket's famous Boston Post Cane, which is always in the keeping of the island's oldest resident.

Among the Latvian families who had gathered to hear John Egle's words in Prospect Hill Cemetery in February 1920, were the Ottisons, who had come to Nantucket five years earlier. Adolph Ottison had left Latvia in 1904, and Anna Emily Feierabend followed in 1908. Their first child, Alma, was born in New Hampshire in 1912, and four years later their son Albert was born in Nantucket. Between the births of the children, Emily's mother Catherine "Katrina" Feierabend joined them in the United States. After 1920 Latvia-born Fred Matison, who had been in the United States longer than any of them, also came to live with the Ottison family in the Pleasant Street home they had purchased. Young Alma Ottison married Allen Holdgate, who was barely older than she was, and the couple resided with her parents. Adolph Ottison and Fred Matison supported the large household by fishing. Between 1914 and 1930 elderly Katrina Feierabend had not learned to speak English and, despite assimilationist pressures during and after World War I, she did not seek United States citizenship.

Latvia, which had been incorporated into Russia in the 1720s, only gained national independence in 1918, after the departure of the families who settled in Nantucket. The federal censuses for Nantucket variously identified the Latvians on the island as Russians and Poles, and their first language as Russian, Polish, "Lettish," and even Yiddish, which was probably an error for Lettish. (In the past Latvians have been called Letts, and their language Lettish.) All the Latvians who were born in the old country and died on Nantucket were interred in Prospect Hill Cemetery.

Finns

In the 1800s Finland endured many political and economic conditions in common with Latvia. Over the course of six centuries as a province of Sweden, the land had been a bloody battleground, as the border between west and east constantly shifted back and forth according to the balance of power between the kings of Sweden and the czars of Russia. In the first half of the 1700s, at a time when Nantucket's English population was burgeoning, Finland's population was crashing. During two grim periods recalled as "the great wrath" and "the lesser wrath," a military scorched-earth policy drove the Finnish population into hiding in the forests for years on end. Destruction of food reserves, lost harvests, and severe winters without adequate shelter decimated the population. In 1808 Sweden finally ceded all of Finland to Russia.

As bitter as the 1700s had been, Finns have not remembered the 1800s fondly either. Whole villages starved to death in the 1860s, and even as late as the 1890s there was hunger in the countryside, as the Russian administration failed to ship food from where it was available to remote areas where it was needed. As in Latvia, the Russian government attempted to suppress a rising sense of national identity by building garrisons in towns around the country and bringing in Cossack troops to intimidate the local population. A russification policy was put in place: Russian was declared the official language of the country, schools were supposed to be conducted in Russian, Russian-language street signs went up in the towns, and Finnish men were conscripted to fight in the Russian army against the peoples of Central Asia.

Finland's own language diversity exacerbated the situation. Unlike Latvian—a language with affinities to both Russian and Polish—Finnish is historically unrelated to either Swedish or Russian. Its linguistic relatives are Estonian, spoken to the south across the Gulf of Finland; several minority languages spoken in northern Fenno-Scandinavia and in Russia; and—more distantly—Hungarian. As Finnish nationalism gathered force in the 1800s, one of its rallying cries was, "Swedes we never were. Russians we can't become. So we must be Finns!"

Yet the language map was not so simple. During its long period as a province of Sweden, the language of church and education in Finland had been first Latin and then Swedish. Having a Swedish surname and speaking Swedish had become indicators of class. Town folk, estate owners, clergymen, and bureaucrats were Swedish speakers. For centuries Finnish speakers had been dependent on them for getting things done—everything from securing employment to bringing suit in court to getting married, naming one's children, and burying one's dead. The published literature of Finland had been written in Swedish. Yet as the wave of Finnish nationalism gathered force, many Finnish intellectuals willingly gave up their Swedish names for adopted Finnish ones and strove—with greater and lesser success—to switch to speaking Finnish.

There was another Swedish-speaking population in the country, however—one that was unwilling to go along with this shift. On the coasts of the Gulf of Bothnia and the Gulf of Finland, farmers and fishermen spoke Swedish as their first language, and they were not eager to relinquish their linguistic heritage. As one descendant of these coastal working people remarked, "There are two kinds of Swedish speakers in Finland: the aristocrats and the fishermen. And the fishermen have always fancied themselves aristocrats." The language issue divided Finn-Swedes (or Finlanders as they are sometimes called) from the majority Finnish population, and the "language wars" carried on for decades.

From Finnish records, it appears that between 1880 and 1920 (when Finland had finally achieved its independence and survived a brief but devastating civil war) over three hundred thousand people, both Finns and Finlanders, left their country to escape poverty, conscription into the Russian army, and the imposition of repressive Russian policies at home. Most went to the United States and Canada. The Swedish-speaking emigrants were more willing to see their children grow up as English speakers than as Finnish speakers in the old country. Everyone was more willing to voluntarily adopt English than to have Russian forced on them.

Initially, young unmarried men outnumbered women among the immigrants. In Massachusetts they found work as quarrymen in Quincy and Cape Ann. On Cape Cod they worked alongside Cape Verdeans in the cranberry bogs, rose to be bog managers, and saved to become bog owners.

Unmarried Finnish women found employment as domestics. Both men and women went to work in the Fitchburg, Massachusetts, textile mills. They founded a Finnish-language newspaper in Fitchburg, built saunas and social halls wherever they settled, and—like the Latvians in Beverly—gathered at festivals and church socials to meet one another, make music, talk politics, and find spouses.

Although there is a cohesive Finnish-American presence on Cape Cod, the Finns resident on Nantucket—few in number, from different hometowns, and married to non-Finns—did not organize. The Kittilä name has carried on through generations on the island. The first John Kittilä was born in Pyhäjoki, a coastal town on the west coast of Finland, in 1895 and came to the United States in time to serve in the U. S. Coast Guard during World War I. His son followed in his footsteps and had a career in the Coast Guard, serving at Sankaty Head and Brant Point Lighthouses and as commander of the South Shoals Lightship, where he made lightship baskets in his free time. His grandson John Kittilä III also became a basket maker, and his great-grandson carried on the name as John Kittilä IV.

In the summer of 1928 Jalmar Kiiski was engaged as swimming instructor and masseur at Royal's Baths, "the most popular and largest bathing establishment on the island." According to the advertisement announcing that summer's opening of the bathing beach, Kiiski already had "many years' experience in the finest and most up-to-date pools and camps of New England" as well as being a graduate of the "Cambridge School of Swedish Massage and Medical Gymnastics, the largest massage school in New England." The 1934 Nantucket telephone book contains a listing under Kiiski's name for a "health service" on Lower Main Street. In the mid 1940s he returned to the island with his family as year-round residents. Although his wife, Gladys Gardner (Lingham) Kiiski, had been born in Brockton, Massachusetts, she was connected to the island through her mother, Nantucket-born Emma Andrews.

In the immediate postwar years the Kiiskis lived on North Liberty Street, their son Richard attended Academy Hill School, and Jalmar Kiiski was employed as the Nantucket agent for Knapp Brothers shoes. Later they moved to Orange Street and then to a shared house on India Street, where the Nantucket street lists for 1953 and 1954 state Jalmar's occupation as carpenter and that of Gladys as housewife. Gladys Kiiski died in August of 1954, and thereafter Jalmar Kiiski's name disappears from the annual street lists.

Two Burgess men, not brothers, took Finnish wives. In 1932 Eugene Francis "Todd" Burgess married a woman from Tampere, a textile-mill town in central Finland. They were married in Port Chester, New York, but thereafter they lived on Nantucket in an area off Lower Orange Street overlooking the Creeks that was and is known as Poverty Point. Todd Burgess supported himself and Anna by driving a taxi and, according to the Nantucket street lists, occasionally serving as the town dog officer. The couple remained childless.

When the Soviet Union attacked Finland in 1939, the *Inquirer and Mirror* reported that Nantucket resident Anna Burgess was a native of Finland and that "Her mother and sister live at the old homestead and her three brothers are serving at the front." Her hometown had been bombed, the report continued, and Anna Burgess had been out of touch with her relatives for the past six weeks.

Three years after Todd Burgess married Anna, Samuel Burgess took Gertrude Majanen for his wife in New York City. For the first eight years of their marriage they lived in New York, and then they moved to Nantucket and lived on Pine Street.

Sam Burgess was not Todd Burgess's brother or even a Nantucket Burgess. He had been born in Pennsylvania of a father from Tennessee and a mother from New Jersey. It was sheer chance that two unrelated men with the same last name should end up living in a community as small as Nantucket with wives from faraway Finland.

Gertrude Burgess had been born Kerttu Kaarina Lemmikki Majanen in 1910. A few months

The multi-ethnic first grade class at Academy Hill School, circa 1926. Back row: Nelson Hearn, John Heath, June Coffin, Gertrude Esau, Della Dunham, David Roberts, Richard Folger, Alma Richards, Susan Larrabee, Ludabina Santos. Middle row: Doris Kittilä, Olga Anderson, Madeline Santos, Olney Cady, Grace Larkin, Evelyn Gibbs, Rodney Locke, Freida Anderson, Arthur Butler, Louis Coffin. Front row: Mary McGrath, Norman Anderson, Euna Raftery, Gilbert Reed, Ethel Gardner, George Sullivan, Bernice Mathison, Mary Lumbert, Philip Moore.

before her twentieth birthday she embarked for New York, where she anglicized her name to Gertrude and eventually married Sam Burgess. Unlike Todd and Anna Burgess, Sam and Gertrude had children—four daughters, the youngest born the year the family moved to Nantucket and settled on Pine Street.

Ten years later both Burgess marriages collapsed in a matter of a few months. According to the 1953 street list, Gertrude Burgess had left Sam on Pine Street and moved in with Todd and Anna on Poverty Point. In July 1953 she filed for divorce from Sam Burgess, and a month later Anna filed for divorce from Todd Burgess. By October both divorces were final. Gertrude kept custody of her oldest daughter and relinquished custody of the three younger girls to Sam, who later remarried.

Anna remarried too. Her new husband was Victor Salmi, a Finn like herself and a carpenter. They continued to live on Poverty Point, where Victor built Anna a sauna with a grand view of the Creeks and Nantucket Harbor. It was perhaps the only free-standing sauna ever built on the island. In the mid 1960s Anna and Victor sold the property and moved away, but the sauna stood for years after they left, looking like an outgrown children's playhouse or a tool shed until it was finally demolished in the 1990s.

The Soviet attack on Finland at the end of 1939 brought warfare with Russia back onto Finnish ground for the first time since 1808. The attempted invasion launched what was known as the Winter War and brought an outpouring of international sympathy and admiration for the outnumbered Finns fighting off the would-be occupiers.

In a series of articles supportive of Finland's resistance, the *Inquirer and Mirror* first identified Anna Burgess as Finnish-born and then, the following month, reported that Hilda Gibbs was also a native of Finland.[1]

Hilda (Österberg) Gibbs was the widow of Sarah P. Bunker's grandson, Maurice Gibbs. For the first three years of her marriage, Hilda had shared living space with Sarah P., and for the eighteen years since Maurice's death, she had been head of the household in Sarah P.'s place. By 1940 the street address was 12 Cliff Road, and hardly anyone recalled that when Hilda had come to live there, it had been North Street.

It is not surprising that it took the *Inquirer and Mirror* over a month to find out that Hilda Gibbs was a native of Finland. She was much older than Anna Burgess and had lived on Nantucket since the 1890s. Born in 1871 in the town of Vasa, down the coast of the Gulf of Bothnia from John Kittilä's hometown, Hilda—unlike John Kittilä and Anna Burgess—did not speak Finnish. She had been raised speaking Swedish and had attended a Swedish-language school.

This is not to say that Hilda was any less a patriotic Finn than the Finnish-speaking immigrants to North America. Like so many others, she maintained a small altar to Finnish nationhood on a table in her home. On a white crocheted doily stood a miniature flag pole with the blue and white Finnish flag, a carved wooden spoon, a carved wooden bird, and three wooden boxes. One box was from Turkey, inscribed inside to Hilda from her maternal aunt Magdalena. Magdalena Berg had it as a souvenir of Finland's involvement in Russia's Central Asian adventures of the 1870s, and she gave it to her niece when she left for America.

In the Turkish box Hilda kept a silver thimble and two doll-size miniature sheath knives typical of her region of Finland.

The second was a lacquered box from Russia with a scene on the lid of a troika drawn by galloping horses through snowy woods. The third was a round box and lid carved from a single piece of Finnish birch wood. A drawer in the

---

1. The Winter War lasted from December 1939 to March 1940. During that time the *Inquirer and Mirror* published articles on December 16, December 30, January 27, February 3, March 9, and March 16 supporting the country and soliciting aid to its citizens via the Red Cross and the Finnish Relief Fund. The March 16, 1940, front-page announcement of "Finland's Triumph" was signed by Joseph W. Cochran, chairman of the local Finnish Relief Fund. The triumph was, in fact, an admission by the Finns that they could not maintain force of arms in defense of their country. They ceded part of their territory in exchange for the rest of it not being occupied. Nonetheless, hostilities resumed later that year and the "Continuation War" was waged until 1944 with the displacement of half a million people, the loss of a hundred thousand Finnish lives, and the permanent disability of many survivors.

table contained a Finnish tourist brochure and an autograph book containing verses in Swedish that Hilda's classmates had written for her when she finished school. In different ways, they all asked her not to forget them when she was far away.

Hilda remembered well the garrisoning of Russian troops in Vasa when she was a girl. A block of red-brick barracks and an Orthodox church had been built in advance of their arrival. One winter day word went out that the troop train was coming, and crowds of townspeople began packing snowballs around stones and holding them under water spigots to freeze them. When the soldiers were marched off the train, they were pelted with ice balls. As an old woman, Hilda remembered with shame that the hated occupiers were teen-aged boys, already half-frozen, far from their homes, and exhausted by days of transport from Russia. Soon their heads and faces were streaked with blood as they marched though a gauntlet of townspeople. And then, she added, their officers made them stand through an interminable Orthodox service in the Russian church before they were permitted to clean up, eat, and rest.

During Hilda's girlhood an air of profound pessimism lay over Vasa, as it did over all of Finland. She had been born in the aftermath of deadly famine. The year she was born, her sister died, and her parents left the countryside for town, where her father went to work in a textile mill. Of the eight more children her mother bore after the move, only four survived childhood.

The oldest of five sisters, Hilda assumed the responsibilities of the son of the family. As her father's helper and his confidante, she was present when a Cossack on horseback menaced him, and she heard of the things that happened to local girls taken into the Russian barracks. Her father told her that like so many young men from their part of the country, she had to go to America and earn money so that her sisters could leave too, and that is what she did. With her she took the Swedish Bible she had received at confirmation. In America she acquired an English-language one, and set to work learning English by comparing biblical passages.

By 1895 Hilda had been in the United States for four years and was working as a domestic on Nantucket. Her sister Ellen had come to work on the island too, and the sisters had a Swedish-speaking Finnish friend, Ida Gref, working here as well. Five years later two more of her sisters, Irene and Edith, had come to Nantucket from Finland. Ellen and Irene were working as domestics in one of the Starbuck mansions—the Three Bricks—on Main Street. Their younger sister Edith had just arrived and was with Hilda, her new husband Maurice Gibbs, and his grandmother Sarah P. Bunker in the old family home on North Street.

Ida Gref continued working for a family on Main Street. When the three sisters and Ida got together with Hilda in Sarah P.'s kitchen on maids days off, they sat down together to chat over knitting, while the house filled with the sounds of Swedish and the fragrance of coffee braids baking in the oven. At four in the afternoon Hilda would carry Sarah P.'s tea up to her room and drop her

Hilda (Österberg) Gibbs and her family. Clockwise from top left: Surfman Maurice Gibbs, Arthur, John, Esther, and Charlotte.

a respectful curtsey, as well-brought-up Finnish girls were taught to and as Finnish maids did all their lives long.

After 1900, the youngest sister, Frida, received her ticket to America too. Next Hilda saved money to help Edith and Frida go to nursing school. By 1910 all Hilda's sisters had moved on, and even Ida Gref had left the island. Sarah P. had gone to her rest, and Hilda didn't curtsey to anyone anymore.

By the time her mother died in Finland, Hilda was herself a widow. It had happened almost without warning. A veteran surfman in the U. S. Coast Guard, Maurice Gibbs had suffered a back injury during a training exercise. Shortly thereafter, while on duty at Madaket Station, he was suddenly "stricken with a peculiar illness." Taken to the Marine Hospital in Vineyard Haven for treatment, he did not recover.

Left with four children—the youngest eleven years old—Hilda set about expanding Sarah P.'s house in all directions to add rooms for boarders. Sarah P. Bunker's old home became unrecognizable as the classic Nantucket house it had been.

Hilda's daughters helped with the paying guests. There were "regulars" who returned every year for a week or two in the third-floor "sky parlor," the sleeping porches, Sarah P.'s own rooms, and the downstairs borning room. Hilda's family members withdrew into what had been the servants quarters behind the kitchen and the carriage house in back. In 1923 the *Inquirer and Mirror* published a high school essay by Hilda's daughter Charlotte about being a surfman's daughter and about playing what has come to be known as the "Nantucket shuffle," relinquishing one's living space to renters and moving into uncomfortable summer quarters. "Houses to be rented receive an extra spring polish," she wrote. "If you are unlucky enough to be living in one, you know how renters always come to look it over at the wrong time; and how they insist on seeing the room where you are dressing, or the kitchen at dinner time."

Fourteen years after her husband's death Hilda began to receive a Coast Guard survivor's pension, which augmented the summer income from her boarders as her children married and brought children of their own into the household.

It was in the middle years of Hilda's widowhood that Finland was plunged into war. The crisis galvanized her household, as everyone down to the youngest grandchild was put to packing relief boxes for relatives in Finland. The struggle for national survival finally brought Finnish speakers and Swedish speakers together across the language divide—both at home and among Finnish emigrants abroad. Back in 1927 three Finnish women—Hilma Koskela, Anna Kosonen, and Vieno Kouvola—had spent a summer in a nearby house on Cliff Road, but Hilda had made no effort to meet them. They were summer people and—more to the point—as Hilda firmly maintained, she didn't speak a word of Finnish. But with the war, patriotism won out over language allegiance. She sang the Finnish national anthem to her grandchildren in Swedish and revealed that she did, after all, know some songs in Finnish too. Language allegiance no longer counted so much.

From the day Hilda's youngest daughter first opened the North Shore Restaurant in 1943, Hilda baked the daily dinner rolls. Kneading bread dough in the summers and knitting countless pairs of red woolen gloves in the winters kept hands, heart, and mind busy for another two

The North Shore Restaurant soon after it opened in 1943.

Courtesy of Frances Karttunen

decades, granting Hilda a life as long as Sarah P.'s had been. Her grandchildren were the sixth and last generation of descended Nantucketers to live in Sarah P. Bunker's old home.

Like Theresa Szabo, young Hilda Österberg had brought a small lingusitic treasure chest with her to Nantucket: her Swedish Bible, her autograph book, and the songs from her childhood.

Swedes

The weaving studio at 64 Union Street is nearly in view of Poverty Point, where Victor and Anna Salmi's sauna once stood, and it is even closer to Nikita Carpenko's former studio and the duck pond. On an afternoon in early 2001, master weaver Margareta (Grandin) Nettles took time away from her loom to read Hilda (Österberg) Gibbs's autograph book. For a woman born in Sweden in 1933 the language of the verses written back in 1885 was old-fashioned, provincial, and sometimes oddly spelled, but Margareta was in no way critical. Neither did she take the shortcut of translating anything into English. Instead, she would tactfully ask, "Do you understand this right here?" and if the answer was no, she would paraphrase the verse in more understandable Swedish until it became clear. By the time the bright winter sunshine began to fade, the verses had been read to the end, and Margareta exclaimed over the pleasure of having spent the afternoon with Hilda's girlhood friends from so long ago and far away.

Such generosity was characteristic of Margareta, who found positive good in many things and most people. Raised in Eskiltuna, a town in central Sweden, and professionally trained in textile design at Stockholm's State School of Art and Design, she came to the United States on a Swedish travel grant in 1966 and soon returned to teach a summer course at the Nantucket School of Needlery. Thereafter she established a studio of her own in New York City, where she met and married James Nettles. In the late 1970s she and her family moved to Nantucket and opened a weaving studio on Union Street. Margareta's sense of design and the excellence

of the products of the Nettles' studio brought so many commissions that for years the studio had a staff of a half or dozen or more. Many aspiring weavers apprenticed there, producing rugs, wall hangings, and other textiles for celebrity clients. When Margareta underwent surgery in 1997, the Nettles family cut back on the studio's production to give full scope to her boundless zest for life. Her death in the spring of 2003 left her immense circle of friends and admirers bereft.

The Union Street weaving studio was not the only one in Nantucket. Not far away on Orange Street Anna Lynn, also from Sweden, has her Weaving Room. Graduate of Stockholm University and a textile design school, Anna also moved to New York City, as Margareta had before her. A friend suggested a spring get-away visit to Nantucket for a milieu more like Sweden. Returning to the island via an association with the Nantucket Island School of Design & the Arts, Anna Lynn became a resident of the island—entrepreneur, wife, and mother.

At the end of the twentieth century, Margareta Nettles, Anna Lynn, and several other Swedish women formed a Nantucket social circle that met regularly for food, handwork, and companionship, just as the Österberg sisters and their friend Ida Greff had a century earlier.

There is a history of Swedish women outnumbering Swedish men on Nantucket. At the end of the whaling era James Sandsbury, born in Sweden, lived on the island. He owned substantial real estate but was approaching 70 and no longer engaged in any occupation. Ten years later, he was making his home with a very large family. Another aged Swede, a sailmaker whose name appears as "Theodore Sohufflin" was recorded in the 1880 census. By then a young shoemaker, O. Magnus Holmberg, had moved to the island with his wife and infant child and departed again. The 1870 federal census, the one that records no Cape Verdeans on the island, also shows no Swedes. Because the economy was at its nadir and there had been a great exodus, this may be true, or—on the other hand—there may have been an undercount of the foreign-born that year. Whatever the case, after 1870 Swedish women began to appear. Three were resident on Nantucket in 1880, nine in 1900, seven in 1910, eleven in 1920, and fourteen in 1930.

These women had come to work, but they stayed as married women. Seven of the nine on-island in 1900 were employed as servants, but six out of seven were married in 1910, and among the Swedish women living on the island in 1920, only the widow Hannah Norcross, who did housework for Gulielma Folger and her sister on Cliff Road, was still working as a domestic. Likewise, in 1930 only one Swedish woman was unmarried and working in someone else's home, in this case caring for an elderly couple.

Two Swedish women married Dunham men. Anna Dunham was born in 1845, arrived in the United States in 1873, married Daniel Dunham, and already had children by the time she appeared in the 1880 census. Forty years later she was still on-island, living alone as a widow. Lalla Dunham had come in 1911, been naturalized in 1918, married Nelson O. Dunham, and become a mother by 1920. By 1930 the couple had four daughters.

The conversion from gas lighting to electric lighting in private homes put electricians to work wiring old Nantucket houses, a project that carried on for decades. In 1900 there were already several electricians on the island. One was Augustus Lake. His wife, Anna Nelson, was born in Gothenburg, a city on the west coast of Sweden, and had been brought to the United States as a girl in 1887. Selma Newman came to the United States three years later and was employed as a chambermaid by the Fish family until electrician George Rogers of Rhode Island married her. They made their home in 'Sconset, and in 1930 their adult son, who had followed his father into the business, was living with them. Also living in 'Sconset in 1930 was Hilda Welch, who was a clerk in her husband's grocery store on Shell Street.

Hulda Mårtensson traveled all the way to Iowa on her way from the old country to Nantucket. In Iowa she married Fred Allen, changed her name, and became Hilda Allen. Later the Allens, their Iowa-born son William, his brother Clifford, and Fred's father operated Allen's Pullman Lunch at the foot of Main Street. Nantucket's railroad had ceased operation at the time of World War I, and all its rolling stock had been shipped off with the exception of one car, which remained next to the American Railway Express building at the foot of Main Street, just beyond the Pacific Club building. At about the time that the railroad went out of operation, the Allen family moved from Iowa to Massachusetts. From the mainland they came on to Nantucket, moved in over the express company, and created a diner in the orphaned railroad car. Like the Kaufman family's restaurant around the corner on South Water Street, the Pullman Lunch diner and its "annex" dining room in the former express office space were perennially popular with residents and summer visitors alike and operated for decades. Hilda Allen lived to within a few days of her hundredth birthday. Her obituary stated, "There was no one on the island who made a better bread pudding or apple pie than did Mrs. Allen."

Ellen Johnson was also employed as a restaurant cook in 1930. The census that year recorded her as head of a household consisting of herself and her three Iowa-born children. Her daughter

The white building behind the Pacific Club became home to Allen's Pullman Lunch. Photograph by John W. Macy, 1928.

was at that time working as an assistant restaurant cook. Caroline Lewis, who had arrived in 1898, had become the wife of Nantucket farmer William Lewis and was living on Orange Street with her husband.

Not all Swedes on Nantucket were Swedish women married to local men. Carl Anderson, born in Sweden in 1879, was already approaching middle age when he married Hattie Parker of Nantucket. At the time he was working as a fisherman, but as a married man he left the water to run a gardening and caretaking business. Unlike many of the foreign-born and their children, Anderson was not reticent about his old-country origin; he publicized it by building a Scandinavian kick-sled for himself, on which he glided around town after snowstorms. Also unlike many other foreign-born men on Nantucket, he did not join the Masonic lodge, instead centering his social life around the Oddfellows lodge and the Wharf Rat Club. He and Nikita Carpenko died within a day of each other in 1961. Unlike Carpenko, Anderson reached the end of his life an octogenarian, father, and grandfather.

In the 1930s an elderly Swedish couple, Eric and Norma Lindqvist, were living with their son, daughter-in-law, and grandchildren on North Liberty Street, and Carl and Holga Stig were operating the Grey Gull Restaurant on Liberty Street, yet another restaurant that became an enduring island business.

Another Swedish couple on Nantucket were Albert and Augusta Rohdin. Albert Rohdin had come to the United States in 1888 and Augusta shortly after. Both were naturalized in 1895. Albert began by fishing on vessels out of Gloucester but soon found his life's work in the U. S. Life-Saving Service, where he advanced through the ranks. By 1910 he was keeper of the Lifesaving station on Muskeget Island. His wife and their four Massachusetts-born children lived on Nantucket and visited Muskeget occasionally.

In 1915 the Life-Saving Service was merged with the United States Revenue Cutter Service to form the United States Coast Guard. Rohdin was promoted to the rank of chief warrant officer and transferred to the Surfside Station (the building now

Captain Albert Rohdin and his crew at Muskeget Lifesaving Station, 1910. Seated by the faking box is Cape Verdean surfman Annibal Martin.

occupied by the Star of the Sea youth hostel) until it was converted into a naval radio-compass facility. Leaving the island, he continued in the Coast Guard until his retirement in 1928. Five years later he suffered a peculiarly Swedish death, suddenly, while shoveling snow at his home in Rhode Island.

As Nantucket's fishing economy expanded, several Swedish men found a way to make a living at it. In 1920 Carl Anderson was one of three Swedish harbor fishermen. One of them, young Helmer Östman, had a Nantucket wife, and the couple with their baby were living with her parents. Ten years later Helmer was still fishing, and the Östman couple had six children and their own home—equipped with a radio, as most fishing families' homes were in 1930.

Commonwealth of Massachusetts death certificates record the birthplace of the deceased, the birthplaces of the parents of the deceased, the father's name, and the mother's maiden name. Throughout rural Scandinavia, family surnames were late to replace the system of patronymics, in which the son of a Swedish man named Anders—

– Courtesy of Grace Marshall

Members of the Anderson and Östman families. Standing left to right: Theresa Anderson, Cora Östman, Hjalmar Alfred Anderson. The children left to right: Edward Östman, Beatrice Anderson, and Olga Anderson. At far left is Frederich Östman, and the baby at the right is Marion Östman.

for instance—would be Andersson, and his sister would be identified as Andersdotter, even after marriage. In the course of emigration the double "ss" in men's names and the "dotter" of the women's did not carry over well, but the areas of North America receiving Scandinavian immigrants are full of Andersons, Olsons, Larsons, Eriksons, Nilsons and Nelsons. When some of Nantucket's residents died in great old age, their mothers' nineteenth-century patronymics were recorded as their maiden names. Carl Anderson's parents were recorded as Anders Oleson and Mary Larsdotter. Hilda Allen's parents were John M. Mårtensson and Ida Amelia Zachrisdotter. Hilda Gibbs, from Swedish-speaking Finland, was the daughter of Johan Erik Träskbacka-Österberg and Ulrika Isaksdotter. In the urban, progressive port of Gothenburg, however, Anna Lake's mother had a forward-looking western surname, Segerlind.

Norwegians

On Christmas Day 1926, Arne Parelius Pedersen and Anna Kristina Nilson were married on Nantucket, joining the island's small Swedish community to its much larger community of Norwegian fishermen, the Norwegian "sen" of his patronymic contrasting with the Swedish "son" of her father's.

Anglicization sometimes obscured the fine distinctions among Scandinavian names and at other times made false distinctions. Olga Hansen wrote, "My maiden name Anderson should have been Andersen, but it was Anderson on my father's naturalization papers, so my father wrote it that way. Also, the two Fleming families: one spelled it with one "m" and the other with two "m"s just because it was spelled that way on their papers. They were brothers!"

By 1938 the roster of Norwegian men currently or recently fishing out of Nantucket included Olaf, Edward, and Hjalmar Alfred Anderson; Ole Borgen; Axel and Arne Christiansen; John Dale; Richard Johansen; Paul, Mathias, Samuel, and Wilhelm Mathison; Sigurd, Rudolf, and Bernt Matland; Knutte and Sigurd Rasmussen; and Rolf Sjölund. Harold Cooke's occupation was listed in the 1930 census as "master: steamboat."

Captain Peder Pedersen, whose name was unofficially anglicized to Pete Peterson, modestly described himself as "boatman," but he had commanded vessels of every sort in a lifetime at sea. He was born in the Lofoten Islands, off the northwest coast of Norway well above the Arctic Circle. Despite their far northern location the islands are not icebound, because the North Atlantic Drift Current sweeping up the coast ameliorates the climate. Between February and April this stream of warm water is the spawning ground for codfish, attracting fishermen from all over Norway. The riches of the fishing grounds are harvested at great risk, however, because the current between the islands is the original Maelstrom, a treacherous area of giant eddies and whirlpools. In the midst of this wild maritime environment Peder Pedersen was born in the 1870s. At age fourteen he left home for the merchant marine and thereafter, during the years preceding World War I, he moved on to operating wealthy men's pleasure boats for them.

Compared to the waters around his home islands, the coasts of Denmark and Germany are relatively benign, and Pedersen spent nearly a dozen years skippering sailing yachts in those waters. With many adventures along the way, he became a United States citizen at the time of World War I, retired again from merchant service in 1922, and took up residence on Pleasant Street on Nantucket. For ten years he was employed by playwright and Nantucket resident Austin Strong, during which time he and Strong organized the Nantucket Yacht Club's children's sailing program. Together they brought into being the "rainbow fleet" of miniature catboats that became the postcard symbol of Nantucket harbor. Pedersen was a core member of the Wharf Rat Club on North Wharf. After his death, his Norwegian sheath knife was presented to the Nantucket Historical Association.

Peder Pedersen's wife Henrietta was from England, Hjalmar Anderson was married to Budapest-born Theresa (Szabo) Anderson, and Rolf Sjölund's wife Eunice was the daughter of Nantucketer James T. Worth. Peder Pedersen's nephew Arne had taken a Swedish wife, and some of the other fishermen had Norwegian wives. Three Norwegian women—Ragnhild Coffin, Bertha Conway, and Machen Hamblin— were married to Nantucket men.

Margarethe Stigum of Bergen, Norway, resided unmarried on Nantucket for ten years. When she

Captain Peder Pedersen, right, with Austin Strong in Strong's boathouse on North Wharf, circa 1945.

Louis S. Davidson photograph, NHA

died young of cancer in the spring of 1940, a lyrical but uninformative obituary was printed in the *Inquirer and Mirror*. It describes her as building something unspecified and doing so artistically. Her death certificate states that her father was Karl Stigum of Trondheim and that she lived on Union Street and sold antiques in a shop. In the late 1930s the Norwegian Pottery Shop, selling modern Scandinavian ceramics, glass, and silver rather than antiques, was located at the site of Nikita Carpenko's studio at Consue Corner. The Nantucket street lists for 1939 and 1940 indicate that Stigum, Carpenko, and another woman, all merchants, shared that address. Among Carpenko's papers are a letterhead for the shop, a price list, and a letter with a reference to working "in the shop." Despite the cryptic initials R.D.W.W. at the end of Stigum's obituary, the writing is a stylistic match with that of Carpenko's own autobiographical writings.

Other Norwegians living and working on land included baker Emil Isaksen; Carl T. Andersen (whose surname was often spelled "Anderson," confusing his identity with Swedish Carl E. Anderson) and his wife Sigrid; Håkon Thorstersen and his wife Birgit; carpenter Richard Johnsen, who was living with his sister Dagny Anderson and her husband Olaf; and trucker Albert Johnsen and his wife Rosalena. Eugene Larsen was keeper of Sankaty Head Lighthouse.

The surname of Joseph Remsen, Larsen's predecessor, appears Norwegian, but he was Nantucket-born. Through his mother and grandmother Joseph Remsen was descended from Gardners, Colemans, Swains, and Bunkers, and he would have considered himself kin to Sarah P. Bunker. Born in 1849, he joined the United States Lighthouse Service, and in the course of his career served as keeper of Brant Point Lighthouse, spent a year on the South Shoals Lightship, and finally became keeper of Sankaty Lighthouse, a position he held for twenty-seven years.

During those years both Charles Vanderhoop and Eugene Larsen served as assistants under Remsen. After serving briefly as Remsen's successor at Sankaty, Vanderhoop returned to Aquinnah as keeper of Gay Head Light. Larsen succeeded Vanderhoop at Sankaty and remained there until his retirement in 1944. Under his stewardship, Sankaty was repeatedly recognized as a model for all the lighthouses in the service, and he received numerous awards for its maintenance and operation.

Eugene Larsen was from Oslo, the second of seven children. Following the custom of the time and place, he went to sea young and while still in his teens served on a British ship before moving to the United States and signing on with the U. S. Coast and Geodetic Survey, where he served as quartermaster on three different ships. Returning to Norway, he met and married Tobine Edvardine "Dina" Reinertsen, an island girl from Korshavn.

Eugene and Dina moved to Oslo but neither found life in the city to their liking, and Eugene returned to the United States, this time to employment as quartermaster on vessels of the U. S. Cutter Service. Early in 1910 he managed to transfer to the U. S. Lighthouse Service and was able to send for Dina to join him on shore.

Their oldest child was a son, born in Norway and named for his father. Mother and toddler traveled in steerage to Boston to begin a new life on islands with lighthouses. One of Eugene's posts was at Thatcher's Island, off Cape Ann, near Gloucester, where the Larsens' oldest daughter, Alice Thatcher Larsen, was born. At Sankaty, the Larsens had five more daughters: Marie Antoinette, Thelma Ann, Ethel Alma, Helen Edith, and Evelyn Doris. Universally known as the beautiful Larsen girls, the sisters made Sankaty a lively place that people—Nantucketers and summer people alike—enjoyed visiting.

Alice Larsen married Nantucket historian Edouard Stackpole, whose family had longstanding connections with the *Inquirer and Mirror*. When Edouard Stackpole's father-in-law died in 1961, the *Inquirer and Mirror* published a tribute to the Larsen family that read in part, "Keeper and Mrs. Larsen made the lighthouse on the bluff a place of beauty and joy. Above all it was their

– Courtesy of Ethel Hamilton

Sankaty Head Lighthouse keeper Eugene Larsen with some of his daughters: From left: Marie, Alice, and Ethel. A visiting girl stands at right.

home. Here, Keeper Larsen was a part of an old tradition. As he gazed out to sea from the tower, he could recall his experiences as a youngster scrambling aloft on a square rigger, or being on the bridge of the cutter *Gresham* during rescue operations after the steamers *Republic* and *Florida* collided off Nantucket Lightship in 1909. Here he recounted his experiences at the two lights of Thatcher's Island or at lonely Minots. Here, in the spotlessness of the lighthouse, he could survey the little domain to which he gave devoted service."

Like the Larsens, many of the Norwegian and half-Norwegian couples had growing families, and they formed a mutually supportive social network. Eunice Sjölund reminisced about summer boat trips to Pocomo, where the young Norwegians shared picnic lunches on the beach, went swimming, played pranks on each other, and danced to accordion music. When the weather was bad and boats were delayed getting home, the fishermen's wives listened to their radios and called each other on the telephone to keep up their courage and reassure each other.

Although Rolf Sjölund settled on Nantucket later than many of the other Norwegians, he arrived with ready-made connections. Years earlier his father had come to the island to work on construction of the jetties at the entrance to Nantucket Harbor.[2] Moreover, Rolf's first cousin Dagny and her fisherman husband Olaf Anderson resided on-island, and Dagny's brother Richard Johnsen lived with them for a time.

The Sjölund family homestead was located on the Oslo Fjord, close to the border between Norway and Sweden. From that fjord it is a straight sail out past the northern tip of Denmark to the North Sea, and thence to the oceans of the world. When Rolf Sjölund's father left home for Nantucket, Rolf was not yet born. The little boy, born in 1906, was already walking and talking by the time his father returned with his earnings from America.

During World War I the Norwegian merchant fleet, which at the turn of the century had grown to be one of the largest in the world, lost about half its vessels to German submarines and mines. Travel to work outside the country was next to impossible, and local work was hard to come by. In a situation comparable to Nantucket's after the American Revolution, a third to a half of Norway's workers found themselves without employment.

The Sjölunds, originally a family of seven—parents, four sons, and a daughter—was hard hit. Two of the four Sjölund brothers died in the war. Rolf's surviving brother took up studies to become a Lutheran pastor, and young Rolf felt an obligation to make life easier for all by leaving home and being, as he put it, one less mouth to feed. In the 1880s it had been possible for Peder Pedersen to ship out at age fourteen, but by 1920, child-protection laws were in place, and Rolf Sjölund had to pretend to be older than his years. Like Pedersen before him, he was fourteen when he succeeded in signing on for seven years in the Norwegian merchant marine. After that, he came to Nantucket and went to work in commercial fishing, proving himself so competent that his cousin-in-law, Olaf Anderson, turned over the operation of his boat *Dagny* to him.

The first boat Rolf Sjölund owned and operated for himself was the *Eunice Lillian*. Then in 1946 the *Carl Henry* was built for him in Fairhaven. The new vessel's maiden voyage to the fishing banks, without benefit of radio or any of the modern navigational conveniences that became available in the postwar years, yielded a record catch of 86,000 pounds of flounder, haddock, and codfish. Over the next quarter century a great many Nantucket men went fishing on the *Carl Henry.*

Captain Sjölund retired from fishing in 1970. At his death in 1984, he held membership in many diverse organizations: Union Lodge, F. & A. M., the Oddfellows, the Pacific Club, the Nantucket Historical Association, and the Anglers Club.

It was Marion Matland's family connections to Nantucket that brought Karsten Reinemo to the island. Her father, fisherman Bernt Matland, moved his family to Nantucket in 1922. He and his wife Caroline (Christiansen) Matland were both born in Norway, and their first three children—including Marion—were born in New York. Two more Matland children were born on the island, where other Matlands and Christiansens were already residing. All the Matlands and Christiansens were making their living from commercial fishing.

Bernt and Caroline gave their two oldest children classic Norwegian names, Ragnhild and Gottfrid. Marion and her younger brothers—Clifford and Kenneth—received names that stood out less at school, and in Nantucket High School Gottfrid chose to go by the name of Karl. Marion attended the Orange Street School until it closed, and then she moved on through the Cyrus Peirce School, the junior high school at Academy Hill, and Nantucket High School. After graduation, she took a job with a bank in Boston, and that is where she met Karsten Reinemo.

The Reinemo family had lived in the vicinity of the town of Holmstrand on the Oslo Fjord for generations. When Karsten was born, they had just survived the hardships of World War I, and he grew up in the economic depression that followed.

---

2. The west jetty was mainly built between 1880 and 1885, and the east jetty between 1891 and 1902, but work continued on both of them until 1937.

Before the Germans occupied Norway in 1940, his father advised him to leave, and young Karsten used the same vehicle for leaving home that Peder Pedersen and Rolf Sjölund had before him, the Norwegian merchant fleet.

Over the next several years—dangerous ones for shipping in the Baltic and North Seas—he worked his way up to the rank of chief steward, the position he held in 1943, when torpedo damage sent his vessel into Boston for repairs. He and Marion Matland met at a church social in Boston, and they married before his ship left port. According to their son, "In the Norwegian merchant marine officers were allowed to take their wives. So when my father married my mother in 1943, she was the only American gal on the vessel. She sailed with him for about a year and a half, and she learned to speak Norwegian fluently, because she was the only lady on board." Her total immersion in spoken Norwegian had taken place under sunny Caribbean skies as the ship ran freight between New Orleans and Haiti.

At war's end, the Reinemos settled in Nantucket, and Karsten joined the men of the island's deep-sea-fishing fleet, working on the *Carl Henry*. In the summers Karsten and Marion leased the restaurant of the Ships Inn from its owner. But the restaurant business was seasonal, and in the winters Karsten had to go out on week-long fishing trips to the offshore fishing banks. In 1965 Gordon MacDonald, the owner of the Downyflake Restaurant, offered to sell it to the Reinemos, and they seized the opportunity to own and operate

The original Downyflake building with its doughnut sign.

Nantucket Historical Association

their own business, expanding it from a two-month-per-year summer operation to a year-round business that opened at 5:30 AM for fishermen and other working people. In 1991, an early-morning gas explosion in the original Downyflake building in the heart of town nearly proved fatal for Karsten, but he survived, and the Reinemo family rebuilt in the business district on the edge of town, where the Downyflake continues to prosper.

Karsten Reinemo worked in his restaurant's kitchen to the end of his days, and he kept on spending wintry mornings on the water scalloping with his son Karsten, whose wife, Julie, is Sarah P. Bunker's great-great-great-granddaughter and Hilda (Österberg) Gibbs's great-granddaughter.

Dutch

Leendert Block served as mate on Olaf Anderson's *Dagny*, Rolf Sjölund's *Eunice Lillian*, and a half a dozen other vessels that fished out of Nantucket and New Bedford. From time to time he was a "transient captain" for a fishing boat when its regular captain was temporarily off. Born in Ymuiden, a North Sea port on the coast of the Netherlands close to Haarlem, Block—like Peder Pedersen and Rolf Sjölund—had gone to sea young on merchant ships and then came to the United States to work in commercial fishing. He enlisted in the U. S. Army at age thirty, was naturalized during his service, and then moved on to the Army Transport Services. At age forty he married a Nantucket woman and settled on the island just when the stock market collapse sent the nation reeling into the Depression. In the next decades he became, in the words of his obituary, "a well-known island fisherman."

In 1920 a dozen men from Dutch families resident on Nantucket were supporting themselves by fishing. William Grice and his wife Frytjes were in their sixties, but William continued deepwater fishing with his unmarried sons Albert, Jacob, and William Jr. One of the Schafer brothers, Peter, had a Dutch-born wife Tina, but his brother, Orvis—just a year younger—had an American wife, as did John Vahlan, John van Evrendeft, and Cornelius

Sanders. Thomas Townsend's wife was Swedish. John Grock and Frederick Young were widowers. H. van Ommeren, minister of the Unitarian Church 1914–21, and William Voorneveld were the only Dutch-born men on the island at the time who were not commercial fishermen.

Arriving ahead of the Dutch fishermen, the Voornevelds had been Nantucket's first family to come from the Netherlands. Hermanus and Madaline Voorneveld were already an aging couple when they moved to Nantucket in 1903 to open a florist shop. Married at the time of the American Civil War, they had brought their large family to the United States in 1883, when their youngest son William was just four years old.

Hermanus Voorneveld was born in Utrecht, an inland city about as far from the coast as possible in the small and sea-oriented country of the Netherlands.[3] For generations the Voornevelds had been horticulturists, a profession that had prospered greatly during the golden years of the 1600s and 1700s when much of the world was delirious with "tulip fever." (The sultan of the Ottoman Empire was one of the best customers of the Dutch horticulturists, buying shiploads of tulip bulbs for his court gardens.) In Nantucket, it was the summer residents, "with hundreds of whom she [Mrs. Voorneveld] came in contact each season," whose patronage made the Voornevelds prosperous.

When eighty-year-old Madaline died in 1916, Dutch clergyman van Ommeren conducted committal services in Prospect Hill Cemetery. Hermanus survived his wife by barely a year, and his graveside rites were carried out by members of the Oddfellows, of whose Nantucket Lodge he had become a member.

Their son William carried on as "Voorneveld the Florist," noted not only for the cut flowers and floral arrangements from the family florist shop, but also as a landscape architect, town tree warden, and superintendent of moth suppression—an important position in the 1930s as the whole Northeast suffered from a plague of gypsy moths. He joined Union Lodge, was an active member of the Congregational Church, and was elected to the Nantucket board of selectmen.

Despite Hermanus Voorneveld's advanced age at the time of his death, the *Inquirer and Mirror* had reported that "The suddenness of his death was a surprise and shock to all the people of Nantucket." Twenty-two years later, the *Inquirer and Mirror* used almost the same words to report the death of his son: "The sudden death of William Voorneveld Sr., Wednesday morning, came as a severe shock to the community." It came as an even greater shock to learn that sixty-year-old William Voorneveld had ended his own life with a bullet from a thirty-eight-caliber revolver, joining the sad company of Frank Oddo and Stanley Ozog (and far, far back, Quak Te), foreign-born men who exited without warning from economically depressed Nantucket.

Despite this shock, the Voorneveld florist business carried on through two more generations in Nantucket with its shop on Centre Street and its gardens and produce stand on Madaket Road.

In the 1920s the fishermen came and went. The federal census of 1930 lists eight Dutch fishermen from four families, not one of them from among the Dutch families who had been on-island in 1920. Leendert Block, Marius Scheele, and Albert Greik had moved to the island with their American wives and children. Four Lamens brothers had also taken up residence—in order of age: Leendert, Martin, Gerard, and Lambertus. They had come from Den Helder, the northernmost tip of the Dutch coast before it breaks up into the Frisian Islands. Leendert and his wife Dirkje, born and married in the old country, had come to Nantucket with their Dutch-born daughter Trina and their New York-born daughter Annie. Martin Lamens's wife was

---

3. The only people from the Netherlands known to have lived on Nantucket in the 1800s were two domestic servants and a ship's rigger. For all intents and purposes, "Holland" is synonymous with "the Netherlands." In the nineteenth century, the country was at one time the Kingdom of Holland and at another time the Kingdom of the Netherlands. Originally the Kingdom of the Netherlands included Belgium and Luxembourg, but they both separated from the kingdom and became independent. Today they have regrouped in an economic union known as "Benelux." "Dutch" is derived from the fact that the language of the Netherlands is a form of low-country German (*Deutch*).

from Florida, but their children, too, had been born in New York. Gerard Lamens's wife was from New York. The youngest brother, Lambertus, arrived as a bachelor and wed Latvian-born Alice Duce. Alice's brother Arnold married Annie Lamens, creating double bonds between the Latvian Duces and the Dutch Lamenses. Annie's older sister Trina married Nantucket carpenter Oscar Ceeley.

Garrett and Susan Huyser came to Nantucket with their children from Long Island in 1923. Almost as soon as they arrived, Susan Huyser was hospitalized with a ruptured appendix and peritonitis, and their infant son died. According to his death certificate, Garrett Huyser Jr. was infected with tuberculosis, and he survived less than three months. Surviving this tragic start, the Huysers stayed and raised a Nantucket family. Before moving to Woods Hole, Albert Greik put up capital for Garrett Huyser to become half-owner of a dragger, but by 1930 Huyser had found a land job as driver for the local office of Railway Express.

The heads of the Dutch families living on Nantucket in the 1920s and 1930s had left home for America before the outbreak of World War I. The Netherlands remained neutral in that war, but like Norway—another North Sea country with a maritime economy—it suffered brutal economic losses. The emigrants had ridden out the war years at a safe distance from the devastation of Europe, but even from Nantucket they could probably discern the clouds of an even worse fate for the Netherlands gathering in the 1930s.

French Canadians

Despite its centuries-long economic exploitation of the sea, Nantucket has never been a locus of boat building. All timber and metal had to be transported to the island, and the harbor has always been a shallow place for sizable vessels. It is little wonder that in the course of half a century the boat yard on Brant Point produced only five whaleships, one in 1803 and the other four between 1832 and 1838: The *Rose* in 1803, the *Charles Carroll* in 1832, the *Lexington* in 1836, the *Nantucket* in 1837, and the *Joseph Starbuck* in

1838. Nantucket's catboats and even the dories of the second half of the 1800s were built off-island. So were the fishing boats of the early twentieth century, which were launched from mainland shipyards in Maine, Massachusetts, and New York.

According to the 1920 federal census, only one man living on Nantucket, Maine-born George Donovan, was occupied as a boat builder. Ten years later Donovan was no longer on the island, but in his place Stanley Butler gave his occupation as boat builder as did an elderly Canadian, Laurence Burrage, who was probably no longer active in his profession. Under boat building and repairs the 1927 Nantucket business directory lists Walter Chase at the head of Steamboat Wharf, Nantucket Boatworks on Whale Street, and the South Beach Boat Yard at the end of Washington Street.

Beginning in the 1920s, however, the island was undergoing a boat-building boom thanks to the arrival of seven French Canadian men. Clovis Mazerolle, in the United States since 1902, had relocated to Nantucket as foreman of a boat-building crew. Two of his employees were boarding with his family on Coffin Street, and three others had brought their families along and were taking in boarders themselves.

It was a full house at 4 Coffin Street in 1930. Clovis and Eugenie Mazerolle had three children, and Eugenie's mother Rose was living with them, too, as well as boat builders Maillet Resther and Jude Rantreau. The other French Canadian boat builders were Emile Trahan, Maxim LeBlanc, Alfie Lombard, and Andre Theriault.

Boat building on Francis Street Beach, 1925.

207

Among the fishing vessels built in Nantucket in the 1920s and 1930s were the *Native* for French Canadian fisherman Fidence Fortin in 1924, the *Margaret* in 1930, and the *Squam* in 1933. They were long-lived vessels. Eight years after launch, the *Native* was still working out of Nantucket. Captain Philip Grant was operating the *Squam* nineteen years after she was built.

In 1930 there were more French Canadian men building boats on Nantucket than fishing from them. Fidence Fortin, his Irish wife Mary, and one Massachusetts-born child were already living on the island in 1920. By 1930, when the Fortins had a second child born on Nantucket and owned a house on Martins Lane, two other French Canadian fishermen had taken up residence. Louis Amiralt had come on his own and was boarding with a French Canadian family on Orange Street, while Alonzo Achison, with his English wife and their two Massachusetts-born children were renting a house on Silver Street. In sum, there were only three French Canadian fishermen living on-island. Among Coast Guard surfmen stationed on the island, Philip Samson was born in Canada and Leo Gamache had a French Canadian father.

This is not to say, however, that there were few French Canadians living on Nantucket. To the contrary, between 1920 and 1930 there had been an influx of French Canadians to the island. The Fortins had been joined by at least thirty-five others (many with American-born children), enough to constitute a visible and audible new ethnic group on the island. Boat building was a strong specialty among them, but it was a subspecialty of the building trade. Two building projects that attracted workers to the island were construction on Steamboat Wharf between 1926 and 1929 and the raising of the new brick Academy Hill School in 1929. Among the French Canadian men living on Nantucket in 1930, seven—including Ulric Trahan, brother of boat-builder Emile Trahan—gave their occupations as carpenters or house builders, and they were supported in their work by a French Canadian plumber, Henry Richard, and two French Canadian house painters, Charles Roy and Joseph

Domis. Prominent among these builders were "Mack" Paradis and Joseph Senecal.

French Canadian families are famously large. Carpenter and cabinetmaker Magloire Paradis was born in Frenchville, Maine, as one of seventeen children. His wife, Marie (Boutin) Paradis, born in Quebec, was one of seven. They were parents of ten daughters and finally a son, Patrick. It is practically a party game among Nantucketers to name the Paradis daughters: Annette, Bernadette, Laurette, Germaine, Claudette, Maximille, Adrinette, Jeanette, Therese, and Georgette.

Mack Paradis's employment by the Taylor Construction Company of New Bedford first brought him to Nantucket in 1926 to work on construction of a large freight building on Steamboat Wharf. Three years later he returned with his family and stayed for the rest of his life. On Nantucket he was known as a highly skilled craftsman, and he trained a number of the next generation of Nantucket carpenters.

Five of the Paradis sisters married into Nantucket families, and Patrick's wife came from Washington, D. C., to live on the island. By 1959, the year Mack Paradis died, there were twenty-three Paradis grandchildren, including Patrick's first son, Nicholas, whose birth guaranteed that the Paradis name would continue on Nantucket.

Patrick Paradis started his own career in the building trades as a carpenter for the Marine Lumber Company. Beginning in 1958 as woodworking instructor at the Coffin School, he too taught future Nantucket carpenters, carrying on his father's legacy. When the Coffin School closed as a vocational school, he transferred to Nantucket High School. Then in 1993, as "owner's representative," he took on the demanding role of liaison among the director, trustees, and contractor in the three-year restoration of the Nantucket Atheneum building, a project on which his son Stephen also worked. Subsequently Patrick Paradis served as clerk of the works during construction at the Nantucket Cottage Hospital, while Stephen Paradis was contracted in the same role for the conversion of the Nantucket Historical Association's Fair Street

Museum building into an archive and research library. Patrick Paradis has since been engaged as clerk of the works for the construction of the Nantucket Historical Association's new museum complex incorporating the Whaling Museum and the Peter Foulger Museum buildings.

Joseph Senecal was born in La Prairie, Quebec. After their June wedding in New Bedford in 1924, he and his bride Laura Marie Richard came to Nantucket, where—according to his son—one of Joe Senecal's first jobs was repairing the Old Mill for the Nantucket Historical Association and getting it back into running condition. It was a job he repeated in 1936 and again in 1949. The machinery he built for the task was still available to English builder John Gilbert when he made repairs to the mill in 1978. Senecal had a carpentry shop on Lily Street, and the high quality of his work was recognized by Nantucket's other builders. The Senecal home on Pleasant Street, close to the mill that he cared for so diligently, remains in the family.

Only a few French Canadian men working on land in 1930 were not involved in the building trades. Three were truck drivers, one was a butcher in a meat market, one was on a grounds crew at a golf club, and one was a farm laborer. Most of the women were "at home" as wives and mothers looking after large families, but one young woman was working as bookkeeper for the Nicoletos brothers, and three women—one born in Canada and two born to French Canadian parents—were waitresses in local restaurants. In weddings a week apart in September, 1930, two of the Latvian-American Duce brothers took young French Canadian brides. Waldemar Duce married Yvonne Marchessault, one of the waitresses, and Harry married Regina Lemieux, daughter of truck driver Joseph Lemieux.

According to the federal censuses for 1920 and 1930, the number of men from the Azores and Cape Verde engaged in fishing declined moderately, and they were mainly engaged in harbor fishing and shellfishing. The number of French Canadian fishermen grew from just one to three, but two dozen Canadian men of English, Irish, and Scottish background moved to the island to work in commercial fishing. The number of Dutch fishermen declined slightly, while the Scandinavian fishermen—mostly Norwegians—increased in numbers. Although their crews were cosmopolitan, the owners and operators of deep-water fishing vessels were mainly Norwegians and English-speaking Canadians.

Fishing boats alongside Straight Wharf in the 1930s. In the foreground are kegs used to ship fish and shellfish off-island.

When Rolf Sjölund's *Carl Henry* joined the Nantucket fishing fleet, most of the other vessels had been built at least two decades earlier. It was the older wooden fishing boats that had assisted Captain Manuel Sylvia in bringing the steamer *Islander* safely to dock in Nantucket in March 1927, avoiding what appeared to be inescapable destruction. When the *Islander*'s steering mechanism failed outside the jetties in a spring storm, Captain Sylvia used her steam whistle to alert people on shore that she was in distress. The *Inquirer and Mirror* reported that:

> *The first boat to go out was one of the small Coast Guard patrol boats, but as the whistle blasts from the steamer continued to sound, some of the large fishing craft followed out of the harbor, among them being the* Victor, *the* Anna C. Perry, *the* John Erickson *and the* Dagny. *Other large fishing boats berthed at the Steamboat wharf were ready to go out to the scene if needed, but owing to the narrowness of the channel between the jetties and in to Brant Point, it was realized that only a small number of boats could operate there without interference.*

Alternately running and cutting the engines, Captain Sylvia kept the steamer off the rocks until high winds and heavy seas lifted and carried her in broadside between the jetties. Once the *Islander* was in the calmer waters of the outer harbor, the *Perry* and the *Erickson* made fast to the steamer to help her keep in the channel as they approached Brant Point Lighthouse. There a crowd stood waiting to see if the steamer could round the point without being driven hard aground. With the fishing boats hugging to her, the steamer swung completely around, touched bottom, and cleared the lighthouse. The fishermen cast off their lines only when it was certain that Captain Sylvia would be able to bring the steamer alongside Steamboat Wharf unassisted. The drama had played out over three and a half hours to an anxious audience of hundreds of onlookers lining the beaches.

As the Depression descended on the nation, the price for which fishermen could sell their catch sometimes fell below operating costs. In June 1932, Captain Paul Mathison chose to donate five thousand pounds of flounder from the *Bernice* to the needy of New Bedford rather than to dump them. His donation was not the first from fishing boats coming in to the city and finding no market for their catch. Previous fish give-aways had been so chaotic that the New Bedford Public Welfare Department had orga-

The steamer Islander *passing stern-first around Brant Point with the assistance of the Nantucket fishing fleet, March 1927.*

nized a procedure for notification and equitable distribution to area families.

Deep-sea fishing is one of the most hazardous of professions, and the Nantucket and New Bedford newspapers often carried news of business failures, physical injury, and loss of life.

Crossing to the Vineyard during the December 1933 freeze-up, Olaf Anderson suffered frostbite of both hands and his windward ear. The newspaper also reported that he had sold the *Dagny*, "one of the most active fishing boats in these waters for a number of years." Having a wealthy patron such as Leeds Mitchell wasn't proof against the Depression either; in the summer of 1938 an advertisement in the *Inquirer and Mirror* announced that Captain John Egle was offering for sale his own "Yawl *Mnemoosha* (The pride of Old North Wharf). All reasonable offers considered."

On New Year's Day 1941, out in the shoals "to the southard" where so many Nantucket whalemen had lost their lives in the early days of whaling, Hjalmar Alfred Anderson was struck by a falling mast aboard the *Alice*. The *Alice* powered back to

– Spinner Collection

The Dagny, built for Captain Olaf Anderson, pulls into Hathaway Braley Wharf in Fairhaven to unload her scallop catch some time in the 1940s.

New Bedford under full throttle, but the medical examiner there determined that Anderson had died almost instantly of his injuries. Theresa (Szabo) Anderson was left a widow with four children.

Captain Jack McDonald was badly injured when the *Gladys & Mary*, on her maiden voyage, was caught out on the fishing banks in the 1944 hurricane. Some years later, at sea aboard the *Carl Henry* in midnight darkness a steel tow cable parted and struck Lambertus Lamens a powerful

The Bernice unloads her catch at L. S. Eldridge's fish house in New Bedford in 1932. The Bernice had been built for Capt. Paul Mathison in Thomaston, Maine.

Spinner Collection

blow to the ribs. Captain Sjölund brought the *Carl Henry* straight in to Nantucket, but Lamens died at the hospital of a ruptured liver. Years before, his brother Martin, described as a "hard-working industrious fisherman," had died of a heart attack on the fishing schooner *Anna Louise*.

On Good Friday 1950 the deep sea scalloper *William J. Landry* was running for New Bedford in an April storm. The crew of the Pollack Rip Lightship sighted her battling heavy seas in blizzard conditions, but they were unable to assist her. Ship-to-shore radio contact continued until midnight, and Captain Arne Hansen, Hjalmar Alfred Anderson's Norwegian son-in-law, put through a reassuring call to his family, but in the early morning hours of Easter Saturday, he perished with his five-man crew, including Theodore Polasky and Earl Blount of Nantucket. Seven children, four of them on Nantucket, were left fatherless.

The *Four Sisters* with a crew of ten from New Bedford disappeared in the same storm. The *Gladys & Mary* and the *Anna C. Perry* were reported missing after they lost radio contact but made port safely, Two years later in another spring storm the *Anna C. Perry,* newly rebuilt and outfitted, was lost with all hands. Her crew of six were from New Bedford and Fairhaven, but her owner was Catherine Flanagan of Nantucket. The *Anna C. Perry* had been built for her father, Eugene Perry.

As the death toll mounted, the entire Nantucket community was stricken. People who were children in 1950 recall the deadly Easter weekend with the same photographic clarity with which Americans know where they were and what they were doing when President Kennedy was shot or when the World Trade Center towers fell. Not so long afterward, Nantucket's fishing families began to move to New Bedford where, as Captain Hansen's widow Olga Hansen wrote, "living was easier and they did not have to make the trip to Nantucket after they sold their fish."

Prospect Hill Cemetery and St. Mary's Cemetery lie across the street from one another. Nantucket fishermen have been interred in both. A drawing of the *Carl Henry* is engraved on the Sjölund family marker in St. Mary's Cemetery, and Norwegian and American flags are placed there on Memorial Day.

The fishing fleet tied up at Island Service Wharf, 1930.

CHAPTER TWELVE

English-Speaking Cousins

There were no titles allowed among Quakers.
Everyone was addressed by the first name. Since
we children were not permitted to use Mr. and Mrs.,
we called all Father's and Mother's friends Uncle,
Aunt, or Cousin. It seemed as if we were related to
nearly everyone in town.
—Deborah Coffin (Hussey) Adams

The English-born families who began settling on Nantucket in 1659 retained the placenames in use among the island's Wampanoag inhabitants. With few exceptions, they did not impose "new" names such as New London, New Haven, New Bedford, much less New York, New Jersey, New England, or New South Wales. Had they all originated in the same English town or shire, perhaps the settlers might have identified their adopted home and its parts with familiar places they had left behind. They were, however, a mixed lot, and in just one generation their Nantucket-born progeny identified with their island home to the exclusion of any Old World place.

That intense local identification, amplified by Quaker inwardness, has been tenacious over the centuries. Cousinhood, on the other hand, has been and remains a broadly inclusive category of great importance to the descended Nantucketers, and its ties know no geographical bounds. Practically by definition, descended Nantucketers have countless cousins at home and abroad. Some of these relationships are tenuous in the extreme—removed, by marriage, and even fictive—but are deeply felt nonetheless.

Britain

Many Nantucketers maintained ties to cousins in England. In the early 1700s, for example, William Gayer Jr. was sent from Nantucket to marry his first cousin in England in order that

his uncle's estate would remain in the family. Nantucket merchants and their families spent years at a time in London, and English businessmen found a warm welcome in Nantucket. Transatlantic bonds such as these added yet another dimension of personal trauma to the American Revolution and the War of 1812, which so devastated the island's economy and from both of which Nantucketers earnestly dissented.

Until the American Revolution, the distinction between people born in England and those born in the colonies was obvious, but ultimately all were fellow English subjects. After American independence, cordiality between Nantucketers and their English cousins persisted to a degree that—in the opinion of some patriots—bordered on the treasonous. In the mid-1800s, when federal census returns finally differentiated between the native and the foreign-born, they revealed a sizable British community living on Nantucket.

In 1850 there were twenty-eight English-born men, four men from Scotland, and six English women residing on Nantucket. The census recorded another eleven transient seamen from England. The whaling economy at that date was beginning to decline, and by 1860 the number of men born in England had dropped to thirteen, while the number of English women was the same as a decade earlier. Only one Scot remained, but a Welsh woman had come to live on-island. The decline continued until the 1890s. Then, from a low of just three English-born women, five English men, and a Scot, the numbers began to rise very quickly. The difference between this new wave of British residents and the those of whaling days is that while the number of men began to rise slowly, the increase in women was quick, the English and Scottish women coming to outnumber the English and Scottish men by nearly three to one. The majority of these women were married and "at home," but single British women were employed as nurses, housekeepers, domestic servants, and laundresses.

In 1850, most of the men from England were engaged in maritime professions, with a near-monopoly on rigging ships. In addition to riggers and seamen, there were ropemakers, a shipwright, a sailmaker, a blacksmith, and one wealthy maritime merchant, Henry I. Defrieze. Among those not directly connected to maritime commerce were a farmer, a shoemaker, and a tailor. Aging John Weston was a pauper living at the asylum for the indigent.

John Boadle, a Quaker teacher living with the Mitchell family, was originally from Birkenhead, a town near Liverpool. In 1829 the Nantucket Society of Friends had written to the Friends of Philadelphia requesting a teacher for young children, and the Philadelphia Friends sent him. In 1838, nearly a decade after his arrival, the Nantucket Friends built a school building on Fair Street where he conducted the Monthly Meeting School. Even as the building was being erected, however, Quakerism on Nantucket was in steep decline. The number of Quaker schoolchildren fell so low that maintaining the school for them was no longer feasible, and the school building was converted into a meeting house. Subsequently, John Boadle conducted a private school for Quaker and non-Quaker children until, shortly after the 1850 census, having spent two decades teaching Nantucket's children, he left the island to open a school in New Bedford. Wherever his school was, and whatever proportion of his students were children of Friends, Quaker plain speech was mandated. The following description of "John's School" was published in 1922:

> At the beginning, John's school was limited to the children of the Society of Friends, but later he took the children of "world's people" too. . . . Whether they were Friends' people or world's people there was one invariable rule for the children; they called John Boadle "John" by his express direction. Sometimes they got into trouble at home (the

> worldly ones) and were told sternly that they must say "Mr. Boadle" and not "John." But once back at school John would have none of it. It ended in his having his own way and the way of the Friends, and he was "John."

With the exception of the transient seamen, most of the British women and men had Massachusetts-born spouses and considered Nantucket their permanent home. Unforeseen economic depression in the wake of the Great Fire of 1846 and the increasing scarcity of whales to be found in the world's oceans, however, sent many of the foreign-born and their families off in search of greener pastures. Between 1850 and 1860 the total number of island residents born in England, Scotland, and Wales dropped by more than half.

Henry I. Defrieze was exceptional. He married into Nantucket's old families not once, but twice. In 1819 he married Elizabeth "Betsy" Coffin, and the couple had four children. Within a year of Betsy's death in 1829, he married the widow Anna Barnard, and they had six more. In the 1830s and early 1840s, he prospered as part owner of at least one whaleship, the *Clarkson*. Then, miraculously, in a period of economic collapse and mass exodus from the island his fortune grew. In 1850, when he was 59 years old and gave his occupation as merchant, his estate was valued at $5,000. In the five years after he was elected to the board of directors of the Pacific National Bank in 1855, it rose to $19,500, and ten years after that, when the census listed his occupation as retired mariner, it had reached $27,000.

His son, Captain Thaddeus Defrieze, served as judge of the Probate Court from 1873 to 1908, but at his death in 1913, he was best remembered as "the last whaling master of Nantucket." A portrait of Thaddeus was presented to the Probate Court in 1948.

Yet the Defrieze family name, so prominent in Nantucket in the 1800s, slipped into local oblivion in the following century, even as settler families' names such as Coffin, Gardner, and Starbuck—to mention but three—were burnished ever brighter through the efforts of the Nantucket Historical

Association, which had been founded in 1894 to preserve and promote Nantucket's history. Henry Defrieze had been one of the world's people, and from Nantucket his progeny had moved off-island into the greater world. Although his son Thaddeus stayed and served the island, Thaddeus's brother George was one of the many Nantucketers who went to California to seek his fortune, and his brother Ferdinand had a career in the U. S. Navy.

As residents of Nantucket the Defriezes had enjoyed great wealth and influence, but that did not assure their name a prominent place in Nantucket history. On the other hand, a man born in England whose assets dwindled to nothing during his life on the island has been afforded durable posthumous celebrity. In the southeast corner of the Old North Cemetery a large stone tablet is inscribed with a succinct biography of one of Nantucket's professional riggers. Robert Ratliff was born in New Castle-upon-Tyne in 1794 and died on Nantucket in 1882, just five days short of his eighty-eighth birthday. In his mid-twenties, he had survived a shipwreck on the shoals surrounding Nantucket and had stayed on as a resident of the island for over sixty years.

In his young life before his rescue from the shipwreck, he had many adventures that appealed to the imagination of Nantucketers. Sea-oriented as they were, and in spite of Quaker abhorrence of war, they found Ratliff's worldly experiences fascinating. He had gone to sea as an apprentice seaman in his early teens, just as Nantucket boys did, but instead of doing battle against whales, he served in the British navy and was a sailor on the British ship *Albion* in the attack on Washington, D.C., during the War of 1812. Then he served on the ship *Northumberland* when it conveyed Napoleon Bonaparte into exile on the island of St. Helena in 1815. His personal recollections of the appearance and demeanor of Bonaparte were so compelling for Nantucket shipowner Frederick Sanford that he commissioned the stone for Ratliff's grave and had included in the inscription that Ratliff had "received marked notice from the great emperor."

Portrait of Robert Ratliff by Eastman Johnson, 1879.

On-island, Ratliff took a Nantucket wife, the widow Judith (West) Robinson, who brought two daughters to their marriage. To support them, he established his own rigging loft on Nantucket's waterfront, where his business prospered. The Ratliffs lived in a spacious house on Quince Street, and Robert Ratliff was noted for his integrity and generosity. In 1842 he invested in shares of the Nantucket Marine Camel Company, a scheme to float heavy ships over the sandbar that blocked entrance to Nantucket Harbor. Then, in 1846, the Great Fire consumed Nantucket's whole business district and waterfront, destroying his loft and everything in it, and burning to within a block of his home. He started over, but Nantucket's maritime economy did not recover. After discovery of gold in California, many of the ships he would have rigged sailed to California, never to return. Four years after the fire, the value of his estate was listed as just one thousand dollars; in 1860 he had managed to build it to $1,600, but ten years later, he had only two hundred dollars left to his name, and the Ratliffs had taken in two boarders. Then Judith died and left him an aged widower. As the couple had been childless, there was no one to look after him, and Robert Ratliff went to the town asylum to live out the last years of his life.[1]

He was by no means friendless there, despite his age and poverty. Sanford and other visitors came to hear his stories of long-past days at the beginning of the 1800s, when Lord Nelson had defeated the Danes in the Battle of Copenhagen and British ships had been frozen into Baltic ice for weeks at a time; about his personal memories of the burning of the White House by British forces in 1814; and of the stoicism and fortitude of Napoleon Bonaparte in the face of his utter defeat. One of Ratliff's visitors was Eastman Johnson, who painted Ratliff's portrait in 1879 and presented it to the Nantucket Historical Association in 1900. The handsome portrait and the large stone tablet in the Old North Cemetery afford a durability to the memory of Robert Ratliff that eluded the Defrieze family.

The 1870 census records the aging of the English men who had once been occupied in the whaling business. Besides retired Henry Defrieze, there were mariners William Rivers, 66, and John Quinell, 57. Of three remaining riggers—Benjamin Jones, 58; Robert Ratliff, 76, and John Gardner, 87—only Jones might still have been engaged in his profession. Ropemaker Thomas Thrift was 87 years old. The generation of English maritime men had passed.

Back in 1850, when just a half-dozen women who had been born in England resided on Nantucket, two of them had unconventional living arrangements. Twenty-four-year old Lucy Hill, white and illiterate, was sharing a household with two black men in New Guinea. Sixty-five-year-old Nancy Folger was also a member of some sort of collective. She was living with six other women, only two of whom were obviously related to one another.

Female heads of household were not uncommon on Nantucket in 1850. Most of them were headed by widows, and the other members of the household, male and female, were clearly family members with the same surname. Nancy Folger, however, shared a household with the following women: Emeline Bartlett, 47, and Ann C. Bartlett, 26; Adaline Fanning, 44; Phebe Beard, 71; and Sally Coffin, 69. With the exception of Ann Bartlett—who was Emeline Bartlett's daughter—and Sally Coffin, each of these women had independent wealth. Nancy Folger's estate was valued at $1,250; Emeline Bartlett's at $1,500; Adaline Fanning's at $500; and Phebe Baird's at $400. By mid-nineteenth-century standards, these were significant sums and especially remarkable for single women. From the census returns, it appears that a group of unattached Nantucket women of means pooled their resources to live together as a small, mutually supportive community within the greater community of Nantucket.

By 1895 the number of women from England and Scotland had risen to thirteen, while only two English men resided on the island. One of the men was baker Thomas Bickerstaff, whose sister Agnes was also living and working on Nantucket.

Agnes Bickerstaff had left England first. Born in 1862, she had come to the United States while still in her teens. In 1880, her brother, just a year younger than Agnes, made the same journey. By 1895, both were on Nantucket, Agnes working as a nurse and Thomas as a cook. Thomas married a woman from Minnesota, and by 1900, they had four children. During those busy years, Thomas was also accumulating capital to go into business for himself. Purchasing a bakery building on Lower Pearl Street, he became proprietor of the Nantucket Domestic Bakery. A half-page advertisement in the 1909 Nantucket directory offers, "Home Made Bread, Pies, Doughnuts, Cakes, &c. A Specialty Made of Catering both to Large and Small Parties." For the next ten years the bakery's advertisement continued unchanged until, in the 1919 directory, an additional line appeared: "Open to Public Inspection at all Times."

Thomas Bickerstaff's family continued to grow. In 1910 the Bickerstaffs had six children, and shortly after that they moved from Hussey Street

---

1. In 1854 parts of a building that had been at the Quaise Farm for the indigent were moved to town to be part of an asylum "for the care of the needy, mentally ill, homeless and diseased." It was not until 1905 that the institution acquired the name "Our Island Home."

— Courtesy of Judith L. Ross

Anna Sisson with her daughters Dorothy, left, and Bettina in stroller with two friends in front of Bickerstaff's Bakery, 1921.

— Nantucket Historical Association

Remains of the ovens after demolition of the bakery building next to the Nantucket Atheneum.

to a house on New Dollar Lane. In 1930 Thomas Bickerstaff was a widower and had retired from baking. A man of considerable self-made wealth, he moved to his daughter's home on Milk Street and occupied himself with gardening. The bakery on Lower Pearl Street was taken over for a real estate office until it was demolished to make way for the Atheneum's garden.

Agnes Bickerstaff made a life-long commitment to nursing. Remaining unmarried, she boarded with the Robinson family on Fair Street and only in the last years of her life moved to Quince Street, to live next door to the former home of her fellow countryman Robert Ratliff.

Another Englishwoman known for her kindliness was Elizabeth Watts of 'Sconset. Universally known as "Nana Watts," she assisted in the delivery of many native Nantucketers, especially those born in 'Sconset, where she generally reached a mother in labor well ahead of a physician summoned from town. She was on hand as Dina Larsen gave birth to five daughters in the keeper's cottage at Sankaty Lighthouse.

Elizabeth (Langton) Watts had been born in the village of Chadderton, near the town of

Oldham, on the edge of Manchester, England. James Watts was born in Wolverhampton, a town on the edge of Birmingham. They met in New York after making their ways separately to the United States in the 1880s. When they first came to Nantucket, they lived and worked on a farm in Quaise, where their daughter Ethel was born. Five more children followed.

Moving from Quaise, James Watts acquired Wayside Farm on Sankaty Road, between the village of 'Sconset and Sankaty Lighthouse. His listing in Nantucket directories varies between florist and gardener. The 1920 census reports him as a gardener on a private estate, and he is said to have planted most of the large privet hedges that afford privacy to 'Sconset's most affluent summer residents.

The Watts family lived on New Street in Siasconset until the 'Sconset Casino, wishing to build tennis courts on the land where their house stood, offered to move it to the Wayside Farm property. So it happened that the Watts family address changed in the 1920s, although they continued to live in their old home.

During World War I the family temporarily relocated to New Bedford to help in the war effort by working in a factory there. Again during the Depression, James Watts moved to the mainland, this time to work for a large florist business in Boston while his family remained at Wayside Farm.

After so many decades in 'Sconset, James and Elizabeth left the village at the end of their lives. When James Watts died in 1942, he had gone to live with his son James at the Wannacomet Water Company property on Cliff Road. Elizabeth Watts resided for a time at Our Island Home and then moved to a mainland nursing home, where she died in 1946. Their legacy to the island is, in part, the great green privet walls of 'Sconset and the children and grandchildren of those Nantucketers Nana Watts helped into the world. Among James and Elizabeth's descendants is Nantucket's retired fire chief and selectman, Bruce Watts.

James and Elizabeth Watts came to the end of their days during the war years of the 1940s. At the same time a young man and a young woman were coming of age in England. The future would bring them together and then to Nantucket, where they burst onto the scene as gifted actors with the Theatre Workshop of Nantucket.

It was Elizabeth Gilbert whose connection to 'Sconset brought her and John Gilbert to the island. Her father, a physician who practiced in the United States, had a summer cottage in 'Sconset that he offered to the young couple for their honeymoon in 1955. They had been planning to relocate from

– Courtesy of the Gilberts

Elizabeth and John Gilbert, 1957.

London to New Zealand, but the weeks in 'Sconset changed their minds. Instead, they brought their considerable talents to the island as permanent residents. Many Nantucketers first made their acquaintance in the Theatre Workshop production of *The Mikado* in 1957.

Nantucket has a history of involvement with the theater dating back to the 1880s, when 'Sconset became the home of an actors' colony. In the decades before air conditioning, the New York theaters closed for the summer and the writers, directors, producers, and actors moved to rural places like 'Sconset to refresh themselves in prepara-

The Theatre Workshop staged elaborate costume productions such as She Stoops to Conquer *in 1962, during the Gilberts' active years. In this scene are Norman Wilson, Gwen Gaillard, and Roger Young.*

tion for the fall season. Nantucket's own community theater had been fostered in part by individuals associated with 'Sconset's professional theater folk.[2]

In the mid 1950s Joseph "Mac" Dixon began his involvement with Nantucket. In 1956 he directed *An Italian Straw Hat,* the first of many well-appreciated productions, and followed it up with *The Mikado.*

The Theatre Workshop actors were not professionals. Norman Wilson, one of the stars of *The Mikado,* was a meat cutter by day. Other actors worked in sales, journalism, teaching, and the like. John Gilbert was employed as a carpenter, and Elizabeth Gilbert managed stores, but despite their youth and their day jobs, the Gilberts brought with them to Nantucket a wealth of experience in singing and dancing for audiences in England. Over the years on-island they took on roles from the comic to the most profoundly serious, with music and without. Among the veterans of the Theatre Workshop, Elizabeth Gilbert was involved in a record number of productions, onstage for thirty-seven and offstage as costume mistress and in other capacities for many more.

As the Gilberts contributed to Nantucket theater, they also became core members of the island business community—Elizabeth as a distinguished needleworker and proprietor of a crafts center, and John as a builder and restorer of historic structures. In 1978 he took over responsibility for putting the Old Mill back in running order once again, and he also worked on most of the Nantucket Historical Association's other properties.

For many years the Gilberts lived and conducted their businesses opposite Nantucket's Quaker graveyard, the inspiration for *The Quaker Graveyard in Nantucket. For Warren Winslow, Dead at Sea,* Robert Lowell's poetic meditation on the bloody combat waged by pacifist Quakers against the world's whales. Because orthodox Friends rejected attachment to earthly remains, there are few headstones on the rolling grassy expanse—"this field of Quakers in their unstoned graves," as Lowell puts it. The Gilberts' quiet neighbors were for the most part also nameless. But from among the world's people a significant headstone presented itself to them on a visit to England in the spring of 2003. In the churchyard of John's ancestral home of Ashford, Kent, they came upon the grave marker of a previous John Gilbert. And then these English cousins set their course westward and returned to their adopted island home.

English Canada

Dear to the hearts of generations of Nantucketers was the Old Nantucket Candy Kitchen that shared the lot on Lower Pearl Street with the Bickerstaffs' bakery. Confectioner Walter Sisson had his business there from 1918 through the 1950s, and each May he and his Canadian wife Anna rewarded every child who participated in Nantucket's Memorial Day parade with an ice-cream cone.

Anna "Nan" Belyea was born in Hartland, St. John, New Brunswick, in 1883 and came to the United States in 1910. By then Walter Sisson, a native of Lynn, Massachusetts, had already been in the candy business on Nantucket for a half dozen years. Together they ran a candy stand on Chestnut Street before moving to Lower Pearl. There, on a large slab of marble in the back of the small building, Anna and the Sissons' two daugh-

Anna and Walter Sisson at the door of their candy store in 1910.

Courtesy of Judith L. Ross

2. Although most of the amateur theatricals on Nantucket were put on by and for the summer residents, Margaret Fawcett, daughter of actors George Fawcett and Percy Haswell, wrote Nantucket historical plays and cast Nantucketers in the roles. Some Nantucketers also gained theater experience by taking part in the annual reviews at the Siasconset Casino. In the 1930s many Nantucket children had the experience of acting and singing in musical comedies, including Gilbert and Sullivan's *Pirates of Penzance,* directed by native Nantucketer Ellen Ramsdell.

ters kneaded, pulled, cut, and wrapped the salt water taffy so popular in coastal New England resorts. In the evenings they sold popcorn to patrons of the nearby Dreamland Theatre. In addition to the candy stand, the building also housed Nan's Souvenir Gift Shop. Their businesses endured for nearly half a century.

It was only after 1900 that English-speaking Canadians arrived in force. Throughout the 1800s, the number of Canadian-born residents of Nantucket had never risen above twenty. A minor specialty of Canadian men during the whaling era had been making packing boxes for spermaceti candles. In 1910 there were just twenty-seven residents from "English Canada," but in 1920, for the first time, the number of Nantucket's residents born in Canada exceeded the number of island residents born in Ireland. By 1930, before the Depression undermined all economic incentive to move to the island, their number had risen to 150.[3]

With the exception of Granville Cranston, who came from Ontario, all the Canadians—both English-speaking and French-speaking—who moved to Nantucket were from the provinces on the Atlantic coast: Nova Scotia, New Brunswick, Prince Edward Island, Quebec, and Newfoundland. This was the part of Canada earliest settled and most populous. There had been two French colonies in the 1600s: New France with its cities of Quebec and Montreal, and Acadia, which was later divided into the provinces of Nova Scotia, New Brunswick, and Prince Edward Island.

After France ceded Acadia to Great Britain in the 1700s, Acadia's French residents were deported, mainly to Louisiana, to be replaced with settlers from England, Scotland, and Ireland. A decade later a few of the Acadians made their way back, mainly to northern New Brunswick.

At the close of the American Revolution about forty thousand American colonists not

in sympathy with the revolution against British sovereignty—people known as "United Empire Loyalists"—moved north, mainly to Nova Scotia. As the result of eighteenth-century politics and war, Quebec today is French-speaking with a minority of English speakers, while Canada's Atlantic Provinces are English-speaking with a minority of French speakers.

During the late 1800s, with North America's focus on westward expansion, the Atlantic Provinces became backwaters eking out a subsistence economy based on fishing, dairy farming, and the production of apples and potatoes. Nonetheless, because of a high birthrate and continuing immigration, especially from Ireland in the wake of the potato famine, the population nearly tripled between 1870 and 1930 and severely taxed the resources of those northern lands with short growing seasons.

Between 1914 and 1918 more than 600,000 Canadian men served in World War I. Initially there had been a promise that Canada would not conscript men for overseas military service, but when voluntary participation in the war effort proved insufficient, conscription was imposed in 1917. After the close of the war, the hard feelings incited by the draft were compounded by demands for higher wages, better working conditions, and subsidized crop prices. Canadians in the Atlantic Provinces sought better opportunities in the United States, and many moved south to New England.

Among the opportunities Nantucket offered was employment by the Nantucket Cottage Hospital, first opened in 1913. Until then Nantucket had managed without a general hospital, sick and injured Nantucketers being treated and cared for in their own homes. With advances in surgery, however, Nantucket's physicians required a sterile operating room. Moreover, the growing population of summer residents faced a

---

3. It is only in 1920 that French Canadians begin to appear in Nantucket census records. However, in 1758, when England expelled the French residents of Acadia and dispersed them among its other North American colonies, over thirty were assigned to Nantucket. A list of thirty-seven individuals, twenty-seven with the surname Dupee [Dupuis?] and ten with the surname Bruse or Brufe, appears on p. 3 of Volume 24, Archives of the State of Massachusetts. Apparently the Acadians did move to Nantucket. In 1764 there were fifty-two "neutral French" living on the island. They were not welcome, and at the August 13, 1766, town meeting it was voted to request the legislature to confirm an order already passed for removing the French from the island. This was in the same period when the selectmen were forcing the departure of other individuals and groups who had moved to Nantucket without invitation and were perceived as undesirable.

sometimes painful dilemma. Unlike the islanders' sturdy homes, many of the summer peoples' cottages were inconvenient and uncomfortable for illness and convalescence, but under those circumstances the discomfort of travel back to the mainland was often unbearable. Voting residents of the town of Nantucket did not assign high priority to the establishment of a hospital on the island, but the physicians and the summer people did. (In response to an accusation that she was against progress and against the hospital, Sarah P. Bunker's neighbor Gulielma Folger retorted, "I was against the hospital until we got money. I didn't think it fair to put it on the summer people.") Doctors John Grouard and Benjamin Sharp called a series of meetings about the problem in 1911 and succeeded in enlisting Nantucket businessman Millard Freeborn and popular novelist Mary Waller to their cause. Funds were raised, a hospital corporation was formed, a location on West Chester Street was chosen, and work began on converting a former private home into a hospital.

To begin with, patients staying at the hospital brought their own private nurses. Three beds were provided in the attic for the nurses, and the hospital's cook slept in the kitchen, which doubled as the nursery for newborns.

Originally intended only for summer operation, by 1915–16 the hospital was open year-round.

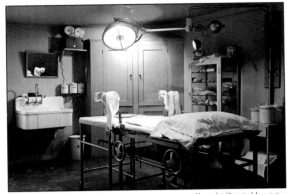

The Cottage Hospital's operating room, 1950.

The influenza pandemic of 1918 brought the first islandwide challenge for the new medical facility and its staff. Of 337 confirmed cases of influenza in the late fall of that year, there were just nine deaths, a far cry from the devastating mortality of the "Indian sickness" of the mid 1700s.

In the course of the 1920s, Nantucketers' use of the hospital increased dramatically. In 1927 there were 416 admissions, 151 surgeries performed, and 224 X-rays taken. As many as seventy births took place each year at the Nantucket Cottage Hospital. The continual need for expansion of facilities was underwritten by ever more elaborate summer fundraisers—fairs and fetes and thrift-shop operations. To expand the staff, the hospital board looked to Canada. In 1930 four of nine nurses

The original Nantucket Cottage Hospital located on West Chester Street.

employed by the hospital had come to the island from Nova Scotia and New Brunswick, as had the cook and two maids.

The tradition of Canadian nursing on Nantucket was, in fact, more venerable than the island hospital itself. In 1870 Maria Thomas of Nova Scotia was supporting herself and her thirteen-year-old son by nursing. She owned Nantucket real estate and had substantial cash savings as well. In 1900 Canadian Annie Reilly, who had been in the United States for a decade, was a private nurse for the King family, and in 1920 Lucy Crompton, a "trained nurse," was providing services for an unnamed private family. In 1910 Carrie Freeman was nurse on a Nantucket farm. In addition to the nurses at the hospital in 1930, Eva Topham was employed as a private nurse.

Eva May Rowley was born in New Brunswick. Unlike the members of the hospital staff, who had for the most part left Canada for the United States in the 1920s, she was already living on Nantucket when the 1895 local census was taken. In 1900 she had been joined by two younger Rowleys: Walter,

a blacksmith, and Burton, who was working as a day laborer. Eva married surfman Leland Topham, and during the 1920s they were proprietors of the Blue Dory Tea Room, first on Liberty Street in the building later occupied by the Grey Gull and later in the Wright Mansion at 94 Main Street. When the marriage failed, Eva Topham turned to private nursing until her death in 1932.

As in the earlier cases of the Irish and then the English, Canadian women on Nantucket substantially outnumbered Canadian men. Besides nursing, the woman did various sorts of domestic service as cooks, housekeepers, maids, and laundresses. Some worked as waitresses in Nantucket's proliferating restaurants. Emma Fraser was a milliner with her own hat shop in the 1920s. Hilda Allen's Canadian daughter-in-law, Evelyn Allen, was a public-school teacher. Most of the English-speaking Canadian women were, however, married and "at home" as were the French Canadian women and the English women on-island. Among the English-speaking Canadians in 1930, there were about two dozen couples in which

Nurses at Nantucket Cottage Hospital, June 1920.

Aquila Cormie's blacksmith shop on Straight Wharf.

Cormie at work at his anvil.

husband and wife were both born in Canada, and about three dozen more Canadian women married to Nantucket husbands. Nantucket Cottage Hospital's hiring of nurses from Canada continued; in the late 1950s and early 1960s four nurses from Newfoundland—Shirley (Reid) Gardner, Betty (Elms) MacDonald, Georgina "Jean" (Holmes) Bennett, and Violet (Pyne) Allen—came to the island, married local men, and stayed.

In early-twentieth-century Nantucket, Canadian men had a near monopoly on blacksmithery. In competition with Irish-American Thomas Warren Sr. and his son Thomas Jr. were young Walter Rowley, aging James Quigley, and partners Frederick Heighton and Aquila Cormie.

Aquila Cormie's life in Nantucket began before 1900. Born in Moncton, New Brunswick, in 1880, he left for the United States at age 17, and soon was working as a farm laborer at Eatfire Spring Farm on Wauwinet Road. He learned smithery from Nantucketer Clinton Parker, and by 1910 Cormie, now a married man and a homeowner, was employed as a blacksmith.

Fredrick Heighton was born in River St. John, Nova Scotia. In 1896 he went to Maine to work as a blacksmith and from there moved on to Ottawa, Illinois. In 1898 he married May L. Jocelyn from Antigonish, Nova Scotia, and they started their family in Illinois.

The advent of the automobile put many blacksmiths out of business, but on Nantucket, where automobiles were prohibited until 1918, there were still plenty of horses. Moreover, the fishing fleet needed the services of smiths to make and repair tackle, dredges, and other equipment for their vessels. May Heighton's sister, Charlotte Holm, who was married to Nantucket farmer Frank Holm, encouraged the Heightons to relocate to the island. They came with their Illinois-born children, and while they were living and working on several Polpis farms, their family increased. Altogether there were twelve Heighton children, including two sets of twins. The next-to-youngest of the Nantucket-born Heightons—Constance—grew up to be newspaperwoman Connie Indio, cofounder and copublisher with her husband Joseph Indio, of the *Town Crier*.

In the 1910 federal census, where the Heightons first appear in Nantucket, Fred Heighton's occupation is listed as farmer, but by 1920 his occupational listing had changed from farmer to blacksmith. In fact, he both farmed and did blacksmithery all his life. Among the farms he rented and operated were the Mitchell Farm and the Devlin Farm in Polpis, Eatfire Spring Farm, and the Snow Farm on Hummock Pond Road. The produce of the farms they worked fed the Heightons' own family, and Fred Heighton had a regular route for distribution of their dairy products and eggs. Besides shoeing horses, he also made fireplace andirons and ironwork fences, including some of the elegant ones still to be seen at residences on Main Street. May Heighton shared the farmwork and also supplemented the family income by working for Polpis neighbors.

Fred Heighton and Aquila Cormie went into partnership to operate a shop on Still Dock, just a short distance from Tom Warren's blacksmith shop on South Water Street. Toward the end of Cormie's very long career—he became something of a curiosity as Nantucket's "last blacksmith," working at his forge, shoeing horses on the sidewalk, and amiably making souvenir rings from bent horseshoe nails for children and tourists. Upon his retirement at age 74, the shop and many of its furnishings were incorporated into the Four Winds Gift Shop, which still occupies his former premises.

Oscar Quigley came from St. John, New Brunswick, to Nantucket as a teenager in 1910. Like Aquila Cormie, he apprenticed to a local tradesman, in this case Nantucketer Nathaniel Lowell, from whom he learned masonry. Retiring after forty years in business as a contractor, he was appointed a member of Nantucket's Airport Commission, serving the town until his death in 1967.

Nantucket had three Canadian barbers by 1920. Frederick Currie had been brought to the United States as a child in 1887. In 1910 he was boarding with a Nantucket family, and ten years later he had his own barber shop. His wife Juliet was born in Denmark and left her home country in 1909. By 1930 the Currie family was quite prosperous.

John Fee of Prince Edward Island was a decade older than Frederick Currie, but he came to Nantucket later. Although he and his large family were living in a rented house in 1920, he too had his own barber shop. The Fees' oldest son was a surfman in the Coast Guard.

John Leslie MacDonald and his wife Rosa of Prince Edward Island were living on Nantucket with their three children in 1910. They had become homeowners, but more than most families, the MacDonalds divided themselves between the United States and Canada. "Les" MacDonald had

been naturalized many years earlier, but Rosa had not become a United States citizen. The oldest of their children, according to the 1910 census, had been born in the United States two years after their marriage, but their second and third children, Wanda and John, were born in Canada and entered the United States for the first time in 1906.

During World War I, Rosa and the children returned to Canada, and Les MacDonald served in the United States armed forces. In 1920, he was back on-island, still married but living alone on Atlantic Avenue, next door to his relative Margaret Hyde, also born on Prince Edward Island, and her Massachusetts-born husband. In addition to his house, he also owned his own barber shop. Ten years later, in 1930, he was sharing his household with two sons and two nephews and no longer listed his occupation as barber. In late middle age he had switched to carpentry and was working with his nephews, one a carpenter and the other a mason.

When Les MacDonald died in 1953, he had been living with his fisherman son, John MacDonald, who had moved from Nantucket to East Providence, Rhode Island. His other children, Wanda and Donald, had long since returned from Prince Edward Island to Nantucket, and it was to Nantucket's Prospect Hill Cemetery that their father was returned for burial.

Nantucket's fishermen had an affinity for Christmas weddings, because Christmas was one of the rare times of the year when everyone was ashore. Like Arne Pedersen nearly a decade earlier, Newfoundlander John J. "Jack" McDonald had such a wedding. He married Mary Genevieve Davis, whose parents were also from Newfoundland, on Christmas 1933. A reception was held at the home of yet another Newfoundland couple living on Nantucket—McDonald's best man, fisherman Ambrose Furey and his wife Ellen.

In the 1930s McDonald and Furey were among at least twenty-six Canadian men fishing out of Nantucket. Jack McDonald—who began fishing at age 16—had left the sea to earn a college degree before emigrating from Newfoundland. Once on Nantucket he became a captain in the island fishing fleet. In 1944 he and Captain Ernest Murley had a new fishing vessel built for them. They named her the *Gladys & Mary* for their oldest daughters.

On September 5, 1944, the *Gladys & Mary*, captained by Jack McDonald with a crew of seven, sailed from Nantucket on her maiden voyage to the off-shore fishing grounds. Two nights later, as they were in the vicinity of the South Shoals Lightship, their barometer began to drop precipitously. Aware that this meant the approach of a powerful storm, they made a run out of the shoals for the relative safety of deep water, but the storm overtook them. The vessel withstood a tremendous pounding from hurricane winds and huge waves that at least twice drove the boat over on her beam ends. Pieces were torn off the vessel, and water poured in through smashed hatches. The generator failed, and the engines stopped running. In the darkness a wave breaking over the stern knocked Captain McDonald down a companionway. Unconscious from the blow, he was in danger of drowning when two crewmen pulled him out of the water below decks. At the mercy of the storm, the *Gladys & Mary* was tossed and battered for hours. Only the fact that she was new-built accounted for her staying afloat. When the storm moved off and left the fishermen in its wake, they

had been swept from south of Nantucket to far east of New Jersey. Twenty-four hours later the *Gladys & Mary* limped into Nantucket Harbor, and Captain McDonald and one crew member went to the Nantucket Cottage Hospital for treatment of injuries sustained in the storm. Having come within a breath of drowning, Jack McDonald went straight back to his vessel, continued fishing for another two decades, and lived to the age of 87.

Tobias Flemming was another Newfoundlander who became a captain in the fishing fleet. He had not come to the United States until the 1920s. Fishing out of New Bedford and Nantucket, while he was still in his twenties, he became one of the youngest captains of commercial fishing vessels in the United States. Over the years he commanded the *Charles Fossey*, the *Catherine T.*, and the *Anna C. Perry*, having the good fortune not to be aboard the *Perry* on her final, fatal voyage. He both owned and operated the *Mary Tapper*. Despite all the hazards of deep-sea fishing, he retired from a long career as a fisherman and died on land in 1973.

The stone marking the Flemming plot in St. Mary's Cemetery is incised with a fishing boat passing Brant Point Lighthouse outward bound with the text: "Dear Lord be good to me. The sea is so wide and my boat is so small." The gravestone of Captain Tobias Flemming proclaims, "Safe harbor at last."

Black Nova Scotians

Back in 1783, some United Empire Loyalists who relocated to Nova Scotia from Virginia plantations took their slaves with them. Thousands of other slaves had been promised their freedom, protection from future enslavement, and land of their own by British colonial governors in exchange for taking up arms against the American colonists. The fledgling government of the United States of America objected to the departure of the Loyalists' slaves and former slaves on the grounds that they were American property that the defeated British had no right to remove from the United States. To resolve the dispute, the British made a cash payment to the United States, certificates of freedom were issued to the departees, and documenta-

The Gladys and Mary at Straight Wharf, June 1953.

GLADYS & MARY
NEW BEDFORD

tion of more than three thousand slaves who had earned their freedom through service to the British was registered in the "Book of Negroes" created for the occasion.

In Nova Scotia the United Empire Loyalists found life difficult. The climate was harsher and the soil less fertile than Virginia's, and replication of the plantation life they had once lived proved impossible. As a result, masters abandoned their slaves to fend for themselves. As for the Black Loyalists who had arrived with their certificates of freedom, few received the hundred acres promised to each who had served. Those who did receive some land had to wait years for it only to find subsistence farming hardly viable. In order to survive, Black Loyalists had to indenture themselves and their children to more prosperous whites or to hire themselves out as very cheap labor, thereby arousing the resentment of others in competition with them for jobs.

In 1791 the Black Loyalists sent a representative to England to seek redress. While there, he approached with an offer of free land for all in Africa, and the following year two thousand of the Black Loyalists embarked on fifteen ships in Halifax, Nova Scotia, and sailed for Sierra Leone. At the same time, a group of Maroons from Jamaica, descendants of former slaves who had freed themselves, were relocated to Nova Scotia. Some of them, too, went on to Sierra Leone. A generation later, during the War of 1812, the number of black Nova Scotians was augmented when once again the British offered slaves in the United States freedom and land in Nova Scotia in exchange for fighting against the United States.

The Maroons in Nova Scotia joined the remaining Black Loyalists and the abandoned slaves in several black communities, including Shelburne on the south coast, Birchtown a bit to the north, and Guysborough, a town reconstituted in northeastern Nova Scotia after a disastrous fire. Like Nantucket's New Guinea, these communities had their own small businesses, schools, and churches.

From Nova Scotia's black communities at least three people made their way to Nantucket in the 1800s. Two women first appear in the 1850 census.

Lydia Boston, wife of seaman Benajah Boston Sr., had previously been married to one of the Nantucket Pompeys. Elizabeth Camben was the wife of West Indian seaman Daniel Camben. Although Pitman Moors was only middle-aged, he had no stated profession in 1850. Nonetheless, by 1860 he owned a modest piece of real estate in New Guinea.

What had brought these Nova Scotia-born people to the island? An old connection between Nantucket and Nova Scotia dated to the period immediately after the war. As the United Empire Loyalists struggled to settle themselves, Nantucket was also struggling to rebuild its whaling economy, which lay in ruins after the American Revolution. Prospects for the return of prosperity seemed dim. Many Nantucketers saw no alternative but to leave the island for locations offering more protection in case of future war. Some went to a well-defended spot high up the Hudson River in New York. Others moved their business to Nova Scotia in order to trade directly with the London market unhampered by United States mercantile regulations.

Just three years after the Loyalists' arrival on ships from New York, ships bringing forty Nantucket families arrived in Dartmouth, near Halifax, Nova Scotia. Nova Scotia welcomed the prospect of the employment whaling might offer to the jobless Loyalists. The Dartmouth community, however, was as short-lived as the one attempted in Dunkirk, France, a few years later. In 1791 it was reported that most of the people who had left the island for Nova Scotia had returned to Nantucket.

Pitman Moors had been born in Nova Scotia in 1800, Lydia Boston in 1803, and Elizabeth Camben in 1819, all after the brief Nantucket experiment at Dartmouth. Perhaps the lines between Nova Scotia and Nantucket remained open for a while after the whaling colony failed, or perhaps each had found a way to the island independently of the others. In 1900 a young woman named Lucy Backus, born in Canada of Canadian parents and classified as black, was working on Nantucket as a hotel cook. During the ensuing century other people of color from the United States, Canada, and Bermuda would follow her lead, coming to work and to live on Nantucket.

CHAPTER THIRTEEN

Northward Voyagers

Sea-going Nantucketers' Children

Nantucket families had moved to Dunkirk (and to New York and Nova Scotia as well) to pursue the wealth promised by the whaling industry to those willing to make personal sacrifices. The Nantucket whaling outposts on land offered housing similar to what the migrating families had left behind. There were Quaker meeting houses for the free practice of worship, and women and children enjoyed the daily company of other Nantucket women and children. In Dunkirk it was useful to be able to speak French, but it was possible to live in an entirely Nantucket household and community.

Once whaling entered the Pacific and ever-lengthening voyages stretched out over years, some captains began to take their wives and children along with them, dropping them off for spells in Honolulu or Lahaina, the whalers' port on the island of Maui, in the company of other whalers' families. This was a situation very different from life in the little communities dispersed on land. While at sea the captain's wife was the sole woman aboard, and her children were her only daily company. The crew members of whalers spoke a welter of languages, and in port the local language might be Spanish, Portuguese, French, or any of a number of Polynesian and Melanesian languages.

Little accommodation was made for pregnancy and birth. Children were born on land if possible, but some births inevitably took place aboard ship. Matilda Joy, wife of Samuel Joy, gave birth to their daughter Anna in Mexico and two years later gave birth to Anna's brother William in Brazil. Maria Winslow was one of the fortunate children to be brought into the world in Hawai'i, but Ida and Emily Winslow were born at sea. Of the ocean-going Grant family, Charles was born on Pitcairn Island, George on Upolu, Western Samoa (then known as Navigator's Island), and Leonora at New Zealand's Bay of Islands. Other sons and daughters of Nantucket had their birthplaces in Peru and Chile and on Norfolk Island, east of Australia. During World War I Lawrence Cady was born in Cuba. For all of them, getting to Nantucket for the first time meant traveling north toward home.

Lahaina, on the Hawaiian island of Maui, was a gathering place for Nantucket whaleships.

Painting by Russell and Purrington, 1845, New Bedford Whaling Museum

Wives from Distant Shores

Although it was next to impossible for a crew member to marry while on a voyage and take his wife home with him, there were a few foreign-born wives from the Caribbean, Latin America, and elsewhere to the south. From St. Thomas in the West Indies came Ann Louisa Ray, daughter of Nicholas and Grace Potter of St. Thomas. In 1850 Ann Louisa was living on Nantucket with her mariner husband. Two Potter men, Peter and Thomas, were also living on the island. Peter, a cooper, was lodging with the Upham family, and mariner Thomas Potter was a Nantucket home-owner with a Nantucket wife and children. Ten years later Ann Louisa's sisters Eliza and Mary had come to Nantucket and were living with one of the Macy families. Ann Louisa bore four children and lived until 1890.

Another woman from the West Indies, Gwendolyn Backus, was the wife of Oliver Backus, purser on one of the steamboats. Like Ann Louisa Ray before her, Gwendolyn had four Nantucket-born children. The family was living on Union Street in 1930.

The 1850 census recorded twenty-year-old Isabella Starbuck, born in Australia, as wife of equally young store clerk Marcus Starbuck. It also recorded Leonore B. Whippey, 23, of some unspecified place in South America, married to George Whippey and mother of a Nantucket-born infant.[1] In 1860 Maria Ramsdell, Francita Goodnow, and Mary Gifford, all Chilean women in their twenties, were living in Nantucket. Maria and Francita and their families were sharing living quarters.

In 1870 the federal census recorded the birthplace of Rosa Ross, wife of James Gardner Ross, as the island of St. Helena, twelve hundred miles out in the Atlantic Ocean off the coast of Africa. Such was its isolation that it was chosen as the place of exile for Napoleon Bonaparte, taken there in 1815 in a ship on which the young Robert Ratliff served.

Jamestown, St. Helena. Uninhabited when discovered in 1502, the island became the home of a small number of English settlers and of imported slaves who were freed in 1832. Its most famous resident was the exiled Napoleon Bonaparte.

Several men from St. Helena came to Nantucket over the years. Among the transient mariners listed in the 1850 census were William Canfield, 22, and William Wright, 24, both classified as white. A decade later another mariner—William Tony, 27—had settled on Nantucket as a newlywed with a Nantucket wife. A great many years later Matthew Ellis, born on St. Helena to parents also born there, was living on Nantucket and working as a school janitor. He had been married but was divorced and living alone in 1920.

It is easy enough to see how seafaring men from St. Helena had made their way to Nantucket, but it is an intriguing mystery how a young, unmarried woman of color could leave such a remote place and travel so very far north to marry James Gardner Ross, a Nantucket barber whose grandfather had been born in Africa. Rosa was 25 years old in 1870 and the mother of two Nantucket-born children. The census classified her as "mulatto," and listed her occupation as "tailoress." Her husband was a nephew of Eunice Ross. Thanks to the successful campaign for school integration waged for and by Eunice Ross, their son J. Gardner Ross, born in 1877, graduated from Nantucket High School and went on to Newton Theological Seminary and a life of service in Baptist churches.

---

1. The Whippey family made something of a tradition of marriages with the world's people. David Whippey Jr. (1801–75) married a native Fijian and lived out his days in Fiji. Nantucket innkeeper William Whippey was born in New Zealand in 1801, most likely of a Maori mother.

Mariners Putting Down Roots

In addition to the five members of the Potter family from the West Indies, there were at least three other men born in those islands and living on Nantucket in 1850. William Hazell was a young ship captain with a local wife and a baby. Another West Indian man resident on the island at the time was Thomas Derrick, a mariner who also had a Nantucket wife and child. Daniel Austin, on the other hand, was an octogenarian pauper living at the town asylum in the company of English-born Philip Walker, an aging farmer who had come to the same fate. The asylum received a state subsidy for the support of the two men. All these residents of Nantucket were classified as white. Among transient seamen from the West Indies in 1850 were four classified as white and four classified as black.

John Thomas, 35 years old in 1850 and classified as black, was from Santo Domingo. Two men from "St. Catherine, South America," lived out their lives on Nantucket. Mariner Joseph Simmonds died on-island in 1864 and Joseph Rose, an elderly widower, in 1873. Although there is a St. Catherine Island off the coast of Santo Domingo, their birthplace was probably Ilha de Santa Catarina off the south coast of Brazil. In the second edition of *Worcester's Gazetteer*, published in 1823, the entry for "St. Catherines, isl. in the S. Atlantic ocean, near the coast of Brazil" reports the island to be green and fertile although plagued with poisonous snakes. The population at the time was 30,000, but the inhabitants were too poor to take advantage of the island's potential: "Their soil, which is very fit for the cultivation of sugar, remains unproductive for want of slaves, whom they are not rich enough to purchase. The whale fishery is very successful." It would have been a wise move for a mariner to ship out of Santa Catarina on a whaler bound for nearly snake-free Nantucket.

In 1860 master mariner William Wood had taken up residence on Nantucket. He had been born in the West Indies in 1810 and is described in the *Barney Genealogical Record* as "of New Bedford," "from the West Indies," and "a stranger." His wife, Eliza Ann Edwards, and three of his children were all born in Massachusetts; but their son Alexander was born in Peru in 1852. Alexander followed his father's profession and, sadly, died at sea at the age of seventeen.

Peruvian-born mariner Joseph Castro—born in Paita, on the coast of northern Peru—was also residing on the island in 1860. His wife Lavina and his stepdaughter Isabella were Nantucket-born. All were classified as mulatto and living in New Guinea.[2] In 1870, although he was fifty years old, Joseph Castro was "at sea" when the census was taken.

In the first half of the 1800s, a man from Suriname named Vanderhoop was assimilated by the Aquinnah Wampanoags, and he and his wife Beulah have many descendants on Martha's Vineyard. Charles E. Delprado, a seaman from Suriname, settled in Nantucket's New Guinea in the 1850s and married a woman from the black community, but unlike the Vanderhoops, they did not establish a family to carry on their name. The young couple was living on Nantucket in 1860, but ten years later they were gone, part of the general exodus from the town's post-whaling-era depression.

There were both transient and settled mariners on Nantucket in the 1800s who had been born in Chile, Peru, and Brazil. In the late 1990s a new wave of Brazilian immigrants began gathering in Hyannis and on Martha's Vineyard. By 2002 a Brazilian convenience store had opened on Nantucket, and the local supermarkets had begun to advertise that cash transfers could be arranged through the Banco da Brasil. In 2003, Isabella Rose Tarcitano, all of whose grandparents live in Rio de Janeiro, was born on Nantucket.

2. Philbrick 1998 says that Dorcas Honorable had a daughter Emmeline (not Lavina) who married a man named Castro and had a daughter named Isabel, who became the wife of former slave and Civil War veteran Hiram Reed. He has confused Dorcas Honorable with Dorcas Mingo. (Although Dorcas Mingo is described in court documents as a "spinster," this does not refer to her marital status but to her profession as a spinner of wool.) Dorcas (Mingo) Wilbur, her daughter Lavina (Wilbur) Draper, and her granddaughter Isabella (Draper) Reed were all classified at one time or another as black or mulatto. Isabella Reed is classified as an Indian in the 1870 census. Although Isabella died in 1882, her mother, Lavina, lived until 1891. Lavina and Isabella were both buried in Nantucket's "colored" cemetery behind Mill Hill.

CHAPTER FOURTEEN

Brotherhood

A reader of obituaries in the Nantucket newspapers cannot fail to be struck by how important fraternal organizations were to foreign-born men in the late nineteenth century and the first half of the twentieth century. Membership in such organizations was so universal that those few obituaries that do not end with mention of special graveside rites by fellow Freemasons, Oddfellows, or Red Men stand out and catch one's attention. Men who belong to one such organization often belong to several, but membership in Nantucket's Masonic lodge has been the rule. Since the mid-1800s it has been rare for an individual to find companionship at the Pacific Club or with the Oddfellows without also belonging to Union Lodge F. & A. M.

This is remarkable in view of the intensely anti-masonic sentiments of earlier times. Nantucket's Union Lodge was founded in 1771, when the influence of Quakerism was in full force in Nantucket. The Friends Book of Objections is replete with cases of men who risked disownment not only for admitting musical instruments into their homes, sailing on armed vessels, and being innoculated against smallpox, but also for consorting with Freemasons. Just a year after the founding of Union Lodge, Quaker elders who sought to dissuade Jethro Hussey from an interest in freemasonry "received from him such unbecoming carriage and behavior as prevented them from doing so." Over a period of three months in 1775, Andrew Worth was "treated with for joining a company in throwing a quantity of oysters out of a vessel without legal authority and for being in fellowship with those called Freemasons both which he refused to give satisfaction." Ultimately, although he made things right about the oysters, he "declined to discuss freemasonry." Both Worth and Hussey were disowned.

Although the action of the Meeting made it clear that Quakerism would not tolerate it, Nantucket men's attraction to freemasonry continued unabated. The cases of Jethro Hussey and Andrew Worth are just two of many such entries in the Book of Objections.

For many of the same reasons that the Society of Friends proscribed freemasonry, so did the Roman Catholic Church, which perceived Masonic ritual as in competition with Christian holy ritual. Faithful Catholics were barred from membership in Masonic lodges, and membership in the Knights of Columbus was offered as an alternative. Over time a great many Catholic men in Nantucket have been members of the Knights of Columbus, but many have also joined Union Lodge.

What was it about freemasonry that was so compelling for Quaker men, Catholic men, and foreign-born men living on Nantucket? In the 1700s, it was still quite a new phenomenon. Although freemasonry has its roots in the period of the construction of Europe's great cathedrals, when stonemasons formed professional guilds throughout Europe, the social function of the Freemasons' organizations and the elaborate rituals in use today developed in the late 1600s and early 1700s. Freemasons consider the formation of the Grand Lodge of England in 1717 to be the foundation event of their organization. From England, freemasonry came to the North American colonies, where it became immensely popular, and its membership included the most influential leaders of the colonies and the founding fathers of the new United States of America. To be a Freemason was to belong to a brotherhood of men of accomplishment.

For the newly arrived foreign-born, membership in a lodge offered, if possible, even more advantages than it did to the native-born and long-established. Immigrants had left behind all the continuities of their family networks. In particular, they were separated from their family gravesites and were generally anxious about who would bury them in the new land and who would look after their survivors. As a result, immigrants were quick to form burial societies, mutual-aid societies, and insurance cooperatives. In places like Nantucket, where ethnic groups were, for the most part, diminutive, freemasonry offered a ready-made alternative. A Freemason knows that his brothers will be at his funeral, where they will speak eloquently and confer dignity on the occasion, and they will continue to offer support to his widow and children.

Most Freemasons were also members of churches, and church membership might seem to suffice for these purposes. In Nantucket, however, where there were no Eastern-rite churches and no Lutheran church, many of the foreign-born had to choose new churches to join; Armenians and Lutherans alike joined the Congregational Church, for instance. But beyond membership of any particular church, Freemasons found fellowship with a broader sector of the community, and as an international organization freemasonry did not discriminate against the foreign-born. Anxiety about mass immigration to the United States in the late nineteenth and early twentieth centuries gave rise to a nativist backlash among citizens who considered themselves descendants of Anglo-Saxon settlers. Languages other than English, foodways other than those considered all-American, and domestic rituals from "the old country" were generally driven underground by outspoken public criticism. The Freemasons, who had themselves suffered from an intense antimasonic movement in the 1820s and 1830s, did not close their door to the foreign-born, and they offered new, inclusive rituals. For men seeking to assimilate into their new American home on Nantucket, freemasonry was a broad, well-tended highway.

Even a partial list of Union Lodge's foreign-born members shows how cosmopolitan Nantucket's Masonic brotherhood has been over the decades: Captain John Murray Jr. (Azores, Portugal), José Reyes (Philippines), Carekin Proodian (Armenia), Emile Genesky (Russia), Antoon Khouri (Syria), John Nicoletos and George C. Anastos (Greece), Eugene Collatz (Germany), Peder Pedersen and Rolf Sjölund (Norway), Leendert Block and William Voorneveld Sr. (Netherlands), Frederick Heighton (Canada), John Gilbert (England). Simon Kaufman was a devoted member of the Wauwinet Tribe of Red Men, but his son-in-law Milton Zlotin was a member of Union Lodge. Lincoln Porte, whose grandfather had come to Nantucket from India and whose grandmother was the descendant of African slaves, was a member. Although living off-island in retirement, Albert Rohdin, born in Sweden, maintained his Nantucket ties, and his obituary concluded: "He was a member of Union Lodge F. & A. M. of Nantucket and took pride in belonging to a lodge with its history dating back to the years before the Revolution."

In recent years, especially since it began admitting women, the Nantucket Rotary Club has to some degree superseded Union Lodge as the premier place for Nantucketers to meet and network, and most recently the Great Hall of the Atheneum has become Nantucket's busiest international gathering place. A grant from the Coffin School to the Nantucket Atheneum funded the purchase of a roomful of laptop computers. Beginning in the summer of 2001, use has grown to over 25,000 computer patrons per year, with usage concentrated in the summer, when Nantucket's highly international workforce fills the hall with people waiting for their turns to receive and send e-mail. Keeping in touch with home has drawn hundreds of young men and women into the library, which they otherwise might never have visited during their seasonal employment on the island. Even a tripling of the use fee in the third summer did not abate the service's popularity. This is without doubt the most vital and appreciated service the Nantucket Atheneum has ever offered to its foreign-born residents.

Part IV
Coming to Work, Staying to Live

Steamboat inbound around Brant Point with summer people and their summer "help." — *Nantucket Historical Association*

Approaching the Twentieth Century

Sarah P. Bunker and Sampson Pompey both survived the century into which they had been born, she dying in 1902 and he surviving until 1909. Both lived in neighborhoods of empty houses vacated by the great exodus of Nantucketers from the island in the 1850s and 1860s. In changed circumstances, they had stayed on and made themselves useful, each becoming a respected community elder. They were both "descended Nantucketers"—she descended from the English settlers, he from those settlers' African slaves.

There was some connection between their families, the nature of which is now forgotten. Although Sarah P.'s great-granddaughter Charlotte Gibbs had been only four years old when Sampson Pompey died, she always spoke in respectfully familiar terms of Mr. Pompey, and to her children she transmitted knowledge of the African Meeting House at a time when its significance had fallen into obscurity for most islanders.

From the vantage points of their family houses—hers on the North Shore, his in New Guinea—Sarah P. and Sampson Pompey witnessed the precipitous decline of Nantucket as a whaling port and its res-urrection as a summer resort. The massive Sea Cliff Inn was built up the street from Sarah P.'s house, and right by her front windows horse-car tracks were laid to carry guests between Steamboat Wharf and the hotel. To the chagrin of neighbors Sarah and Gulielma Folger, poles were planted on North Street, now renamed Cliff Road, to carry telephone service to the houses along the Cliff.

A similar transformation took place beneath the front windows of the Pompey house. The thorough-fare leading away from Pompey's Corner, labeled "New Guinea" on maps as late as 1858, became Atlantic Avenue, gateway to the South Shore.

When Patience Cooper was on trial for the murder of Phebe Fuller in the 1860s, the neighbor-hood was full of vacant houses. During her long years of incarceration, sixty-eight houses were demolished and the debris used to construct a roadbed for paving from the corner of Main and Pleasant Streets to the intersection of Pleasant and York Streets, the site of the African Meeting House. From there the paving continued via Atlantic Avenue with the goal of reaching a prospective development that had been named Surfside. Seventeen years into the project, the brick- and stone-paved road had passed Sampson Pompey's house and extended as far south as a rise in the land then known as Shear Pen Hill.

In the summer of 1882 the *Inquirer and Mirror* urged a volunteer effort on the part of "our citizens and the fishermen who have teams and labor, and who are constantly using this road" so that "we may see Atlantic Avenue extended to the shore this fall." A paved road to Surfside would benefit the "stablekeepers and such as let teams (especially those who have complained that the railroad has usurped their business)." The main purpose of this project, however, was to get tourists to Surfside. In the words of the *Inquirer and Mirror*: "As we gain notoriety as a summer resort, our visitors will bring their own teams, when a drive to Surfside will be one of the real enjoyments." While being entertained with shore dinners out there, off-islanders might be induced to buy lots on which to build houses.

Great effort went into promoting the Surfside development, but it failed nonetheless, at the expense of the sixty-eight houses described in the *Inquirer and Mirror* as "ancient landmarks which were situated in the various streets and suburbs of our town"—a forgotten act of urban clearance exceeded in magnitude only by what the Great Fire had laid waste in 1846. The successful devel-opments turned out to be Wauwinet, accessed by boat up the harbor, and Siasconset, reached by the Milestone Road. Soon the railroad that had been built from town to Surfside was extended to 'Sconset, and traffic on the road past Sampson Pompey's house diminished to a trickle.

Of the four mills that had stood above New Guinea on Popsquatchet Hills only one survived to be acquired in 1897 by the recently founded Nantucket Historical Association. In 1900 the once bustling village downhill from the mill grounds had become a backwater inhabited by a small number of black families and transited mainly by tourists attracted to the panoramic views from what was now called Mill Hill. There were other approaches from the west and north, however, so visitors did not have to pass through the old black neighborhood if they chose not to.

View from New Guinea toward the mill grounds in the late 1800s.

CHAPTER FIFTEEN

The Twilight of Whaling-Era New Guinea

Sampson Dyer Pompey and his wife, Susan (Kelley) Pompey, were among the relicts of the old African-Nantucketer community that lingered on after the collapse of the whaling industry. Their parents had been influential people. Stephen Pompey was a mariner and Trillania (Dyer) Pompey was a neighborhood organizer active in promoting public health in New Guinea. They had married in 1825 and in 1829 purchased from a group of white owners the house that still stands at 3 Atlantic Avenue.

Their son Sampson, born the following year, grew up to be an even more imposing figure. Following in his father's footsteps, he went on his first whaling voyage at age seventeen, and the 1850 and 1860 censuses record father and son both employed as seamen. When the Civil War broke out, Sampson was past thirty and still unmarried. He enlisted in the Navy as an ordinary seaman on the U. S. bark *Kingfisher*, and after taking part in the Union's blockade of the Confederacy and cruising in the Gulf of Mexico was discharged as an able seaman.

His service in the Civil War was a defining moment in his life. When the Nantucket Post of the Grand Army of the Republic was established in 1891, Sampson Pompey was a charter member. His membership had been sponsored by Josiah Fitch Murphey, justice of the peace and fellow veteran, who at the same time sponsored the membership of Hiram Reed, former slave from Missouri. Reed had been emancipated by the Union Army and sent to Nantucket, whence he immediately enlisted in the infantry, returning after his service to live out the rest of his life on the island. Whenever a group photo of the G.A.R. veterans was taken, the two black men turned out with their aging white comrades-at-arms, all in their uniforms. Unlike

mainland posts, Nantucket's G.A.R. was racially integrated thanks to Sampson Pompey, Hiram Reed, and Josiah Fitch Murphey.

Immediately upon his discharge from the army in 1865, Hiram Reed had found himself a Nantucket wife, Isabella Draper. Sampson Pompey had married even sooner, on January 7, 1863, but for a while after he and Susan Kelley married, she continued to live with her parents while he went to sea. He also did some fishing and farming and worked as a cooper, a profession held over from whaling days. Later he became active in acquiring and selling real estate in and around New Guinea, and from time to time he contributed items to the *Inquirer and Mirror*.

Susan Kelley's father had been born in Virginia in 1811 of Virginia-born parents, and he was employed as a mariner until late in life. He finally

Civil War veterans Sampson Pompey (seated) and Hiram Reed (behind) among fellow members of the Grand Army of the Republic, 1909.

Nantucket Historical Association

left the sea in his sixties and became a laborer on shore. Susan's mother, Harriet (Simons) Kelley, was from an old New Guinea family with Wampanoag heritage. Susan was born during the Nantucket public schools integration battle, and by the time she was ready to attend Nantucket High School, it had long been open to all. She began her studies there in 1856 at age thirteen and left school in 1859.

Newspaperman Arthur Elwell Jenks described Susan Pompey as, "an honored representative of a respected colored family of Nantucket, intelligent, industrious, active in good word and work from girlhood to womanhood." As a married woman she served as secretary and treasurer of the Summer Street Baptist Church and executive associate of the Women's Relief Corps, duties she maintained almost to the end of her life.

Since Sampson Pompey was thirteen years older than his wife and they married late, it is hardly surprising that they remained childless. Even without children to raise and educate, however, the Pompeys began to lose ground as the Nantucket economy shifted from the sea to tourism. Bit by bit Sampson and Susan Pompey sold off family-owned land, including what had been passed down to them by Trillania Pompey. They sold a spare house in New Guinea, and then they mortgaged their own house at 3 Atlantic Avenue. By 1900 Sampson was "retired" but without any retirement income.

In the midst of their financial anxieties, Sampson could not have been prepared for losing Susan. When, in 1904, she died of breast cancer after enduring "intense physical suffering," Arthur Jenks wrote, "To her aged husband now left alone in his sorrow, the sympathy of our community is extended." Sampson Pompey responded by placing a card of thanks in the *Inquirer and Mirror* with the following text:

I desire to extend my sincere and heartfelt thanks to those who, in one way and another, extended to my beloved wife and myself kindness and courtesy, both during her illness and after her decease. May the great giver of all good richly reward you, one and all, for the kindnesses bestowed.
— Sampson D. Pompey.

Sampson and Susan Pompey in front of their house at 3 Atlantic Avenue, circa 1895.

Nantucket Historical Association

He lived on alone for another five years in the Atlantic Avenue house where he had been born and had always lived while on land. There was no foreclosure on the unpaid mortgage, and his neighbors, the Porte sisters and Emma Lewis, put hundreds of dollars into his support. In his last years he donated a portrait of Captain Absalom Boston to the Nantucket Historical Association. The fact that the portrait came from 3 Atlantic Avenue has led to the mistaken identification of the house as Absalom Boston's own home. It was, in fact, the home of two generations of Pompeys, upstanding contributors to their community.

Almost at the end of his life, Sampson Pompey dressed once more in his Civil War uniform for a G.A.R. group portrait. A short time later, on April 29, 1909, he died of old age. The surviving Civil War veterans and the women of the Relief Corps honored him at his burial, and the *Inquirer and Mirror* printed a tribute, recalling that Sampson Pompey was "faithful in the performance of his civil and religious duties. His great talent in whistling, song, and recitation entertained many who will never forget him."

The Porte sisters who had lent money to Sampson Pompey in his last years were the businesswomen daughters of Christina (Pompey) Porte, who lived next door at 5 Atlantic Avenue. Christina and her Calcutta-born husband, William Porte, had bought the house in 1849, and Christina was photographed standing out front, next to a newly planted tree, shortly before her death in 1895. Four generations of Christina Porte's family members—her mother, herself and her husband, her children, and her grandchildren—had resided at 5 Atlantic Avenue up until the death of Ida Porte at age 97 in 1961.

Christina and William Porte and many of their New Guinea neighbors were among the thirty founding members of the Pleasant Street Baptist Church when the African Baptist Church reorganized under the Reverend James Crawford in 1848. Over the next ten years the membership in the church doubled, taking in Trillania Pompey (who rather soon departed), her daughter-in-law-

to-be Susan Kelley, and Susan's schoolmate Annie Nahar, among others. A church member from the beginning was Ann Crawford, wife of the Rev. Mr. Crawford. A decade later, when he heroically redeemed Ann's sister Dianna Williams and Dianna's daughter Cornelia Read from slavery in North Carolina, they came to Nantucket and promptly joined the church.

With her mother, Cornelia Read joined a household consisting of her aunt and uncle, her uncle's mother Mary, and her cousin Juliana who was four years her junior. Although it offered a new life in freedom, it was hardly a salubrious environment. Elderly Mary Crawford suffered from dementia, and Ann Crawford died soon after welcoming Dianna and Cornelia to her home. James Crawford then married Dianna, but both she and Mary Crawford died in 1860, leaving the household in the hands of young Cornelia and Juliana.

Despite having lived in slavery, Cornelia Read was literate, and beginning in February 1863 she carried on an intense correspondence with William B. Gould, an equally literate black sailor in the Union Navy. When Gould received a letter

An undated essay on "The Negro, his Friends and Foes" in the Civil War diary of William B. Gould.

From Diary of a Contraband, courtesy of William B. Gould IV

William B. Gould, circa 1880, and Cornelia (Read) Gould,
circa 1890. They were married in the African Meeting House in 1865.
— From Diary of a Contraband, *courtesy of William B. Gould IV.*

William and Cornelia Gould with their children in the late 1880s. Back row:
Lawrence, Herbert, William, Jr., and Medora. Front row: Luetta, James,
Cornelia, William, and Ernest. Medora was the only one of the Gould chil-
dren born on Nantucket. — From Diary of a Contraband, *courtesy of William B. Gould IV.*

from Cornelia, he sometimes responded within the day. When mail was slow or interrupted, he jotted despairing notes in his diary. According to Gould's diary, he and Cornelia had known each other as children in South Carolina, and during his years of service in the Civil War their courtship bloomed. When opportunity presented itself, Gould visited Cornelia in Nantucket, and on November 22, 1865, they were married by James Crawford in the African Meeting House.

The Goulds remained on Nantucket until after the birth of their daughter Medora and then moved to Dedham, Massachusetts, where they raised a large family and were active not in a Baptist Church but in the Episcopal Church of the Good Shepherd. Gould, like his fellow veteran Sampson Pompey, was a member of his local G.A.R. post and paid annual visits to Dedham public schools on Memorial Day just as Nantucket's Civil War veterans did, down to the very last survivor.

In 1995 William B. Gould IV, Charles A. Beardsley Professor of Law at Stanford University Law School, came to Nantucket in search of his family history and became a strong supporter of the restoration and reopening of the African Meeting House, where his great-grandparents had been married in 1865. *Diary of a Contraband: The Civil War Passage of a Black Sailor,* his account of the first William B. Gould and of Cornelia Read, was published by Stanford University Press in 2002.

Lucretia Wilkes, a contemporary of Sampson Pompey, was also his neighbor. She had been born in 1828 to Peter and Rhoda Boston's daughter

Mahalah and Mahalah's Virginia-born husband William Collins. In 1850 Mahalah Collins joined the Pleasant Street Baptist Church, and at about the same time her daughter Lucretia married Nantucket-born Joseph Wilkes. A decade or so later, Joseph Wilkes died at sea and left Lucretia a widow with two children, Isabella and Edgar. To make ends meet they lived with Mahalah and helped with her laundry business. After Isabella grew up and married, Lucretia went to a live-in job as a domestic and took Edgar with her. By the time she at last had a home of her own on Pleasant Street in 1880, she was living alone.

Her solitude was not to last. Edgar had been living off-island, where he married Emma Roach, daughter of black Nova Scotians. In 1895 Edgar, Emma, and their three children—the oldest named after her aunt Isabella—had come to live on Nantucket. Also in 1895 Isabella's husband, Alexander Lewis, had brought their son William C. Lewis to the island, leaving him to live with his grandmother while attending school.

In short order the family of Edgar and Emma expanded to six children, and they bought a house of their own on Orange Street. Edgar Wilkes supported his large family by working as a day laborer and later as a caretaker. As custodian of the African Meeting House, he personally closed its doors for the last time in 1912.

Throughout their long lives on Nantucket, Edgar and Emma Wilkes had managed their resources with great care. After their children were grown, they left Orange Street for a house they bought on North Wharf and later moved once more to Sparks Avenue, where they both lived past their ninetieth birthdays.

A long-lived woman herself, Lucretia Wilkes in her old age had gone to live with her son and his family during the years when they still lived on Orange Street. In 1909 she died within months of Sampson Pompey.

Baptism in the Pleasant Street Baptist Church required long and prayerful preparation followed by public testimony about one's personal coming to God. William and Christina Porte had joined the church in 1848, but Christina Porte did not complete her spiritual journey to baptism until 1856. Two years later Susan Kelley was among a large group of church members giving testimony and receiving baptism. It was not until January 31, 1897, that a diary entry noted "Mr. Pompey baptized." However late Sampson Pompey's final commitment may have been, ultimately this whole group of neighbors was linked through their asso-ciation with the church that met in the African Meeting House in its latter days.

Sampson and Susan Pompey, the Porte sisters, Emma Lewis, Hiram Reed, Lucretia, Edgar, and Emma Wilkes, and—with the exception of Cornelia (Read) Gould—the extended family of their pastor James Crawford, were all laid to rest in the cemetery behind Mill Hill. With their departure—aside from the occasional burial in an old family plot—the old cemetery fell into disuse.

In a sense, Sampson Pompey and Lucretia Wilkes had played out roles much like those of Abram Quary and Dorcas Honorable as last remnants of their people. Sampson and Susan Pompey had been childless, while Lucretia's grandchildren had grown up and departed from a very changed Nantucket—one in which whaling, the African Meeting House, and the "colored" cemetery were fast fading from living memory. New people had come to the island to do different kinds of work for different people. Another black community was already evolving without roots in the old world of the Pompeys and the Bostons.

Family enclosures and headstones for New Guinea's most prominent citizens remain, although no known descendants of the early African Nantucketers reside on the island.

Patricia Butler photograph

Chapter Sixteen

The Summer Trade

Drawing by George Gardner Fish of a whaleship and two steamboats at Steamboat Wharf, 1852. – Nantucket Historical Association

In 1850 Nantucket's population was 8,452, already down by 1,560 from the pinnacle it had reached in 1840. Between 1850 and 1870 the population dropped by fifty percent, down to 4,123. Contributing to this decline were two circumstances that drew able-bodied men away from the island: the discovery of gold in California in 1849 and the Civil War, which began in 1861. In the years between the Gold Rush and the conclusion of the Civil War in 1865, Nantucketers who remained on-island endeavored to build a new economy based on agriculture, dory fishing, small manufactures, and tourism. It was tourism that was to become Nantucket's economic backbone, but it took some years in coming. When it finally did, it forced Nantucketers into a pattern of frantic work during short summers alternating with long off-seasons of inactivity and unemployment. Still, they could not do it all, and to fill the gap seasonal workers began coming to the island, either on their own or attached to families as live-in domestics.

Prior to the Great Fire of 1846, lodgings on the island ranged from rough seamen's boarding houses to rooms in private homes offering reliable travelers a "genteel" experience. There was even a large establishment, the Washington House, on the corner of Main and Union Streets that approached the character of a hotel. A Main Street fire in 1836, precursor of the Great Fire of the following decade, destroyed the Washington House, and a hiatus ensued despite the perceived need for a proper

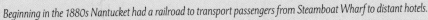

Beginning in the 1880s Nantucket had a railroad to transport passengers from Steamboat Wharf to distant hotels.

Nantucket Historical Association

— Nantucket Historical Association

Shortly after the Great Fire of 1846 Jared Coffin's Broad Street residence was purchased by the Nantucket Steamboat Company and converted into the Ocean House Hotel.

hotel. It was only in the late 1840s, after the Great Fire had burned right up to the front door of Jared Coffin's large brick residence at the intersection of Broad and Centre Streets, that the Nantucket Steamboat Company purchased the building and made it over into the Ocean House Hotel. By then, paddlewheel steamers were providing regular passenger service to the island, tying up at the wharf at the foot of Broad Street.

Almost simultaneously a vacation hotel, the Atlantic House, opened in Siasconset with land transportation provided from Steamboat Wharf. The village even had its own ice cream stand, saving patrons the long trip to ice cream parlors in town. The health benefits of sea bathing for men, women, and children were promoted, and enterprising Nantucketers who had not been lured away to California offered lodgings, meals, and entertainments. Despite the economic doldrums left in the wake of the Great Fire and the collapse of whaling, elm trees were planted in town and pine trees out on the sheep commons (which were romanticized as "moors"), while gas lighting was introduced to downtown streets, businesses, and residences—all with the prospect of making Nantucket more attractive to visitors. Throughout the 1850s and into the early 1860s there were constant efforts to attract vacationers.

Then came the Civil War. The monument at the intersection of Main, Milk, and Gardner Streets reveals only part of the war's impact on the island community, which had not long before been largely Quaker and pacifist. The seventy-three names inscribed on the obelisk are those of Nantucket's war dead. Hundreds of Nantucket men, white and black, had left to fight for the Union, and when the war concluded many of the survivors moved on to new off-island opportunities without ever return-

The Atlantic House in Siasconset

Nantucket Historical Association

ing home. No names of black Nantucketers are inscribed on the monument. Of the twenty who enlisted from the island, almost all served in the Union Navy, and all survived.

Advertising for vacationers ceased during the war years, and at war's end Nantucket's endeavor to become a summer resort had to begin anew. In the latter half of the 1860s and into the 1870s hostelries and ice cream parlors again proliferated, sailing and fishing began to be viewed as amusements, and saltwater bathing was again encouraged. Party boats began running up and down the harbor, delivering passengers to shore dinners and bathing beaches.

By the 1880s the islanders' schemes and invest-ments had paid off to the point of producing rather too much of a good thing. On August 12, 1882, the *Inquirer and Mirror* reported:

It is a lamentable fact that the influx of visitors is too great at present for the accommodations we have to offer, the hotels being obliged to turn away guests daily, while private boarding houses are filled to overflowing. Hotel landlords agree that their business this year is beyond all expectation, and that before another season opens "something has got to be done."

Even the newspaper couldn't keep up. In the same issue it announced an augmented print run because, "Our last edition of over 1500 copies was inadequate to supply the demand." Nantucket was being compared to Newport as a summering place and was struggling to define itself as offering a very different experience.

Wauwinet, destination of the large catboats that took passengers on pleasure trips up-harbor, was a great draw. The original Wauwinet House, a dance pavilion and chowder house at the head of a small dock, was erected in 1876 and was an imme-diate success.

For the summer of 1882, the owner of the Wauwinet House brought a Chinese man to the island to make the chowder. The writer of the "Here and There" column in the June 24 issue of the *Inquirer and Mirror* included an item

Dory fishing for sharks off the beach at Siasconset was entertainment for summer visitors in the late 1800s.

that "Fong Sing, the head cook at the Wauwinet House, is not a 'Heathen Chinee.' He was one of the early converts to Christianity under the Rev. Dr. Simmon's missionary enterprise in New York." That said, the *Inquirer and Mirror* spent the whole summer making jests about Wauwinet's "heathen Chinee," even in the column that had first introduced him to the newspaper's readers. "Here and There" opened with doggerel verse in the July 8 issue:

> Now to think they should bring
> A pure heathen Chinee,
> Just the real live thing
> From the Empire of tea,
> And then carry him out to Wauwinet,
> It's really surprising to see.
> We don't know his name,
> We shall call him Sam Lee,
> Good enough is the same
> For such low chaps as he,
> Who bring cheap Mongolian labor
> To run the land of the free.

Readers picked up on the conceit. On August 12, a contributor to the newspaper wrote:

> A "heathen Chinee" is now employed as a cook at the Wauwinet House by the new proprietor, but as he was taught how to make clam chowder by Mr. Small, who possessed the art to perfection, and as the Chinese are noted for having the facility of imitation, future visitors to that place will probably find the clam chowder as good as ever.

Although Edward Underhill indulged in much the same sort of nineteenth-century jocular style in promotional brochures for his cottages in Siasconset, the butt of his humor was not the exotic foreigner but the colorful Nantucketer and the hypochondriac tourist. In the persona of one old sea captain or another, he wrote philosophical advice in what is known as "eye dialect"—spelling intended to suggest nonstandard pronunciation—and he made summer visitors out to be lacking in one thing or another that was bound to be available in 'Sconset. Even more than the remoteness of Wauwinet, the quaintness of Siasconset's fish-

The Lillian *and another catboat with the steamer* Island Belle *at the Wauwinet dock. The* Lillian *and the* Island Belle *both went into service in 1876.*

ing village with its unconventional residents was a draw for visitors, and in Underhill it had attracted an unusually perceptive developer.

Edward Underhill was born in 1830 in Wolcott, New York. At age sixteen he lost several fingers in an accident, and although limited by his disability, he learned to take shorthand and became a court stenographer. He also developed into a prolific writer. During the Civil War, while employed as a correspondent for *The New York Times*, he was taken prisoner by the Confederates, tried as a spy, and imprisoned. After his release, he was instrumental in the professionalization of court stenography in the state of New York.

Becoming prosperous, he first invested in a vineyard in Chatauqua County. This he sold in order to go into resort development in Siasconset, where he put $20,000 into buying property and building new cottages modeled on the old 'Sconset fishermen's cottages. An energetic promoter of seaside vacations in the village, he was credited by the *Inquirer and Mirror* with the extension of the railroad track from Surfside to 'Sconset.

One of the Underhill Cottages on Evelyn Street.

Edward Underhill's connection to Nantucket via his own Quaker heritage was reinforced through his marriage to Evelyn Stoddard. She and both her parents had been born in Hudson, New York, where Nantucketers had migrated during whaling days. Two of the streets along which the Underhill Cottages were built are Evelyn Street, named for his wife, and Lily Street, named for his daughter.

Among the cottages that he built, the China Closet was Edward and Evelyn Underhill's personal summer home. World travelers, the couple acquired a vast collection of chinaware. In the

Children around a derelict fish cart in Siasconset with houses on and below the Bank in background.

On the lawn of the Cashman Cottage, North Bluff, Siasconset.

"Sandanwede," built by Edwin J. Hulbert near Jetties Beach in 1881.

summer of 1895, architectural historian Henry Chandlee Forman's grandmother visited the China Closet, where Mr. Underhill showed her and her companions "his beautiful collection of old china…many rare and curious pieces" with which they had furnished their cottage. There were plates, teapots, and bowls on every surface, horizontal and vertical, even affixed to the ceiling.

Not all of Underhill's Nantucket writings were promotional. He also produced a series of historical studies of Siasconset architecture titled "Some Old Houses on 'Sconset Bank." In time, Henry Forman would take on Underhill's passion for the 'Sconset's very old houses and their history and become their twentieth-century interpreter.

The popularity of Siasconset proved durable. No other location or development ever approached its success. Separate summer listings do not appear in the Nantucket directories until after World War I, but of about 435 entries under summer cottages and residents in the 1919 directory, slightly over thirty percent are in Siasconset. Wauwinet, by comparison, has just twenty entries.

The 1927 directory shows explosive growth of the summer population. The cottage and resident listings total nearly 700, and again, just over thirty percent are in Siasconset, while Wauwinet's entries had grown by only seven. Quidnet, Squam, and Monomoy also attracted a few summer residents each.

Codfish Park, boardwalk, swimmers at the waterline circa 1885.

In town, the edge of the Cliff was lined with large houses built for sweeping views up-harbor and out across Nantucket Sound. Then the flatlands of Brant Point and Hulbert Avenue filled in with houses right on the beach. Some of the summer houses in and out of town were indeed cottages, while others that people called cottages were very large, albeit uninsulated and somewhat unfinished within. A few of the summer houses were true mansions, although not on the scale of those in Newport. What they all had in common, even those that could genuinely be called cottages, were servants quarters for live-in "help."

The summer population needed luggage transported, food cooked, linen washed, clothes pressed, beds made, carriages and—later—automobiles maintained and driven. Residences that stood empty as much as nine months of the year had to be opened in advance of summer arrivals and closed again in September. Between Memorial Day and Labor Day someone had to keep sweeping out the beach sand, warding off mildew, weeding the flower beds, and cutting the lawns to make the summer a time of untroubled leisure for the island's visitors.

Compensation for these services was modest, but economically strapped Nantucketers took on the jobs. During the summers Nantucket schoolboys cut lawns and schoolgirls made beds in order to save money for after graduation. Married women opened and closed houses to augment their family incomes, and Nantucket men became winter caretakers for off-island property owners.

Only the most parsimonious were able to accumulate capital this way. A small business with cheap labor provided by family members and low-paid employees offered the best shot at prosperity. Among the family businesses in turn-of-the-century Nantucket were boarding houses, restaurants and catering services, gardening and landscaping services, livery stables, pleasure craft, and laundries. Among the entrepreneurs engaged in those endeavors were families of Cape Verdean, African-American, Afro-Caribbean, and Wampanoag heritage who saw opportunities in the summer trade and reached out to seize them.

The West Family

John R. West and his wife Elizabeth moved to Nantucket from New Bedford with their three children in the early 1880s. Five more West children were island-born. Raised to value education and to be industrious in furthering the family enterprises, the Wests were a model turn-of-the-century middle-class family.

Like the residents of old New Guinea, both John R. and Elizabeth West were of Wampanoag and African descent. John R.'s mother was recognized as a Chappaquiddick Wampanoag through her mother, Lucy Wamp. Her father, Abraham Brown, born in Rhode Island and apparently a descendant of slaves once belonging to Robert Brown, had become a prosperous farmer on Chappaquiddick and in 1840 was serving as one of the Overseers of the Indians there. On this side of the family, there were connections to Martha's Vineyard by birth and to Nantucket's black Gardner family through a previous marriage. John R.'s wife, Elizabeth (Howard) West, was a descendant of Paul Cuffe, whose father was an African who had worked himself out of slavery and whose mother was a Wampanoag.

In 1885 John E. West purchased a house in Nantucket for his son and daughter-in-law, and ownership of the house on New Street has remained in the family to the present. Four years after its purchase Elizabeth, independently of her husband, bought property on nearby Atlantic Avenue, on the opposite side of the street from Sampson and Susan Pompey's house.

John R. West at the helm of the Gertie, with little girls in Sunday best.

Courtesy of Adele Ames

The family had enjoyed advances in employment from Tobias West, whose occupation in Philadelphia was consistently listed as "dealer," to his sons, John E. and Tobias Jr., both barbers, on to John R. who also began his business life in New Bedford as a barber.

At one time barbering had been an almost exclusively black trade, but immigration had changed that. In Nantucket the black barbers of earlier times had been succeeded by Irish, English, Canadian, and Portuguese men. For a while there was even an Irish woman barber. In the face of this competition the Wests succeeded with their own hairdressing shop and a laundry service, managed by Elizabeth. John was, moreover, listed in the Nantucket directory of 1919 as owner of the *Gertie*, on which he took visitors out day-sailing.

The 1919 directory also has a listing for young Carlton West under "livery." In time he would become a fixture among Nantucket's independent taxi drivers. His older brother, John E. West, was an electrician employed at the Nantucket power plant.

The eldest of the West children, Gertrude, completed the "classical course" at Nantucket High School—the only member of the class to achieve that—and was valedictorian of the graduating class of 1898. From Bridgewater Normal School, Grace Brown Gardner, daughter of Nantucket's representative to the Massachusetts legislature and every inch a descended Nantucketer, wrote to Gertrude of her frustration at not being able to attend the January graduation exercises in Nantucket. She praised Gertrude's accomplishments and encouraged her to prepare for a career in teaching.

This was not a courtesy letter from an older woman. Grace had been valedictorian of the Nantucket High School class of 1897. Not long after writing to Gertrude, she came back to Nantucket and did her practice teaching at the Siasconset School before going on to teach in the New Bedford schools and at Framingham Normal School. Forty-four years after writing her letter to Gertrude, Grace retired to Nantucket and devoted herself to compiling Nantucket historical research material. She died in 1973 at age 93.

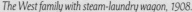

The West family with steam-laundry wagon, 1908.

W. B. Douglas photograph, courtesy of Adele Ames

– Courtesy of Adele Ames

Gertrude (West) Ames and James Ames.

During Grace Brown Gardner's entire career, women teachers were expected, indeed required, to remain unmarried, and she did. Had Gertrude West followed in her friend's footsteps, she too would have remained unmarried and childless, but she chose another path.

Her wedding to James Ames of New Bedford took place in the West family home on July 1, 1909. The bride was attended by three of her sisters and two friends, and the best man was James Ames's brother. The *Inquirer and Mirror* reported the evening wedding in detail. A New Bedford newspaper added details about the bride and groom—that Gertrude was "a reader of considerable ability" and James was "a popular man about town and was once a member of the famous Thailan Dramatic Club." On July 2 the couple departed on a honeymoon trip to New York, after which they took up residence in New Bedford.

Nearly a century after they parted, there has been a remarkable convergence of Gertrude's and Grace's ways. Gertrude conveyed her commitment to education to her son, James Bradford Ames, who earned two degrees in chemistry from the Massachusetts Institute of Technology as one of its earliest nonwhite graduates. Shortly before his death, he pledged his support for the restoration of the African Meeting House—just blocks from the West family house on New Street—and the documentation of the black families who had lived in the neighborhood. In his memory his wife, Adele Ames, established the James Bradford Ames Fellowships for the study of African-American and Cape Verdean history on Nantucket. From 1996 through 2004 ten scholars had been beneficiaries of James Bradford Ames Fellowships, and most, if not all of them, have spent many hours poring over the invaluable scrapbooks of Nantucket newspaper clippings assembled in her retirement years by Grace Brown Gardner.

In time the West sisters who had been attendants at Gertrude's wedding also married and moved to New Bedford. Ruth West, who had not been part of the 1909 wedding party, connected the family once again to Wampanoag heritage by marrying Darius Coombs of Mashpee in 1916.

Instead of taking his bride away to the mainland, fisherman Darius Coombs came to live on Nantucket and bought a house on Upper York Street. His brother Otis moved his family to Nantucket as well and became a homeowner on Orange Street. Six Coombs cousins were attending Nantucket public schools when Darius died in 1932, leaving Ruth to carry on by herself. In the depths of the Depression she advertised as a dressmaker who (like tailor Paul Levine) could construct copies of garments. She also offered remodeling and "fur work." In the 1940s, while still maintaining her house on Nantucket, she moved to New Bedford.

The West family took pride in their Wampanoag heritage, and in her later life Ruth (West) Coombs, a gifted singer, adopted the persona of "Princess Red Feather." Dressed in buckskins with feathers in her hair, she made public appearances to promote Wampanoag history and culture. When she died in New Bedford in 1964, her body was returned to Nantucket for burial with Darius in the Coombs family plot in Prospect Hill Cemetery.

When the 1930 census was taken, Carlton West was the only child of John and Elizabeth still living at home at 18 New Street. He was thirty-two years old, still single, a veteran of Coast Guard service during World War I, and a member of the local post of the American Legion. Nantucket was a place rich in nicknames, and from boyhood his had been "Grit," because as a boy his first venture into business was distributing *Grit Magazine*, the self-described "good news" publication founded in 1882.

From delivering magazines, young Carlton moved on to delivering trunks and suitcases by horse and wagon to hotels and summer residences, and then, when the ban on automobiles on the island was lifted after World War I, he went straight into the taxi business.

Soon after the local prohibition against automobiles was lifted, nationwide prohibition of the sale and distribution of alcoholic beverages was imposed. During the thirteen years until Prohibition's repeal, Nantucket was an active locus of bootlegging and rum-running, and colorful stories have become part of Nantucket oral history. Not all of what went on was lighthearted.

Some of the young veterans of the American Legion were occasionally appointed as special police officers. As a member of this squad, Carlton West was diligent in reporting scofflaws and suspicious activity. Late in the days of Prohibition he reported a car driven erratically as it left a business on New Street, close by the West family home. Police responding to his tip raided the building in time to catch men trying to dispose of alcohol by pouring it down a sink. When violent retaliation was directed against the Nantucket police force, Carlton West was its first victim. He nearly lost his life.

Late on the night of December 1, 1930, he received a telephone call to drive three men to the cranberry bog. As he turned off Milestone Road, one of the passengers struck West a hard blow to the head, the first of many. The men then took over the wheel and pulled him into the back seat of his taxi. Tied, gagged, and blindfolded, West regained consciousness to feel the car bumping to a stop. His assailants then stripped him to his underwear, helping themselves to his wallet and watch. They discussed drowning him in Gibbs's Pond but gave up on the plan because they were unable to drive the car close to the water. Then they set out to find a place to throw him into the surf.

As they drove, one of the men taunted West, saying that they were being paid five hundred dollars to take him for a ride, and that their next victims would be State Police Sergeant Joseph Fratus and Nantucket Police Sergeant Lawrence Mooney.

Among themselves the men spoke Portuguese.

During hours of driving, stopping, and moving on again, the men prodded West in the ribs with what he took to be a revolver, hit him repeatedly on the head with a blackjack, and forced alcohol into his mouth, but they

– Louis S. Davidson photograph, NHA

Taxi operator Carlton West.

apparently lost their focus on drowning him. In the early morning hours they abandoned him— unclothed, bound, gagged, and severely beaten—in the back of his taxi in the middle of Prospect Hill Cemetery.

When he was sure they were not coming back, West managed to free himself and, despite pain and weakness from blood loss, drove himself to the police station.

Within the day Joseph Cruz, John Vincent, and Russell Barrows were under arrest for assault with the intent to kill. Under interrogation they alleged that their attack and the two subsequent ones to be carried out against police officers had been plotted over the weekend, and that they expected to be paid off by a local man enraged by the recent raid on New Street. Shackled together, they were transported to New Bedford to await trial.

In July 1931 Cruz, Vincent, and Barrows each pleaded guilty to assault with intent to rob and assault to commit murder. The judge sentenced John Vincent to a term of eight to ten years in state prison, Joseph Cruz to five years and a day in the Concord Reformatory, and Russell Barrows to an indeterminate term in the Concord Reformatory.

Carlton West, already "well-known among residents and summer visitors," continued with his taxi service. He married, divorced, remarried and was widowed, and to the end of his life he lived in the West family house on New Street. The Aquinnah Wampanoags recognized him as one of their own. When he died in the summer of 1969, the Byron L. Sylvaro Post of the American

Legion carried out their ritual for fellow veterans at the funeral home, and Chief Lorenzo Jeffers of Aquinnah came to attend his funeral and burial in Prospect Hill Cemetery, the place where his night of terror in 1930 had ended.

Of all the West children only three survived Carlton—his brother John E. West, who had long ago moved to Boston, and the eldest two of his sisters, Almira "Flossie" Williams and Gertrude Ames, both of New Bedford.

Purveyors of Food and Drink

In 1889 Charles A. Grant acquired the property on South Water Street that many years later would house the Opera House Restaurant. He and his wife Rachael operated a saloon on the premises, and the income from their business made it possible for them to own their residence on Coon Street mortgage-free. When Grant died in 1897, Rachael carried on, supporting herself, their son Charles S. Grant, and a foster daughter as well.

Young Charles was living with his mother on Coon Street and fishing for a living when Prohibition closed down the family-owned saloon. Looking for a different revenue-producing use for their commercial building, Rachael and Charles Grant let it out to an Orange Street neighbor, Anna Correia.

Anna Hinton, born in North Carolina in 1893, had married Cape Verde-born Manuel Correia of Nantucket. Anna and Manuel moved into the Grant's former saloon, and Anna turned it into a bistro-style restaurant with red-checked tablecloths and silverware in mason jars on the tables. In 1930, in addition to herself and Manuel, there were three workers residing on the premises: two French-Canadian waitresses and an elderly widow named Martha Helm, whose occupation was described in the 1930 census as helper in the restaurant.

In 1933 Charles Grant married Ruth Jones of Georgia, and as Rachael Grant grew old, Ruth Grant took over the property management from her. The restaurant on South Water Street apparently never had an advertising budget and does not appear in Depression-era newspaper ads, but it was known by word-of-mouth as "Ruth Grant's restaurant," even though Anna Correia was proprietor of the business through 1938.

Like The Modern, the Nicoletos brothers' establishment on Main Street, the South Water Street restaurant did not survive the Depression. In 1939 Anna and Manuel were still living in the building, but he was working as a laborer elsewhere and Anna's occupation had changed to "housekeeper." The next year the Correias moved back to Orange Street, where they lived until the 1960s.

With the closing of the restaurant, the Grants' building stood vacant for several years. Then, during World War II a Servicemen's Club opened just opposite on South Water Street. Nantucket schoolboys gravitated to the Servicemen's Club, and it was felt that they needed an appropriate place of their own. A Boys Club had been organized in Nantucket in the 1890s, fallen into abeyance, and been revived in 1908. Members played basketball in the gymnasium of the Athletic Club on South Beach Street, and there had been plans for checkers and pool tournaments. Nonetheless, despite annual town appropriations to support it, by 1913 the Boys Club was again defunct. When it was resurrected yet again during the 1940s, the Athletic Club building had long since been taken over by the Nantucket Yacht Club, and it was difficult to find a meeting place.[1] The Grants offered their South Water Street building, and Boys Club activities began there in 1944.

---

1. The Athletic Club had been founded as a year-round club for Nantucketers with special summer rates for nonresidents. Summer members became so numerous that the Athletic Club agreed to let the Yacht Club run programs on its premises from the time the Nantucket schools let out in June until Labor Day, returning the clubhouse with its gymnasium, bowling alleys, billiard and pool tables, library, etc., to the Nantucket resident membership for the balance of the year. During World War I, the U.S. Navy took over the property, and both the Athletic Club and the Yacht Club suspended activities. When the property was to be returned to private ownership in 1920, the Yacht Club managed to acquire it for its own exclusive use, renaming itself the Nantucket Yacht Club. In the February 18, 1933, issue of the *Inquirer and Mirror* a long article appeared under the headline "Nantucket Needs Gymnasium Most at Present Time" stating that, "It is superfluous to point out the benefits to be derived from a gym on Nantucket…in these days of curtailed employment…giving the young people something else to do besides hanging around the street corners and spending their time in various loafing places.…It has been claimed…that the town did have a gymnasium at one time…but…that the gymnasium privileges were abused, and that the town discontinued it for that reason only—a rather senseless argument in the light of what really happened."

The arrangement was not to last long, however. Harold and Gwen Gaillard approached the Grants about opening another restaurant on the premises, and the Boys Club had to move on. In their place the Gaillards created the Opera House Restaurant, a Nantucket institution that endured for forty years, from 1945 to 1985.

In interviews over the years Gwen Gaillard characterized the Opera House, with its Gay Nineties decor, vaguely French cuisine, and piano bar, as "Nantucket's first naughty restaurant." In the days after the end of World War II it certainly was a departure from the ambiance of other restaurants on the island. But the legend has eclipsed the facts that all the way back in 1927 the Nicoletos brothers advertised a piano in The Modern, and that the Gaillards created the Opera House Restaurant and Bar in a space that had been a real 1890s saloon and then a bistro almost to the end of the 1930s. Despite the success of the Opera House, moreover, the Gaillards did not acquire the deed for 4 South Water Street from Ruth Grant until

1969. For a full eighty years this revenue-producing commercial property had remained in the hands of a black Nantucket family.

Florence and Isabel Carter of Philadelphia were teachers who spent their summers on Nantucket. Although their parents, postal worker John Carter and seamstress Mabel (Pugh) Carter, were Philadelphians, they were devoted summer residents of Nantucket to the point that they arranged to be laid to rest on the island. To that end they acquired a family plot in the cemetery behind Mill Hill, where fewer than a dozen burials had taken place since the turn of the century.

Mabel Pugh had grown up in Windsor, North Carolina, a town on the coast road from Norfolk, Virginia, to Charleston, South Carolina. Due south of Windsor on that road is New Bern, North Carolina, where Anna Gardner—teacher in Nantucket's African School—went to teach at a Freedmen's school in the wake of the Civil War.

Mabel's grandmother, Sarah, had belonged to Liberty Hall, a plantation in Windsor. Like New Bern,

Windsor lies on a river emptying into the vast sounds separated from the Atlantic Ocean by the barrier islands of the Outer Banks. During the summer, the people from Liberty Hall were transported by barge to Nag's Head on the ocean side, roughly half way between Kitty Hawk and Cape Hatteras.

In the second half of the 1800s North Carolina's Outer Banks followed the same course as Nantucket in becoming a summer resort for urbanites who could afford to flee the crowd diseases and heat of the cities. By the late 1880s trains from mid-Atlantic cities connected with regularly scheduled steamboat service from Elizabeth City, a bit northeast of Windsor, to Nag's Head.

As a child growing up in Windsor, Mabel Pugh, daughter of Belle Pugh—property owner and restaurateur—made the summer trip to Nag's Head just as her grandmother Sarah and her fellow plantation workers had two generations previously. In 1898 Mabel left Windsor to marry John Carter and live in Philadelphia. After operating a small neigh-

– Nantucket Historical Association

The Opera House Restaurant.

borhood grocery store for awhile, John succeeded in securing a position with the U. S. Post Office. As barbering had been the prestige occupation for African-American men through the first half of the nineteenth century, employment in the postal service was the prize of the succeeding decades.

"Beer and Ale" sign on the Grant family's building on South Water Street prior to Prohibition.

Nantucket Historical Association

John and Mabel (Pugh) Carter, 1927.

With the income from John's federal employment and Mabel's skillful dressmaking, the family was able to move into a good neighborhood in Philadelphia and to create a comfortable and attractive home. There was no escaping the disease environment, however. The plantation in swampy Windsor had suffered so from mosquito-borne diseases that its residents had fled to Nag's Head in the summers. Philadelphia was every bit as pestilential, with epidemics spread by insects, contaminated water, and human contact. Mabel and John Carter's daughter Florence fell victim to an urban epidemic and nearly died of it.

In the summer of 1925 Mabel Carter visited Nantucket in the company of a fellow seamstress who had come to sew for summer residents. Nantucket's beaches recalled the North Carolina coast familiar to her from childhood, and she returned to Philadelphia with a plan to provide a respite from city summers for her own daughters. Over the year 1926–27 the Carters built Windsor Cottage on Prospect Street just a little way downhill from the windmill and nearly opposite the road to the cemetery. It was at the time the only black-owned summer residence on Nantucket. To support it, John Carter planted a large garden each year and kept Rhode Island Red chickens, while Mabel Carter divided her dressmaking business between Philadelphia and Nantucket. Their summer house became a gathering place for black college students employed on the island during summer vaca-

tions, and—at a time when it was difficult for black visitors to find accommodations—the Nantucket Information Bureau directed them to Windsor Cottage to rent the Carters' guest bedroom.

Mabel Carter died in December 1948, and John followed her in death just six weeks later. Florence and Isabel, both school teachers, carried on, operating a boxed-lunch business from Windsor Cottage. Customers would wait in the front yard while their orders were filled: sandwiches, coleslaw, and a brownie for ninety-nine cents. After two summers of working from home, the sisters moved their Florabel Carter's Boxed Lunch business downtown to 23 Federal Street. Seasonally for several years the sisters operated a combination antiques shop and lunch service for beach-goers, bicyclists, and boaters.

Florence (Carter) Smith died in 1967 at the age of sixty, while Isabel (Carter) Duckrey, born in 1900, lived until 1995. Both found their final resting places next to their parents in the cemetery so close to Windsor Cottage.

Summer residents with large houses up on the Cliff, down on the Point, and out on the Bluff in Siasconset employed caterers and bartenders for their private parties. Many of the people who provided those services were themselves seasonal residents on Nantucket. Before they founded their boxed-lunch business, the Carter sisters were among the caterers for the people collectively referred to, according to Florence Carter's daughter Isabel, as "'richwhitefolks,' spoken in one word in our milieu." Jessie Fisher, who owned a house in Codfish Park, Siasconset's black community, often teamed up with her neighbor Clarence Wilson to provide catering and bartending for parties at the east end of the island.[2]

Clarence Wilson also provided refreshments for the black patrons of Frank Scott's dance hall in Siasconset, but always with an eye out for the police. After the repeal of Prohibition, there were still very few liquor licenses on Nantucket, and Frank Scott had no chance of procuring one. But

---

2. Their predecessor had been Nantucket's celebrated Abram Quary. Writing around 1880, George F. Worth, who had been born in 1809, recalled that after giving up whaling, Quary had a second career as "the prince of Nantucket caterers," without whom "no evening entertainment was deemed complete."

Men at a table in the Chicken Box.

Willie House, founder of the Chicken Box.

the spirit of Prohibition persisted. If alcoholic drinks could not be offered legally, then they were brought in brown bags or soda-pop bottles and shared around. Knowing at which restaurants owners and staff would serve food and look the other way about what was poured into coffee cups or water glasses was part of the adventure of Nantucket after dark.

Before the Chicken Box, there was the Dodo Club. Lacking a liquor license, the Dodo Club was, nonetheless, known to the Nantucket police for its "midnight entertainment and drinking soirees." In the summer of 1949 partners Willie House and Hancy Jones took over the premises, expanded them, and opened a fried-chicken restaurant. Like its predecessor, the Chicken Box was open past midnight and lacked a liquor license, so it was inevitable that former Dodo Club patrons would come in and carry on the old traditions.

In the early morning hours of an August night a worker just off his shift at another restaurant visited the Chicken Box for a snack. When he pulled out his own whiskey flask, and refused to share, a brawl broke out. Willie House called for police assistance. Two officers came, and in the course of breaking up the fight one of them drew his gun and fired into the air. When it was over, the Chicken Box was littered with broken dishes and smashed furniture.

It is a wonder that Willie House didn't pull up stakes and go find a more peaceful outlet for his honey-fried chicken, but he stayed on and made the Chicken Box an island institution. Three years into the operation, he bought out his partner and carried on for more than two decades as the reigning

monarch of nightlife on Nantucket. Muddy Waters performed at the Chicken Box and so did a host of other musicians. There was music, there was pool, and in time there was a liquor license. For Willie House, it was a great deal of work, but he thrived as his own boss.

It had been a long road to sole ownership of a successful business. Willie Augusta House had been born the seventh of nine children in Mayfield, Kentucky, and he bootstrapped himself up in life without a high school education. As a young man, he worked in construction. Employment by summer residents brought him to Nantucket, and teaming up with Hancy Jones had made it possible to get a toe in the door of property ownership. From there on it was all hard work, careful management, and the secret chicken recipe. A memorial tribute referred to House as "the black Colonel Sanders of Nantucket."

Fried chicken became less a feature of the Chicken Box as music, beer, and pool went into ascendance. The place was still rowdy, and the police still visited. In the early 1970s House backed off a bit from running the place and gave matrimony a try. Marriage didn't suit him, however, and ended in divorce. In 1977, without divulging his chicken recipe, he sold the Chicken Box for vastly more than the original buying price and tried to take it easy. The work ethic was so ingrained in him, however, that he launched a lawnmower business almost immediately.

Prospering as a nightclub and live-music venue, the Chicken Box endured without chicken in the fryer and House behind the bar. For nearly two decades after its sale, one of its most faithful patrons was Willie House. In 1995 he was laid to rest in Newtown Cemetery, right inside the fence with a sightline across Sparks Avenue to the Chicken Box. On the side of his memorial stone facing in toward the cemetery are his name, birth and death dates, and the text, "The Lord is my Shepherd." On the street side of the stone is engraved, "Founder of the Chicken Box." Every December it is adorned with a Christmas wreath.

Casting Off the Cloak of Invisibility

The cooks, housekeepers, maids, butlers, and chauffeurs who traveled to and from Nantucket to provide domestic service in summer residents' houses are nearly invisible in Nantucket records. Unlike their employers, they do not appear on the property tax rolls, in the "summer cottages and summer residents" section of the town directories, or listed in the telephone books. Because of their transient presence on the island, they—like the cosmopolitan seamen of Nantucket's whaling days—rarely appear in the federal census returns. The names of some women and men who were well known and are still remembered from their

many summers on the island are nowhere to be found in print. In photos from Nantucket's early days as a resort there appear people whose identities have been utterly lost.

Only when they married Nantucket residents, bought property, or happened to appear in captioned newspaper photos, did seasonal workers become visible. Even then, records of Nantucket's black residents are less complete than records of its white residents, and to the extent that they exist, they tend to be less accurate.

A case in point is that of Virginia-born Ella (Gay) Duvall, grandmother of Selectman Frank Spriggs. She worked for years as a domestic for the Dickson family of Washington, D.C., traveling with them to the island every summer. When one of the Dickson sons took up year-round residence on the corner of Winter and Liberty Streets, she stayed on as his housekeeper. Upon her marriage to Cape Verdean Antone Rose on January 2, 1912, the town's

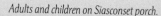
Adults and children on Siasconset porch.

Conductor William I. Sandsbury and a young boy at train station.

Children in Pump Square, Siasconset, 1904.

annual report listed both of them as Nantucket residents, yet Ella does not appear in federal census returns for Nantucket until 1930. By that time she had brought her mother, Hattie (Tyler Gay) Matthews to Nantucket to live out her final years.

Hattie Matthews died in 1927, yet the only Nantucket record that mentions her is her daughter Ella's 1951 death certificate. Ella and Hattie came into public view when Frank Spriggs began telling their story and his own. In 1942 he had been sent from segregated Washington D.C. to Nantucket, to spend the summer with his grandmother, and three years later he returned to live with her year-round, attending Nantucket schools from fifth grade through his junior year at Nantucket High School. When Ella Rose died, he had to leave and finish school on the mainland, but his classmates considered him a permanent member of the NHS class of 1953.

Frank Spriggs had felt isolated as an African American in the Nantucket schools, but the contrast with life in segregated Washington made a profound and lasting impression: "I couldn't believe the difference in life here, when I came as a child. I was accepted as a black person—no, I was accepted as a *person*." He recalled Nantucket in the 1940s and 1950s as having been "really ahead of most of the country in terms of race relations."

Eventually, in retirement, he moved permanently to the island with his wife Bette, sought elective office, and won handily.

Another mother-and-daughter pair on Nantucket were Charlotte (Bell Bentley) Bagwell and her daughter Mattie Pina. They were both born in Coushatta, Louisiana, on the Red River just south of Shreveport.

Although it is named for the Koasati Indians who migrated through the area from their native Alabama in the latter half of the 1700s, the small town of Coushatta (current population 2,300), is a predominantly African-American community whose economy still derives from the surrounding cotton fields, a ranch, and a sawmill. When Charlotte was born to Solomon and Millie Bell in 1880, it was into a world as distant from Nantucket culturally as it is geographically. Eighteen years later, when Mattie was born, Coushatta was still isolated out in the pine woods.

Like Mabel Carter, Charlotte was a seamstress, and she supported herself and her daughter by working as a dressmaker. In time, mother and daughter migrated to Kansas City, Missouri, where Mattie went to work as a nursemaid for the children of a wealthy family, and it was that employment that brought her to Nantucket in the 1930s.

On September 11, 1938, Mattie stepped out of the obscurity shrouding seasonal domestic "help" by marrying Fogo-born Cape Verdean John C. Pina. Their marriage certificate is the first notice of her presence on Nantucket, recording her birth in Coushatta, her mother's maiden name as Charlotte Bell, her father as George Bentley, and her residence in Nantucket beyond the numbered addresses on Lower Orange Street. She was forty years old, and it was her first marriage.

John Pina was forty-two years old, and it was his first marriage as well. He had been living on Cherry Street with the Mendes family and was employed as a truck driver for the Island Service Company. At the time, the Island Service Company provided ice not only for the holds of Nantucket's fishing fleet, but also house-to-house delivery for home ice boxes. Mattie was fond of saying that she had "married the iceman."

The first year after their marriage they lived together on Lower Orange Street, and then for a while they moved yearly, from Orange Street to Eagle Lane to Coon Street to 22 Atlantic Avenue. By 1946 they were residing at 10 Atlantic Avenue. In every street listing from their marriage onward, John Pina's occupation was listed as truck driver, and Mattie's as housewife.

In 1950, John and Mattie—in their early fifties and childless—had been joined by Mattie's mother, Charlotte, and a young woman named Ella Mae Herring, both having arrived within the year from Kansas City. Charlotte and Ella Mae were living at 10a Atlantic Avenue. By then Charlotte was 69 years old, and her occupation was simply listed as "at home." Ella Mae was just 20.

The following year they had taken in an additional boarder at 10a, and according to the street list, Mattie had also moved into 10a with the women, leaving John alone in 10 Atlantic Avenue. The following year, 1952, there is no listing at all for 10 Atlantic Avenue, and there is no sign of John Pina. He had moved off-island, where he died. According to Mattie, she was contacted about having his body returned to the island, but she turned aside the suggestion. Mattie's death certificate lists her as a widow, but there is no death certificate or probate record to mark the passing of the iceman with whom she had shared her life for fourteen years.

From that time on Charlotte and Mattie lived together. Mattie continued to list her occupation as housewife, but to support herself and her mother she did cooking and domestic work. A receipt from 1970 indicates that her neighbor, Florence

As late as the 1950s the old New Guinea neighborhood, as viewed here from Sparks Avenue toward Williams Lane and Cherry Street, remained the place where people of color were most likely to find a house to rent or buy. Knights of Columbus Hall, originally Alfonso Hall, is the second tall gable from the right.

Higginbotham, paid Mattie $2.50 per hour to help out at her house.

A life begun amidst the cotton fields of Louisiana had made both mother and daughter tough. Despite multiple life-threatening conditions, Charlotte lived to the age of eighty-three before being laid to rest in the cemetery behind Mill Hill. Her death certificate indicates that she was the widow of Walter T. Bagwell and does not mention George Bentley.

Mattie outdid her mother and lived to the middle of the summer of 1999, within weeks of her 101st birthday. When she died, Walter Bagwell was listed as her father, but he was probably her stepfather. No one seems to know where or when any of the men in this story—Bentley, Bagwell, or Pina—came to rest, but Mattie Pina lies next to her mother in the old cemetery founded by and for African Nantucketers. By virtue of living to be a centenarian, she had become a local celebrity at the end of her life, completely visible to all.

According to her obituary, Sadie Pride of Beaufort, South Carolina, had begun coming to Nantucket in the mid 1930s. For years she worked as a cook for the Harris family at 99 Main Street and eventually bought a house of her own on Fayette Street. As a homeowner and registered voter, she appears in the annual street lists until the year before her death. At the time of Nantucket's three-hundredth birthday celebration in the summer of 1959, she was living in her own home, but dressed in an eighteenth-century costume she took part in that year's Main Street Fete, posing on the front steps of 99 Main for photographers.

Throughout her years on Nantucket she was an active member of the Summer Street Baptist Church, and her warm and outgoing personality won her many friends. Nonetheless, when her health began to fail, she felt that she needed to return to Beaufort. Her obituary, with a photograph of her in the Fete costume, was sent to the *Inquirer and Mirror* in May 1965 for publication on the day of her funeral in Beaufort.

The eighteenth century had begun with acceptance of slavery on Nantucket and ended with its absence. The heritage of that century was New Guinea's free community of Nantucket-born descendants of African slaves, people who could properly be called African Nantucketers. During the nineteenth century, Nantucket became a refuge for people in flight from slavery, and New Guinea absorbed people from the slave states of Missouri, Louisiana, South Carolina, Maryland, and Virginia as well as free black Nova Scotians, West Indians, Cape Verdeans and a few Pacific islanders. All of these people, despite their different histories and cultural diversity, became united in the experience of being perceived as "black"

and thereby relegated to residence on the southern margin of the town.

The beginning of the twentieth century brought seasonal workers from Cape Verde for the fall cranberry harvest and others from the southern states and the Caribbean as summertime domestic help. By the end of the twentieth century, the expansion of "rump seasons" in the spring and fall had created a new need for seasonal workers, bringing Jamaicans to Nantucket on six- and nine-month visas to work in hotels, restaurants, and stores. Whereas earlier domestic workers who came to the island for the summer months had generally lived-in with their employers, Jamaicans on Nantucket typically live in worker housing provided by their employers. These circumstances—as earlier, when Cape Verdeans were housed in shanties on the cranberry bogs—congregate newcomers. On the one hand, employee housing can afford mutual support and cultural continuity, but on the other hand it isolates people and exposes them to group stereotyping.

Despite Nantucket's demographic changes, the pattern of the first half of the nineteenth century has been perpetuated, with people considered "black" either living in space provided by their employers or residing in the part of town identified with and for blacks—the old New Guinea neighborhood plus the waterfront, Washington Street, Lower Orange Street, and Sparks Avenue.

Sparks Avenue—running from Atlantic Avenue to the rotary where Orange Street ends—took the place of the old gated livestock fence that demarcated the south edge of town. Not only did Edgar and Emma Wilkes reside on Sparks Avenue in the last years of their lives, but Dr. Alwyn Potter and his family owned a house there, too. Dr. Potter was a graduate of Tufts University and Meharry Dental College and a lieutenant colonel in the Dental Corps of the U. S. Army. He and his wife, Vivian Potter, were enormously appreciated in postwar Japan, where he was stationed from 1953 to 1958. During those years Vivian Potter taught English and led a Girl Scout troop in Yokohama. Returning to a dental practice in Nantucket, Dr.

Potter was a member of the Rotary Club and was active in the music program of the Summer Street Baptist Church. Nonetheless, the Potter family—like the Carter family—lived on what Isabel Carter Stewart has described as the "edge of what had been circumscribed as the black quarter."

Along with the residence pattern, the old Nantucket Quaker division of the world into a specific "us" versus the undifferentiated "world's people" lives on as "white" versus undifferentiated "black." This peculiar kind of color blindness in which everyone who is not perceived as white is lumped together has led to moments of considerable irony. Isabel Carter Stewart wrote of one of her "few black friends, the daughter of a respected island dentist" being refused admission to a children's program at Jetties Beach in the 1950s. More recently Nantucket High School students working at vacation-time jobs have been bemused by summer residents' compliments on their unaccented English and queries about how late they can stay on in the fall. On the other hand, some Nantucketers returning home are startled when a Jamaican man opens the door to the plane, smiles warmly at the arriving passengers, and says, "Welcome to our island."

It takes an effort to bear in mind that not all people considered black are African Americans. Even if the term "American" encompasses—as it should—Canadians, "African American" does not describe the historical experience of people of Cape Verdean, Bermudian, or West Indian heritage, to say nothing of those Native Americans, Pacific islanders, and Asians who once were also "black." Blackness is a matter of how people are perceived and how they are treated. In that sense, African Americans, Cape Verdeans, West Indians, and others as well, have had and continue to have common cause in dealing with discrimination, inequities, and prejudice.

Now, as in the past, racial perception of color tends to obliterate appreciation of the great variety of working people who have come to call Nantucket home for part of the year or, inevitably, home for good.

CHAPTER SEVENTEEN

Codfish Park

Early Siasconset had been no more than a row of rudimentary shelter huts for men working shifts as they watched for whales from a lookout mast erected on 'Sconset Bank. Some of the island's oldest buildings survive from those days, either free-standing (*Auld Lang Syne*, *circa* 1675) or as rooms within larger buildings (part of *Shanunga*, *circa* 1680). The handful of parallel streets running along the Bank, closely lined with small seventeenth- and eighteenth-century buildings, has been described as a medieval village, and it was this essence of quaintness upon which Edward Underhill capitalized in the late nineteenth century.

The evolution of 'Sconset from whale station to fishing village was not seamless. Alongshore whaling gave way to offshore voyaging on "the deep" in the first half of the 1700s, but dory fishing from the beach below 'Sconset Bank only began with the delivery of the island's first dory to carpenter-turned-codfisherman Asa Jones in 1857. By then 'Sconset already had its first tourist hotel. Just when increasing numbers of visitors began coming to seaview rooms and verandas along the Bank, the beach below the Bank was being built up with improvised fish houses. As the sought-after healthful breezes came onshore from the Atlantic, they picked up the smell of desiccating codfish and wafted it upwards.

Young woman posed on a dory with Codfish Park and buildings on the Bank in background.

Nantucket Historical Association

Fishing shacks and barrels along 'Sconset Bank, circa 1870.

Tourists and dories below the Bank in the 1890s.

On the beach where saltwater bathing was encouraged, bathhouses competed for space with dories and fish carts. Far from repelling visitors, however, the fishing scene provided a popular backdrop for early photographers, who posed women and children in and around the hauled-out dories.

Codfish Park occupied an apron of land that had not existed a half-century earlier. The shoreline had only recently begun making out to seaward. "In 1814," Edward Underhill wrote, "and thence forward for many years, the beach was so narrow in front of 'Sconset, that in heavy gales the surf washed over it to the foot of the Bank, and twice within Capt. Joy's recollection, it [the Bank] was washed away and houses had to be removed. A street to the eastward of the one now on the edge of the Bank thus disappeared."[1] The situation had not improved at mid-century. According to J. Clinton Andrews, "In 1852, the ocean was washing the foot of the bank at 'Sconset, which was eroding away in storms. A barn with a horse in it was washed away one night. Gradually the erosion lessened, and then the beach started to build up. By 1883, fish houses—shacks to dress fish and to store gear and green salt fish—were being moved to 'below the Bank' on the sand then being deposited

by the ocean and creating a widening strip of land. My grandfather had built the first one a short time previously. The beach continued to build."

Fish houses and fish carts were not the only mobile structures that came to rest on the new land. When the railroad was extended in 1884, the terminus was below the Bank. To serve 'Sconset passengers, part of the Surfside depot was dismantled and re-erected on the beach at Codfish Park.

Because it was new land, it was also no one's land and everyone's land. Buildings thrown together from scavenged lumber and driftwood were intended as temporary structures, and the notion of establishing title to beach sand was ludicrous. It hardly seemed possible at the time that a village would come into being down on the beach, but Codfish Park followed a trajectory much like that of New Guinea, becoming Nantucket's second black community.

As the old village became a popular resort, developments sprang up on its flanks to the south (Sunset Heights) and to the north (Sankaty Bluffs). The newly built houses had quarters for the domestic servants who accompanied summer residents to 'Sconset. For married domestics with families of their own, however, living-in meant

---

1. The situation has now reversed again, with buildings in Codfish Park lost to the sea in the 1990s and the bank farther north at Sankaty Head so frequently undercut that the lighthouse is in danger of toppling over into the sea. The keeper's cottage where the Larsen family once lived is long gone.

Railroad depot in Codfish Park, with large hotel on the Bank in the background. —Nantucket Historical Association

months-long separation from their children every year. In time, some sought to live apart from their employers in order to bring their families with them to the island for the summer. Cheap housing was available in Codfish Park. Some summer residents purchased houses there for their employees, but as time went by and nest eggs accumulated, the domestics bought houses for themselves. As families moved in, whether as renters or home owners, they brought with them a new sense of community. In 1939 William O. Stevens wrote of the evolution of the Park:

> Between the village and the beach is the settlement of the squatters, known as Codfish Park. This in recent years has spruced up amazingly and is growing flowers and flaunting new shingles and fresh paint as gay as you please. But it was not always thus. There are still little cabins in the Park that suggest something of the way all the Siasconset houses were built, with a stray window here and an old door there and a piece of tiling for a chimney. In the days when offshore fishing flourished, the Park was somewhat dégagé. Entrails and heads of fish were blithely tossed about, which under the summer sun became extremely obsolete. Now that the fish refuse to be caught off this beach any more, the inhabitants grow nasturtiums and take in washing for the "summer people" up the bank, and the place is nothing if not genteel.

What Stevens did not state explicitly was that most of the people living in Codfish Park in the summer were black.

Because of the seasonal nature of their work, domestics were not generally counted by the census. In 1920 the three black families in 'Sconset who do appear in the federal census for that year—the Deans, the Scotts, and the Wades—lived on New Street, which parallels Milestone Road leading into the village from the west. A decade later, in 1930, no black families lived on New Street. They had moved to Codfish Park.

Few of the dwelling houses in the Park were winterized. Their inhabitants departed with their employers in early September and returned for Memorial Day weekend. Many spent nine months of the year at primary residences in New York City. Gradually, however, the Park became the year-round home of numbers of hardy souls.

The Deans, Scotts, and Wades had all moved to Codfish Park, and there they had been joined by the Dicksons, the Fords, the Williamses, the Phillipses, and Walter Kelly. In time the Wilsons and the Mauldins moved in. Phyleatus and Priscilla Lyburtus, domestic workers who married on Nantucket in the summer of 1930, became year-rounders. Codfish Park residents hailed from Louisiana, Alabama, Mississippi, North Carolina, Virginia, West Virginia, Washington D.C., Pennsylvania, Ohio, and Illinois.

The 1938 street list enumerates thirty-four adults living permanently in the Park. Unlike the predominantly African-American summer population, the year-rounders were a racial and ethnic mix. In addition to the African-American

263

Lyburtuses and Mauldins living below the Bank, there were the Azorean Santos family; their Danish son-in-law Folmer Stanshigh; Massachusetts-born Elmer Davis; his wife Theresa Bridget Davis—born in County Galway, Ireland; and their boarder Mattie Finnegan. The Wilsons were from Bermuda.

Lying far out in the Atlantic due east of Charleston, South Carolina, and nearly seven hundred miles from New York City, Bermuda is the most northerly group of coral islands in the world. Of its hundreds of islands and islets, twenty are inhabited and, in fact, densely populated. The islands first appear on a map in the early 1500s. A century later, the shipwreck of a group of English colonists on their way to Virginia brought Bermuda to the attention of England. Most of the colonists who had fetched up there moved on, but the Virginia Company sent sixty more to stay and settle the islands.

By 1620 enslaved Indians and Africans were being transported to Bermuda. Their experience there was different from that of field slaves on plantation islands to the south and on the American mainland. Despite Bermuda's warm climate and lush vegetation, labor-intensive agriculture has never been a feature of the economy. Most food was and is imported, with little in the way of exports. As in Nantucket, people of color in Bermuda worked as domestic servants, craftsmen, and boat builders, but unlike in Nantucket, they soon outnumbered the English. As in the Azores, a burgeoning population on limited land inevitably produced a demographic crisis that could only be alleviated by emigration, but that could happen only once the black population was free to leave.

Slavery continued in Bermuda, however, until 1834, when it was abolished throughout the British Empire. Thereafter, the white minority continued to control the government and the economy of the British crown colony until forced to begin to share its power with the black majority in the 1970s. During the near century and a half in between, the people of Bermuda eked out a living by taking part in mercantile trade between North America and the West Indies and by salvaging ships that came to grief in surrounding waters. During the U.S. Civil War, some Bermudians profited from

Fish houses at the foot of 'Sconset Bank in the 1890s.

blockade running and privateering. Later, during Prohibition, money was to be made by rum-running, but by then Clarence Wilson had left.

Clarence Fitzgerald Wilson was born in 1901. After World War I, he moved to the United States and worked at a series of jobs as cook, houseman, gardener, and butler for New York families. Florence Adlina De Shields, born and educated in Bermuda, made a brief visit in 1922 and returned to work for a family in Connecticut two years later.

Clarence and Florence met in New York in 1924 and married the next year. After a few years, they moved to New Jersey, where Clarence worked as chef for the officers at the naval air station in Lakehurst. Then, in the pit of the Depression, with children to raise and educate, he lost that job, and the family moved back to New York City to patch together part-time jobs in an effort to stay afloat.

Many of the very wealthy with summer houses on Nantucket managed to float above the economic disaster and take advantage of the pool of cheap labor to expand their domestic staffs. During the 1930s, actor Regan Hughston's twenty-eight-room house in Siasconset was maintained by a summertime staff of at least eight, including a cook, a chauffeur, a gardener, and several maids. In 1938 they were joined by Clarence Wilson, who had been hired as butler. He remained with the Hughston family for fifteen years.

From 1938 to 1943 the Wilson family endured six-month separations, with Florence and the children staying behind in New York while Clarence went to Nantucket. He arrived two weeks in advance of the Hughstons to open their house for the summer, served the family through October, and then closed the house after their departure. Florence was hired as Mrs. Hughston's personal maid in 1941, and beginning in 1943 the Wilson family was able to stay together throughout the year.

To begin with, the Wilsons—parents and children—lived in the servants quarters of the Hughston estate, but in the late 1940s they bought one house in Codfish Park, and in 1950 they acted on a tip about another house coming up for sale there and succeeded in buying it, too. Once they

— Courtesy of Joan Wilson-Godeau
Clarence and Florence Wilson, 1991.

had their own housing, Florence Wilson informed the Hughstons that they could no longer continue to employ her without contributing to Social Security for her eventual retirement benefits. At her insistence, the estate owners began to pay into Social Security for all their domestic employees. Probably not coincidentally, Clarence Wilson left the Hughstons and for the next two decades split his employment between winters working in New York for William Lindsay White, an editor at *Reader's Digest*, and summers working for John B. Fitzpatrick, a summer resident with a house on Nantucket harbor at Shawkemo. This arrangement made it possible for the Wilson family to continue to spend every summer in Codfish Park.

These summers were cherished by the Wilsons. There was the pleasure of living in their own house on the beach, and during summer vacation from school there was also intellectual stimulation for a family that valued learning. The Hughston family had bought fine books for the Wilsons' youngest daughter, Joan, whose voracious childhood reading led in time to a career in education.

Clarence Wilson customarily reached out beyond his family, extending a hand to each and every newly arrived black domestic. According to Joan, "When new domestics would come, he would make it his business to go and introduce himself and try to help them to assimilate and adjust. That's important on an island like Nantucket. However friendly it may be, it is a white island, and there are so few of us."

Although the majority of families living in Codfish Park in the summer were black, they lived in close daily contact with two distinct white populations—a large number of wealthy summer residents who lived above them on the Bank and a smaller number of year-round working families, some of whom lived above and others down below in the Park. This intimacy with the dominant white presence made the Wilsons uneasy. At the same time that their daughter Joan was taking singing and dancing parts in the amateur theatricals staged by the summer residents at the 'Sconset Casino, she was hearing the word "nigger" bandied about freely. For many African Americans the N-word is so unspeakable that their voices drop to near inaudibility if they feel they must say it. From the lips of white 'Sconseters, however, it sounded loud and clear, and as often as not it was directed at her.

"Part of the beauty of Nantucket is that you can be pretty comfortable here and that you don't find a lot of hostility," Joan said in 2003. "But there is still the separation. And by the time I got to be ten years old, my mother started sending me to camp in the summertime, because she felt that as I grew older, I would be more and more shunned as a black kid. My mother was quite aware of the fact that I would no longer be accepted in the circles with these white children, and that was the case. So she said, 'I've got to do something else, and as wonderful as Nantucket is, I want my child to have a broader experience.' So for five years, from the age of ten to fifteen, I went to camp on the mainland. First I went to a YWCA all-black camp, and then I went to an integration camp also run by the YWCA."

Going to camp reduced Joan Wilson's time on Nantucket to a couple of late summer weeks before the opening of school, but it never diminished her sense of rootedness in Codfish Park and its black community. The Wilsons' backyard was a gathering place for the neighbors to enjoy Clarence Wilson's famously fine cooking and to talk over work, plans, and problems, a tradition that continues to the present. So it was that a photo album, one of only a very few collections of photographs documenting Nantucket's community of black domestics, was handed down to the Wilson sisters.

Aerial view of Codfish Park (center), 1927.

The album originally belonged to Jessie A. Fisher, a neighbor in Codfish Park who frequently teamed with Clarence Wilson in the catering and bartending business. Most of the photos in the album are of Jessie Fisher herself and of black residents of the Park, including the Wilsons. There are also photos of African Americans in town, of Nantucket's Cape Verdeans, and of white summer residents. Along with the photographs of people, there are also some of landscapes and of houses in 'Sconset. Most are not labeled with the names of the people in them or the date, but clothing and automobiles in the photos provide clues to when they were taken. Remarkable are the photos of cars and aircraft of the 1930s and 1940s. Some photos even date back to the beginning of the 1920s. The album is a precious repository of twentieth-century black history on Nantucket.

The era of black domestic service finally passed in the mid-1960s, largely—if not fully—put out of business by evolving technology, by the Civil Rights movement, and by people like Florence Wilson insisting on appropriate compensation for their work and decent opportunities for their children. One effect of this was the whitening of Codfish Park. There has been no younger generation of black seasonal workers to take the place of aging and departing members of the Park's black community. Many of their houses have been bought and gentrified as summer rental properties.

Jessie Fisher, identified as "Siasconset caterer," outside her house in Codfish park.

Nature, too, has changed Codfish Park. In the 1990s the beachfront that had once been so wide began to erode again, and owners of houses along the east side of Codfish Park Road who did not move them out of harm's way saw them washed out to sea, curtains flying in the wind. The Wilsons' land-side house suddenly had an unobstructed ocean view across the street. Obtaining building permits and insurance has become an issue. Although the 1990s brought Nantucket a surge of black workers from Jamaica, they are not, for good reasons, settling in Codfish Park.

A visitor today would need a historical marker to learn about the black history of the little village below 'Sconset Bank.

Larger houses atop the Bank overlook the modest ones in Codfish Park in the 1930s.

CHAPTER EIGHTEEN

Meccas and Entertainments

Over the centuries, maintaining a life of one's own has always been a struggle for people employed as servants. For house slaves, indentured servants, and wage earners alike, domestic service has almost inevitably meant living-in. Those fortunate enough to have regular days off have had to seek some place to go, since domestics could hardly expect to receive visitors in the homes of their masters and mistresses.

Privacy has not been part of the bargain. On the contrary, masters—and mistresses in particular—have universally taken scrupulous interest in governing the most intimate details of their servants' lives. Sometimes this has been for the good when, for instance, mistresses have taken a hand in educating their young servants or providing an elderly retainer with security to life's end. Nantucket's Absalom Boston benefited from his boyhood employment by Anna Gardner's grandparents, and later in life he paid regular social visits to the family. Eunice Ross's sister Sarah, having outlived her employers, continued to make herself at home in their house and died there. Even in cases of mutual devotion, however, the inequality and paternalism of the relationship could not fail to exact a toll on domestics' dignity and freedom of expression.

The crowning virtue of a domestic was to be ever available, ever agreeable, ever eager to please. In 1954 William White wrote of Clarence Wilson,

Two women in maids' uniforms stand in the background of this group photograph, 1880s.

Nantucket Historical Association

"Nothing delights him more than to have a large dinner party suddenly sprung on him. Most curious of all is his disposition. Surely he must have his share of life's crosses to bear. But it is part of his professional code—its object being to make you happy—never to let you know that they exist." Clarence Wilson described his relationship to his summer employer, John Fitzpatrick, in less lyrical terms. He was, he remarked wryly, Fitzpatrick's "general flunkie."

Having one's own home, going out to work and returning home after work, no matter how late, is heady liberation from living-in. In its incipiency New Guinea was a village of former slaves now in possession of their own dwelling houses on their own land. It is hardly to be wondered at that the residents of New Guinea threw themselves with such enthusiasm into buying, selling, and consolidating real estate. Generations later, when Nantucket became a summer resort for the well-to-do, domestics who accompanied them to the island were constantly on the lookout for the chance to buy houses for themselves, and many of them succeeded.

The process took time, however, and in the meantime the choice—if there even was one—was between living in servants quarters or renting a room. Available rooms were in short supply, since only a few people were willing to rent to black seasonal workers—or to black summer visitors for that matter. Generally, the rooms available were in the homes of domestics who had acquired houses of their own and were letting rooms to meet taxes and mortgage payments. Among the people who took in roomers were Ruth Grant, Florence Higginbotham, and Louise Phillips. As mentioned above, it was known to the Nantucket Information Bureau that the Carters on Prospect Street would take in black visitors.

Those private homes, the black equivalent of the homes in Nantucket that had offered travelers of the 1800s a "genteel experience," afforded hospitality to many more black summer residents than the few they could accommodate as roomers. They became the homes away from home to which

domestics on "help's day off" (Sundays and every other Thursday) could come to spend time with friends, play cards, smoke cigarettes, and get away from their employers' houses. Joan Wilson-Godeau described Louise Phillips's household as a "mecca."

– Courtesy of Joan Wilson-Godeau

Louise Phillips, born in Virginia in 1908, lived to age 94 in her home on West York Lane.

> *Her house was always a mecca for people who were domestics. She always would have gatherings for them, and every summer they would come back, and she'd entertain them. She was a wonderful person. She had friends from all over who worked for people here. They came from Texas and from St. Louis. There was a driver from St. Louis who would come every summer and spend time with her because he would drive this family—this very wealthy couple—here, and they would house him at Mrs. Phillips, and they were such good friends.*

Isabel Carter Stewart described her family's home hospitality in a similar vein:

> *Our modest little Windsor Cottage became a gathering place on Thursdays and Sundays for the more upscale and successful among those working "in service." There were wonderful stories of young men studying to be doctors and dentists and lawyers who snagged summer jobs at the posh hotels, all gathering in our front yard or on the porch.*
>
> *Later, in the late thirties and early forties, friends of my mother and aunt gathered as young marrieds, whether they were vacationing or also working "in service."*

Mizpah, the York Street home of Florence Higginbotham, stood next to the long-closed African Meeting House and was another of the gathering places where domestics could come together on their days off. Among the entertainments at her house were tea-leaf readings and fortune telling. David Barrett, who still lives on York Street recorded his childhood impressions of the socials taking place next door:

On Sundays there would be not really a scheduled gathering, but there were always a lot of people coming and going, and I interpreted it—as did my mother and father—as a left-over sort of a get-together since there was no church anymore. She always had people coming and going. You could smell food, and a lot of maids would stop—on their way to work I think, because they had their uniforms on. And there was a bench along the porch to the left of the front door going in, and somebody was always sitting on that.

Among the Higginbotham papers preserved at the Museum of Afro-American History in Boston are a great many letters and postcards from women who had stayed at Florence Higginbotham's house, worked with her, and become her good friends over the years. They remained faithful correspondents to the ends of their lives.

In addition to the home gathering places, black domestics on Nantucket had a dance hall to go to. Back in the 1820s John Pompey had operated one in New Guinea, and a generation later Trillania

Pompey organized neighborhood dances with music provided by New Guinea fiddler Henry Wheeler. Then, in the latter half of the 1800s, the flight of people from New Guinea left the churches, the shops, and the dance floor empty. Over in Alfonso Hall, between Williams and Cherry Streets, dancing had shifted to the Azorean *chamarrita*. Carpenter Frank Scott, a resident of Siasconset since before 1920, saw an opportunity and built a dance hall. Vivian (Wilson) Richardson described it as a large building at the end of an unpaved road not far from Sankaty Lighthouse. In the 1930s and 1940s it was yet another mecca for Nantucket's black domestic workers—a place to take in music and enjoy the company of others. It served its purpose until Willie House opened the Chicken Box back in town at the end of the 1940s, and the memory of Frank Scott's dance hall with its hardwood floors and sandwiches catered by Clarence Wilson was cherished for many years afterward.

Blackface minstrel shows were popular entertainments for white Nantucketers for over a

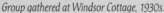

Group gathered at Windsor Cottage, 1930s.

century. On the mainland professional minstrel troupes had come into being in the years before the Civil War, reached a peak of popularity, and then lost place to vaudeville and burlesque at the end of the century. Long after the demise of minstrel halls and touring companies, however, minstrel shows persisted, carried deep into the twentieth century in the movies and by amateur players. Nantucket was no exception.

On June 25, 1847, the *Nantucket Inquirer* advertised the arrival of Rice and Company's "Original and Inimitable Band of Ethiopian Opera Serenaders in their celebrated songs, glees, parodies, choruses, conundrums, etc." They had played Palmo's Opera House in New York and the Melodeon in Boston before coming to the island for two shows at Pantheon Hall on Main Street. Nantucket was still rising from the ashes of the Great Fire of the summer before, and the towns-people were more than ready for some comedy.

One evening in the summer of 1849, aboard the barque *Russell* making a passage around Cape Horn to San Francisco, five young crew members—two Nantucket boys and three "strangers"—put on a minstrel show at sea. A passenger wrote to her mother back home, "I heard a general roar of laughter. I looked up and there came skipping out of the steerage five 'Christy Minstrels' with their music in their hands and dressed to order—faces and hands blackened, their red lips and white teeth made visible by a broad grin, looking nearer like negroes than ever a negro did like himself. Then commenced their negro songs, conundrums, and dances, and for half an hour our lungs were well exercised."

In the 1860s there seems to have been a disconnect between the high seriousness of abolition and the horrors of the Civil War on one hand and audience enthusiasm for minstrel shows on the other. When Sam Sharpley brought his minstrel troupe to Nantucket in September 1869 for two performances in the Atheneum's Great Hall, readers of the *Inquirer and Mirror* were urged to attend, because the performers would "no doubt furnish our citizens not only with a rich musical treat but fun enough to last them through the coming dull winter."

Perpetuated by local groups, the shows remained in favor on the island right up to the days of the civil rights struggles of the 1960s. In the 1930s and 1940s, the Oddfellows and the Red Men regularly staged minstrel shows, and even the Nantucket High School seniors got into the act, presenting one in the spring of 1939. The next year there was a special "All Girl" minstrel show. On March 1, 1952, the *Inquirer and Mirror* reported that "a large group of black-faced Red Men, augmented by a couple of ebony Pocahontases, and stove-polished lovers of the merry minstrels, opened the annual Red Men's minstrel show…" Among the performers in blackface was Cape Verdean Herbert Cabral.

Why, it may be asked, did minstrel shows hang on so long in Nantucket, where they were perceived as fine off-season entertainment to be put on by members of civic-minded organizations

Eugene and Annie (Nevins) Perry with grandson Charles Flanagan, all in costume for a Red Men's parade in front of the Dreamland Theatre, 1930s.

Courtesy of Catherine Flanagan Stover.

271

for fellow citizens? In hindsight, the notion of people blackening their faces, painting on exaggerated red lips, and burlesquing African Americans is offensive, yet it was not so perceived by most Nantucketers as recently as the 1950s.

Perhaps minstrel shows could linger on Nantucket past their time precisely because islanders were relatively unexposed to authentic African-American culture. Just when the minstrel show was first rising in popularity, Nantucket's old black community was melting away. The Cape Verdeans who took their place in no way identified themselves with the specifically African-American stereotypes that were stock-in-trade of the shows, and Nantucket's new black seasonal workers left the island every fall before the kick-off of the minstrel-show season. Growing up on Nantucket, William Higginbotham felt he was the only African-American child on the island year round. A bit later Frank Spriggs, ultimately destined to be elected to Nantucket's board of selectmen, felt the same way. In the Nantucket school-registration records from the early to mid-twentieth century, there are very few nonwhite children whose families did not focus on their Cape Verdean or Native American roots. In any case, no one at the time raised a voice of objection to the racial stereotyping of the shows.

Discomfiting as minstrel shows are from the perspective of the twenty-first century, they did accomplish more than just hold African Americans up to ridicule. They were a first conduit for the blackening of American popular entertainment. When white men (and women and even some black men) covered their faces with charred cork and went out on the stage to sing and dance, they were playing at being black, performing to songs that purported to be African-American music and that sometimes approached the real thing. Having stepped into those shoes, white performers in blackface tried on different ways of talking, different ways of making music, different ways of carrying themselves. The style was infectious, and they were never quite the same again. Neither were the members of their audiences who sang along with them and repeated their "conundrums." American ver-

nacular culture was changed by the minstrel shows just as it was, far more powerfully, by black entertainers of the twentieth century.

One of the whitest of Nantucket venues was the Main Street Fete, a fund-raising event to support the Nantucket Cottage Hospital. The first was held on Main Street in 1921. It was repeated in 1923 and continued every other summer for decades. During a Main Street Fete, the street was closed to traffic from above the square all the way to the Civil War monument, and owners of Main Street houses opened them to the public. Grandparents' clothes were brought out of attic trunks to dress participants as the families of nineteenth-century whaling captains and merchants. Playwright Austin Strong and artist Tony Sarg, both summer residents, contributed their considerable talents to the fetes, and islanders and tourists alike were more than happy to pay entrance fees to have a look at the interiors of some of Nantucket's most imposing mansions.

For the 1923 fete, Strong conceived a bit of street theater. Attired as a returning China trade captain, he led a procession of men dressed as crewmen up Main Street. On his arm was Katherine Adams, another summer resident, robed in silk as his Chinese bride. At their side marched Arthur Watkins, an African-American boy in the role of cabin boy. When they reached the corner of Main and Pleasant Streets, the crewmen formed an honor guard for the wedding couple, while Arthur Watkins danced a jig for the onlookers. Not a trace of a family named Watkins is to be found in town records. Arthur must have been the son of seasonal workers. Only a half-dozen photos and his name in a newspaper caption record his presence on the island and his performance during the summer of 1923.

Main Street Fetes fell into abeyance, but the event was resurrected for Nantucket's three-hundredth birthday celebration in the summer of 1959. Nantucket women were encouraged to sew old-time costumes for themselves and their families, and all summer the town was full of little girls in pinafores in the company of women in hoop skirts or Quaker scuttle bonnets and men in knee breeches and broad-brimmed Quaker hats. Amidst the evocations of the past, Sadie Pride, in colonial ruffles and mobcap, pushed an antique wicker baby carriage back and forth between 99 Main Street and the Pacific National Bank. Graciously pausing for photographs, she was the epitome of dignity as she played her role of nursemaid to a wealthy Nantucket family back in the time when slavery had still been part of living memory on the island.

Ellen Ramsdell was born in Nantucket in 1898, a descended Nantucketer on her father's side and of Azorean heritage on her mother's. Blessed with extraordinary musical talent, she went to the New England Conservatory, and then, during the Depression, returned home as music teacher in the island's public schools. During the 1930s she accomplished the seemingly impossible, directing junior high school students in productions of Gilbert and Sullivan.

In 1935 she took a break from fast-paced and under-appreciated political satires with a thoroughly silly operetta. In *Jewels of the Desert* Nana, "beautiful child of the desert" and daughter of "a fierce Arab chieftain," falls in love with "a strange Arab" while an American professor is pursued by a titled English woman. Among the supporting characters are Ceasar, a "colored gentleman from the U. S. A." and Cheeko, "the Lieutenant's Arab boy." Florence Higginbotham's son William had the role of Cheeko rather than of Ceasar. The roles available to him seem to have been limited to "a colored gentleman" and a servant referred to as someone's boy. As with the minstrel shows, there was no local perception of the operetta as offensive or demeaning, but Bill Higginbotham, who—like Ellen Ramsdell—was musically gifted, felt himself more marginalized than encouraged in the school music program. His sixth-grade report card from the Cyrus Peirce School records generally excellent grades, straight As in art, excellent attendance, and abysmal grades in music.

Out on the east edge of the island, the Siasconset Casino Association had incorporated itself in the spring of 1899. The fifteen original members were stockholders in the association, each holding from one to five shares, and membership was rigorously

Arthur Watkins dancing in the 1923 Main Street Fete.

273

exclusive. According to the bylaws adopted at the time, shares were transferable to other persons, but any stockholder wishing to do so had first to offer them for sale back to the corporation.

The Casino building was erected over the winter of 1899–1900. When it formally opened on August 4, 1900, the actors' colony, which had been using the village's Union Chapel and the railroad station below the Bank as performance venues, finally had an auditorium with proper seating and lighting. Productions began at once and continued on through the century, long after suspension of the railroad service that had originally transported audiences to 'Sconset.

A staple of the 'Sconset Casino summer programs from 1947 to the 1960s was an annual variety show called *On the Isle*. Some of the songs in the revue were satires of old standards, but a significant number were written for the occasion. At age ten, just before her mother sent her off to camp, Joan Wilson had a scene all her own in the 1947 show. In 1953 she soloed as a *chanteuse*, and the next summer's show featured "In Person—Joan Wilson." Nonetheless, when it came to casting the 1988 revival of *On the Isle*, she was passed over, as she was again in 1999 when *On the Isle* was revived once more for the hundredth birthday of the Casino. One of the songs in the 1988 revival had been written for the 1953 show in which she did appear. Its ambiguous title was "My Siasconset Maid."

Participation in *On the Isle* productions was not limited to summer residents of Siasconset; a few of Nantucket's year-round resident musicians were regulars in the casts of the 1940s and 1950s. Conversely, the Nantucket Community Orchestra had a few summer members, but it was primarily an organization of year-rounders that had its origin in the Theatre Workshop productions of *An Italian Straw Hat* in 1956 and *The Mikado* in 1957. The 1956 show required musicians, and the Gilbert and Sullivan musical of the following year needed even more.

Community-wide recruitment of musicians brought together about two dozen local musicians, Herbert Cabral and Richard Mauldin among them.

After playing for *The Mikado*, the group decided to continue together, and the Community Orchestra was born. Cabral and Mauldin stayed with the orchestra for its life span, which extended from the 1950s on throughout the 1960s, and both served terms as officers.

Benefit of the Siasconset Casino

Dramatic and Musical Entertainment
Saturday Evening, Aug. 4, 1900

THE CASINO
Under Management of Miss Mary Shaw

Programme.

OVERTURE—March—The 'Sconset Hungarian Orchestra.
Miss Annette Norton, Miss Helen Galvin, Mr. Tom Streeter, Mr. Harry Roberts, Miss Mary Chittenden.
PIANO SOLO—Waltz by Boldini.............Miss Lucy Drake

"A FALSE START"
A Trifle by Julian Sturgis, Esq.

CHARACTERS

Lady Roedale..........................Miss Mary Shaw
Nora.................................Miss Percy Haswell
Harry................................Mr. Walter Hale

INTERLUDE—An Innocent Young Maid............Orchestra
SPANISH DANCE..Miss Agnes Everett and Mr. Allan Rowe
RECITATION—"Seein' Things at Night"
Miss Margaret Galvin
SONG AND DANCE (from "The Geisha") "Monkey on a Stick"
Miss Percy Haswell.
NEGRO SONG AND DANCE.................Mr. Arthur Shaw
SUNFLOWER QUARTETTE...................The Mysteries
WALTZ SONG—"Singing Girl"...................Orchestra

To conclude with

"A GENTLE JURY"
by Arlo Bates, Esq.

CHARACTERS

Forewoman—Mrs. Julia Linthicum.
Miss Skinner......................Mrs. G. H. Gilbert
Miss Sharp........................Miss Agnes Everett
Mrs. Dyer.........................Miss Percy Haswell
Mrs. Faint........................Mrs. R. P. Carter
Mrs. Blake........................Mrs. Walter Hale
Mrs. Jones........................Miss Annette Norton
Mrs. Small.....................Miss Margaret Chittenden
Miss Fort.........................Miss Marie Meltzer
Mrs. Fritz........................Miss Alice Ladue
Miss Fuss......................Miss Louise Patterson
Miss Feathers.....................Miss Marie McKay
Sheriff..........................Mr. George Fawcett

Doors open at 7.45.
Performance will commence after arrival of evening train.
Tickets $1.00, 75 cents and 50 cents.

on sale at Congdon's Pharmacy and at the door.

A special train will be run over the Nantucket Central Railroad on the evening of the entertainment. Tickets for round trip 50 cents. Good for the 3 p. m. and evening boat trains. Only good to return on special train leaving for Nantucket after the performance.

Ladies are requested to remove their hats during the performance

Nantucket Historical Association

274

Henry Wheeler and young Thomas Boston had been the violinists of New Guinea. Violinist Richard Mauldin was the resident musician of Codfish Park. Born in Philadelphia in 1903, he and his family moved to the Park in the early 1940s. In Nantucket he found employment as a mechanic at the local Chevrolet dealership, did some caretaking for summer residents, raised his family, and played first violin in the Community Orchestra. Codfish Park remained his home to the end of his ninety-four years.

In general, townspeople were as insensitive as most summer residents to the tacit discrimination that pervaded island life. In the summer of 1930, the short-lived *Nantucket Beacon* (the first of two newspapers bearing that name) reported that at Nantucket's agricultural fair that year, "Everybody has Gala Time….Old and young, men and women, little boys and little girls. Yes, even 'black and white'"—the wording and the shudder quotes implying that when it came to inclusiveness, race was more remarkable than age or gender. From white audiences enjoying the performance of white entertainers in blackface to white audi-

ences accepting the occasional black person among white performers had been a stretch. It was a longer stretch yet for a mixed audience to come together while a black person commanded a venue whites considered their own. That had happened when Fredrick Douglass rose to speak at the Atheneum, and it happened again when, close to the end of his life, he spoke to a crowd filling to beyond capacity the Unitarian Church, at that time Nantucket's largest meeting hall. Booker T. Washington was an honored speaker in that same space, but, like Douglass, he was a visiting celebrity. A long time had to pass before a familiar presence on the island could lead Nantucketers to put aside their uneasiness about race. The time did come, however, thanks to a black woman with an angelic voice.

Like Richard Mauldin, mezzo-soprano Josephine White Hall also came from Philadelphia, but she had begun life in Orange, Virginia, the oldest of twelve children. Gifted with an extraordinarily intuitive sense of music, she first sang in public at age six and went on singing in churches all her life. She was eighteen when she moved to Philadelphia, and another ten years passed

Nantucket Community Orchestra rehearsal, 1958. Richard Mauldin is at left in violin section and clarinetist Herbert Cabral is seated third from right, middle row.

William Haddon photograph

before she began formal music training, first in Philadelphia, then in New York, and finally in Germany. In the 1950s and 1960s she made three European tours under the aegis of the U. S. Department of State, performing a range of popular, folk, and classical music. Closest to her heart, however, were the spirituals of her childhood church.

Throughout her musical career, White Hall continued to work as a domestic and to sing for guests at her employers' parties. While working for a family in Haverford, Pennsylvania, in the summer of 1952, she came with them to Nantucket. This was a time when television was new to the island, and reception was abysmal. Crowds of people still gathered downtown after supper to sing to the accordion of Herbert Brownell. Main Street "sings" were a cherished summer tradition, and White Hall simply stepped forward, sang "Swing Low, Sweet Chariot," and entered the hearts of Nantucketers.

The attraction was mutual. Nantucketers loved White Hall, and she loved them and their island. Determined to spend summers on Nantucket ever after, she returned the following year with her daughter and took whatever jobs she could get that did not interfere with her singing. She worked mornings as a chambermaid at a guest house, taught voice in the afternoons, and conducted the choir of the Summer Street Baptist Church. Ruth Grant made her home and piano available for practice and teaching, and Cape Verdean Mathilde Rose rented a room in her house on New Street to White Hall and her daughter. Eleanor True, organist at the Congregational Church, and Marguerite Fordyce, organist at St. Paul's Episcopal Church, became good friends with White Hall and arranged occasions for her to sing in churches, at private parties, in concerts, and—despite the ill treatment Marian Anderson had recently received from the Daughters of the American Revolution—for the local chapter of the D. A. R. Despite objections from some members of Nantucket's black community, White Hall felt that singing for the D. A. R. was a vindication and a road to reconciliation.

With time, the difficulty of finding a place to rent on Nantucket threatened to put an end to White Hall's summers on the island. Her solution was to become a live-in, uniformed maid for Sara Barnes Roby, an art collector with a summer home on Orange Street. White Hall put a good face on the compromise she had made by viewing it as an opportunity for her to meet artists and musicians in Mrs. Roby's home.

In 1981 she sang in the first Noonday Concert series in the Unitarian Church, and she appeared in the series every summer thereafter for fifteen years. In 1993 she gave a concert on her seventy-fifth birthday, and in August 1996 she sang a special benefit concert to raise money for school supplies for Bosnian refugees. For her adoring Nantucket public it was their last opportunity to hear her gorgeous voice filling the space of the Unitarian Church. Having exited to a standing ovation, she returned and urged everyone in the audience to touch another person and promise to do something to make the world a better place. Then she walked the aisle one more time, shaking hands left and right. Leaving Nantucket for the last time, she went to her native Virginia to devote her remaining time to her young voice students there. Two years later Nantucketers were grieved to hear of her passing.

If ever a person raised everyone around her above any possibility of racial prejudice, it was Josephine White Hall. A century earlier Anna Gardner—known as "Black Annie" for her devoted service to African Americans—had withdrawn from the Religious Society of Friends and taken up membership in the very Unitarian Church in which White Hall lifted her voice and Nantucket's conscience for so many years. United in that heaven in which White Hall so fervently believed, there could be no closer kindred spirits than Annie and Jo.[1]

---

1. In Nantucket Historical Association Manuscript Collection 335, folder 650, there is a photocopy of a newspaper clipping without date that reads in part, "The last teacher of the 'Bear Street School' that we can find any record of was the late Anna Gardner, a woman of great literary ability who was an ardent abolitionist and a friend and admirer of Frederick Douglass. Owing to her interests and close associations with the cause of slavery, she was often referred to as 'black Annie,' not in a tone of disrespect by any means, but designating her as the Anna Gardner who was the friend of the colored man."

CHAPTER NINETEEN

Bringing It Back to Town

Florence Higginbotham

Contrary to what some Nantucketers imagined, Florence Higginbotham was not a Gypsy. She was born in Richmond, Virginia, in 1894. Her parents were Alice Stewart and Landon Clay, and she had an older brother and an older sister who lived out their whole lives in Virginia.

Leaving home in her mid-teens, young Florence Clay went north for work. One of the jobs she found was with the White House Coffee company in Boston, and from there she accompanied friends to Nantucket to do summer domestic work in Siasconset. When her friends returned to Boston in the fall, she remained on the island. In October 1917 she married Robert D. Higginbotham, who was also employed in 'Sconset. One of their witnesses was 'Sconset midwife Elizabeth "Nana" Watts, who remained Florence's friend through thick and thin. Thin years were soon to follow.

Robert Higginbotham, four years his bride's junior, soon joined the U.S. Navy as a cabin steward. From his ship as it cruised to Rio de Janeiro in the winter of 1918-19, he sent a series of postcards to "my Dear Wife," the last dated June 30, 1919. When she filed divorce papers in 1923, she gave his place of residence as Los Angeles and dated his desertion of their marriage to the summer of 1919. In 1921 Florence Higginbotham gave birth to her only child, William Caroll Higginbotham, whom she and her friends called "Bunny."

Edward Underhill, 'Sconset's energetic promoter and developer, had died in 1898, leaving his cottages, all thirty-six of them, jointly to his wife Evelyn and his daughter Lily with the stipulation that the women not sell the cottages. The income from their summer rental was to support the two women for the rest of their lives. At the death of one, the other would become full owner. In 1921

Evelyn Underhill was living alone in the China Closet with all the chinaware she and Edward had collected. She had lost her husband, her stepdaughter, and most recently her housekeeper. She was seventy years old and in need of help in managing the cottages.

– Museum of Afro American History

Young Evelyn Stoddard (later Underhill), circa 1880.

Three months after William's birth, Evelyn Underhill had Florence Higginbotham and her baby come to live with her in the China Closet. It was the custom of 'Sconset families to provide housing for their African-American employees in Codfish Park, but as Florence Higginbotham wrote to William in 1969, "They [the Underhills] never owned any property

Young Florence Clay (later Higginbotham) in a catboat with Nantucket historian Alexander Starbuck, circa 1917.

Nantucket Historical Association

277

down bank, that is why she wanted me to come and live with her." So began a remarkable relationship between the two women.

Florence Higginbotham and her son William, 1922.

The China Closet, where Florence and William Higginbotham lived with Evelyn Underhill in the 1920s.

For the rest of the 1920s the two women and the boy lived together in 'Sconset in the summers. As William grew, they moved from the China Closet to another of the Underhill cottages, the Double Decker, to get away from all the breakable china. At the end of each summer season they would close the cottages, take the boat to Woods Hole, and go to Mrs. Underhill's mainland home in Waltham, where William began school.

Then, as Evelyn Underhill approached her eightieth birthday, her fortunes spiraled downwards. Losses followed losses as her husband's uninsured rare-book collection was destroyed in a warehouse fire and the stock market crash of 1929 wiped out other Underhill investments. The women decided to stay on in Nantucket in the winters, and William transferred from his Waltham school to the Siasconset School, which he attended in 1930 and 1931 before transferring to the new Cyrus Peirce School in town.

The move to town was a reversal of the roles of Mrs. Underhill and Mrs. Higginbotham. When Florence Higginbotham had been a young single mother, Evelyn Underhill had taken her and William into the China Closet. Now Florence Higginbotham took the elderly Evelyn Underhill into her home. In 1920, she had invested in a house at 27 York Street, buying it from Edward and Elizabeth Whelden for $200 to use as a rental property. Her tenant, Harold W. Folger, described as "one of the last of the dory fishermen of this vicinity," died in bed there.

Adding a front porch and a sunroom to the house, Mrs. Higginbotham moved Mrs. Underhill with her family photos and her china collection to York Street. For the remaining years of her life, Evelyn Underhill lived under the care of her former housekeeper. When her niece and her husband came to visit, Florence Higginbotham withdrew to the back of the house, but otherwise the two women and William lived as a family. The women passed the time together—smoking cigarettes, reciting poetry to each other, listening to the radio, doing jigsaw puzzles, and working on scrapbooks. Some of the scrapbooks were of celebrities and the world of high fashion. Florence Higginbotham kept a scrapbook of articles about African-American history. Among her newspaper clippings was "Mizpah," a poem about separation based on the Book of Genesis, chapter 31, verse 49: "The Lord watch between me and thee when we are absent one from another." She took the name of her house from the text.

William made new friends on York Street and sought his mother's permission to join the Catholic Church, to which his friends belonged. Florence Higginbotham and Evelyn Underhill were not churchgoers but encouraged William to follow his own inclinations.

Bit by bit, through the Depression years, the women sold off furniture and pieces of the china collection to support their household, keeping notes about the sales. A Spode platter went for thirty-five cents and a Wedgwood teapot for forty-five cents. Nonetheless, despite their straitened circumstances, Florence Higginbotham made another investment. In June 1933 she bought the lot adjacent to her York Street house, land on which stood the African Meeting House.

On September 7, 1911, the fifteen surviving members of the Pleasant Street Baptist Church—including the Porte sisters, Joseph and Emma Lewis, and Edgar and Emma Wilkes—had sold the African Meeting House to Henry C. Chase for $250. The deed describes the building as "the 'African Baptist Church' situated in that part of said Nantucket called 'Newtown,' on the corner of Pleasant and York Streets." It references a deed transferred from Jeffrey Summons to the trustees of the African Baptist Society on Valentine's Day, 1826, and asserts the right of the fifteen people whose names are affixed to the document to sell the property. The transfer of deed was finally recorded on November 14, 1911, and shortly after that church custodian Edgar Wilkes turned the key in the lock for the last time.

Upon conveying the property to the trustees of the School Fund for Coloured People and the trustees of the African Baptist Society, Jeffrey Summons had stipulated that a school be kept in the building in perpetuity, but subsequent to the integration of the public schools in the 1840s the children of New Guinea went to classes elsewhere. For the next forty years, up until his death in 1888, the Pleasant Street Baptist Church met there under the leadership of the Reverend James Crawford. In the end, the aging church members relinquished the historic building to the white proprietor of a trucking business. Henry Chase installed a large sliding door across the front and converted the Meeting House into a garage.

At his death in 1932 Chase left his business, two trucks, fifty chickens, and $1000 cash to his young son Maxwell Chase. When Florence Higginbotham approached the Chases in 1933 about selling the Meeting House to her, Maxwell was already married although he was just eighteen years old. Henry's widow—who, for the purpose of probating her late husband's will, had been named Maxwell's legal guardian—handled the sale, and Maxwell's wife Grace signed away her dower rights to the property. Mrs. Higginbotham paid a thousand dollars in cash and another two thousand dollars in four scheduled payments of $500 each. In July 1934 the final installment was paid, and the African Meeting House was hers free and clear.

The transit from 'Sconset to the old New Guinea neighborhood was complete. The Underhill Cottages had long since ceased to support Mrs. Underhill. In a document executed in August 1932, Evelyn Underhill had sold to Florence Higginbotham "all the personal property, including household furniture and personal effects, now situated in the building numbered 27 York Street in said Nantucket." Two weeks later she signed another document, witnessed by two of her close friends from 'Sconset, stating that "I have given Florence Higginbotham my watch and rings for her faithful services to me for the many years she has been with me."

On April 17, 1935, Evelyn Underhill died at the age of 84 years.

Throughout his childhood William Higginbotham had the security of both his mother and Mrs. Underhill at home. He went to church, belonged to a Boy Scout troop, and was a delivery boy for the New Bedford *Standard-Times*. He was popular with his age mates. During the Depression many families could not afford even used bicycles for their children, but Bill Higginbotham had a

William Higginbotham (back row, center) with New Bedford Standard-Times delivery boys, circa 1936.

Courtesy of Constance Indio

279

very nice one. Arline Bartlett, granddaughter of Nana Watts, recalled that he regularly lent her his bicycle so she could go for a ride with her friends. He was, she said, "always very obliging one way or another, always willing to share." Christine Santos added, "Bill was older than me and a real good dancer. All the girls wanted to dance with him." According to Francis Pease, "He and I used to play trumpets in the school band. He was a much better trumpet player than I was." Eileen McGrath expanded on this: "We had a school band in the seventh, eighth, and ninth grades. They sent a man down from away, either once every week or once every two weeks, to give instructions. We were a motley bunch, I'll tell you. But Billy really had great talent, and he *did* play the trumpet, and he was developing his lip. He was learning to be very good. He played the trumpet beautifully. We were just very fond of him."

Nonetheless, the mid 1930s brought painful changes. The Catholic Church had disappointed him, and just at adolescence he lost Mrs. Underhill, whom he had regarded as a grandmother. His mother had to take winter employment on the mainland, leaving him to live with a York Street neighbor during her absence. Despite his earlier successes in school, he was made to repeat ninth grade. Dark-skinned, bigger than the younger boys in the class, he began to suffer from feeling out of place. Florence Higginbotham decided that her son needed to leave the island and go to school with other African Americans. Calling on the influence of some of her friends and stretching her resources to the limit, she sent him to Palmer Memorial Academy in Sedalia, North Carolina, for the last three years of high school.

In 1941 William was admitted to Virginia State College for Negroes in Petersburg, Virginia. Although he intended to earn a degree in electrical engineering, the school required that he meet broad liberal arts requirements. His course schedule indicated that he was to take courses in elementary German and Latin and intermediate French.

Upon enrolling in college, he changed his name from William to Wilhelm. The college did

not go along with the change; on the deposit for his entrance fee, "Wilhelm" is crossed out and "William" written in its place. Father Cleary of the Holy Family Church in Petersburg addressed him as Wilhelm, however, when he invited him to join the Catholic students at school receiving Holy Communion together at a Mass in December 1941. During that fall semester he was also in demand to play trumpet solos in the college chapel. This bright beginning came to naught at the end of 1941, however, when he dropped out of school and stayed out for over a decade. When he did return to college, it was in San Francisco, where he earned a bachelor's degree in history from San Francisco State University in 1960 and then did course work in anthropology preparatory to embarking on a master's program in anthropology.

Once William had left for Sedalia, Florence Higginbotham was alone and on her own. In the summers she worked as *sous chef* at the Nantucket Yacht Club. Nana Watts's granddaughter Arline Fisher got a job there as a waitress when she was just twelve years old, and for six summers she carried food from the kitchen where Florence Higginbotham prepared it to the club members in the dining room. Arline's classmate Eileen McGrath worked as a waitress there, too, and both appreciated how Florence Higginbotham's sense of humor and accepting nature made things easier for them to work under "an irascible Irish woman named Mrs. McGovern." Eileen McGrath recalled that "Mrs. Higginbotham was very cheerful. Nothing passed her by. She was able to see what was going on, and in a way she smoothed the way for us with Mrs. McGovern, because I would have been scared if I hadn't had somebody with a good sense of proportion. She always laughed, no matter how bad it was."

Working nights at the Yacht Club, Florence Higginbotham did domestic work by day. A letter of reference preserved among her papers states that "Florence Higginbotham is an excellent cook and a very neat cleaner, sober and trustworthy." Another says, "We have only good references to give about her." Four letters mention the opening of houses for the summer and closing of them for the winter.

As demonstrated by her bankbooks, during even the hardest of times, Florence Higginbotham always managed to put by part of her earnings as savings. With Nantucket's seasonal economy, it was necessary to hoard every penny from the summers and to take off-island jobs in the winters. Thrift did not ruin her sense of style, however. In photos from the early days, young Florence strikes model's poses in a fur coat. She carried clothes elegantly on her tall, slender frame, and her walk was elegant, too, according to her next-door neighbor, David Barrett:

> She had a wonderful gait, almost a strut—a very proud, erect woman. I would always marvel at her when she would walk, because she would have a very colorful bandanna or a hat and a lot of jewelry. She always had, to my recollection, a walking stick. Not a cane, but a stick, and it was in perfect rhythm with her gait. You know how some people don't know how to use them at all? Well, she had it down. She was good.

It was her colorful clothes, head cloths, makeup, and jewelry, as well as her willingness to read tea leaves that led Nantucketers to regard Florence Higginbotham as a Gypsy. About her there hung an air of exoticism that they could not fathom. When Arline Fisher married Franklin Bartlett in 1941, Florence Higginbotham made a large garland of all sorts of vegetables and had the young couple's photograph taken framed by the garland. Arline speculated that it symbolized, "the fruit of my womb or something. I don't know what she meant." Florence Higginbotham also suggested that Franklin and Arline make their first home next door to Mizpah in the African Meeting House. They declined but settled not far away on Pleasant Street.

Although she was not a churchgoer, Florence Higginbotham explored religious thought with characteristic broadmindedness. In one of the scrapbooks is a clipping that asks, "Is Witchcraft a Thing of the Past?" and there are also four pages of handwritten notes on "Gods and Goddesses" (Babylonian, Norse, Greek, and Roman). When William was baptized in the Catholic Church in August 1932, she gave him *The Gems of Prayer: A Manual of Prayers and Devotional Exercises for the Use of Catholics.*

Another publication among her papers is *A Sketch of the Life of Prophet Jones, 1850–1914*, the biography of the Reverend Andrew Jones, born of slave parents in Virginia in 1854. In a conversion experience in 1883, he was believed to have been given the gift of prophecy. The pamphlet states that he predicted the Johnstown flood, the Galveston flood, tornadoes, earthquakes, the Spanish-American War, and the death of President McKinley. The pamphlet concludes with the message from Jones that "God is displeased with the country, because of her cruelty to the Negro; who was born here, and has assisted in many ways in making the country what it is."

In the 1950s Florence, perhaps once again responding with sensitivity to her son's religious explorations, wrote to Wilhelm in California, "…Another Sunday and as usual I am writing you as I have always done since you went to Sedalia to school. Maybe someday when I am not among the living…you will see that I have never broken my promise to Allah that I would write you every Sunday as long as I could use my right hand. May Allah bless you always as he has blessed me."

Her richest blessing was her circle of friends. From the early days in 'Sconset she had Nana Watts, Jessie Fisher, Ida Foss, and Susie Lyle. There were many more women and not a few men who visited her when they were on-island, and sent her letters and postcards from their off-island travels. One of her roomers, Pennsylvania-born Florence Voisanger, made Florence Higginbotham the sole beneficiary of her estate. According to Voisanger's obituary, published in the *Town Crier* on August 12, 1955, she had no surviving relatives, and her last address in life was 27 York Street.

The ultimate comfort at Mizpah proved to be Cape Verde-born Frank Correia, who became Florence Higginbotham's year-round roomer in 1945. The neighborhood pig butcher was in his mid-sixties at the time he moved in and made himself useful tending Florence's yard and garden.

For over a decade and a half, despite advancing age and infirmities, he was a companionable presence in her home.

After leaving his studies at Virginia State College at the end of 1941, Wilhelm had returned to Nantucket for a while, but he needed to get on with a life of his own. In 1945, following in the footsteps of so many residents of New Guinea in times past, he went west. On November 5 he and his mother bought a steamboat ticket to Woods Hole for their Dodge sedan. The ticket was good for return within fourteen days, but the return half was never used because Florence and Wilhelm were driving cross-country. On November 17, Florence sent a postcard to Frank at Mizpah announcing their arrival in Bakersfield, California. She also made a list on a Bakersfield envelope of "States we passed through going west in 1945—Florence and her son Bill Higginbotham from Nantucket, Mass." The Dodge had barely made it to their destination. On November 21 they had to pay $113.03 for an engine overhaul. Then Florence bade farewell to her son and went home to Nantucket.

After a couple of years in Bakersfield, Wilhelm moved to San Francisco, where he eventually married and started a family. As Wilhelm grew more distant, Frank Correia eased life at Mizpah by contributing toward the household expenses winter and summer, but most of all, as a companion at home and on the road. In 1948 Florence went to see Wilhelm on her own, traveling by train to San Francisco via Chicago, but after that Frank kept her company on the long trips. From about that time, when friends wrote to Florence, they would include a greeting to Frank. The two stayed together for seventeen years, separated at the last only by old age and ill health.

Florence had written a weekly letter to her son since the late 1930s, and she continued to do so through the 1950s, although she did not always mail them. Week after week she wrote of Frank's increasing debility, of cold weather, of loneliness, of how seldom she heard from Wilhelm, and how much she yearned for more contact with her grandchildren. Then she would add the letter to the others already in the drawer. Concluding her August 16, 1959, letter, she wrote, "I am not posting this because I think you do not want to hear from me every week but I write every Sunday as usual." She did not mention that diabetes was dimming her eyesight. In 1962 it would take her legs and leave her wheel-chair bound.

David Barrett mourned the loss of his neighbor's queenly stride:

> I went away into the military and came back, and my mother filled me in about different things going on and that Florence had lost both of her legs. There were many days of the week when my mother would make an extra plate, and I would take a tray to Mrs. Higginbotham. She was at a card table in her living room, and I would come in and put it down and get whatever silverware she needed from the kitchen. I would sit over there and talk to her, and she was always very lighthearted. Even sitting there with no legs, she was always positive and wanting to know how I was, how my mother was. Of course, my mother would go over, but during mealtime it was easier for me to run the dinner over. Being young, I didn't really know how to say it, but I could see through the front hall into the little bedroom, which had a cot and her prostheses, the two legs, leaning up against it. One time I asked her about the legs. Why don't you try them? As positive a person as she was, I couldn't fathom the negative approach to the legs. To me, all she had to do was put them on and she could be back. But of course they were not as technical and as effective as prostheses are today. It seemed so sad that for whatever reason it wasn't comfortable.

Confined to a wheelchair, Florence could no longer look after Frank, and he had gone to live at Our Island Home. Six years later he was transferred off-island to Taunton State Hospital where he died of pneumonia at the age of eighty-five.

Wilhelm's marriage had ended in divorce at about the same time that his mother suffered the amputations. Despite the wheelchair and her failing eyesight, she welcomed two of his children to

Mizpah. The circumstances were all wrong for her twelve-year-old granddaughter, who arrived for the summer of 1967 and soon returned to California, but her grandson David then came to help out and to attend Nantucket High School in 1967–68 and again in 1969–70.

In 1969, on the occasion of the first moon walk, Wilhelm wrote to his mother from California, "With your clarity of mind you can probably remember the horse and buggy days, the coming of the automobile, and the advent of the airplane. Now you have witnessed a journey through space in a rocket ship. I would like to hear your reaction. When we have recovered from this moon madness, we will return to the history of Nantucket which is still in the works."

But clarity was slipping away. In 1971 Florence Higginbotham grew increasingly weak and disoriented, and in December of that year she was admitted to Nantucket Cottage Hospital and then transferred to the hospital in Taunton where Frank had died in the summer of 1967. Death came to her on January 8, 1972. Her grave in Prospect Hill Cemetery is marked with a handsome stone readily visible from the street.

Florence Higginbotham's legacy to her son and ultimately to Nantucket was the African Meeting House still standing on the corner of York and Pleasant Streets, where it had been built in 1825. Whatever her intention had been when she made such an investment of her savings to purchase it in the 1930s—whether to guarantee that only she would choose her next-door neighbors or to preserve the most significant vestige of Nantucket's African-American heritage—she had kept it from demolition for nearly four decades, and handed it on to Wilhelm.

Return of the African Meeting House

Nearly a century and a half old, the Meeting House was unrecognizable as the public building it had been. The south-facing entrance, once graced with a Greek key motif atop the door and flanked by windows, had been replaced with a sliding garage door. A line of maple seedlings had thrust up under the western sill, and between the

The African Meeting House prior to restoration.

283

fence and the building a tangle of sorrel, chicory, burdock, and milkweed grew eavesward. Over years of paving and repaving, the surfaces of Pleasant Street and York Street had been built up by a foot or more, leaving the Meeting House below grade and at the mercy of run-off from the streets. Down in a depression and buried in weeds, the Meeting House seemed low and dark. It challenged the imagination to picture church services being held inside, much less a chandelier suspended from the ceiling.

Architectural studies of the Meeting House indicate that boat builders' skills had been brought to the construction of its elegantly coved ceiling. This is hardly surprising, for during whaling days, New Guinea's yards had been full of smithies, cooperages, and small boat-building shops. After purchasing the property in 1933, Florence Higginbotham had rented out the building—which she and Wilhelm both referred to at times as a barn—for similar purposes. During World War II, according to neighbors David Barrett and Arline Bartlett, boat building staged a return. Barrett recalled his father's distress at further alteration of the former church:

> At one point Mike Lamb rented the Meeting House and called it "the garage." He stored an outboard motorboat in there, and the boat fit in, but the motor stuck out, so he cut a hole in the door. My father was wild about the hole in the door with the shaft and the propeller sticking out. He couldn't get over it. "So disrespectful," he said.

Arline Bartlett added:

> Mike actually built the boat in there. It was the first plywood boat that was built on Nantucket. It was a PT boat, a kind the servicemen had during the war. It was the first time you could use plywood, so Mike built the plywood boat in there.

The interior was a wreck. To accommodate Henry C. Chase's trucks, the pews and the front platform had been removed and additional layers of flooring put down. Motor oil dripping from the trucks eventually soaked through to the original wooden floor boards beneath. A shed extension had been pushed out from the back wall obliterat-

– Museum of Afro-American History
Fallen plaster and exposed lathes in the African Meeting House.

ing the window that had once cast light down the aisle. The side windows were boarded up, so the only light admitted to the interior came through the opening cut into the garage door and through a gap where the bottom of the door no longer met the rotted sill. Unheated in winter, unventilated and leaking year round, the building was permanently damp, and the moisture attacked wood and plaster alike. Bit by bit the upper walls and ceiling cracked, and pieces fell away from the laths.

Worse was to come. Shortly after Florence Higginbotham's death the east wall fell, taking windows and wainscoting with it. It is a tribute to the skill of the original builders back in 1825 that they had hung the walls like curtains on a sturdy wooden frame, so the fall of one did not bring down the building. Rescuers raised it back into place and braced it. In California Wilhelm Higginbotham took out a loan to pay Nantucket builder Carl Borchert for the temporary stabilization.

By now public recognition of the historical significance of the building was growing, initially thanks to the efforts of businessman Morgan Levine, who had rented the Meeting House from Florence Higginbotham for winter bicycle storage and was fascinated to learn of its history as a black church. Levine, who had been active in civil rights work in Florida, brought Ruth Batson, long-time Boston civil rights activist, to Nantucket to see it for the first time.

The publication in 1978 of Barbara Linebaugh's monograph, *The African School and the Integration of Nantucket Public Schools, 1825–1847*, put forward a precisely documented history of the central role of the building in the struggle for integration of the island's public school system. In 1979 Byron Rushing, then president of the Museum of Afro-American History in Boston, came to see it and entered into discussion of its history with Levine and Nantucket historian Edouard Stackpole. Within the year the Department of the Interior had designated the rapidly deteriorating Meeting House a Historic American Building.

Levine contacted an architectural firm in Cambridge, Massachusetts, for an initial site visit and survey of the building and received an estimate of $3000. When his approach to the Nantucket Historical Association for funding of the survey yielded no results, Levine turned to private sources. In the meantime Rushing wrote to Wilhelm Higginbotham requesting access to the property and the interior of the Meeting House so that the survey could be carried out. Rushing promised full cooperation of the museum and concluded, "I visualize the African Baptist Church fully restored to its appearance when black people last worshipped there. I see it interpreted as an architectural artifact of African-American history in Nantucket, used regularly again as a meeting place, and the center for walking tours and other interpretation of black Nantucket and for research into the rich history of Afro-Americans on the island."

The survey was carried out in 1982 and generated a report that restoration was feasible. Despite the damage from the fallen east wall, "most of the original timber frame and roof structure remain. These remnants provide all the necessary information to reconstruct the building to a high degree of accuracy." Then, despite the report's urgent warning that the building was in imminent danger of collapse, the project stalled for several years.

Disappointed, Levine believed that Wilhelm Higginbotham was uninterested in saving the building. From his 1969 letter to his mother and his subsequent payment to Borchert, however, it is evident that Wilhelm did not intend to abandon it to what has come to be known in Nantucket as "demolition by neglect." Having earned a degree in history and studied anthropology, he embraced the notion of returning the Meeting House to its rightful place in Nantucket's history, a project he and Florence Higginbotham had apparently once conceived of together. It was understandably difficult to relinquish this project to anyone else. When the Nantucket Interfaith Council contacted him in October 1987, to reiterate the danger of collapse and to inquire whether his interest was in restoration or simply in stabilization of the building, he replied that he and his son David envisioned full restoration but were unwilling to have title to the property pass from the Higginbotham family. At that time he suggested a long-term lease of the property at a nominal rental fee, restoration of the building according to available historical documentation, and that the Meeting House, once restored, "be used in the community spirit thereof."

Two years later lack of sufficient financial resources and the failing health of his son, who was living with multiple sclerosis, convinced Wilhelm Higginbotham that restoration of the Meeting House was beyond them. When Ruth Batson and Kenneth Reeves—at the time, mayor of Cambridge, Massachusetts—approached him on behalf of the Museum of Afro-American History, he entered into negotiations to sell the building to the museum. The sale was closed in March of 1989, the museum paying Wilhelm Higginbotham and his partner Angeleen Campra $50,000 for the property. Ruth Batson and Henry Hampton of Cambridge, producer of the television documentary "Eyes on the Prize: America's Civil Rights Years, 1954-1965," guaranteed the mortgage taken out by the museum to make the purchase.

The African Meeting House, standing in its decrepitude as Nantucket's last unrestored historic building, caught the imagination of a range of Nantucket residents—black and white, year-round and summer, descendants of the early English settlers, sons and daughters of Cape Verdean immigrants, and the more recently arrived as well. Upon reading an article by Edouard Stackpole about the African Meeting House in the summer

1988 issue of *Historic Nantucket*, Helen Seager, long-time summer resident on Pleasant Street, had declared, "If they ever do anything with that building, I want to be involved." Upon retirement in 1992 she dedicated herself to advancing the vision for the Meeting House that had been articulated by Byron Rushing. Ruth Batson, with Seager's assistance, organized a like-minded group of Nantucketers into the Friends of the African Meeting House on Nantucket, and Seager served as the convener of the group for the next decade. Museum board member Mary Fernandes, with deep roots in the Nantucket Cape Verdean community, served as the museum's Nantucket project coordinator.

Working closely with the staff and the board of the Museum of Afro-American History, the Friends set about an intensive educational campaign, putting the history and the potential of the Meeting House before the public. Consequently, the 1990s were a dynamic period. At the beginning of the decade, the Meeting House was barely standing, braced and wrapped in tar paper, nearly swallowed up in a sea of rank weeds. In the summer of 1992 the yard was mowed in anticipation of a rededication ceremony that took place on August 8. On that day Ruth Batson offered remarks; Kenneth E. Reeves issued a proclamation; and honored guest Captain William Pinkney, first African American to sail solo around the world, spoke briefly. After the ceremony, speakers and guests moved on to Nantucket High School, where Captain Pinkney delivered an address and Nantucket resident Mildred Daniels spoke on behalf of the Friends of the African Meeting House. A concert of gospel music followed, brought to a conclusion by Josephine White Hall with "Lift Every Voice and Sing," the song known as "The Negro National Anthem."

In September of the following year a symposium on "Island Issues on Freedom and Civil Rights" was held at the Atheneum. Moderated by Joan Wilson of Codfish Park, the topics were not limited to Nantucket issues. Roberta Ostroff introduced the audience to the early Nantucket years in

– Beverly Hall photograph, Museum of Afro-American History

Josephine White Hall in door of African Meeting House as archaeological work began in 1993.

the life of Mary Ellen Pleasant, later known in San Francisco as the "mother of civil rights." Speakers also explored the commonality of black experience on the islands off the south coast of Massachusetts. In addition to Marilyn Richardson describing the career of Captain Absalom Boston, Lamont Thomas spoke on Captain Boston's role model, Cuttyhunk-born Captain Paul Cuffe. Elaine Weintraub, teacher in the high school on Martha's Vineyard spoke of Chappaquiddick's Captain William Martin, and Carrie Tankard discussed the Martha's Vineyard chapter of the NAACP. On the weekend of the symposium an exhibition of "Images of the African Meeting House" opened at the Main Street Gallery.

Also in 1993, outdoor archaeological work directed by Boston University archaeologist Mary Beaudry began at the entrance to the Meeting House. Coming to see its progress, Josephine White Hall entered the old building for the first time. Slipping through the small opening in the door, she stood alone within its walls and sang "Bless This House" as archaeologist Ellen Berkland and the volunteer workers listened outside, transfixed by her song.

Some five years later, when the floorboards were taken up at the start of the interior restoration, trenches were excavated directly beneath the Meeting House. Since then there have been periodic public programs to exhibit the artifacts found under and around the building. As technology evolves, it is expected that more archaeological research will be carried out at the site.

Fundraising for the restoration was under way, A grant of $50,000 for the exterior restoration was received from the Massachusetts Historical Commission on condition of the Museum of Afro-American History raising a matching $50,000. Support was received from the National Trust for Historic Preservation, Nantucket's Tupancy-Harris Foundation, and the Unitarian Universalist Church of Nantucket. An anonymous donor contributed $10,000, and Joan Wilson successfully solicited one donation of $5,000 and several smaller donations from friends. Over the decade $120,000 was donated, in large part in contributions of under a thousand dollars. The donations made at annual Martin Luther King Birthday observances were directed to the restoration as were the proceeds of the premier of a musical written and produced by Nantucket residents. Gallery openings, parties, and benefit performances continued.

Members of the Friends of the African Meeting House began leading walking tours of Nantucket's Black Heritage Trail® from the head of Steamboat Wharf through the town to the African Meeting House with stops along the way at points of particular significance. Helen Seager wrote the original text of the Black Heritage Trail® brochure, and she prepared talking points for docents who sat shifts in the yard of the as yet unrestored Meeting House to tell visitors about the building's history and the plans for its future. The Reverend John Leggett, a summer resident from Pittsburgh, compiled and continually updated loose-leaf notebooks of supporting information for walk leaders and docents.

In 1996 Adele Ames, inspired by the progress in returning the Meeting House to its rightful place in Nantucket, established the James Bradford Ames Fellowships to support scholarly research into the history and heritage of African Americans and Cape Verdeans on Nantucket. Since completion of the restoration the annual lectures by Ames

The African Meeting House in 1907.

Alexander Starbuck photograph, NHA

Sylvia Watts McKinney, Ruth Batson, and Mildred Daniels break ground for the restoration of the African Meeting House, October 14, 1996.

Interior of the restored African Meeting House.

Fellows have been delivered in the Meeting House during the summer.

During Preservation Week in May 1996, a sign was unveiled formally announcing the restoration project. Unfortunately, the sign, produced at the cost of $1,200 by local artist Noelle Walters, was in place only a month before it was stolen. Despite appeals in the newspapers for its return, it was not recovered until two years later, when it was found in pine woods about a mile from the Meeting House. Although this was the most egregious theft from the site, it was not the only one. Over the period 1993 to 1995 outdoor furniture used by the docents and two other signs were taken, returned, and made off with again. In the months immediately after the sign's disappearance, however, local businesses donated materials to Walters for a new one, which was in place in time for the formal groundbreaking for the exterior work.

A late-nineteenth-century photograph of the Meeting House guided African-American archi-tect John James in returning the building to its appearance in the days when the Reverend James Crawford had served the congregation of the Pleasant Street Baptist Church. Once structural work was under way, it was discovered that there had been alterations to the facade after the building ceased to be used as a school. At some time the entrance had been made larger, and the two windows flanking the door had been made smaller and higher. Thus, the restoration was to the later appearance of the building, not to its undocumented appearance at the time of its original construction. This fact was taken into consideration in planning the interior restoration.

Upon completion of the archaeological work, the ground breaking took place in October 1996. On hand were Sylvia Watts McKinney and Ruth Batson from the Museum of Afro-American History to join with Mildred Daniels of Nantucket in turning the first earth and opening the door for the workmen. A significant find occurred the next month. Up in the rafters workmen found the church collection box. At this time an appeal was made for panes of old glass to replace broken ones in the original windows and also for period hardware.

In January 1997 a charette—a meeting for public discussion—was held to explore options for the interior restoration. The wainscoting removed from the building provided vital information about the original paint colors used in the interior, the placement of the front platform, and the height and spacing of the pews during the latter half of the 1800s when the building was in use exclusively as a church. Given this information, it was the church interior rather than the earlier schoolroom interior that was settled upon.

In addition to substantial local newspaper and magazine coverage, the restoration project attracted national attention. An article appeared in The *New York Times*, and a segment was included in a series of broadcasts of the PBS series *This Old House* broadcast from Nantucket.

The July 1997 completion date for the exterior restoration was marked by the visit of a group of parishioners from St. Benedict the Moor Church in Savannah, Georgia, with their priest, Nantucket-born Father James B. Mayo. Picnicking in the yard of the Meeting House they met with local supporters of the restoration, and presented them with a donation.

In 1998, while fundraising and benefits continued, the Museum of Afro-American History sought bids for the interior restoration. Once again the Massachusetts Historical Commission contributed to the funding. From that point, work went forward quickly. On June 25, 1999, a ribbon-cutting was attended by two hundred people, and in August a parade from Steamboat Wharf along the Black Heritage Trail® to the African Meeting House was led by re-enactors of the all-black Massachusetts 54th infantry, the Glory Brigade of the Civil War. On Orange Street the parade stopped for a moment of tribute to Anna Gardner, whose parents had protected the Cooper family from being carried off into slavery. Then the marchers continued on, turned right on York Street into the old New Guinea neighborhood, and came to the fully restored African Meeting House. The work had been accomplished with months to spare before the dawn of the year 2000.

Exterior of the restored African Meeting House.

Frances Karttunen photograph

Conclusion

How is it that this work about people ends with a report on the restoration of a building? What relevance, really, do surveys, matching grants, benchmarks, and ceremonies have for the long story of *The Other Islanders*?

In its original conception, the conclusion was to have been about who was resident on Nantucket in the year 2000: Jamaicans, Central Americans, Brazilians, Russians, Latvians, Lithuanians, Estonians, Icelanders, Turks—to say nothing of people from every corner of the United States of America. Then, as research went ahead, it became clear that from 1850 onward it was federal census returns that provided the first opening into each decade of Nantucket history. The specific details of the census are kept confidential for seventy-two years, however, with only impersonal statistics accessible in the meantime. It will be 2012 before the 1940 returns for Nantucket pass before the eyes of impatient historians and genealogists, 2022 before the first post-World War II census returns are available for inspection. To write a recent history of Nantucket's residents requires a different research strategy and a different researcher as well.

As it stands, *The Other Islanders* advances into the postwar years only when a particular story rooted in the past moves forward on its own momentum. The story that begins with the building of the African Meeting House in 1825 and ends with its reopening in 1999 is the longest story of all. It opens in a black community borne along on a wave of maritime prosperity, reaches a crisis when the African School no longer meets the needs and expectations of its constituency, undergoes transformation under the Reverend James Crawford as prosperity recedes, descends to a nadir of neglect and yet endures until the Meeting House is brought back to a wider Nantucket community than ever it served in the past.

Even more than its near contemporaries, the Nantucket Atheneum and the Coffin School, the African Meeting House has engaged a great diversity of people for the better part of two centuries, and of the three sites, it came the closest to being extinguished from collective memory. All along the way there have been helping hands, and in the end, it was only because the hands have been of many colors and have reached out from Baptists, Quakers, Unitarians, Methodists, Congregationalists, Episcopalians, Catholics, Jews, Muslims, and the determinedly nonreligious that the doors of the Meeting House opened to the residents of Nantucket in time for the new millennium.

Nantucket's history is long and densely populated. Despite the length of *The Other Islanders*, the story of all Nantucket's people is still only begun. Perhaps you have found your grandparents or your neighbors in these pages. If not, please follow John Egle's lead and commit your story to cassettes or writing for the future. In that way Nantucket history will continue to grow ever broader. The more we preserve and share, the better our island community will be.

Epilogue

Artist C. Robert Perrin produced paintings of misty Nantucket scenes full of translucent ghosts of Nantucketers past—sea captains and Quaker ladies. I envision more of these Perrinesque scenes. Residents on Manta Drive hear children's laughter; fifteen chairs stand in a circle in the middle of the field where schoolmaster Benjamin Tashama is waiting for his students to take their seats and settle down to the day's lesson. In sober Quaker attire Zaccheus Macy and the two Richards—Richard Mitchell and Richard Macy—pause by the fence to exchange greetings in Wampanoag. Gertrude West and Grace Brown Gardner stroll arm-in-arm to York Street to admire the restored African Meeting House, and there they meet Phebe Ann Boston and Eunice Ross engaged in a quiet conversation with Anna Gardner. Next door Florence Higginbotham and Evelyn Underhill serve tea and cookies to Absalom Boston and Jeffrey Summons. Three women, all called Bridget, purchase codfish from Sampson Pompey. Susan Pompey, Hannah Boston, and Maria Whippey pick beach plums along the margin of Prospect Street and wave to people gathered on the front porch of Windsor Cottage. Patience Cooper and her half-sister Trillania Pompey bring flowers to the nearby cemetery. On Memorial Day Prospect Hill Cemetery is aflutter with flags as ghosts of Latvians and Armenians clean and decorate their own graves, quietly acknowledging that it is better to have come to rest here than in their homelands. The parade has already disbanded, and next door to the Atheneum Anna Sisson scoops ice cream cones for Hiram Reed and his comrade-in-arms Josiah Fitch Murphey. On Straight Wharf a group of curious Native Hawaiian boys gather around Ning Der's model of the Unitarian Church while Quak Te's ghost sails out past the jetties, embarking at last on the long journey home. John Pompey and Frank Scott have gotten together with Willie House to audition some bands, the chamarrita is being danced in the parking lot of Father Griffin Hall, and a trio of Cape Verdean musicians knocks on the door of a house on Washington Street. Sitting on catboats hauled up on Francis Street Beach incorporeal Norwegian fishermen and French Canadian boat builders share a smoke, and over on Cliff Road Sarah P. Bunker's shade finally floats downstairs to join my grandmother for a cup of coffee in the kitchen.

Sarah P. Bunker, witness

Index

Selected Bibliography

Locations of primary documents:

The Congregational Library, Boston: Gideon Hawley Papers

Nantucket Atheneum: manuscript collection and town censuses

Nantucket Historical Association: manuscript and image collections and the Barney Genealogical Record

Nantucket Probate Court: wills and estate inventories from 1706 forward

Nantucket Registry of Deeds: transfers of property, mortgages, deeds of manumission, early court records

Nantucket Superior Court: court records from 1721 forward

Nantucket Town Clerk: vital records, town meeting records, town reports, selectmen's journals, street lists, voters list, early records

United States Federal Census returns for Nantucket County

Unpublished sources:

Adams, Deborah. 1917. "Memories written in San Francisco in 1917 by Deborah Coffin Hussey Adams, edited by her only daughter, Elizabeth S. Adams." Nantucket Historical Association MS. Collection 138, Folder 5.50.

Fine, Jacob. N.d. Nantucket Historical Association MS Collection 407. The pages of "The Nantucket Story" are numbered 1–46, and those of "Nantucket Personalities" are numbered 1–47.

Freeborn, Millard F. 1929. "A short historical sketch of the farming industry on the island of Nantucket dating from the latter part of the 17th century to the present time 1929." Typescript. Nantucket Historical Association MS. Collection 92, folder 1.

Hanaford, Phebe Ann. Diary fragments, 1857. Nantucket Historical Association MS. Collection 38, Folder 2.

Macy, Obed. Addenda to *History of Nantucket* "Copied from a book of Obed Macy's when he was an old man." Nantucket Historical Association MS. Collection 96, folder 20.

_____. Manuscript journal, 1814–1822. Nantucket Historical Association MS. Collection 96, journal 3.

Macy, Richard. Account book. Nantucket Historical Association MS. Collection 10, Accounts Book 422.

Mitchell, Eliza. 1894–96. *Book of Reminiscences*. Nantucket Historical Association MS. Collection 23.

Mitchell, Leeds, Jr. 1978. "An American Egle." Nantucket Historical Association MS Collection 335, folder 508.

Published sources:

A. M. M. Letter to the editor of the *Inquirer and Mirror*, memoir of "our worthy colored colony," July 29, 1895.

Almeida, Raymond Anthony, ed. Ca. 1978. *Cape Verdeans in America: Our Story*. Based on original manuscripts by Michael K. H. Platzer and Deirdre Meintel Machado. Boston: Tchuba: The American Committee for Cape Verde, Inc.

Andrews, J. Clinton. 1990. *Fishing Around Nantucket*. Nantucket, Mass.: The Maria Mitchell Association.

Banks, Charles Edward. 1911. *The History of Martha's Vineyard, Dukes County, Massachusett*. 3 vols. Boston: George H. Dean.

Barney, Joseph S., Henry D. Robinson, and A. Wilson Starbuck. 1865. *Catalogue of Names Embracing All Scholars Who Have Ever Been Pupils of the Nantucket High School, from its Organization, April 16, 1838, to the Present Time, July 1, 1865*. Nantucket: Hussey and Robinson Printers, *Inquirer and Mirror* Office.

Bolster, W. Jeffrey. 1997. *Black Jacks: African American Seamen in the Age of Sail*. Cambridge and London: Harvard University Press.

Booker, Margaret Moore. 2001. *Nantucket Spirit: The Art and Life of Elizabeth Rebecca Coffin*. Nantucket: Mill Hill Press.

Bradford, William. 1963. *Of Plymouth Plantation, 1620–1647*. Samuel Eliot Morison, ed. New York: Alfred A. Knopf.

Bragdon, Kathleen J. 1996. *Native People of Southern New England, 1500–1650*. Norman, Oklahoma, and London: University of Oklahoma Press.

Brasser, T. J. 1978. "Early Indian–European Contacts." In the *Handbook of North American Indians* vol. 15, *Northeast*, edited by Bruce Trigger. Washington, D.C.: Smithsonian Institution. Pp. 78–88.

Busch, Briton Cooper. 1985. "Cape Verdeans in the American Whaling and Sealing Industry, 1850–1900." In *American Neptune* 45, No. 2. Pp. 104–16.

Byers, Edward. 1987. *The Nation of Nantucket: Society and Politics in an Early American Commercial Center, 1660–1820*. Boston: Northeastern University Press.

Carreira, António. 1982. *The People of the Cape Verde Islands: Exploitation and Emigration*. London and Hamden, Conn.: C. Hurst & Company and Archon Books.

Chyet, Stanley F. 1970. *Lopez of Newport: Colonial American Merchant Prince*. Detroit: Wayne State University Press.

Coleman, Elihu. 1825. *A testimony against that anti-Christian practice of making slaves of men, wherein it is shewed to be contrary to the dispensation of the law and time of the Gospel, and very opposite both to grace and nature*. New Bedford: reprinted for Abraham Shearman, Jun. 1825. [Originally published in 1733.]

Collections of the Massachusetts Historical Society for the Year 1794, series 1, vol. III. Reprinted by Munroe and Francis, Printers to the Massachusetts Historical Society, 1810.

Crèvecoeur, J. Hector St. John de. 1986. *Letters from an American Farmer* and *Sketches of Eighteenth-Century America*. Albert E. Stone, ed. New York: Penguin Books. [*Letters from an American Farmer* originally published in 1782, drafted in 1770s.]

Dorman, Franklin A. 2000. "Researching Descendants of Nantucket Slaves." In *Historic Nantucket* 49, no.4. Pp. 9–16.

Doughton, Thomas L. 1997. "Individuals in the Earle Report by Tribal Group" (drawn from the 1859 *Report to the Governor and Council Concerning the Indians of the Commonwealth*). Available at www.geocities.com/quinnips/earle.

Eliot, John. 1666. *The Indian Grammar Begun; or, An Essay to Bring the Indian Language into Rules for the Help of Such as Desire to Learn the Same for the Furtherance of the Gospel Among Them.* Cambridge, Mass.: Samuel Green and Marmaduke Johnson.

_____. 1669. *The Indian Primer; or The way of training up our Indian Youth in the good knowledge of God, in the knowledge of the Scriptures and in an ability to Reade.* Cambridge, Mass.: Samuel Green and Marmaduke Johnson.

Farnham, Joseph E. C. 1923. *Brief Historical Data and Memories of my Boyhood Days in Nantucket.* 2d edn. Providence, R.I.: Snow and Farnham.

The First Resident and Business Directory of Nantucket, Edgartown, Cottage City, Vineyard Haven, Tisbury, West Tisbury, and Chilmark. 1897. South Braintree, Mass.: J. & E. Kyte Directory Company.

Fleming, Walter L. 1970. *The Freedmen's Savings Bank: A Chapter in the Economic History of the Negro Race.* Westport, Conn.: Negro Universities Press. [Originally published 1927]

Foreman, Henry Chandlee. 1966. *Early Nantucket and Its Whale Houses.* New York: Hastings House.

Freeman, James. 1807. "Notes on Nantucket." In *Massachusetts Historical Society Collections*, second series 3. Pp. 38–94.

Gardner, Anna. 1881. *Harvest Gleanings.* New York: Fowler and Wells.

Goddard, Ives, and Kathleen Bragdon, 1988. *Native Writings in Massachusett*, 2 vols. Philadelphia: The American Philosophical Society.

Gookin, Daniel. 1970. Historical Collections of the Indians of New England, Of Their Several Nations, Numbers, Customs, Manners, Religion and Government, before the English Planted There. Worcester: Towtaid. [Originally published in 1792.]

Gould, William B. IV. 2002. *Diary of a Contraband: The Civil War Passage of a Black Sailor.* Stanford: Stanford University Press.

Guba, Emil E. 1965. *Nantucket Odyssey: A Journey into the History of Nantucket.* Waltham, Mass.: Published by the author.

Halter, Marilyn. 1984. "Working the Cranberry Bogs: Cape Verdeans in Southeastern Massachusetts." In *People and Culture in Southeastern Massachusetts,* vol. III. Pp. 69–83. New Bedford: Spinner Publications.

_____. 1993. *Between Race and Ethnicity: Cape Verdean American Immigrants 1860–1965.* Urbana and Chicago: University of Illinois Press.

Harms, Robert. 2002. *The Diligent: A Voyage Through the Worlds of the Slave Trade.* New York; Basic Books.

Hart, Joseph C. 1995. *Miriam Coffin, or The Whale-Fisherman.* Nantucket: Mill Hill Press. [Originally published 1834.]

History of Union Lodge: Union Lodge F. & A.M., Nantucket, Massachusetts, 1771—History—1941. Early Records and Activities. Lodge of Sorrow. 1941. Nantucket: The Inquirer and Mirror Press.

Horsman, Reginald. 1981. "Nantucket's Peace Treaty with England in 1814." In *The New England Quarterly,* LIV (June 1981). Pp. 180–98.

Hough, Franklin B. 1856. *Papers Relating to the Island of Nantucket, With Documents Relating to the Original Settlement of That Island, Martha's Vineyard, and Other Islands Adjacent, Known as Dukes County While Under the Colony of New York.* Albany, N.Y. [Facsimiles of original documents.]

Kinross, John Patrick Douglas Balfour (Lord Kinross). 1977. *The Ottoman Centuries: The Rise and Fall of the Turkish Empire.* New York: William Morrow and Company.

Lancaster, Clay. 1972a. *The Architecture of Historic Nantucket.* New York: McGraw-Hill.

_____. 1972b. *The Far-Out Island Railroad: Nantucket's Old Summer Narrow Gauge.* Nantucket: Pleasant Publications.

_____. 1993. *Holiday Island: The Pageant of Nantucket's Hostelries and Summer Life from Its Beginnings to the Mid-Twentieth Century.* Nantucket: Nantucket Historical Association.

Lancaster, Mary. 1997. "Mattie Pina on the South, the ice man, and on 'Broadway.'" In the *Nantucket Beacon*, July 2, 1997.

Landberg, Fern R. 1997. "Island retreat: Jews find on Nantucket a spiritual haven by the sea," *Greater Boston Jewish Times: The Jewish Advocate*, July 25–31, 1997.

Lapidus, Ira M. 1999. "Sultanates and Gunpowder Empires: The Middle East." In *The Oxford History of Islam*. John L. Esposito, ed. New York: Oxford University Press. Pp. 347-393.

Leach, Robert and Peter Gow. 1997. *Quaker Nantucket: The Religious Community Behind the Whaling Empire.* Nantucket: Mill Hill Press.

Lepore, Jill. 1999. *The Name of War: King Philip's War and the Origins of American Identity.* New York: Vintage Books.

Little, Elizabeth A. 1980. "Probate Records of Nantucket Indians." *Nantucket Algonquian Studies* No. 2.

_____. 1981a. "The Mattequecham Wigwam Murder." *Bulletin of the Massachusetts Archaeological Society* 42. Pp. 15–23. [Included in "A Portfolio of Nantucket Studies 1976–1986," deposited at the Nantucket Historical Association.]

_____. 1981b. "The Writings of Nantucket Indians. *Nantucket Algonquian Studies* no. 3.

_____. 1981c. "The Indian Contribution to Along-Shore Whaling at Nantucket." *Nantucket Algonquian Studies* no. 8.

_____. 1983. "Indian Place Names at Nantucket Island." In *Proceedings of the 15th Algonquian Conference, October 28–30, 1983.* Edited by William Cowan. Ottawa: Carleton University. Pp. 345–62.

_____. 1985. "Prevailing Winds and Site Aspects: Testable Hypotheses About the Seasonality of Prehistoric Shell Middens at Nantucket." In *Man in the Northeast* 29. Pp. 15–27.

_____. 1986. "Observations on Methods of Collection, Use, and Seasonality of Shellfish on the Coasts of Massachusetts," *Bulletin of the Massachusetts Archaeological Society* 47. Pp. 18-27.

_____. 1990a. "Indian Horse Commons at Nantucket Island, 1660–1760." *Nantucket Algonquian Studies* 9.

_____. 1990b. "The Nantucket Indian Sickness." In *Papers of the Twenty-first Algonquian Conference.* Edited by William Cowan. Ottawa: Carleton University. Pp. 181–196.

_____. 1994 "Abram Quary of Abram's Point, Nantucket Island." *Nantucket Algonquian Studies* 16. Nantucket: Nantucket Historical Association.

_____. 1996a. "Daniel Spotso: A Sachem at Nantucket Island, Massachusetts, circa 1691–1741." In Grumet, 1996. Pp. 193–207.

_____. 1996b. "NAGPRA: List of Nantucket Indian Skeletal Materials at NHA." *In Nantucket Archaeological Study 14: NAGPRA Studies for the Nantucket Historical Association 1993–1996.* Nantucket: Nantucket Historical Association. [North American Graves Protection and Repatriation Act. Articles within this collection are not consecutively numbered.]

Little, Elizabeth A., and J. Clinton Andrews. 1982. "Drift Whales at Nantucket: The Kindness of Moshop." In *Man in the Northeast* 22. Pp. 17–38.

Lobban, Richard A., Jr. 1995. *Cape Verde: Crioulo Colony to Independent Nation.* Boulder, San Francisco, and Oxford: Westview Press.

_____. 1996. "Jews in Cape Verde and on the Guinea Coast." Paper presented at the University of Massachusetts-Dartmouth, February 11, 1996. www.umass.edu/specialprograms/caboverde/jewslobban

Lothrup's Nantucket, Massachusetts, Blue Book and Directory. 1927. Boston: Union Publishing Co.

Macy, Obed. 1880. *The History of Nantucket.* 2d edn. Mansfield, Mass.: Macy and Pratt. [Originally published 1835.]

Macy, William F. and Roland B. Hussey. 1916. *The Nantucket Scrap Basket.* Nantucket: The Inquirer and Mirror Press.

Macy, Zaccheus. 1790. Memorandum of 29/8 mo./1790. Reproduced in Silvanus Macy 1868, p. 97.

_____. 1792a. "A Short Journal of the First Settling of the Island of Nantucket…" 17/5mo/1792 Nantucket Historical Association MS. Collection 96, folder 44. Published in *Collections of the Massachusetts Historical Society, for the Year 1794,* vol. III. Boston: printed in the year 1794, reprinted by Munroe & Francis, 1810. Pp. 155–60.

_____. 1792b. "A letter from Zaccheus Macy, forwarding to the Historical Society an account of the former Indian divisions of the island, etc." 2/10mo/1792. [Reprinted in O. Macy 1880, pp. 253–59. Also reprinted in Starbuck 1924. Pp. 120–123 and in Sussek 1981 with a facsimile of the manuscript.]

Mandell, Daniel R. 1996a. *Behind the Frontier: Indians in Eighteenth-Century Eastern Massachusetts.* Lincoln, Nebraska, and London: University of Nebraska Press.

Massachusetts Soldiers and Sailors of the Revolution, vol 2. 1896. Boston: Wright & Potter Printing Company, State Printers.

May, Samuel J. 1857. *Memoir of Cyrus Peirce.* Pamphlet reprinted from *Barnard's American Journal of Education for December 1857.* Nantucket Historical Association Pamphlet NAN 920 P35.

Mayhew, Experience. 1727. *Indian Converts or Some Account of the Lives and Dying Speeches of a Considerable Number of the Christianized Indians of Martha's Vineyard, in New England.* London: J. Osborn and T. Longman.

Melville, Herman. 1856. "The 'Gees." In *Harper's New Monthly Magazine* XII, no. 70 (March 1856). Pp. 507-09.

Miles, Mary. 2003. *Nantucket Voices, Volume One.* Nantucket: Trimtab Publications.

_____. 2004. *Nantucket Voices, Volume Two.* Nantucket: Trimtab Publications.

Mooney, Robert F. 1988. *The Wreck of the British Queen.* Nantucket: Mill Hill Press.

_____. 1997. *The Church of St. Mary Our Lady of the Isle, Nantucket, Massachusetts: A Chronicle in Celebration of Its First Century, 1897–1997.* Nantucket: Wesco Publishing.

Morison, Samuel Eliot. 1936. *Harvard College in the 17th Century.* 2 vols. Cambridge: Harvard University Press.

Morris, Paul C. 1996. *Maritime Nantucket: A Pictorial History of the "Little Grey Lady of the Sea."* Orleans, Mass.: Lower Cape Publishing Company.

The Nantucket Directory. 1919. Boston: Union Publishing Co.

Nordyke, Eleanor C. 1989. *The Peopling of Hawai'i.* 2d edn. Honolulu: University of Hawai'i Press.

Ó Gráda, Cormac. 1992. "For Irishmen to Forget?' Recent Research on the Great Irish Famine." In *Just a Sack of Potatoes? Crisis Experiences in European Societies Past and Present.* Edited by Antti Häkkinen. Helsinki: Finnish Historical Society. Pp. 17–52.

Osthaus, Carl R. 1976. *Freedmen, Philanthropy, and Fraud: A History of the Freedman's Saving Bank.* Urbana, Chicago, and London: University of Illinois Press.

Parsons, Elsie Clews. 1921. "Folk-Lore of the Cape Verde Islanders." In *The Journal of American Folk-Lore,* 34, no. 131. Pp. 89–109.

_____. 1923. *Folk-Lore from the Cape Verde Islands.* Memoirs of the American Folk-Lore Society, XV, part I. Cambridge, Mass., and New York: The American Folk-Lore Society in co-operation with the Hispanic Society of America.

Philbrick, Nathaniel. 1994. *Away Off Shore: Nantucket Island and Its People, 1602–1890.* Nantucket: Mill Hill Press.

_____. 1998. *Abram's Eyes: The Native American Legacy of Nantucket Island.* Nantucket: Mill Hill Press.

Prince, Nancy. 1850. *Narrative of the Life and Travels of Mrs. Nancy Prince.* Boston: Published by the author.

_____. 1990. *A Black Woman's Odyssey Through Russia and Jamaica: The Narrative of Nancy Prince.* Introduction by Ronald G. Walters of Johns Hopkins University. New York: Markus Wiener Publishing. [Based on the 1853 second edition of *Narrative of the Life and Travels of Mrs. Nancy Prince.* There was a third edition in 1856.]

Reed, Robert R. 1995. "Remembering Willie House." In the *Inquirer and Mirror,* January 12, 1995.

"Report on the NHA Symposium: Nantucket and the Native American Legacy of New England." In *Historic Nantucket* 43, no. 4. Pp. 98-100.

Report to the Governor and Council Concerning the Indians of the Commonwealth Under the Act of April 6, 1859. 1861. Boston: William White, Printer to the State.

The Resident and Business Directory of Nantucket. 1909. Boston: Boston Suburban Book Co.

The Resident and Business Directory of Nantucket. 1914. Boston: Union Publishing Co.

Rogers, Francis M. 1979. *Atlantic Islanders of the Azores and Madeira.* North Quincy, Mass.: The Christopher Publishing House.

Rosenthal, Irving. 1989. "Nantucket's Congregation by the Sea." In *K'Fari,* June 1989. Cabot, Vermont: The K'Fari Center, Inc.

Russel, Howard S. 1980. *Indian New England Before the Mayflower.* Hanover, N.H., and London: University Press of New England.

Salisbury, Neal. 1982. *Manitou and Providence: Indians, Europeans, and the Making of New England, 1500–1643.* New York and Oxford: Oxford University Press.

Salvador, George Arnold. 1969. *Paul Cuffe, The Black Yankee, 1759–1817.* New Bedford: Reynolds-DeWalt Printing.

Salwen, Bruce. 1978. "Indians of Southern New England and Long Island, Early Period." In the *Handbook of North American Indians,* vol. 15, *Northeast.* Edited by Bruce Trigger. Washington, D.C.: Smithsonian Institution. Pp. 160–76.

Schütz, Albert J. 1994. *The Voices of Eden: A History of Hawaiian Language Studies.* Honolulu: University of Hawai'i Press.

Seager, Helen. 2002. "Portuguese Islanders and the Old Mill." In *Historic Nantucket* 51, no. 1. Pp. 10-14.

Somakian, Manoug Joseph. 1995. *Empires in Conflict: Armenia and the Great Powers, 1895–1920.* London and New York: Tauris Academic Studies.

Sowell, Thomas. 1981. *Ethnic America: A History.* New York: BasicBooks.

Speck, Frank G. 1928. *Territorial Subdivisions and Boundaries of the Wampanoag, Massachusett, and Nauset Indians.* Indian Notes and Monographs 44. Edited by F. W. Hodge. New York: Museum of the American Indian, Heye Foundation.

Stackpole, Edouard A.. 1946. "Patience Cooper and Nantucket's Murder-Mystery of Years Ago." *Inquirer and Mirror,* April 6, 1946.

_____. 1972a. *Life Saving Nantucket.* Nantucket: Nantucket Life Saving Museum.

_____. 1972b. Whales and Destiny: The Rivalry Between America, France, and Britain for Control of the Southern Whale Fishery, 1785–1825. Amherst: University of Massachusetts Press.

_____. 1975. "The Fatal Indian Sickness of Nantucket that Decimated the Island Aborigines." *Historic Nantucket* 23, no. 4. Pp. 8–13.

_____. 1981. *Rambling Through the Streets and Lanes of Nantucket.* New Bedford, Mass.: Reynolds-DeWalt.

_____. 1988. "A plan has been advanced for the restoration of the old African Baptist Church on Nantucket." In *Historic Nantucket* 36, Number 1 (Summer 1988). Pp. 7–10.

Starbuck, Alexander. 1924. *The History of Nantucket: County, Island, and Town, Including Genealogies of First Settlers.* Rutland, Vermont: Charles E. Tuttle Company. [Republished 1969.]

Starbuck, Mary Eliza. 1929. *My House and I: A Chronicle of Nantucket.* Boston and New York: Houghton Mifflin Co.

Stewart, Isabel Carter. 2004. "Summering in Windsor Cottage." In *Historic Nantucket* 53, no.3. Pp. 5–7.

Sturdevant, Lucy Huston. 1922. "Two Quaker Teachers." In *Proceedings of the Nantucket Historical Association,* July 26, 1922. Pp. 48–54.

Sussek, Marie. 1981. "Zaccheus Macy's 1792 Account of the Indians of Nantucket: Three Versions." In *Nantucket Algonquian Studies* 7. Pp. 1-17.

Thomas, Joseph D. 1990. "They Picked Cranberries." In *Cranberry Harvest: A History of Cranberry Growing in Massachusetts.* Edited by Joseph D. Thomas. New Bedford: Spinner Publications. Pp. 84–89.

Thomas, Lamont. 1986. *Rise to Be a People: A Biography of Paul Cuffe.* Urbana and Chicago: University of Illinois Press.

Turner, Mary. 1982. *Slaves and Missionaries: The Disintegration of Jamaican Slave Society, 1787-1834.* Urbana, Chicago, and London: University of Illinois Press.

Underhill, Edward F., 1961. *The Old Houses on 'Sconset Bank: The First History of Siasconset, Nantucket Island. America's Most Unique Village,* edited by Henry Chandlee Forman. Nantucket: Myacomet Press.

"Union Lodge, Nantucket, Mass.: Historic Gleanings." In *The New England Craftsman,* February, 1906. Pp. 154–167.

Vital Records of Nantucket, Massachusetts, to the Year 1850. 5 vols. 1928. Boston: New England Historic Genealogical Society.

White, Barbara Linebaugh. 1978. *The African School and the Integration of Nantucket Public Schools, 1825–1847.* Boston: Boston University Afro-American Studies Center.

Whitten, Paul F., 1960. *The Friendship Baskets and Their Maker: José Formoso Reyes.* NHA pamphlet NAN 920 R 33. Copyright 1960 by José F. Reyes. Photographs by the author, price list in rear. ["Reprinted with permission and generously underwritten by the Nantucket Basket Makers and Merchants Association," 2002. Available at the Nantucket Lightship Basket Museum.]

Williams, Jerry. 1982. *And Yet They Come: Portuguese Immigration from the Azores to the United States.* New York: Center for Migration Studies.

Williams, Roger. 1973. *A Key Into the Language of America.* John J. Teunissen and Evelyn J. Hinz, eds. Detroit: Wayne State University Press. [Originally published in London, 1642.

Wilson, Margaret Fawcett. 1958. "They Suggested It Themselves, Thus Began the Boys' Club." In the *Inquirer and Mirror,* August 22, 1958.

Wood, David H. 1994. *The Lightship Baskets of Nantucket: A Continuing Craft.* Nantucket: Nantucket Historical Association.

Worcester, J. E. 1823. *A Geographical Dictionary or Universal Gazetteer, Ancient and Modern, in Two Volumes.* Boston: Cummings & Hilliard.

Zlotin, Zelda. N.d. *Once More at Cy's: A Wonderful Walk down Memory Lane.* Nantucket: Published by the author.

At Nantucket High School, students pass beneath the skeleton of a finback whale.

Martha Carl photograph, NHA

About the Author

Martha Carl photograph

Of Finnish heritage on one side of her family and a twelfth-generation descendant of Nantucket's English settlers on the other, Frances Ruley Karttunen is a year-round resident of Nantucket, Massachusetts. "I confess to being a coof, brought home to Nantucket ten days old on the steamboat," the author writes. A graduate of Nantucket public schools, she went to Radcliffe College for a bachelor's degree and earned a PhD in linguistics from Indiana University. During thirty years at the University of Texas at Austin, she conducted research in Mexico, where she compiled a dictionary of one of the Indian languages spoken there.

She also held three Fulbright appointments at Finnish universities and was a visiting professor at universities in Sweden and Hawai'i. In 1987-88 she served as Program Director for Linguistics at the National Science Foundation. Her writing includes Between Worlds: Interpreters, Guides, and Survivors, as well as books and articles on linguistics, social history and Latin America. Since retirement she has been colibrettist of an opera about the Conquest of Mexico and spent four years researching and writing *The Other Islanders.*

Spinner Publications, Inc.

As a nonprofit cultural organization, Spinner Publications is committed to the publication of books that promote the history and culture of people in southeastern New England and foster the understanding of the diverse groups that live in the region. We are grateful to many individuals and organizations, including the Massachusetts Cultural Council and the Henry Crapo Charitable Foundation, whose generous support has helped us achieve these goals.

164 William Street • New Bedford, MA 02740 • 508-994-4564
www.spinnerpub.com • spinner@spinnerpub.com